Participatory Healthcare

A Person-Centered Approach to Healthcare Transformation

Participatory Healthcare

A Person-Centered Approach to Healthcare Transformation

Editor, Jan Oldenburg

Associate Editor, Mary P. Griskewicz

Foreword by Dr. Paul Kleeberg · Afterword by Dr. Danny Sands

CRC Press
Taylor & Francis Group
Boca Raton London New York

CRC Press is an imprint of the
Taylor & Francis Group, an **informa** business
A PRODUCTIVITY PRESS BOOK

CRC Press
Taylor & Francis Group
6000 Broken Sound Parkway NW, Suite 300
Boca Raton, FL 33487-2742

© 2017 by HIMSS
CRC Press is an imprint of Taylor & Francis Group, an Informa business

No claim to original U.S. Government works

Printed on acid-free paper
Version Date: 20160426

International Standard Book Number-13: 978-1-4987-6962-4 (Paperback)

Library of Congress Cataloging-in-Publication Data

Names: Oldenburg, Jan, editor. | Griskewicz, Mary P., editor.
Title: Participatory healthcare : a person-centered approach to healthcare transformation / editor, Jan Oldenburg and associate editor, Mary P. Griskewicz
Description: Boca Raton : Taylor & Francis, 2016. | Includes bibliographical references and index.
Identifiers: LCCN 2016003446 | ISBN 9781498769624 (hardcover : alk. paper)
Subjects: | MESH: Patient Participation | Delivery of Health Care--methods | Professional-Patient Relations | Medical Informatics | Anecdotes
Classification: LCC R727.3 | NLM W 85 | DDC 610.69/6--dc23
LC record available at https://lccn.loc.gov/2016003446

Visit the Taylor & Francis Web site at
http://www.taylorandfrancis.com

and the CRC Press Web site at
http://www.crcpress.com

Printed and bound in the United States of America by Publishers Graphics, LLC on sustainably sourced paper.

Contents

_____
* Only advanced degrees are listed.

Foreword

You hold in your hands a book that contains the keys to transforming our healthcare system from one in which patients are receivers of care to one in which they are collaborators in care.

We are in an interesting transitional time. Historically, physicians were the holders of knowledge and truth. Physicians from Hippocrates to those in the midtwentieth century were expected to make decisions for patients, and patients were expected to do the things that were "ordered." Toward the latter part of the twentieth century into the twenty-first century, a proliferation of information available to everyone is shifting this balance of power. The Gutenberg printing press revolutionized science and religion in the fifteenth and sixteenth centuries by giving everyone access to primary sources and enabling others to let their works and voices be heard. The Internet and social technologies have made this access several orders of magnitude easier. No longer do we have to go to the library and search bound texts or research articles to learn about health and disease. Today, detailed and timely health information is keystrokes away and many resources are written in easy-to-understand language from reliable sources. Now that we have access to this information, we are able to become better educated and ask more intelligent questions of physicians and caregivers. This allows us to play a greater role in decisions affecting our health. Since we are now in a better position to be able to manage our own health and be active participants in the decision-making process, the old medical paradigm needs to change.

Jan Oldenburg, the principal editor/author of this book, has had a lifelong experience with the healthcare system; her brother and sister had significant health issues growing up and their healthcare struggles were the stuff of family folklore. Later, her experience as a patient, parent, and partner to a patient helped her to see firsthand the benefits of patient engagement. This experience has driven her to work inside the healthcare system to incorporate technology, behavior, culture change, and system redesign in care delivery. It has made her passionate about advocating for a system that is "person centered," one that is designed from the perspective of patients and caregivers.

Her first book, *Engage! Transforming Healthcare through Digital Patient Engagement* (HIMSS, 2013), highlighted the benefits of providing patients with access to digital tools to empower their healthcare experience.

This book serves two purposes: It gives us a road map of the path forward to a collaborative care environment and enables us to hear patient stories that highlight the importance of heading down this path. Though it is especially useful for providers and patients, there is something in here for others as well: caregivers, the family, the healthcare facility, the chronic care manager, and the health IT implementer.

At the outset, Jan introduces you to the contributing authors of this book. Each of them is passionate about transforming care so it addresses the needs of patients and their caregivers. Each writer gives concrete examples of how healthcare could be better and illustrates places where these tools are in place and working. The second section of the book is dedicated to patient stories.

These stories not only tell of the challenges and barriers people have encountered but also of ways in which they would like to see the system change, leveraging technology to make the process of getting care easier and understanding disease simpler, as well as how they could become more of a partner in making decisions about their treatment and care.

I have had the honor of working as a family physician in a small community. I got to know my patients and they got to know me. We would meet in the grocery store or in the park—sometimes in the emergency room and sometimes in labor and delivery. It was the type of medicine that is still practiced in broad sections of this country and it really gave us the opportunity to know each other. I practiced at a time when patients were beginning to explore the Internet to do research on their own, and I found that this made my job a bit easier and more fun. When they were armed with information, we could be more collaborative.

I also have experience as a patient. To be honest, I expected things to be further along than they are. Despite the introduction of new technologies to improve patient–provider interactions, there are still bugs that need to be worked out and innovative ways in which technology could be used but isn't yet. New and radically different technologies tend to be very disruptive and require a change in the way people do things in order to optimize their effectiveness. This workflow redesign takes time and, since lives are at stake, many are reluctant to relinquish old ways that have worked so well for so long. The chapters in the first section and the stories in the second section take us through a journey of how medical care can be made better and why it is important.

And now the chapters in Section I will be discussed.

The New DIY Health Consumer

In this chapter Jane Sarasohn-Kahn describes how healthcare consumers, driven by the experience of online ease in managing other aspects of their lives and the increased out-of-pocket cost of care, have become more demanding about having the information they need to make informed decisions in healthcare. She gives examples of how both traditional and nontraditional companies have stepped in to try to fill this gap. This chapter is valuable both to providers of care, so they can be prepared to meet increasing customer needs, as well as to patients, so they know what to expect, what to demand, and where to find that which already exists.

The Science and Practice of Health Behavior Change: A Consumer-Centric, Technology-Supported Approach

In this chapter, Susan Butterworth and Catherine Serio address the emotional needs of patients and ways in which both technology and touch can begin to address these needs and help patients make and sustain health behavior changes. Redesigning the system so it meets the needs of patients and caregivers is not strictly a technology solution, though technology can help. It is also redesigning the process so it addresses the psychological and emotional aspects of the person. This chapter is valuable to anyone who is involved with patients and families in managing chronic disease. It describes how technology can give patients greater access and control over their disease while connecting them with their caregivers, providers, and others like them.

High-Tech and High-Touch Primary and Chronic Care

In this chapter, Jan Oldenburg takes the connected health consumer one step further. Though there is always the possibility of "convenience care," convenience is not the most important quality we want from our care providers. We want a trusted relationship with someone who knows us. Appropriately designed and implemented technology can help strengthen this bond. This chapter, written for both the consumer and provider, gives ideas and concrete examples of where this is working and how it can be made better.

Acute Care and Hospitalizations

Few people are hospitalized because they want to be. Most go to the hospital because they have to. The hospital is a busy and confusing place where many nurses, providers, therapists, and aides come and go. The faces change; people often arrive unannounced, do their tasks and leave. In this chapter Jan Oldenburg talks about the challenges faced by patients and their caregivers and cites solutions other organizations have implemented to address these issues of unpredictability and confusion. This chapter is written for hospitals to help their patients' stays be more predictable—so that they and their caregivers and loved ones know what is going on and what to expect. Many of these technology solutions are simple ones and examples are given of where they are working.

Achieving Whole Health

In this chapter, Mary Griskewicz reminds us that health is much more than just the absence of disease. Whole health involves spiritual, social, behavioral, environmental, and financial health. Designing a consumer and caregiver health system that is focused on health, rather than on just the absence of disease, must take all of these factors into account. It also needs to incorporate complementary therapies in an integrated fashion. This chapter, written for a broad spectrum of health providers as well as individuals, helps bring this concept into focus and provides examples of how different technologies can be used to assess different aspects of our health.

Family Caregivers, Health Information Technology, and Culture Change

This chapter focuses on the information needs of families. Written primarily for software developers and implementers, it clearly spells out what is needed in health information technology and the way the technology is used in order to provide information of value to families. There is a clear need for this because families are the first line of defense against rehospitalization or the exacerbation of chronic conditions.

Programs That Work to Promote Partnership and Engagement

This chapter, written for the provider of care as well as patients and their families, pulls everything previously discussed together and gives a number of examples where technology and culture change have been leveraged to promote a partnership between providers of care and patients and their families. It describes many practical examples of where these initiatives are working, along with references and links to resources for further information.

Section II: Patient and Caregiver Stories Introduction

Here, Jan Oldenburg gives a perspective on the stories that follow and the lessons we can learn from patient and caregiver experiences. She provides context for the way the stories bring home the importance of redesigning the system so that it meets the needs of those who need it most.

Section II: Patient and Caregiver Stories

This section contains a series of patient stories. Each story speaks for itself. Each provides a different perspective on our current sytem and why making it more "person centered" would benefit us all. At the end of each story, key observations for policy and practice are highlighted to make the connection to necessary changes. These stories provide us with the reason why it is so important for us to undertake this effort.

So sit back, enjoy this book, and think of how it could be if we worked together to make it so.

Paul Kleeberg, MD, FAAFP, FHIMSS
Family physician
Former chair, HIMSS board of directors
Apple Valley, Minnesota

Preface

This book is inspired by stories. On the one hand are the stories of patients and caregivers, who share their experiences and perceptions of what it is like to traverse our healthcare system; outsiders in a system that was supposed to be designed to serve them. On the other hand are the stories of those working inside the system to make it more patient centered, more convenient, more healing: doctors, nurses, administrators, entrepreneurs, and even IT staff. Together these stories weave the fabric of our current system, and bring reasons for hope and optimism—often generated by the very incidents that currently produce impatience and frustration.

Stories are powerful. Jonathan Gottschell writes about the emerging science of storytelling and what it reveals about the impact stories have on our attitudes, fears, hopes, and values. He notes that studies show that "in fact, fiction seems to be more effective at changing beliefs than writing…designed to persuade through argument and evidence."[1] We have tried to use both types of persuasion in this book. The chapters in the front of the book emphasize the stories of people and places that are "getting it right." They showcase innovations and practices that highlight the nuts and bolts of transformation, which takes place one person and one initiative at a time. At the same time, we interviewed many people who have been patients in the healthcare system or care for others who are patients (or both!). Their stories illustrate the lived experience of sickness and illustrate the complexity that people experience in contacts with the healthcare system. Some stories tell of great care, healing relationships, and empowering technology, and some stories highlight the opposite end of the spectrum. Both types of storytelling and both types of experiences offer lessons that can help us improve.

In writing the book, *Engage! Transforming Healthcare through Digital Patient Engagement* (2013, HIMSS Press), we argued that patient engagement, especially using digital tools, is good for the whole healthcare system. We especially focused on persuading physicians that engaging patients in their own care was a good thing, supporting all three dimensions of the triple aim: improving the health of populations, enhancing the experience of patients, and reducing the per-capita cost of healthcare. This book is a companion piece to *Engage!* Its intended audience is both healthcare insiders—physicians, nurses, administrators, and payers—and patients and caregivers. Our goal is to help accelerate an ongoing shift in healthcare to be more convenient, collaborative, and patient centered.

My work in this space is rooted in my lived experiences as a patient, caregiver, and partner as well as my professional experiences as a change agent, intrapreneur, systems developer, product manager, consultant, and implementer. As a result of those experiences, I firmly believe that healthcare must change for the good of patients as well as the good of healthcare workers. This book stands on the shoulders of others: not just the authors and patients who have contributed chapters and stories, but also the many people who work daily on aspects of healthcare change and transformation—both from the inside as healthcare workers and from the outside as patients and patient advocates. I have had the joy of working with amazing colleagues within two integrated delivery systems: HealthPartners and Kaiser Permanente. I've also worked with wonderful people within Aetna who are building accountable care organizations (ACOs) and seeking to improve the system. In my consulting career as an independent, at Evantage and EY, I've had the opportunity to work with consultants, health systems and payers who are committed to making life better for the patients and caregivers they serve. This book is a salute to all the people whose mission, day by day, is to care for others and make healthcare better.

This book also honors the people who are brave enough to share their health stories honestly and openly in the hopes that others can learn from them. Each story we tell serves to illustrate something important about what is both right and wrong with healthcare today. Often it is small interactions that make major differences in patient experiences—and we have to look and listen closely to understand what those small differences are. We could only tell a small fraction of the world's moving, inspiring, and infuriating patient stories in this book, but we hope these stories will inspire you to ask more questions, listen with more attention, and see every patient experience as an opportunity to make a positive difference.

Changing the world of healthcare requires that we first change ourselves. We hope this book helps you in some small way move forward on the journey of transformation.

Jan Oldenburg, FHIMSS

Note

1. http://www.fastcocreate.com/1680581/why-storytelling-is-the-ultimate-weapon

Editors

Lead Editor Jan Oldenburg, FHIMSS, is passionate about making healthcare more engaging, more convenient, and more healing. She focuses on consumer and patient experience at the intersection of healthcare and technology. In her roles as independent consultant, mentor to start-ups, Senior Manager at EY, Vice President of Patient and Provider Engagement in Aetna's Accountable Care Solutions Division, and Senior Leader in Kaiser Permanente's Digital Services Group, she has experience across a broad spectrum of health plan and provider operations.

Jan's focus areas are innovation design, digital product design and management, as well as culture change. She is a passionate believer that empowering consumers with knowledge, digital tools, and access to meaningful clinical information is a key component to healthcare transformation.

Jan is a past president of the Northern California HIMSS board, an HIMSS Fellow, and cochair of the National HIMSS Connected Health Committee. She frequently speaks and writes about patient and physician engagement. Jan served as the primary editor of *Engage! Transforming Healthcare through Digital Patient Engagement*, published by HIMSS Press in March 2013. She also authored the "Personal Health Engagement" chapter of the third edition of *Medical Informatics*, published in March 2015 by HIMSS Press. Jan also wrote the "Patient Portals: Enabling Participatory Medicine" chapter of *The Journey Never Ends: Technology's Role in Helping Perfect Health Care Outcomes*, published by CRC press in February 2016, as well as numerous journal articles. Jan earned a BA in English and philosophy from Luther College in Decorah, Iowa, summa cum laude, and coursework towards a PhD in English from the University of Minnesota. You can follow her on Twitter at @janoldenburg.

Associate Editor Mary P. Griskewicz, MS, FHIMSS, is director of sales for the Health Information Management Systems Society (HIMSS), the largest U.S. cause-based, not-for-profit healthcare association. It is focused on the optimal use of information technology and management systems for the betterment of healthcare. Mary has received national awards for her work in education and leadership in healthcare IT and is an HIMSS Fellow.

Mary leads HIMSS strategic sales efforts for the HIMSS annual conference, the organizational affiliate and academic membership programs, and the HIMSS Personal Connected Health Alliance's Connected Health Conference and HX360 conferences.

Mary has authored many blogs and articles as well as edited several books. She has drafted federal legislation and provided congressional testimony on the adoption and use of health technology for patients and providers. Mary was responsible for launching the HIMSS connected patient committee and community, and she directed HIMSS clinical and business intelligence, ambulatory, and payer and life sciences initiatives for HIMSS.

She has extensive industry experience as a former lobbyist and executive in healthcare management and information technology working for General Electric, IDX Systems, TekSystems, CIGNA, Aetna, Hospital of St. Raphael's, and Anthem Blue Cross and Blue Shield.

Mary also serves as a visiting scholar for medical and professional associations nationally and has instructed at Yale's Executive in Healthcare Master's program. Currently, Mary teaches at Northeastern University's Master's in Information Technology program and the University of New Haven's Healthcare Administration program. She is also a founding board member of Connecticut Health Partners.

She earned a master's degree in industrial relations from the University of New Haven and a bachelor's degree in political science/public administration from Central Connecticut State University. You can follower her on Twitter at @mgriskewicz.

Contributors

Susan W. Butterworth, MS, PhD, is the principal of Q-consult, LLC, and has been involved in the health promotion and chronic disease self-management field since the word "wellness" was coined. She earned her doctoral degree in adult education and training with a cognate in health promotion from Virginia Commonwealth University. Her special area of expertise is the practical application of behavior change science, such as motivational interviewing-based health coaching and other patient engagement strategies, to various healthcare settings. She has been awarded multiple National Institutes of Health (NIH), Health Resources and Services Administration (HRSA), and other grants to study the efficacy and impact of health management interventions and is well published on the theory and outcomes of behavior change science.

Dr. Butterworth was an associate professor at Oregon Health & Science University for nearly 20 years. While there, she taught at both the Schools of Medicine and Nursing and founded Health Management Services, which was awarded Best Wellness Vendor by Health Industries Research Companies in 2007, 2008, and 2009. She is an active member of the Motivational Interviewing Network of Trainers and oversees workforce initiatives for healthcare organizations that wish to implement an evidence-based, patient-centered approach.

Jane Sarasohn-Kahn, MA, MHSA, is a health economist, advisor, and trend-weaver to organizations at the intersection of health, technology, and people. Jane founded THINK-Health after spending a decade as a healthcare consultant in firms in the United States and Europe. Jane's clients are all stakeholders in health: technology, bio/life sciences, providers, plans, financial services, consumer goods, and not-for-profits. Jane also founded the Health Populi blog in 2007.

Jane advises clients on strategy via environmental analysis, scenario and strategic planning, and health policy analysis. She serves on several advisory boards including CanSurround, the US Health Efficiency Index, GE Ventures, the Health 2.0 Conference, HealthBank, Intuit's American Tax & Financial Center, the Society for Participatory Medicine, and WEGO Health. Jane also sits on the HIMSS Connected Health Committee.

Jane was named one of the #HIT99 in August 2015, one of Healthcare IT Leaders top 50 healthcare IT influencers on Twitter in July 2015, and one of fifteen influencers shaping digital health in 2014 in March 2014.

Jane earned an MA (economics) and MHSA (health policy) from the University of Michigan. While Jane loves her work, she is even more passionate about family and home, Slow Food and her local CSA, and living a full and balanced life. Follow Jane along with nearly 20,000 others on Twitter @healthythinker. See more on Jane at www.janesarasohnkahn.com.

Catherine D. Serio, MS, PhD, is senior director of the behavior change strategy, Healthwise, and is a licensed psychologist with 25 years of experience translating behavior change research into healthcare. Dr. Serio is passionate about leveraging behavioral science to empower healthcare providers and patients to partner in improving health. Dr. Serio earned her MS and PhD in clinical psychology from Virginia Commonwealth University. She completed a postdoctoral residency in rehabilitation medicine at the Medical College of Virginia and an externship in family therapy at the Family Therapy Practice Center in Washington, DC.

In 1995, Dr. Serio joined the University of Washington's Family Medicine Department as an associate clinical professor. She trained primary care physicians and allied health professionals in best practices of behavioral science, including patient-centered behavior change and motivational interviewing. She is a member of the Motivational Interviewing Network of Trainers (MINT), an international organization of trainers committed to promoting the use, research, and training of motivational interviewing. In 2007, Dr. Serio joined Healthwise, a nonprofit consumer health company, where she leads the application of behavioral science into health content and interactive, digital tools that are used by millions of people each year. Dr. Serio consults with healthcare systems around the country to support their implementation of behavioral science into healthcare.

John Sharp, MA, MSSA, PMP, FHIMSS, is senior manager, consumer health IT for the Personal Connected Health Alliance at the Health Information Management Systems Society (HIMSS). His focus is on patient engagement technologies. He is active on social media as @John Sharp and blogs weekly on LinkedIn about connected health. He is also adjunct faculty in the Health Informatics Master's program at Kent State University, where he teaches clinical analytics. He is also a project management professional. He earned his bachelor's and master's degrees from Case Western Reserve University in Cleveland, Ohio. He has published several book chapters and journal articles on topics ranging from social media in healthcare to e-research and patient registries. He works at the HIMSS Innovation Center in Cleveland.

John became interested in patient engagement through a long-term career in healthcare that began in oncology social work. Initially finding value in initiating face-to-face support groups for cancer patients and families, he moved on to be an early adopter of online patient support and education through groups like the Association of Cancer Online Resources (ACOR). As he moved into information technology full time, he helped to develop user-friendly websites including patient education and later supporting patient-centered research. After being a member of HIMSS for more than 10 years, he joined the staff in 2013 with a focus on patient engagement.

MaryAnne Sterling, CEA, is the cofounder of Connected Health Resources, focused on healthcare transformation through the eyes of patients and their families. She serves as patient research partner and ambassador for the Patient Centered Outcomes Research Institute (PCORI), as consumer ombudsman for the National Association for Trusted Exchange (NATE), a member of the ONC Health IT Policy Committee's Consumer Workgroup, and is a former executive in residence for the HIMSS Foundation, Institute for e-Health Policy.

MaryAnne has been a caregiver and advocate for her aging parents for nearly 20 years. She is a renowned speaker and educator on family caregivers and their health information technology needs and often shares her experience having multiple parents struggling with dementia. Her personal story has been featured in *Kiplinger*, the *New York Times*, *USA Today*, and the *Wall Street Journal*.

She earned her bachelor's degree in biology and biotechnology from the University of Nebraska at Omaha. You can follow her on Twitter at @SterlingHIT and learn more at www.connected healthresources.com.

Paul Kleeberg, MD, FAAFP, FHIMSS, is currently a medical director with Aledade, Inc., but has been focused on Health IT and clinical practice optimization nearly since he left Stanford and his residence in family medicine at the University of Minnesota. His passion for the work of participatory healthcare comes from being a provider and a patient. He says, "My patients had much better outcomes when they were activated and engaged. It enabled us to work as a team. It made my job more fun and I believe it led to better outcomes. Now, as a patient, I have come to know what is possible and have high expectations of my providers. I want to be allowed to be engaged in my care and be free of unnecessary obstacles. I also believe that person-centered care will improve quality, reduce costs and improve the overall health of the population." Dr. Kleeberg has represented the information technology needs and challenges of rural providers with the ONC Policy Committee, the Senate Finance Committee staff, with the President's Council of Advisors on Science and Technology and the HIMSS Board of Directors.

Daniel Z. Sands, MD, MPH, is passionate about healthcare transformation. A practicing physician with training and experience in clinical informatics, Dr. Sands has worked in a variety of capacities in the healthcare IT industry for 25 years. He spent almost 14 years at Beth Israel Deaconess Medical Center, where he developed and implemented innovative systems to improve clinical care delivery and patient engagement, including clinical decision support systems, an electronic health record, and one of the nation's first patient portals. This was followed by leadership positions at Zix Corporation and Cisco. Dr. Sands is the recipient of numerous healthcare honors, including recognition in 2009 by *HealthLeaders Magazine* as one of "20 People Who Make Healthcare Better." He is the coauthor, with e-patient Dave deBronkart, of *Let Patients Help* and a cofounder of the Society for Participatory Medicine. Dr. Sands holds an academic appointment at Harvard Medical School. He is a popular speaker and consultant, who blogs at http://www.drdannysands.com/ DrDannySands.com and is active on Twitter as http://www.twitter.com/DrDannySands @DrDannySands.

ESSAYS FROM THE FIELD: HEALTHCARE REIMAGINED FROM THE PATIENT AND CAREGIVER PERSPECTIVE

I

Chapter 1

Introduction

Jan Oldenburg, FHIMSS*

> This is the legacy of patient empowerment: all of us taking responsibility for our own well-being, and medical professionals respecting the right of patients to make their own well-informed health care decisions... Shared decision-making lies *between* "doctor's orders" and "patient's choice" and follows the ethical standard of acting in the patient's best interest.[1]

> My obligation is to "prove the patient right" and to connect to their humanity above the connection to their patient-ness... If we are human to human first and patient to physician second, we are anchored by a higher reality than "medical" and it's more meaningful and more fun.[2]

Nearly everyone has a health story to share: The person sitting beside me on the plane whose life and career have been shaped by caring for a disabled child. An old friend whose cancer experience is still top of mind. A colleague's friend, who is still making sense of the way illness altered his perceptions of what is possible. Someone's daughter, a physician herself, struggling with the way her mother died. A doctor surprised by the way it feels to be a patient.

People are eager to tell their stories of health, illness, and recovery. Getting sick, whether with an acute, chronic, or terminal illness, forces people to take stock of who they are and how physical health factors into their sense of self. Telling the story helps people make sense of their illness, put it into context, and give it meaning. The people who shared their stories for this book often mentioned the hope that by telling their story, they might make things better for others who are living through similarly life-altering events. This book is written to share their stories, honor their courage, and reimagine healthcare as it might be if it were designed to put the needs of patients and caregivers first.

When we first began interviewing patients and caregivers, we expected to hear about hassles, about unnecessary complexity, about confusion and frustration. We heard all of that. We also heard people express the desire for technology to make the process of getting care and understanding disease simpler and easier, more like interactions in the rest of their lives. Most importantly,

---

* @janoldenburg

however, we heard a deep longing for human connection with their medical care teams, for choice in their experiences, to be listened to with respect and treated as a partner in making decisions about treatment and care.

The people we spoke with also challenged all of us in healthcare to think differently. They challenged us to innovate, to use our imaginations to redesign the experience, they asked us to: Develop new tools to help them stay healthy, explore alternative ways to interact with physicians, invent medical devices that better meet their needs, and design hospitals that promote healing. Many of them expressed the desire to be on the inside, helping us invent a future that incorporates both useful technology and better ways to connect with the medical professionals who help them care for themselves.

The book opens with Section I's essays by experts in the field highlighting how care, treatment, and interactions could be different were they redesigned from the perspective of patients and caregivers. The essays also explore changes that are already underway both in individual interactions and at the system level. In Section II, patient and caregiver stories bring the experience of illness to life, highlighting how we can learn from the lived experiences of individuals. Together they showcase how technology can be applied to solving patient and caregiver problems by empowering them with information and tools and freeing up time to build sustaining and healing relationships.

Participatory Medicine

Patients increasingly want to be involved in and take responsibility for their own care. A recent study conducted by Public Opinion Strategies highlights this desire. Study respondents were asked to rate their favorability toward the following statement about informed decision making on a scale from 0 to 100: "Informed medical decision making is an idea in health care that patients should receive information about all of the treatment choices and options available to them for a specific disease, illness, or procedure before they decide, in conjunction with their doctor, on the appropriate treatment choices." Nearly 70 percent of respondents rated the statement with a score greater than 80.[3]

The idea that patients both *want* and have a *right* to share in decisions about their health is not new. The Informed Medical Decisions Foundation, now a part of Healthwise, was founded in 1989 with the mission of improving the way doctors and health systems communicate with patients about their treatment options.[3] Michael Millenson traced the evolution of the participatory medicine movement back to Dr. Spock in an excellent article entitled, "Spock, Feminism, and the Fight for Participatory Medicine.[4] In the article he discusses the need for a balance between patient autonomy and physician authority, suggesting that the new model of care "takes into account the medical evidence, physician experience and patient preferences and values as part of an 'intense collaboration.'"[5]

There is evidence that providing patients with information about their conditions, treatment options, and costs produces patients who are more involved in their own care and that those patients have better outcomes. Judith Hibbard has done much of the pioneering work in this area by developing the patient activation measure (PAM) and then studying the differences in outcomes between highly activated patients and less activated patients. Her studies show that more highly activated patients have better outcomes, choose lower cost treatment options, are more satisfied with their care overall, and are less likely to suffer adverse health consequences.

Online Tools

Emerging evidence shows that giving patients access to their data via online tools also increases activation levels.[6] In a recent survey conducted by the National Partnership for Women and Families, also referenced in Chapter 2, "The New DIY Health Consumer," 79 percent of those surveyed said online access to their own data increased their knowledge of their own health and 78 percent said it increased their ability to communicate effectively with their doctor.[7] These findings are echoed by some of the research from organizations that have opened clinical notes to patients, such as the VA. In a 2012 study following opening clinical notes to patients, the authors found, "Our findings support prior qualitative research that shows full health record access is empowering for patients and caregivers."[8] Other studies show improved adherence to agreed-upon medication regimens as a result of online access to health data and prescription refill capabilities.[9,10]

The National Partnership for Women and Families survey, mentioned earlier, found:

> The more frequently individuals access their health information online, the more they report that it motivates them to do something to improve their health. A dramatic 71 percent of those using online access three or more times per year report this, compared with 39 percent of those who used online access less often.[7]

These findings are congruent with data provided by the ONC (Office of the National Coordinator for Health Information Technology) in 2015 from the 2013–2014 Consumer Survey of Attitudes toward the Privacy and Security Aspects of Electronic Health Records and Health Information Exchange, which are discussed more fully in Chapter 8, "Programs That Work to Promote Partnership and Engagement."[11]

It's clear that people are interested in access to their clinical data and the ability to perform healthcare tasks digitally. Research is demonstrating that online tools support individuals in taking responsibility for their health and result in feelings of empowerment, higher activation levels, and better clinical outcomes.

Human Connection

But the ability—and the desire—to perform more tasks digitally and to gain access to one's data digitally does not mean that people are satisfied with less human connection in their healthcare.

Patients' desire to be involved in their own care and to have access to their health data in order to understand the choices available to them does not mean that everyone wants complete autonomy. Most people want collaboration and trust, and both take time to develop. It sometimes feels as if we have lost both the time for and the art of engaging in conversations between doctors and patients, which are seen as indulgences in a culture of hurry. What is lost when we don't build in time for those conversations is more than a warm empathetic connection. What is lost for patients is the opportunity to get help making sense of illness and to be known in a way that is both empowering and healing. For doctors, what is lost is the connection to their mission and the opportunity to renew their commitment to their work.

A trusting, empathetic relationship with your doctor can be a significant benefit to overall health. A study on the components of a healing relationship found that there are several key factors in physician behaviors that make for a healing relationship. The first is valuing and honoring patients in a nonjudgmental way by being truly present to them and finding ways to form an emotional connection with them. The second is managing the power dynamic by engaging patients as partners in their care and consciously working to increase patients' power. The third is abiding with the patient over time with the conscious commitment not to give up on the person. The study authors note that there are three relational outcomes from these processes that contribute to a healing relationship: "trust, hope, and a sense of being known."[12]

Attitudes about the relationship between patients and doctors are changing in ways that seem likely to create more positive interactions. There's no simple way to measure the change in attitudes toward patient-centered care, but there are some promising indications. According to the Beryl Institute's report on the State of Patient Experience 2015, 87 percent of the institutions surveyed felt that patient experience is extremely important, and many are putting in place the structures to manage and improve it.[13] Similarly, the 26th Annual Health Leadership study from 2015 showed that 87 percent of respondents indicated that patient satisfaction will be the top priority at their organization in the course of the next 12 months.[14] The Beryl and Planetree Institutes are leading the way in formalizing and teaching the design of human- and patient-centered care environments. All across healthcare, organizations are creating the position of chief experience officer, a role "at the center of driving culture transformation and unifying quality, safety, and experience strategies to improve care delivery."[15,16]

The Chapters and Authors

The writers of this book are passionate about the opportunity and the need to redesign healthcare from the perspective of patients and caregivers. Each chapter explores a different aspect of healthcare and the transition that is underway. The writers showcase examples of world-class systems that are already in the process of this transformation, and imagine what care could look like with additional technology to support patients and caregivers. Some of the tools and capabilities described help patients take ownership of their own health; others focus on helping caregivers better support their loved ones, and still others highlight the way technology is changing the location and context of care.

The writers of the chapters have stories of their own and come to this work out of a deep belief in and commitment to the transformational impact of collaboration between patients and caregivers. While their professional biographies are covered in the front matter of the book, the statements here describe their passion for this work.

Jane Sarasohn-Kahn, MA, MHSA, frequently writes and blogs about healthcare transformation. Jane wrote Chapter 2, "The New DIY Health Consumer." Jane believes that we cannot achieve the triple aim in healthcare—that is, driving population health outcomes, creating enchanting healthcare experiences, and lowering per capita costs—without patient, consumer, and caregiver engagement. And without understanding people's needs—both clinical and the social determinants of health—we cannot reimagine the health system to gain the trust and the full participation of patients.

Catherine Serio, MS, PhD, cowrote Chapter 3, "The Science and Practice of Health Behavior Change: A Consumer-Centric, Technology-Supported Approach." Catherine explains that her work is fueled by an experience as a patient. She says,

> As a freshman at the University of Texas, I became very ill and could not walk. The doctors were unable to diagnose my condition for six weeks. During this time, I experienced the vulnerability of being a patient. I was stuck in a hospital bed, sharing a room

with old, sick people, and powerless. Once my condition was diagnosed and treated, I decided to dedicate my career to the cause of empowering patients. I wanted to break open the medical paradigm that treats people as illnesses, not as unique, whole human beings. In this pursuit, I became a health psychologist and have enjoyed the privileges of teaching physicians, treating patients, building self-management tools, and advocating for a patient-centered approach to healthcare. We have much more to do. Yet there is so much at stake. Health is our most precious commodity. I hope to preserve mine and empower others to do the same.

Susan Butterworth, MS, PhD, who cowrote Chapter 3 with Catherine Serio, describes what inspired her work by saying,

> I was born into a family with a long line of doctors and nurses. My expectation was that I would probably follow in their footsteps. However, after working several summer jobs in hospital departments such as cardiac rehabilitation and physical therapy, I realized that I wanted to work on the prevention side of healthcare. The health promotion and wellness field was barely developed, but that's where I set my sights. The terms may have changed over the years—health promotion, wellness, disease management, health management, patient activation—but my mission never has. I continue to look for ways to incorporate best practices of behavior change science into interventions that are effective in the healthcare setting. Our clients (formally our patients) deserve it!

MaryAnne Sterling, CEA, authored Chapter 7, "Family Caregivers, Health Information Technology, and Culture Change." She says,

> This work literally found *me* when I became the caregiver and advocate for my aging parents, who had multiple chronic conditions and/or dementia. My frustration at the lack of resources available for family caregivers inspired me to begin influencing health policy and establish my own healthcare start-up to design technology tools that meet the information needs of patients and family caregivers.

John Sharp, MA, MSSA, PMP, FHIMSS, wrote Chapter 8, "Programs That Work to Promote Partnership and Engagement." He has promoted the idea that patients and families should have access to information about their illnesses to cope with the challenges they face. An uninformed patient is more fearful, anxious, and potentially confused about participating in his or her care. That can only lead to bad outcomes. John has always had a scientific approach to his work and scans the literature daily for studies that demonstrate the outcomes of patient engagement technologies; that is, he looks for what works. His current passion is to help physicians and other healthcare providers understand how these patient-facing technologies can be part of modern clinical practice, integrate into their workflow, and improve the health outcomes of their patients.

Mary Griskewicz, MS, FHIMSS, authored Chapter 6, "Achieving Whole Health," and is the associate editor for the book. Mary also shared the story of becoming responsible for her mother's end-of-life care, Story 5, "Becoming My Mother's Voice." Mary believes that we can only achieve whole health by using all of the resources available to us. Patients, consumers, and healthcare providers are not one dimensional and our approach to supporting health and wellness should be multidimensional to match them. This includes innovative and new technologies and, yes, alternative approaches to care. The most important aspect for achieving whole health is for healthcare providers to partner with and "listen" to consumers, patients, and family caregivers.

Jan Oldenburg, FHIMSS, served as the principal editor of the book and wrote Chapter 1, "Introduction"; Chapter 4, "High-Tech and High-Touch Primary and Chronic Care"; and Chapter 5, "Acute Care and Hospitalizations," as well as many of the patient and caregiver stories. She says,

> I grew up hearing my mother tell stories about challenging the healthcare system to get appropriate care for my brother and sister, each of whom had a significant health issue in early childhood. I found my life's work at the intersection of my desire to be a writer, my experiences designing and implementing transformational IT systems, and my personal experiences as a patient, parent, and partner to a patient. My husband and I agreed to tell the story for the first time of his "widow-maker" heart attack in the book, Story 24, "Very Bad Genes and Very Bad Luck." I believe deeply in the transformative power of both technology and story, and hope this book can help expedite change.

Several people wrote their own stories for this book, and each person whose story we shared collaborated deeply in the process. We are proud and honored to have the opportunity to share all the health narratives incorporated here.

Conclusion

We still have a significant distance to travel in ensuring that patients, caregivers, and consumers experience a new kind of healthcare that is convenient and participatory. They need and deserve healthcare experiences that are convenient, that take into account their personal wants and needs, in which they are listened to and treated with empathy, and where they are supported with access to their own clinical data and supplied with tools that help them maintain health, manage disease, and recover from illness. Isn't that a future we all want to be a part of creating?

Our goal for this book is to spur new conversations between patients and providers as well as within healthcare institutions: conversations that lead to transformational change in the way we think about the role of patients and caregivers, the way we bring them into partnership with us, and the tools we offer them to help them manage their health and healthcare.

Notes

1. http://blog.stevenreidbordmd.com/?p=946
2. http://www.patientdriven.org/2013/03/a-patient-centric-definition-of-participatory-medicine/#comment-83641
3. http://informedmedicaldecisions.org/wp-content/uploads/2011/05/Perspectives_Patient_Involvement.pdf
4. http://www.medscape.com/viewarticle/770392_3
5. https://tamhscbioethics.files.wordpress.com/2012/10/physician-recommendations-and-patient-autonomy-finding-a-balance-between-physician-power-and-patient-choice.pdf
6. http://healthaffairs.org/blog/2013/02/04/february-health-affairs-issue-new-era-of-patient-engagement/
7. http://www.nationalpartnership.org/research-library/health-care/HIT/engaging-patients-and-families.pdf

8. http://www.jmir.org/2013/3/e65/
9. http://www.jmir.org/article/viewFile/jmir_v17i10e226/2
10. http://journals.lww.com/lww-medicalcare/Abstract/2014/03000/Use_of_the_Refill_Function_Through_an_Online.3.aspx
11. https://www.healthit.gov/sites/default/files/briefs/oncdatabrief30_accesstrends_.pdf
12. http://www.ncbi.nlm.nih.gov/pmc/articles/PMC2478496
13. http://c.ymcdn.com/sites/www.theberylinstitute.org/resource/resmgr/Benchmarking_Study/2015-Benchmarking-Study.pdf
14. http://www.himss.org/2015-leadership-survey
15. http://www.the-hospitalist.org/article/rise-of-the-chief-patient-experience-officer/
16. http://www.vocera.com/public/ein/whitepapers/wp-cxo-survey-2015-report-ein.pdf

Chapter 2

The New DIY Health Consumer

Jane Sarasohn-Kahn, MA, MHSA*

Introduction

As the evolution of man and woman continues, people are morphing into a species of homo informaticus[1]—information and media seeking beings using many technology platforms and channels. People manage money online through financial service company websites, forcing changes in banks' business models. Travelers book airline reservations on portals, driving most travel agents out of business. People self-develop and share photos via digital means, making the Main Street photography shop largely extinct.

DIY Comes to Healthcare

These do-it-yourself (DIY) behaviors have come to managing health: welcome to the new DIY health consumer, who seeks transparency, access, convenience, and control in his or her health-life. This person has more financial skin in the game in healthcare, is more price sensitive, and is challenging providers' and suppliers' legacy business models.

Americans may be ready for a brave new world of healthcare, a Harris Poll found, with a plurality of health consumers interested in digital tools to check blood pressure (48 percent), check heart and heart rate (47 percent), use apps to track physical activity (43 percent), do general blood tests (41 percent), and check glucose level (39 percent).[2]

Heath consumers with online access to electronic health records (EHRs) are accessing their online records in a variety of ways.[3] The most popular features used by over one-half of consumers with online access to their EHRs are reviewing test results, viewing medical history, e-mailing the doctor or staff, scheduling appointments, reviewing a care plan, accessing immunization records,

---

* @healthythinker

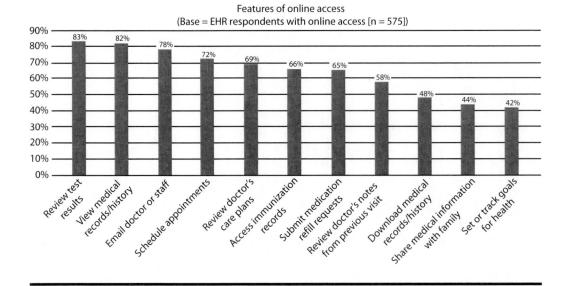

Figure 2.1 Consumer use of online health IT tools. (From National Partnership for Women & Families. "Engaging Patients and Families: How Consumers Value and Use Health IT." December 2014. With permission.)

submitting medication refill requests, and reviewing the doctor's notes from a previous visit. As Figure 2.1[4] illustrates, nearly one-half of people have downloaded their medical records and 42 percent set or track goals for health online.

In addition to people engaging with medical information via expanded access to electronic health records, a growing cadre of citizen-scientists are joining together in peer-to-peer social networks to support each other and share personal health information. The vast majority of people with a medical condition who use social media would be willing to share their health data to help doctors improve care and would also be willing to help other patients like them. Furthermore, 94 percent of social media users also believe their health data should be used to improve care for future patients who may have the same or a similar condition.[5] In communities like PatientsLikeMe (www.patientslikeme.com), DiabetesMine (www.diabetesmine.com), Stupid Cancer (www.stupidcancer.org), and SmartPatients (www.smartpatients.com), among dozens of other online patient networks, people crowdsource research and crowdfund money for healthcare. See Dana Lewis's Story 16, "Managing Diabetes with a Do-It-Yourself Pancreas System," for a personal view on this phenomenon or Hugo Campos's story, Story 4, about trying to get access to the data from his implanted cardiac defibrillator for examples of deeply involved patients.

Health Costs Drive Health Engagement

With more financial responsibility, combined with personal access to digital information via many platforms, people have begun to stretch their DIY health muscles with digital health programs that are available from employer benefits, health insurance, online portals, and mobile tools that have been developed as direct-to-consumer sources enabling access to cost, quality, scheduling, and payment for services.

People with more financial skin in the healthcare game are more likely to act more cost consciously, according to the Employee Benefits Research Institute (EBRI) 2014 EBRI/Greenwald & Associates Consumer Engagement in Health Care Survey.[6] As people have gotten more experience managing consumer-directed health plans (CDHPs, usually high-deductible health plans coupled with health savings accounts), they have become more familiar with the plans' features—especially the nature of the deductible, which makes the consumer essentially self-insured up to the point when the deductible is reached.

Two-thirds of CDHP enrollees feel they are familiar with their health plan, compared with only 34 percent of people enrolled in traditional health plans (those without any deductible). EBRI found that most people enrolled in CDHPs tend to be cost-conscious decision makers, checking whether their plan covers care, asking for generic drugs instead of brand name prescriptions, checking the price of a health service before getting care, and talking with the doctor about treatment options and costs.

But cost doesn't always equate to *value* in healthcare, which can be in the eye of the beholder: patient, consumer, caregiver, or payor. Michael Porter, longtime researcher into value chains, in the *New England Journal of Medicine*, wrote:

> Value should always be defined around the customer, and in a well-functioning health care system, the creation of value for patients should determine the rewards for all other actors in the system. Since value depends on results, not inputs, value in health care is measured by the outcomes achieved, not the volume of services delivered, and shifting focus from volume to value is a central challenge.[7]

In the eyes of healthcare consumers, value is elusive: Almost 70 percent of US adults think that healthcare costs are unreasonable, across generations and insurance status. Furthermore, people bundle other factors into their value equation in healthcare beyond cost, including customer service, accessibility/availability, coordination and follow-up, and "bedside manner" of clinicians.[8]

Two High Healthcare Costs Getting More Transparent: Prescription Drugs and High Deductibles

The most visible healthcare out-of-pocket cost for many consumers is for prescription drugs, for which value can be in the eye of the beholder in several respects: balanced with the direct cost they bear, people also take into account several factors including the side effects related to a drug, convenience (e.g., single or multiple doses), polypharmacy (too many drugs required to take at the same time), and bottom-line, overall effectiveness for their condition, among other factors that are barriers to drug adherence. But cost remains a top reason patients don't take medications as prescribed, a critical challenge as specialty drug prices are the fastest growing cost of the healthcare bill.[9]

Over one-half of US adults have done something potentially dangerous to ration their drug spending, *Consumer Reports* discovered in a 2015 survey.[10] These actions, taken among people who had a prescription drug benefit, included 19 percent who skipped filling a prescription because of cost, 17 percent who skipped a dose without professional approval, and 7 percent who cut pills in half, again without approval.

Patients aren't connecting the dots between self-rationing prescription drugs due to cost in the short term and facing potential longer term healthcare costs due to future adverse events caused by avoiding the initial expense.

The growth of high-deductible health plans (HDHPs) is also exposing health consumers to healthcare "sticker shock." A 2015 Kaiser Family Foundation study found that only one in three nonelderly households with incomes above the federal poverty level had sufficient cash to pay for a midrange annual deductible of $1200 for an individual or $2400 for a family.[11] Despite health reform's title as the "Affordable Care Act," there remain a plurality of people for whom healthcare costs are still too great a cost to bear.

Health Consumers Need Accessible and Reliable On-Ramps to Trusted Information

While most consumers want to be more engaged in their healthcare, very few have been able to effectively access cost and quality information. The Kaiser Family Foundation April 2015 Health Tracking Poll[12] found that very few consumers had used price or quality information in healthcare as illustrated in Figure 2.2.

An unsolved challenge for consumers is that hospital rating systems vastly differ, as observed by a study published in Health Affairs comparing the hospital comparison tools developed by

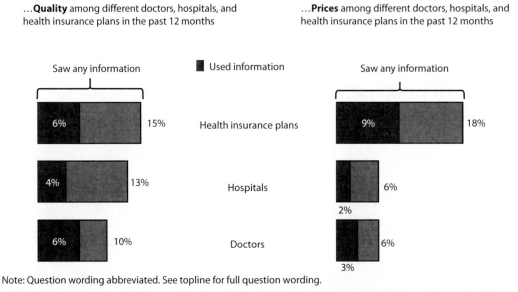

Figure 2.2 Consumer use of price or quality information in healthcare. (From B. DiJulio et al., Kaiser Health Tracking Poll: April 2015, The Henry J. Kaiser Family Foundation, April 21, 2015. With permission.)

Consumer Reports, Healthgrades, the Leapfrog Group, and *US News & World Report*. No hospital was ranked first by all four sources, and some hospitals were ranked highly by one source but poorly by another. Such grade variations are apt to confuse consumers who seek consistent ratings across the hospitals from which they seek services.[13]

Providers Begin to Embrace Consumers' DIY Health

Patients want to be partners in their health: When people receive clear information about their choices, most want to be an equal decision maker in choosing healthcare (found in the Institute of Medicine's [IOM] Roundtable on Value & Science-Driven Health Care[14] and illustrated in Figure 2.3). When patients are engaged with their data, healthcare quality improves, the IOM also asserted in this report. "The ability of individuals to access and use their online medical records serves as one of the cornerstones of national efforts to increase patient engagement and improve health outcomes," noted the leadership team of the National Coordinator for Health IT in their National Action Plan to support consumer engagement via e-health, published in Health Affairs.[15]

While most US adults hadn't yet accessed an online health portal at the end of 2014, Xerox found that most people would be more interested and proactive in their personal health if they had online access to their medical records.[16] In 2014, nine in ten US hospitals and four in five office-based physicians had adopted an electronic health records system.[17,18] The growing presence of electronic health records in both hospitals and doctors' offices is, potentially, providing an accessible on-ramp for health consumers.

Doctors' proficiency with using health IT in patient care has substantially increased since Accenture surveyed US physicians' use of health IT in 2012. The number of US doctors who routinely use digital tools like secure e-mail to communicate with patients has more than doubled since 2012, to 30 percent. Services available to patients online, too, have grown, to 58 percent of doctors offering prescription refill requests, 55 percent offering medical record access (largely through EHR portals), and 24 percent adopting telemonitoring to track patient health online.[19]

Both physicians and patients seem poised to jointly embrace people's use of digital health technology: Most patients (84 percent) and most doctors (69 percent) believe that technology

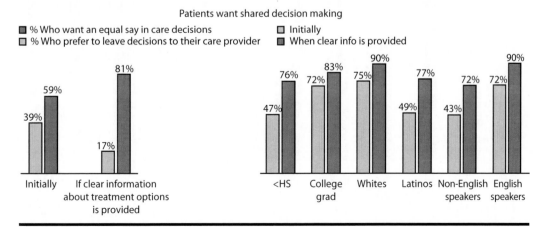

Figure 2.3 Consumer attitudes regarding involvement in health decision making. (From Institute of Medicine. "Partnering with Patients to Drive Shared Decisions, Better Value, and Care Improvements." Meeting Summary, August 2013. With permission.)

should be used by patients to assist in the diagnostic process, found the 2014 WebMD/Medscape survey.[20] Most physicians (86 percent) believe that health apps will increase their knowledge of patients' conditions, 72 percent believe apps will encourage patients to take more responsibility for their health, and one-half think apps will increase the efficiency of patient care.[21]

Patients are broadly concerned, though, about the paperwork they see in health providers' workflows. Hospitals are "drowning in paperwork," which concerns three in four US adults worried that paperwork cuts into the time health providers can spend with patients, according to a Harris Poll conducted for Ricoh.[22] On the upside, most patients feel more connected to providers who don't spend a lot of time on paperwork during a visit. And 60 percent of patients said they'd rather seek treatments online for non-life-threatening conditions than deal with hospital paperwork to see a healthcare professional.

To support patient self-care outside the healthcare setting, several healthcare providers are working to support clinicians who want to prescribe digital health tools and apps to patients. Ocshner Health System launched the "O Bar," a "genius bar" à la Apple retail stores, to recommend mobile health apps to physicians along with selling digital health devices such as WiFi-enabled scales, glucose monitors, and blood pressure cuffs.[23] The Cleveland Clinic started up ADEO,[24] offering mobile apps, software, and digital tools in a marketplace for health providers looking to adapt digital health both inside the institution and for patients.

Providers would be wise to embrace consumers' DIY self-care engagement. More than 40 percent of US consumers would be willing to switch physicians to gain online access to electronic health

Interest in using an app for a smartphone or tablet,
by health-related function, 2014
(among those who never used an app for a smartphone or tablet)

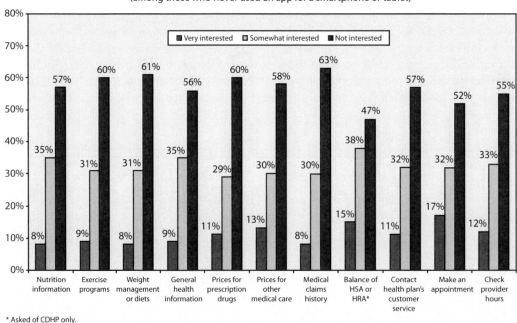

* Asked of CDHP only.

Figure 2.4 Demand for health apps among people who have never used an app for a smartphone or tablet. (From P. Fronstin, and A. Elmlinger, EBRI/Greenwald & Associates, "Consumer Engagement in Health Survey," EBRI Issue Brief, No. 407, December 2014. With Permission.)

records, according to an Accenture study.[25] Health consumers are also looking for a range of digital tools to help manage health. EBRI's survey found demand for health apps among people who have never used an app for a smartphone or tablet, from managing nutrition, weight, and exercise to making appointments, searching their medical claims history, and contacting a health plan, as highlighted in Figure 2.4. Furthermore, with greater financial stakes in physical health, more people seek help for fiscal management as well.

Growing Need for Help with Personal Health Financial Management

Public Agenda's survey research published in the report "How Much Will It Cost?" details consumers' challenges with personal health spending.[26] The report shows that a majority of US consumers want help managing health spending, including accessing websites that show providers' prices, estimates from providers on how much their bill will be before leaving the office, and financial incentives from insurance companies if the consumer chooses a less expensive provider.

Providers' support for patients' management of health finance can better the patient as well as the providers' bottom-lines; in late 2014, a growing number of consumers had trouble paying for healthcare, a pain acutely felt by providers as well, Transunion found.[27] Some hospitals and insurers have launched cost estimators for patients to access before they receive services, such as the Saint Alphonsus Hospital online price estimator tool, and CIGNA health plan's cost estimator, which is available via the CIGNA portal as well as part of the Walgreens mobile app. UnitedHealthcare's online bill payment service enables plan members to pay bills via the myClaims manager portal that integrates with patients' claims. In 2015, there were dozens of start-up companies addressing the healthcare transparency market, such as Benefitter (www.benefitter.com), Bloom Health (www.gobloomhealth.com), Castlight Health (www.castlighthealth.com), Change:Healthcare (www.changehealthcare.com), My Health and Money (www.myhealthandmoney.com), Patient Pay (www.patientpay.com), PokitDok (www.pokitdok.com), Simplee (www.simplee.com), Stride Health (www.stridehealth.com), SwiftPayMD (www.swiftpaymd.com), and Symbiosis Health (www.symbiosishealth.com), among others. Guroo (www.guroo.com), a tool developed by the nonprofit Health Care Cost Institute, has assembled data from several large national health insurance plans on prices for 70 common services based on what insurers pay providers.[28] Many of these provide cost-comparison and estimation tools for consumers to use when shopping among alternative providers and procedures. However, health-engaged consumers will need comparative physician-level quality data and information about their out-of-pocket costs, a level of personalization and granularity missing, thus far, from the commercialized products.[29]

The Home Is the Ultimate Hub for Health

As many US consumers trust large retailers and digital companies to help them manage their health as they do healthcare providers, according to Strategy&'s 2014 survey.[30] "There's a new boss in US healthcare: the consumer," the report asserts. As Figure 2.5 illustrates, the biggest reason consumers might engage with a retail or digital company to help them manage health is because the price, quality, and trust attributes of products and services fetched in retail and online are more transparent in those venues than in healthcare services and products—whether seeking price

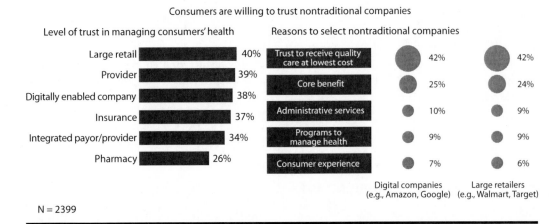

Figure 2.5 Consumers are willing to trust nontraditional companies. (From J. Estupinan et al., The birth of the healthcare consumer: Growing demands for choice, engagement, and experience. © 2014 PwC. All rights reserved. PwC refers to the PwC network and/or one or more of its member firms, each of which is a separate legal entity. Please see http://www.pwc.com /structure for further details. No reproduction is permitted in whole or part without written permission of PwC. Reprinted with permission.)

variations for receiving an MRI in a community or getting the cost for a specialty drug for which a consumer might bear a 40 percent coinsurance share.

Thus, new entrants are coming into people's daily lives via industries long missing from the health ecosystem; these include:

- TD Bank gifted free Fitbit activity trackers to new customers opening bank accounts in January 2015, linking financial wellness and saving money with overall health.
- Grocery stores and food companies are launching apps to help people manage various aspects of gut and overall health.
- The life insurance company John Hancock developed a new type of life insurance for customers who want to lead active lifestyles and make healthy choices to gain points for these activities, lowering annual premiums.
- Telecommunications companies have begun to leverage their reach into people's homes, with Cox Cable partnering with The Cleveland Clinic to provide remote health monitoring into subscriber/patient homes through their joint venture, Vivre Health.
- Consumer electronics companies, such as Apple, Google, Microsoft, and Samsung, are expanding health data ecosystems that collect and organize consumer-generated health data from wearable trackers and smartphones.
- Lifestyle brands, such as UnderArmour, are extending their reach from consumer goods companies into health and wellness. UnderArmour acquired MapMyRun and MyFitnessPal, and will morph well beyond a sporting goods company into a health data and wellness organization.

Together, these new entrants will enable people—health consumers, patients, and caregivers—to access services and self-care well outside brick-and-mortar healthcare institutions (specifically, hospitals and physician offices). Telehealth options, increasingly available at the pharmacy, workplace, and via smartphone app (such as MDLIVE accessed via the Walgreens app, or American Well's AmWell app) will redefine "where" healthcare is delivered.

The person's home will increasingly be his or her health-and-medical home. Hospitals have begun to try the patient's home as an inpatient/at-home setting, looking for a new site of care in the growing reimbursement regime of value-based payment.[31] As more "things" get embedded with sensors in the emerging era of the Internet of Things for health, people will be generating data about daily living that can be aggregated, analyzed and repurposed to inform them on how to improve daily decisions about sleep, movement, nutrition, mood, and other factors that bolster—or diminish—personal health.[32]

Conclusion

Think of the new DIY health consumer as living life as a "new health citizen"—engaging in life, liberty, and the pursuit of health. As Benjamin Franklin, one of the signers of the Declaration of Independence, wrote in the first half of the eighteenth century, "Trusting too much to others' care is the ruin of many."[33] This prescription for self-care does not have an expiration date even two-and-a-half centuries since it was written.

Impact

To understand more about the impact of these issues in the lives of real people, please read the following patient and caregiver stories in Section II of this book:

Story 1   "A Cost-Conscious Consumer: 'And What Will That Cost Me?'"
Story 4   "Give Me Autonomy, Not Engagement"
Story 14   "Learning from Others' Mistakes"
Story 15   "Living Well with Lupus"
Story 16   "Managing Diabetes with a Do-It-Yourself Pancreas System (DIYPS)"
Story 18   "Overcoming Adverse Childhood Events"
Story 22   "Technology Can Make Pain Less Painful"
Story 25   "Visualizing Symptoms"
Story 26   "Wasting My Time"

Notes

1. EY. "How to Copilot the Multichannel Journey," June 2014. http://www.ey.com/GL/en/Newsroom/News-releases/news-30000-consumers-from-34-countries-reveal-new-global-trends.
2. Harris Poll. "Americans May Be Ready for a Brave New World of Healthcare." November 13, 2014. http://www.harrisinteractive.com/NewsRoom/HarrisPolls/tabid/447/mid/1508/articleId/1520/ctl/ReadCustom%20Default/Default.aspx.
3. National Partnership for Women & Families. "Engaging Patients and Families: How Consumers Value and Use Health IT." December 2014.
4. http://www.nationalpartnership.org/research-library/health-care/HIT/engaging-patients-and-families.pdf.
5. Grajales, Francisco, David Clifford, Peter Loupos, Sally Okun, Samantha Quattrone, Melissa Simon, Paul Wicks, and Diedtra Henderson. "Social Networking Sites and the Continuously Learning Health System: A Survey." Institute of Medicine. January 23, 2014. http://nam.edu/perspectives-2014-social-networking-sites-and-the-continuously-learning-health-system-a-survey/.

6. Fronstin, P., and A. Elmlinger. 2014 EBRI/Greenwald & Associates Consumer Engagement in Health Survey, EBRI Issue Brief, no. 407, December 2014. http://ebri.org/publications/ib/index.cfm?fa=ibDisp &content_id=5470.

7. Porter, M. E. "What Is Value in Health Care?" *New England Journal of Medicine* 363 (2010):2477–2481, with permission.

8. Deloitte. "The quest for value in health care: A place for consumers." June 2014.

9. Medscape. "Patients Not Taking Their Drugs? Ways You Can Change That." February 3, 2015. http://www.medscape.com/viewarticle/837405.

10. *Consumer Reports.* "Are You Paying More for Your Rx Meds?" August 13, 2015. http://www.consumer reports.org/cro/news/2015/08/are-you-paying-more-for-your-meds/index.htm.

11. Kaiser Family Foundation. "Many Families Would Struggle to Pay a Typical Health Insurance Deductible, New Analysis Finds." March 11, 2015. http://connect.kff.org/many-families-would-struggle -to-pay-a-typical-health-insurance-deductible-new-analysis-finds?utm_medium=social&utm_source =email.

12. Kaiser Family Foundation. April 2015 health tracking poll. http://kff.org/health-reform/poll-finding /kaiser-health-tracking-poll-april-2015/.

13. Austin, J. M., A. K. Jha, P. S. Romano, S. J. Singer, T. J. Vogus, R. M. Wachter, and P. J. Provonost. "National Hospital Ratings Systems Share Few Common Scores and May Generate Confusion instead of Clarity." *Health Affairs* 34 (2015): 3423–3440. http://content.healthaffairs.org/content/34/3/423 .abstract.

14. Institute of Medicine. "Partnering with Patients to Drive Shared Decisions, Better Value, and Care Improvements." Meeting Summary, August 2013. http://iom.nationalacademies.org/Reports/2013 /Partnering-with-Patients-to-Drive-Shared-Decisions-Better-Value-and-Care-Improvement.aspx.

15. Ricciardi, L., F. Mostashari, J. Murphy, J. G. Daniel, and E. P. Siminerio. "A National Action Plan to Support Consumer Engagement via E-Health." *Health Affairs* 32, 2 (2013): 376–384.

16. Xerox. Consumer survey conducted by Harris Poll among 2,017 US adults, September 2014. Published December 16, 2014. http://news.xerox.com/news/Xerox-EHR-survey-finds-Americans-open-to-online -records.

17. The Office of the National Coordinator for Health Information Technology. "Adoption of Electronic Health Record Systems among US Non-Federal Acute Care Hospitals: 2008–2014." ONC data brief, no. 23, April 2015. http://dashboard.healthit.gov/index.php.

18. US Department of Health and Human Services, The Office of the National Coordinator for Health Information Technology. "Update on the Adoption of Health Information Technology and Related Efforts to Facilitate the Electronic Use and Exchange of Health Information." Report to Congress, October 2014.

19. Accenture. "Despite Increased Use of Electronic Medical Records, Fewer US Doctors Believe It Improves Health Outcomes, Accenture Survey Shows." April 13, 2015. https://newsroom.accenture .com/industries/health-public-service/despite-increased-use-of-electronic-medical-records-fewer-us -doctors-believe-it-improves-health-outcomes-accenture-survey-shows.htm.

20. WebMD/Medscape Digital Technology Survey, September 2014. http://www.medscape.com/view collection/33223.

21. Research Now. "Are Mobile Medical Apps Good for Our Health? A New Study by Research Now Reveals That Doctors and Patients Say 'Yes.'" March 17, 2015. http://www.researchnow.com/en-US /PressAndEvents/News/2015/march/research-now-study-are-mobile-medical-apps-good-for-our -health-infographic.aspx?language=en-US.

22. Harris Poll for Ricoh Americas Corporation. "With hospitals 'drowning in paperwork,' patients look to Internet for treatment." April 13, 2015. http://www.ricoh-usa.com/news/news_release.aspx ?prid=1554&alnv=pr.

23. Farris, M. "Ocshner 'bar' Has Apps Good for What Ails You." WWL-TV, Channel 4, New Orleans, February 11, 2015. http://www.wwltv.com/story/news/health/2015/02/11/ochsner-bar-app/23262855/.

24. Cleveland Clinic. "New Company ADEO to Deliver Proven Healthcare Solutions Directly to Customer." December 2014. http://innovations.clevelandclinic.org/About-Us/News-Media-%281%29 /Newsletter-Pages/122014_ADEO.aspx#.VUeYDPm6eM8.

25. Accenture. "More than Forty Percent of US Consumers Willing to Switch Physicians to Gain Online Access to Electronic Medical Records, according to Accenture Survey." September 16, 2013. http://newsroom.accenture.com/news/more-than-40-percent-of-us-consumers-willing-to-switch-physicians-to-gain-online-access-to-electronic-medical-records-according-to-accenture-survey.htm.

26. Public Agenda. "How Much Will It Cost?" March 17, 2015. http://www.publicagenda.org/pages/how-much-will-it-cost.

27. TransUnion. "TransUnion Healthcare Report Finds Both Patients and Hospital Administrators Feeling the Squeeze of Increased Costs." April 22, 2015. http://newsroom.transunion.com/transunion-healthcare-report-finds-both-patients-and-hospital-administrators-feeling-the-squeeze-of-increased-costs.

28. Health Care Cost Institute. "Health Care Cost Institute (HCCI) Launches Guroo—To Provide Consumers with Free Access to a Health Care Transparency Tool." February 25, 2015. http://www.healthcostinstitute.org/news-and-events/health-care-cost-institute-hcci-launches-guroo-%E2%80%93-provide-consumers-free-access-healt.

29. Yeglan, J. M., P. Dardess, M. Shannon, and K. L. Carman. "Engaged Patients Will Need Comparative Physician-Level Quality Data and Information about Their Out-of-Pocket Costs." *Health Affairs* 32, 2 (2013): 328–337.

30. PwC and Strategy&. "The Birth of the Healthcare Consumer, 2014." http://www.strategyand.pwc.com/reports/birth-of-healthcare-consumer http://www.strategyand.pwc.com/global/home/what-we-think/reports-white-papers/article-display/birth-of-healthcare-consumer.

31. Lamas, D. J. "Admitted to Your Bedroom: Some Hospitals Try Treating Patients at Home." New York *Times*, April 27, 2015. http://well.blogs.nytimes.com/2015/04/27/admitted-to-your-bedroom-some-hospitals-try-treating-patients-at-home/?_r=0.

32. Sarasohn-Kahn, J. "How the Internet of Things Can Bolster Health." *Huffington Post*, March 9, 2015. http://www.huffingtonpost.com/jane-sarasohnkahn/how-the-internet-of-thing_1_b_6801342.html.

33. Franklin, Benjamin. *Poor Richards Almanac*. Philadelphia Printing Office, 1732–1759.

Chapter 3

The Science and Practice of Health Behavior Change: A Consumer-Centric, Technology-Supported Approach

---

Catherine D. Serio, MS, PhD*,
and Susan W. Butterworth, MS, PhD

Introduction

Every Tuesday night, John stopped by his mom's place on the way home from work. John and Maggie enjoyed their weekly routine of sharing dinner and the day's stories and then watching television. On this Tuesday evening, during a commercial break, Maggie stood up and walked into a wall. John called to his mother. But Maggie, dazed and wobbly, didn't respond. She shook her head, turned and walked across the room into a different wall. Again, she shook it off, backed up, and walked into another wall, unaware of her son's cries for help. Maggie was having a massive stroke. When the ambulance arrived, Maggie resisted with all her strength and begged her son, "No doctors. No doctors."

Five hours later, 52-year-old Maggie, mother of two grown sons and grandmother of two more boys, was dead. In the hours just before her death, doctors evaluated her unconscious body and diagnosed Maggie with diabetes—a treatable condition. But the diagnosis came too late. Too late because Maggie hadn't seen a physician in over 10 years.

Maggie was a beautiful young woman with a beauty queen's curves and a dark complexion—gifts from her Portuguese heritage. Motherhood changed her figure and her weight. She gained 12 pant sizes and 200 pounds. No one loathed that change more than Maggie herself.

---

* @catserio.

On a family boat trip one summer afternoon 11 years before, Maggie (age 41) slipped and broke her ankle. The ambulance crew had to use a crane to lift her off the boat before taking her to the hospital. As if that weren't embarrassing enough, the doctor paid more attention to her weight than her ankle: "How did you do this to yourself? Don't you know how bad obesity is for your health? An ankle fracture is just the beginning…you're going to have all kinds of health problems if you choose to continue living this way."

Maggie felt disrespected and humiliated. After that visit, she vowed she would never see another doctor. She was never successful in getting the excess weight off, but she certainly didn't need a doctor to tell her she was fat. The next time she saw a doctor, Maggie came in feet first on a gurney. The doctor's only duty was to pronounce her dead.

Maggie's story didn't have to end that way. Our medical and cultural paradigms failed her. Our medical model focuses on organ systems and diseases processes, not people. People are a collection of conditions, such as "pancreatic disease" (rather than "a person with diabetes") or "cerebral vascular accident" (instead of "someone having suffered a stroke."). When faced with a behavioral issue, such as obesity or not taking medications as prescribed, our medical culture permits us to judge patients as having character flaws. We fail to affirm healthy behaviors while focusing on perceived character flaws. But the failure isn't an individual's character. The flaw is in our reductionist, judgmental paradigms—the very paradigms that convince providers that people like Maggie, who react in a negative way to our approach, are "noncompliant." We blame the client instead of questioning the efficacy of our approach.

This chapter is an invitation to do your part to change these faulty belief systems and help lead an authentic consumer-centered healthcare revolution, rather than just paying lip service to being "patient centered." Previous chapters described how consumer-centered practice is critical to the triple-aim bottom line: patient experience, health outcomes, and costs. This chapter will help deliver that value by suggesting how to engage people to find their voices, own their health, and change their health behaviors.

Our Patients—Our Partners

Inviting people like Maggie to "reclaim ownership of their health" may sound airy and empty. But the science behind respecting a person's autonomy is as solid as our knowledge that the earth is round. Risky health behaviors—ranging from addiction to obesity to not following recommended treatment regimens—are not changed without people's consent and participation. None of us has the power to control another person's actions (unless we choose a career as a prison guard). All of us are empowered by personal choice and autonomy. When someone tells us what to do, our inner 13-year-old crosses his or her arms, squints his or her eyes, and says "Just try and make me!" If you're skeptical that this applies to adults, try changing a law to restrict access to buying guns or to ban sugary beverages in your city. Adults value autonomy and demand choice.

For those of us in healthcare, *our* behaviors need to shift in order to create a patient-centered culture and promote health behavior change. Traditionally, providers have been directive and authoritative. We tell people what to do and how to do it. And it works in acute medical situations. However, chronic condition management, which accounts for about 85 percent of healthcare today, is a different story. When we push people to change their lifestyle behaviors, they push back. When they don't follow their treatment plan, we label them as noncompliant, difficult, or unmotivated. We don't treat them like consumers who need a different type of service. We treat them like Maggie. The outcomes of our efforts are humbling:

- 50 percent of US adults do not take medications as prescribed
- 35 percent of US adults are obese
- 15 percent of US adults still smoke
- 42 percent of US adults get recommended influenza shots, leaving 58% unprotected[1]

These are the standard outcomes that come from using the current behavior change model. Although policies and interventions can influence behaviors, these continuing problems underscore the fact that *we* do not change people. Individuals own their changes and their own choices. And yet, healthcare reimbursement is shifting to hold care organizations accountable for patient outcomes. This poses a paradox for healthcare leaders: How can we be held responsible for something we don't control…especially when patients won't do what we tell them to do? Take a cue from Americans traveling abroad to a country where they don't speak the language. If you speak English to locals and they don't understand, the answer is not to speak English more loudly. Try learning some of the native tongue instead.

The native tongue—and common experience for most of us—is that changing our behavior isn't easy. Acknowledging that fact is powerful and humbling. When we acknowledge this challenge with the patient, a trusted connection forms. That connection deepens through authentic listening, where we are curious and seek to show empathy and understanding. As the trust deepens, people share their ambivalence about change, and that opens the door for us to support and guide them along the way toward greater health. Most of us—when heard in a respectful way—will choose health and the benefits that accompany it. This creates an opportunity for all parties—patients, providers, and healthcare organizations—to align around a shared purpose: Connected, healthy patients. When individuals choose their own goals, they invest in achieving them. When clinicians are free to listen to their patients, they have deeper connections with them. When organizations encourage people to own their health, they advance population health. Gone is the binary notion of "compliant" or "noncompliant" patients. One empowered individual at a time, we are moving together toward triple aim outcomes.

Misalignment Manifested

Alignment of medical care to client goals and preferences is not typical in healthcare today. The dominant medical culture follows the "assess–diagnose–treat" paradigm in keeping with the organ-based training model. Endocrinologists treat the pancreas. Internists treat high blood pressure. Neurologists treat strokes. Each organ has its home. Clinicians figure out ("assess") what is wrong with the organ ("diagnose"), then prescribe the patient a "treatment" plan. This process creates an expectation that change comes from outside, not within, the patient. Things will be done to the patient, not with him or her. Unfortunately, the patient's inner strengths and ideas for change are unseen and unharnessed.

This condition-centric model influences the entire system of care. Organs, like the heart or kidneys, sometimes even have their own centers. Reimbursement follows suit. ICD-10 is the coding system for submitting medical claims, most of which map to an organ system. Our medical record systems were designed following the model of medical billing systems—collecting the data necessary to submit the correct diagnostic code to get paid.

New models of payment are beginning to reward population health metrics. Fee for value is positioned to overtake fee for service (consider the Medicare Access and CHIP Reauthorization Act of 2015).[2] But medicine hasn't yet reached the tipping point. Today's cultural norm remains focused on assess–diagnose–treat an illness or an organ. Listening to and partnering with clients in order to activate them to take charge of their health is not yet a core cultural component—and reimbursement certainly hasn't caught up to the extra time it can take. Bold healthcare leaders have the opportunity to differentiate their organizations by making them the best "listening communities." Those who facilitate such a culture shift will find themselves well positioned for the coming accountable care paradigm shift. When payment follows client experience and health outcomes (which depend on behavior change), *true* client-centered "listening communities" will lead the way.

Behavior Change Drivers

The actions we take are influenced by a myriad of factors including our zip code and educational and marital status. Poverty harms health. So does the rapid rise in consumption of processed foods and the disappearance of open space and clean air. Policy advocates are making inroads toward researching these environmental drivers through research on social determinants of health.[3] Behavior change is not an individual sport. But an individual can do his or her part with the right coaching and support from the healthcare ecosystem. The next section describes factors that influence our behaviors at an individual and relational level.

The First Conversation

There is a saying that "the most important conversation is the one between a person's own two ears." Internal drivers of behavior change are a complex assembly of beliefs and values (see Figure 3.1). Our thoughts shape our beliefs, which shape our actions. Philosophers and writers have observed this across history. Shakespeare said, "There is nothing either good or bad but thinking makes it so." Twentieth-century cognitive scientists have proven that thoughts are a powerful behavior change lever. Someone who believes that he or she is powerless to effect a health outcome is unlikely to try. Just as a person who can imagine himself or herself taking a step in a different

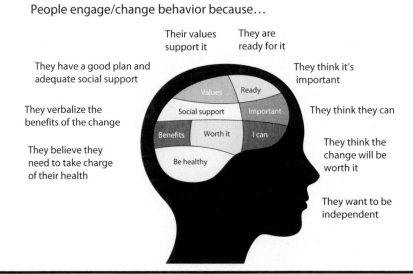

Figure 3.1   Internal drivers of behavior change: a complex assembly of beliefs and values.

direction is that much closer to taking it. Our thoughts interact with our actions—and both exist in the context of the surrounding environment. Foundational psychological theories describe this interplay, models apply these theories into practice, and there are key themes that run across them all. See Figure 3.2 for an overview of key behavior change theories and models, along with key concepts.

Key Theories, Models & Concepts to Behavior Change Practice

Social Cognitive Theory

The key principle of SCT is Reciprocal Determinism: the belief that there is an on-going relationship between three factors: (1) the person (including their cognition or thoughts and various personal factors); (2) their behavior; and (3) their external environment

Self-Determination Theory

Based on the assumption that people will naturally move towards better mental and physical health if the proper support is provided, the SDT identifies extrinsic and intrinsic factors that motivate people.

Theory of Planned Behavior

People will have more motivation and be more likely to adopt a behavior if they: feel that the suggested behavior is positive; they perceive themselves as being able to perform it; and if they think their significant others want them to perform the behavior.

KEY BEHAVIOR CHANGE CONCEPTS
across theories and models

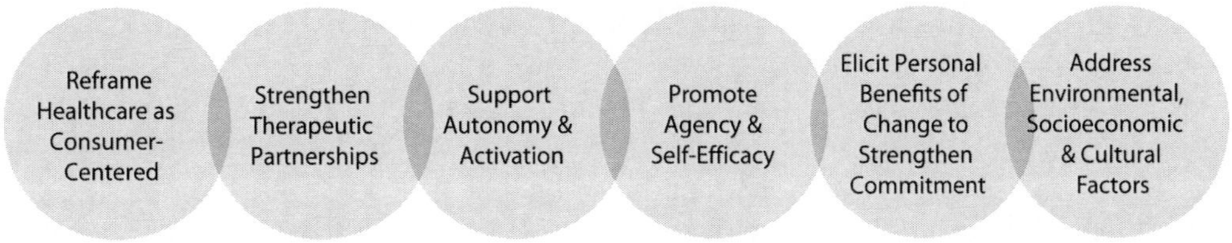

Reframe Healthcare as Consumer-Centered

Strengthen Therapeutic Partnerships

Support Autonomy & Activation

Promote Agency & Self-Efficacy

Elicit Personal Benefits of Change to Strengthen Commitment

Address Environmental, Socioeconomic & Cultural Factors

Health Belief Model

The HBM rests on the foundation that people: have the desire to avoid illness, or conversely get well if already ill; and believe that a specific health action will prevent or cure illness. A person's course of action depends on the person's perceptions of the benefits and barriers related to health behavior.

Transtheoretical Model

The foundational principle of the TTM is that by using approaches that match a person's level of change readiness, the clinician can facilitate and accelerate movement through the stages of change. TTM identifies effective approaches for each stage.

Chronic Care Model

The CCM identifies the essential elements of a health care system that encourage high-quality chronic disease care: (1) the community; (2) the health system; and (3) the delivery system design, decision support and clinical information systems.

Sustainable Change Logic Model

The Logic Model was based on extracting higher categories of change and mapping proven behavior change techniques into each category. There are 5 goals needed to support sustained behavior change: Awareness, Learning, Motivation, Behavior and Sustainability.

Figure 3.2   Overview of key behavior change theories, models, and concepts.

Conversations That Move Us

Therapeutic relationships play an important part in supporting individual behavior change. Any of us can get stuck in our inner dialogue. A trained guide can help us reveal and redirect that inner narrative so that we talk ourselves toward change, not away from it. Effective change conversations begin with empathy—an expression of caring without judging, which enables the first step along the behavior change path. Multiple studies demonstrate that clinicians who demonstrate empathy and alliance with patient goals generally have patients with higher activation, better results, and fewer medical complications.[4,5]

Different schools of psychology (interpersonal, cognitive, etc.) study the impact of counseling on behavior change. Cognitive behavioral therapy (CBT) is a particularly effective counseling intervention for depression, anxiety, and other conditions. A CBT therapist helps people uncover automatic thoughts and behaviors, such as negative ("I think I can't") self-talk that blocks any movement toward change.

For any counseling technique to work, the guide's first task is to establish a therapeutic alliance characterized by trust, empathy, and honoring the individual's autonomy. As described earlier, this approach is not yet core to the culture of medicine, which is rooted in the expert model (assess–diagnose–treat). Yet, the therapeutic relationship is a prerequisite to advance behavior change conversations. Overtly sharing power may be helpful by acknowledging that you have expertise in a subject, such as diabetes or heart disease, but your patient is the expert and authority over his or her life and health choices.

TRADITIONAL VERSUS EVIDENCE-BASED APPROACH TO DIABETES VISIT

Consider the following case study with a typical patient, comparing the traditional approach with an evidence-based approach.

Mrs. Thompson comes into the office for her annual exam. She is obese and has hypertension and diabetes. Allison, the nurse, is dismayed when she reads from the chart notes that Mrs. Thompson has gained five more pounds and her A1c has increased from 7.5 to 9.2.

Traditional approach—Allison explains again to Mrs. Thompson the importance of weight loss to her health and questions her about checking her blood sugar and taking her medications. She gathers a food log of what Mrs. Thompson has eaten for the last few days and tells her what is not healthy or good for her conditions. She provides and reviews the same educational handouts that she gave Mrs. Thompson on her previous visit. Lastly, she tells Mrs. Thompson what her health plan should be and how to enact it. The session lasts 20 minutes. Mrs. Thompson leaves feeling humiliated and condescended to, acutely aware of Allison's dismay and judgment.

Evidence-based approach—Allison explores what Mrs. Thompson feels is going well with her and provides affirmations. Mrs. Thompson brings up the weight herself and Allison asks her what she knows about the relationship between her weight gain and A1c level. She then asks Mrs. Thompson to consider what the overall benefits would be if she was able to lose just 10 percent of her body weight. She elicits some ideas about weight loss from her and explores how her living situation or environment may create barriers to following this plan. Lastly, Allison asks Mrs. Thompson for realistic next steps that she feels confident she can begin. Allison ends the session with a genuine affirmation about Mrs. Thompson's knowledge, insights, and efforts to manage her health. The session lasts 20 minutes. Mrs. Thompson leaves feeling encouraged and ready to take renewed action.

Health Coaching

A major theme in today's healthcare environment is the concern about how best to effect patient engagement, encourage treatment adherence and self-care management of chronic conditions, and ensure better clinical outcomes. Health coaching has emerged as a popular intervention that can be used in diverse healthcare settings, as well as in-person, telephonic, and online. Unfortunately, there is wide variation in definitions, roles, and practice in the health coaching realm. A recent meta-analysis analyzed health coaching studies for evidence of effectiveness and to identify key features of successful programs.[6] Of the 15 studies used in the analysis, fewer than half used rigorous methodology, such as control groups, random assignment, and other factors that limit bias. Significant improvements were noted in lifestyle behaviors such as nutrition, physical activity, weight management, and medication adherence in well-controlled studies. Common features of effective programs were goal setting, motivational interviewing (MI), and collaboration with healthcare providers. Although more rigorous study clearly is needed, health coaching is proving to be a promising modality for health and disease management, and one area for further study is how to bring effective health coaching through a variety of channels, from in person to telephone- or application based.

Motivational Interviewing (MI)

Different health coaching techniques have their place, but recent reviews have identified MI as the most widely studied most effective and most standardized approach. MI is an engaging, person-centered approach that was founded over 30 years ago by William R. (Bill) Miller, a clinical psychologist and addictions counselor, although it has now been adapted for brief encounters in healthcare settings. It is described as a "collaborative, goal-oriented style of communication with particular attention to the language of change."[7] The main principles of MI are (1) partnership—the clinician forms a collaborative relationship with the person and uses a guiding style, rather than a directive one; (2) acceptance—the clinician approaches the individual in a nonjudgmental manner, showing support for autonomy/choice and providing support for self-efficacy and activation with empowering affirmations; (3) compassion—the clinician places the needs and interests of the individual in front of his or her own agenda or needs; and (4) evocation—the clinician selectively elicits and reinforces what is called "change talk" in order to strengthen the person's commitment to the agreed upon treatment plan or lifestyle change.

The most exciting research to date has been in this change talk area and on the influence that clinicians can have on their clients' motivation for change. Change talk is one type of client talk (see "Client Talk" sidebar) and it consists of statements verbalized by someone about his or her perspective on change—the desire for, ability to, and reasons and need for change—along with commitment, activation, and steps already being taken toward change.[7] If engagement is successful, multiple recent studies have found that change talk can be evoked during a session. This change talk is a positive and powerful predictor of treatment follow-through and is correlated with positive clinical outcomes.[8] In addition, a more recent clinical trial also linked the clinician's reflection of change talk, along with evoking it, to better clinical outcomes.[8] The end result of this research has been an increased emphasis on training clinicians to strategically evoke and reflect change talk from the person in order to increase the odds of the individual taking action. Effective MI practitioners employ a complex skill set that requires the same amount of preparation, practice, and feedback as learning to speak a foreign language or to play a musical instrument. MI coaches need coaching themselves. Unfortunately, the standard of care today is for health coaches to participate

LEARN MORE

For more information and a complete bibliography of MI literature go to www.motivational interviewing.org

in one-time MI training but not receive the ongoing feedback and coaching required to become truly proficient in the skill. Imagine the string section in a fifth-grade orchestra. Young violinists often miss the notes and squeak over strings to the point of audience discomfort. Expecting a health coach to use MI proficiently after a single training session will likely result in a similar jarring and discordant experience.

Tailoring for Success

The areas reviewed establish behavior change fundamentals: (1) individuals form self-concepts that either drive or inhibit their efforts to make healthy changes and increase self-efficacy; (2) therapeutic relationships are established based on empathy, trust, and honoring personal choice. Once a partnership is formed, the practice of MI helps to uncover personal motivators for change ("change talk"), increasing a sense of confidence and likelihood to take action.

CLIENT TALK

There are three types of client talk that provide indications of how a client is feeling about his/her readiness for change and the interaction with the practitioner:

Change talk: statements in favor of change: the desire, ability, reasons, and need for change, along with commitment to, preparation for, and steps already being taken toward change. The more change talk that is evoked during an encounter, the higher will be the commitment strength to the change and the more likely a positive clinical outcome. Examples: "I want to start exercising." "I think I could do that." "I want to see my grandchildren grow up."

Sustain talk: statements that represent ambivalence about change, including the barriers and challenges of making the change or following a treatment plan. This is a type of counterchange talk that is a normal and expected part of the change process. It is important for the clinician to genuinely validate and explore sustain talk if it's a sticking point to action; however, the clinician shouldn't dwell there if moving onto change talk is possible. Examples: "It's just so hard to get started." "Smoking helps me unwind." "I just forget to take them."

Discord: statements that represent an interpersonal tension between the client and practitioner. This is another type of counterchange talk that occurs when the practitioner fails to resist the righting reflex (need to direct or fix) and falls back into the traditional medical model approach. Unlike sustain talk, discord is an indicator for the practitioner to change his or her approach. Examples: "You just don't understand how hard this is for me." "I'm tired of people nagging me about this." "Yeah, I've tried that but it doesn't work for me."

Setting a broader context for "action" helps those facilitating behavior change as well as those attempting it. When action is broadly defined, individuals who are not ready to do one behavior, such as start exercising, may be willing to try something else, such as tracking a behavior. "Taking action" can be defined as engaging someone at *any* point along a behavior change continuum to increase motivation and confidence. Behavioral science is not binary ("motivated" or "unmotivated") but rather a continuum of needs and readiness. Tailored interventions support people "where they are" along that continuum so that anyone may be engaged without feeling pushed or set up for failure.

James Prochaska and his team at the University of Rhode Island led the early research on tailoring interventions to the stages of behavior change. In 1983, they developed the transtheoretical model (TTM), which leverages multiple psychological theories to describe the behavior change process.[9] The TTM has four core constructs: stages of change, processes of change, decisional balance, and self-efficacy. People are assigned to one of five stages from precontemplative (not desiring change) to maintenance (trying to sustain change over time). Based on the stage, interventions are tailored to the needs of each individual stage. For example, someone in contemplation may be invited to consider the pros and cons of quitting smoking as a way to explore personal ambivalence. In contrast, people in the preparatory stage are ready to try a new behavior and might receive a checklist of actions to prepare their environment, such as emptying junk food from the pantry as a step toward a healthier diet. TTM interventions show positive effects on smoking cessation as well as other lifestyle risk factors and treatment adherence.[10–12]

At the University of Oregon, Judy Hibbard and her team developed a behavior change segmentation model using the concept of "patient activation."[13] Their research built on the "team-based model of chronic care"[14] that supports individuals' self-management needs including knowledge, skills, and confidence. Hibbard described a continuum of activation levels, ranging from individuals not actively managing their health to those with healthy routines and high self-confidence. Hibbard's research and that of others building on her model show that patient activation levels correlate with results such as improved health outcomes and lowered costs.[15]

The emergence of different behavior change models and theories poses a problem of unification. Which approach or theory is best? How do we unify our approach to standardize interventions and advance behavior change research? Two different research teams at Cardiff University in England are addressing this challenge. The first team, led by Abram and Susan Michie, is cataloging proven interventions (behavior change techniques, or BCTs) across models.[16] To date, Michie and her colleagues[17] have identified 93 BCTs and created a taxonomy to organize them. Cataloging the active ingredients of behavior change can be compared to the work of pharmaceutical scientists who have isolated drug treatment at the neurotransmitter level. This allows pharmacists to consult with medical teams and recommend drugs tailored to precise biochemical causes. This tailoring approach has led to at least 11 chemotherapies for small-cell lung cancer, as one example.[18] Using Michie's taxonomy, effective behavior change interventions can be tailored to where someone is in his or her behavior change journey. But which framework would be used to segment behavior change stages? The field needed a unified theory of behavior change. Fortunately, Dr. Glyn Elwyn's Cardiff team cracked the code on this problem.

Elwyn and his colleagues sought to build a metamodel of behavior change science.[19] They systematically reviewed all of the papers published between the years 1947 and 2010 on health behavior change and four chronic conditions: type 2 diabetes, coronary artery disease (CAD), chronic obstructive pulmonary disease (COPD), and asthma. A total of 3,885 papers were identified and further reviewed against criteria including use of an established behavior change theory and sound methodology (concurrent control with random allocation). Social cognitive theory was the most widely applied model (41 percent of studies), followed by the transtheoretical model (13 percent).[19]

Using findings across theories, Elwyn and his team extracted higher categories of change and mapped proven behavior change techniques into each category. Their model, the "sustainable change logic model," identified five goals needed to support sustained behavior change: awareness, learning, motivation, behavior, and sustainability. Within each goal, they mapped the BCTs from the Michie framework that were used in the intervention (Figure 3.3). Once someone's needs along the logic model are identified, proven interventions are suggested. In the same way that ibuprofen is proven to reduce inflammation and ace inhibitors reduce blood pressure, the logic model shows us which behavior change techniques, when matched to an individual's needs, are most effective.

Knowing an individual's needs is necessary in order to match him or her to the correct logic model category. A recently developed six-item questionnaire[20] helps coaches or consumers themselves identify which needs are most important to the individual at the time. The questionnaire targets a lifestyle goal, such as losing weight or quitting smoking, or managing a chronic illness, such as diabetes or coronary artery disease. The tool places people into logic model categories: awareness (gaining knowledge), learning (building skills), motivation (increasing importance),

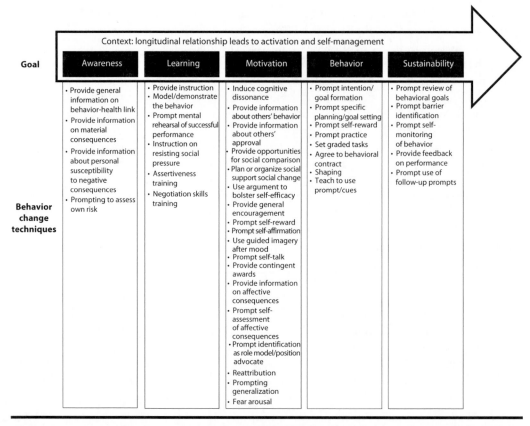

Figure 3.3 Sustainable change logic model highlighting five goals needed to support sustained behavior change mapped to behavior change techniques from sustainable change sequence: a framework for developing behavior change interventions for patients with long-term conditions. (From G. Elwyn et al., *European Journal for Person Centered Healthcare*, vol 2, no 2, 2014. With permission.)

behavior (taking action), and sustainability (overcoming barriers). Once placed, the individual may receive the behavior change techniques effective in that stage. A brief tool to match people with proven change strategies shows great potential to infuse more behavioral science into healthcare. To externally validate the tool, however, additional research in clinical settings is needed. All of this research forms the theoretical basis for techniques that can be applied in a variety of settings to support behavior change: in traditional clinicians offices; in primary care offices, where more and more therapeutic interventions are being delivered; through health coaching programs and behavior change technologies.

Behavior Change Enabling Technology

There is a high-stakes game at play in American healthcare: We are gambling on the idea that technology will improve health outcomes. From electronic health records to population health software and beyond, new or increased technology accounts for 40 to 50 percent of annual healthcare cost increases.[21] This investment could launch a radical, person-centered transformation in American health. Alternatively, the billions of dollars being spent each year could mainly generate profit for the companies developing the technology and the providers selling it.

A patient-centered technology agenda could transform health in revolutionary ways that empower citizens. In some corners, such as social media, the revolution has already begun. "PatientsLikeMe.org" (PLM) built a digital home for people to find their tribes—people struggling with similar illnesses, common or rare. On PLM, people compare treatment responses, learn self-management tricks from others, or participate in research. The Internet gives voices of support and inspiration a digital platform for social connection. Technology holds additional promise, including health advocacy as embodied by those who shared their stories in this book as well as "e-Patient Dave": A cancer survivor and champion of patient empowerment, Dave deBronkart encourages healthcare leaders to "empower, engage, equip, and enable" patients. How can the health technology industry use its leverage to be a force for good, a force to empower individuals no matter what their current readiness to change may be?

Designing for Behavior Change

In this digital era, there are many ways to reach people—none more important than the smartphone in the hands of 64 percent of the US population. Health interventions can be served directly to consumers—an opportunity that launched more than 165,000 new mobile health apps. Unfortunately, the volume of apps is more impressive than the usage data. Fewer than 1 percent of health apps are used more than two times. Sadly, the most person-centered, robust behavior change intervention may be buried in one of those 165,000 apps. The problem is that no one will find that app without breaking through the crowd by creating a sticky experience that rivals that of the game Candy Crush. As behavioral interventions are served up via technology, collaboration with other disciplines and experts, including persuasive design and "gamification," is critical.

Dr. B. J. Fogg has created a lab that mashes up the worlds of technology, design, and behavior change. In his book, *Mobile Persuasion*,[22] Fogg and coauthors describe how to design engaging mobile experiences by integrating concepts of play, simplicity, and meaning. They also address tailoring for different audiences from the young (digital natives) to older people living with chronic conditions. Infusing the competencies of persuasive and user-centered design with the latest science on behavior change is the key to scaling behavior change interventions to reach broad populations.

Wearable Devices

When we connect apps to personal devices, a feedback loop is created. A person's data—hours of sleep, time spent exercising, heart rate—can be fed into a health app. That app can support behavior change techniques (see Figure 3.3) such as getting social support by sharing data and encouragement with someone else working on the same goal. Other techniques include setting goals, such as steps per day, and tracking progress over time. If goals are met, people may be cued to challenge themselves by increasing that goal. If goals aren't met, users could be helped to identify and overcome barriers.

Trials on wearable devices are just emerging and more data are needed. A recent randomized controlled trial on postmenopausal, overweight women demonstrated that wearing a Fitbit alone did not result in increased physical activity levels.[23] However, women who wore the Fitbit, went through an instructional session, and received a one-month follow-up call had significantly improved activity levels. This suggests that effective recipes for behavior change interventions will need to mix behavior change techniques, wearable devices, and some human touch to have the greatest impact.

Web-Based Interventions

Is human touch necessary to support behavior change? Or is it possible that our future will include interacting only with computers that serve as a healthcare extender? When our healthcare workforce is not large enough to meet the demands of 76 million aging boomers, the idea of leveraging technology to close the gap is worth considering. And then there are the 41 million digital natives in the United States for whom technology is accepted as part of every experience.

The research on health interventions that are solely technological is nascent, yet promising.[24] Those individuals who report benefiting from web-based support tools share the following characteristics:

- They see the experience as benefitting their personal health.
- They like the convenience of 24/7 access.
- They appreciate content that is tailored to their preferences.
- They prefer anonymity for sensitive topics, such as HIV/AIDs and substance abuse.

Research suggests that individuals who are comfortable with human–computer interaction will answer difficult questions more honestly since the computer is not judging them. Others report distrusting the system and being unlikely to disclose personal information in order to protect their confidentiality.

Big Data, Precise Tailoring

Looking at things in the closest way—beyond the perception of the naked eye—is an ancient pursuit. The invention of glass dates back to the first century when Romans noticed that viewing objects through glass made them appear larger. Fast-forward 500 years to 1595, when Dutch spectacle makers discovered that if you put multiple lenses in a tube, the magnification level was greater still. This insight led to the creation of the first microscope. Today, we continue in the quest to look closely at things—but the lens we use is data. And there is an unfathomable amount (nearly one zettabyte or the equivalent of about 250 billion DVDs) of it to sort through.

CASE STUDY: IORA HEALTHCARE

The theme of this chapter is simple: Put patients first and behavior change outcomes will follow. A new primary care model, Iora Healthcare, is building their practices with a "patients-first" culture and their outcomes prove that their culture is working. Iora's clinical outcome scores, validated in partnership with the Dartmouth Institute for Health, exceed industry averages by 10 to 20 percent for control of hypertension and diabetes.[25] Their patient satisfaction scores, as measured by the 2014 CAHPS survey, range from 75 to 89 percent. In the eyes of any healthcare executive, these are outcomes to die for. They all begin with culture.

Dr. Rushika Fernandopulle, Iora cofounder, believes that healing comes from continuous, caring relationships. Every aspect of the Iora model—now in over 20 cities across the United States—is built on a culture revolving around patients and supported by a nontraditional, interdisciplinary team. For each Iora physician, there are five additional team members: a nurse, a social worker (to support behavioral health needs), and three health coaches. Hire the right people who are conversant in empathy, says Fernandopulle, and you get the right culture.

The Iora model approach to behavior change begins with getting the relationship right. Coaches send Happy Birthday messages to their members. They follow an "apprentice model" of self-management where the patient observes the action first (such as home blood pressure monitoring) and then staff observe and coach the patient doing the same action. All of this is wrapped into a motivational interviewing framework that honors individual autonomy, explores personal motivation, and builds on past successes.

On top of culture, Iora's two other core tenets are its systems and business model. Both align with the patient-centered culture. Iora is building its own electronic health record, called the "Collaborative Care Platform," which enables patients to not only read their medical records, but also to *write* in them. The technical system is being developed, from the ground up, with patient needs and preferences front and center. Iora likewise gives careful thought to the physical environment of each clinic so that it harmonizes with the needs of the population. Everything from hours of operation to clinic signage to exam room seating is customized to the target populations' preferences.

Dr. Fernandopulle hopes to get patients off the transactional assembly line of healthcare and into healing relationships—relationships with caring at the core, health coaching routinely practiced, and individuals inspired and supported in their unique journey with health. Focus on patients and the behavior change outcomes will come. Iora is delivering on this promise.

Earlier in this chapter, we addressed how tailoring can improve behavior change outcomes. "Big Data," as it is called, has the potential to tailor interventions to the household or even individual level. All of us generate data over the course of our lives: the things we buy, the shows we watch, and the healthcare we seek. These data sets are currently being mined and combined to determine which interventions could be most impactful for a certain type of individual. One healthcare system, for example, found that women who like baseball are more likely to try to have a vaginal delivery after a previous C-section. Big data can predict who will respond to an e-mail intervention and who needs a phone call, as well as who might respond better to a stop smoking intervention that focused on the perils of secondary smoke inhalation vs one that focused on personal health benefits. Big data companies claim (and we await proof) that big data will keep more people at home than end up in hospitals.

The prospect of precise and personalized interventions, aligned with behavior change science, is promising. Ideally, the two fields will merge to create the greatest good. To do so, the process of how big data sets are used must be transparent. Without transparency, there is no trust. And without trust, there is no behavior change. Big data will make healthcare systems smarter about how they use resources. But the potential to help each individual is there—if the conditions of transparency are met.

Conclusion: If We Build It, Change Will Come

Maggie didn't have to die at 52. She avoided healthcare out of the fear of being shamed and embarrassed again. Today, most people have a bit of Maggie in them. We know we could do something different, something to improve our health. But we don't always know how to change. Even if we know how, we struggle to find the "why" of change—the motivational trigger to help us step outside our comfort zone and toward new actions. Changing our own behaviors and organizational culture is not easy. But it is possible and the science of change is solid.

We can start with changing language and thoughts: Instead of patient, try "person"; instead of "noncompliant," think "ambivalent"; instead of telling someone, "here's what you have to do," change to "here is something that may be helpful." We can train and empower staff to create a person-centered paradigm, a culture of listening to and partnering with consumers and patients. We can respect autonomy and choice and evoke people's personal reasons to change. We can assume that people have the wisdom to solve some of their own problems if we provide the right support. We can explore importance and confidence. We can use tailored interventions that guide people toward "success experiences" that increase confidence. We can offer real-time support through the transparent use of technology, including social platforms, aligned with individual needs and preferences.

When these behavior change levers are activated, the balance of powers shifts. People see themselves and their choices as important determinants of their health. The expert model, where providers hold sole decision-making authority and accountability for outcomes, changes to a true partnership model. People feel empowered to own their health. Healthcare professionals remain critical team members. But in a consumer-centric approach, we are health consultants, not health custodians.

Every Maggie out there needs some help and deserves some hope. And providers need that, too. They struggle under pressure to see more patients and produce outcomes. And when it comes to supporting behavior change, many providers feel ineffective. Our existing model of care no longer works in an era of chronic illness and accountable care. But there is a better way. We can put behavior change science into practice. We can lead through inspiration and empowerment. Let's create a culture of listening, a bias for partnership, and a path toward making change possible.

Impact

To understand more about the impact of these issues in the lives of real people, please read the following patient and caregiver stories in Section II of this book:

Story 12	"Healing with Faith, Food, Friends, Family, and Laughter"
Story 18	"Overcoming Adverse Childhood Events"
Story 23	"Transformation Is Always Possible"
Story 24	"Very Bad Genes and Very Bad Luck"

Notes

1. http://www.cdc.gov/DataStatistics/
2. http://www.thelancet.com/journals/lancet/article/PIIS0140-6736(08)61690-6/abstract
3. http://www.cdc.gov/socialdeterminants/
4. http://link.springer.com/article/10.1007/s10488-015-0655-8#/page-1
5. http://journals.lww.com/academicmedicine/Fulltext/2012/09000/The_Relationship_Between _Physician_Empathy_and.27.aspx
6. http://www.ncbi.nlm.nih.gov/pubmed/20809820
7. http://www.guilford.com/books/Motivational-Interviewing/Miller-Rollnick/9781609182274
8. http://www.ncbi.nlm.nih.gov/pubmed/24462244
9. http://psycnet.apa.org/journals/ccp/51/3/390
10. http://www.ncbi.nlm.nih.gov/pubmed/11456079
11. http://www.ncbi.nlm.nih.gov/pubmed/15367070
12. http://www.ncbi.nlm.nih.gov/pubmed/16846327
13. http://www.ncbi.nlm.nih.gov/pmc/articles/PMC1361049/
14. http://www.ncbi.nlm.nih.gov/pmc/articles/PMC2690311/
15. http://content.healthaffairs.org/content/34/3/431.short
16. http://www.ncbi.nlm.nih.gov/pubmed/18624603
17. http://www.ncbi.nlm.nih.gov/pubmed/23512568
18. http://www.cancer.org/cancer/lungcancer-non-smallcell/detailedguide/non-small-cell-lung -cancer-treating-chemotherapy
19. http://www.bjll.org/index.php/ejpch/article/view/736
20. www.healthwise.org
21. http://www.thehastingscenter.org/Publications/BriefingBook/Detail.aspx?id=2178
22. http://captology.stanford.edu/resources/mobile-persuasion-book.html
23. http://www.ncbi.nlm.nih.gov/pubmed/26071863
24. http://www.ncbi.nlm.nih.gov/books/NBK38648/
25. http://www.iorahealth.com/real-results/

Chapter 4

High-Tech and High-Touch Primary and Chronic Care

Jan Oldenburg, FHIMSS*

Introduction

Some of us are old enough to remember the television character of Dr. Marcus Welby as the epitome of the primary care doctor: He was passionate about the care he delivered, made house calls, and was willing to try unorthodox treatments. Most importantly, however, he had time to establish trust with his patients, talk to them about their lives—not just their illnesses, and offer wise advice. The relationship he had with his patients was personal as well as professional, and medical encounters took place in the context of family and community.

Contrast a visit with Dr. Welby with what frequently happens in a primary care visit today. Your doctor is likely to be in a hurry: New interns spend an average of 8 minutes per patient and standard doctor visits are generally 15 minutes each, perhaps a bit longer if the visit is for an annual exam.[1,2] Your doctor may interrupt you, as, on average, doctors interrupt patients after 18 seconds of conversation, making it hard for the patient to tell a coherent story or maintain a train of thought.[2] Even if you are seeing your designated primary care physician (PCP), it can feel impersonal. You may have been anticipating a visit, made heroic efforts to get to the clinic for the appointment on time, or have deeply researched your condition and symptoms, only to feel frustrated and disappointed by the lack of time to explore all of your health concerns, have a real conversation, or get to more complex issues during your visit. These constraints make it difficult to build a trusting relationship with your doctor.

The writer Anna Quindlen addressed this issue in an address to US medical students in 2013, challenging doctors to get to know their patients as individuals. She said, "Isn't that why patients would be just as happy to have someone listen to their heart at Walmart? If no one knows her name at the doctor's office; she can go somewhere cheaper that doesn't know her name and pick up T-shirts for the kids at the same time."[3] Many physicians mourn the loss of a more personalized style of practice as much as their patients do.

---

* @janoldenburg.

Compounding the difficulty of developing a trusted primary care relationship, job changes, moves, or insurance coverage with a narrow network of doctors may force people to choose new doctors frequently because physicians they previously bonded with are now "out of network." While these changes are intended to manage the quality and cost of care, by making it more difficult to build long-term relationships with your doctors, they may have unintended negative impacts on care and health outcomes. This is especially likely to be true for patients with chronic conditions, where building a working partnership based on a long-term understanding of how the person responds to triggers and treatments can be crucial to appropriate treatment.

Given the current obstacles to getting satisfactory care from a known and trusted provider, it is not surprising that consumers often focus on convenience when looking for care, flocking to urgent-care settings and apps that help them find a doctor who is available NOW, searching for information about self-treatment, or opting for a telemedicine visit. Both patients and doctors may desire long-term trusting relationships, but may have given up hope they can be established in the current system.

Much is lost when this scenario becomes the norm. There is evidence that a relationship with a provider whom the patient trusts, who abides with the person over time, who displays empathy and compassion, and who treats the patient as a partner in his or her care can be a powerful element of healing.[4] New studies suggest that the placebo effect is empowered by a trusting relationship with a doctor and—as long as trust is present—works *even when* the doctor tells the patient it is a placebo treatment.[5,6]

Technology can certainly help solve these problems, but it matters that we are solving the right problems. Dr. Jordan Schlain addresses this issue in a blog post entitled, "Is Healthcare Designing the Wrong Patient Experience?"[7] He challenges organizations that focus on patient experience without consideration for building better relationships, saying, "Instead of healthcare focusing on staging an experience for patients, why are we not designing opportunities for us to truly connect with our patients?" He quotes Seth Godin, "In a world of abundance of choice and endless options, there is a premium on credibility and trust."[8] To restore credibility and trust, Schlain suggests that healthcare needs to focus on the four *T*s of patient expectations: time, trust, transparency, and transitions. Technology needs to support all of these, creating environments, space, and time in which trust can be established.

One of the ways to accomplish this is to incorporate patients and caregivers into the design process to ensure we create capabilities that address diverse needs and interaction styles. While some patients are focused on autonomy and self-efficacy, others want more guidance from their physician—and what an individual patient wants and needs from his or her physician may vary over time, depending on the severity of the condition, the amount of anxiety it generates, and other factors in the person's personal life and mental health.

In Chapter 2, The New DIY Health Consumer, we looked at a number of ways that consumers are taking charge of their own healthcare, choosing services, tools, and doctors that support and empower them in their health and healthcare journeys. In Chapter 8, Programs that Work to Promote Partnership and Engagement, we explored evidence that patient access to their own health information is making a difference in patients' ability to take responsibility for their own health. In both cases, we highlighted technologies that add convenience and simplicity to patients' lives.

Since we are likely to get the kind of healthcare system we envision, it's important to imagine a system that acknowledges and supports individuals' desire for convenience, autonomy, *and* long-term relationships: high-touch medicine that is also convenient and uses technology to support and enable both self-care and physician-based care, with transparent economics that make it clear what it will cost and why. In new models of primary care, the patient serves as the quarterback of his or her own care, and the PCP serves as the head coach who creates and tailors the game plan, equipping the patient with the right tools and support to successfully drive the care plan forward.[9] This chapter will explore capabilities that can help us achieve this desired future.

Do I Need Care? And If I Do, What Kind of Care Do I Need?

A cough that nags on and on, disrupting sleep. A knee that aches after a walk. An acute sore throat. An exacerbation of chronic asthma or psoriasis. All of these are examples of minor illnesses that cause individuals to run an internal calculation about whether it is bad enough to see a doctor or whether it will clear up on its own. There are many components to that calculation: How much will it cost to go in? How long will I have to wait—on the phone, for an appointment, in the office? Can a doctor fix this? Will I feel foolish because it's nothing? What if I don't go and something is seriously wrong? Can I feel better with over-the-counter medications instead?

Often, in this period of indecision, we consult "Dr. Google." A Pew Internet survey published in early 2013 found that 72 percent of adults have looked online for information about health, and a full 35 percent of Americans went online specifically to try to diagnose a health issue they or someone else had. Of those "online self-diagnosers," 46 percent found confirmation that they should see a doctor or healthcare professional.[10]

Many online sites and apps feature symptom checkers aimed at helping consumers assess the severity of a health issue. A 2015 study in the *British Medical Journal*, however, highlighted research from Harvard and Boston Children's Hospital showing that current symptom checkers are often inaccurate. After inputting patient vignettes into 23 symptom checkers, the researchers found that "symptom checkers have deficits in both diagnosis and triage, and their triage advice is generally risk averse"—encouraging patients to seek care even when it is not necessary.[11]

Insurers and healthcare organizations have nurse phone lines to help patients make the decision whether and where they need to be seen, reducing the anxiety of "going it alone." This can be especially critical as there are situations where delays in seeking treatment put one's life at risk. Researchers have found that "every 30-minute delay in treatment following AMI (acute myocardial infarction) increases 1-year mortality by 7.5%, and almost half of the 167,000 annual stroke deaths in this country occur before the patient reaches the hospital."[12] People delay treatment for a variety of reasons, and programs that help people make such decisions faster and more accurately can save lives.

Problems also occur when people too frequently go to the emergency room for care. This is especially an issue in lower income populations where individuals may not have a primary care physician. Washington state has created a program that connects Medicaid patients to primary care physicians who can help them manage their health and conditions over time, reducing the cost of emergency room treatments while connecting patients to more appropriate sources of care than emergency rooms. "In the first year of the program, emergency department visits by Medicaid enrollees declined by 9.9 percent and the rate of visits by frequent users (those with more than four visits in a year) fell by 10.7 percent. The savings for 2013 totaled $33.6 million."[13]

In the future, symptom checkers will likely be able to access a patient's full medical history as well as current symptoms and biometric measurements. Using artificial intelligence, they will accurately diagnose illness, recommend next best actions, and even initiate emergency calls to 911 or alerts to the patient's doctor. These kinds of tools could free physicians for more complex problem solving while directing individuals to the appropriate level of care.

Finding a Trusted Partner

"Fit" with your doctor doesn't matter nearly as much for a short consultation by phone or in an urgent-care setting as it does when you are trying to find a long-term physician relationship. Many people who are looking for a primary care relationship turn to their insurer's provider directories to support the effort. These sites are not always a trustworthy source of information, however, as many insurers have difficulty keeping their directories up to date and accurate. One of the top complaints about payers is the quality of their provider directories. In several states, exchange participants have filed lawsuits, charging that they were misled by false information in payer provider directories.[14,15] A California regulatory study of this issue found that provider directories available to the public had significant errors, with up to 25 percent of listed physicians not available.[16] The Centers for Medicare and Medicaid Services (CMS) have recently taken action to improve the quality of provider directories by instituting tighter requirements for Medicare Advantage and Exchange plans, hoping to make it easier for prospective members to determine which providers are included in specific networks as well as which providers are taking new patients.[17]

A growing number of third-party services and applications attempt to help patients with the task of physician selection based on community ratings and other characteristics. These include HealthGrades (www.healthgrades.com), ZocDoc (www.zocdoc.com), and WebMD (www.webmd.com). A few sites go further, providing more detailed search information and attempting to pair prospective patients to physicians who are a "match" for their conditions, personality, and even emotional style.[18] There is evidence that connecting patients and doctors who fit in terms of beliefs and expectations is important to fostering trust in the relationship, though it has limits when it supports prejudices about whether a doctor of a different race or sex can be adequate.[19]

Some provider organizations are taking on this challenge by providing deeper and more searchable information about their providers. Group Health NW, for example, allows prospective patients to search for providers by gender, specialty, language spoken, medical group affiliation, and wheelchair access, as well as whether they are accepting new patients, are board certified, offer maternity care, offer electronic prescribing, or have an electronic medical record. Many Kaiser Permanente regions provide personal profiles of physicians as shown in Figure 4.1 from the Southern California Region,[20] where physicians personalize their entries in the "about me" section by highlighting background material, biography, how they practice, and how they thrive. This gives patients a better sense of the person behind the white coat when they are making their selection.

Industry-wide, more advanced search tools are likely to support consumers in finding doctors that are a match to their needs, conditions, personality, and desired style of support.

Getting an Appointment

Many conditions that would previously have required in-person visits to the doctor are now being handled through virtual means. Spurred by the Accountable Care Act (ACA) and CMS incentives, models of care that reward physicians and practices for outcomes rather than activities mean that providing convenient capabilities can be cost effective for everyone. The nationwide expansion of urgent care centers, from 8000 in 2008 to more than 9300 today, is also a sign of the rapid growth of this after-hours alternative to the doctor's office.[21] The expansion as well as the consolidation of physician practices with hospitals has also led far more primary care physicians to offer extended office hours and same-day appointments in an effort to compete for the loyalty of their patients.

Telemedicine is also emerging as a promising technology for convenient care. Google has tested offering telemedicine visits associated with searches. In test markets, users who search on

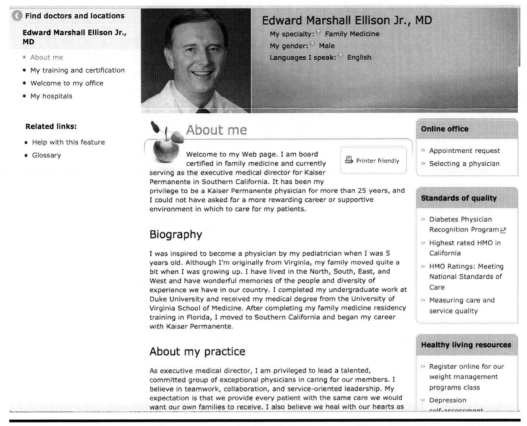

Figure 4.1   Illustration of Kaiser Permanente personalized provider directory page and Edward Marshall Ellison, Jr. directory entry used by permission of SCPMG and Dr. Ellison.

something like "knee pain" have been offered the opportunity to have a telemedicine visit with a doctor "in the moment."[22] This type of activity is growing, as Walgreens recently announced a partnership with MDLive to offer similar telehealth services.[23] Many insurers also cover services such as Teledoc or MDLine to provide members with convenient access to online consultations. These approaches focus on short-term consultations that help consumers decide what kind of care they need and treat minor ills—one-off consultations rather than lasting relationships.

Some health systems are using telemedicine in ways that support *both* convenient care and ongoing connection, so that consumers don't have to choose between the two. For example, Target announced a partnership in Southern California with Kaiser Permanente to offer Kaiser Permanente nurse practitioners and telemedicine services in Target stores.[24] CVS links its retail clinics to local provider organizations to ensure continuity of care, as this example highlights: "ProHealth patients throughout Connecticut will have access to clinical support, medication counseling, chronic disease monitoring, and wellness programs at CVS stores and MinuteClinic, the retail health care division of CVS Caremark."[25] In both of these examples, the clinic care becomes an extension of the primary care team, sharing data and building continuity of care.

One Medical, a concierge practice, has built its services around convenience, including same-day appointments, e-mail access to the patient's doctor, and the ability to schedule telemedicine visits if the patient is out of town. Capabilities are emerging to enable more immediate communication methods, such as texting, to be done in a Health Insurance Portability and Accountability Act (HIPAA)-compliant way.

Individuals who have access to a patient portal can often make, view, change and cancel appointments online. Patients who schedule their own appointments are more likely to show up for them, reducing clinic no-show rates and smoothing the flow of patients in each practice.[26] Increasingly, patients have the option to schedule phone visits, group visits, or telemedicine visits in addition to the standard clinic visit.[27] These types of capabilities can offer convenience without disrupting core physician/patient relationships.

Kaiser Permanente, one of the leaders in providing digital health services, finds that in some geographic areas, more than 50 percent of patient office visits now occur virtually, either by phone, e-mail, or televisits.[28] Kaiser Permanente has been successful in moving clinical visits to other settings in part because incentives are aligned to promote the most efficient setting of care while ensuring that quality of care is maintained and improved. Its portal also enables patients to send their care team questions via secure messaging or to send a list of symptoms or questions in advance of a visit to make it more effective for both parties.

Dr. Ron Dixon accomplished positive outcomes at Massachusetts General Hospital Beacon Hill Internal Medicine Associates, where he is the director of the virtual practice pilot. They've created and implemented a virtual visit platform that enables patients to enter information about their situation online and physicians to respond within a day. He reports that virtual visits are five times more efficient than in-person visits. "When he reads notes from a patient and responds, it takes an average of 3.6 minutes compared to 18 minutes for an in-office visit when factoring in taking vital signs, asking the patient questions, and recording answers by hand and then in electronic notes."[29] This program works especially well for monitoring and managing chronic disease, and it allows patients to be conveniently monitored by physicians with whom they already have a relationship.

Telemental health also has great promise, as organizations are finding that it is possible to offer both brief psychiatric interventions and long-term therapy effectively using telehealth capabilities.[30] The VA is one of the leaders in using telemental health services to help veterans who may live far away from therapists.[31] A 4-year study of telemental health among veterans found that hospitalizations for psychiatric issues dropped by more than 25 percent among the population receiving telehealth care.[32] For those with posttraumatic stress disorder (PTSD), care may be combined with an application developed by the VA and Department of Defense, called, PTSD Coach. It helps veterans track PTSD symptoms, links them to local sources of support, provides accurate information about PTSD, and teaches helpful individualized strategies for managing symptoms.[31] The VA is just beginning a clinical trial of PTSD Coach, but a preliminary evaluation conducted in 2014 found its use promising.[33]

Consolidating Records

When consumers visit a new physician, they generally need to bring along medical records that tell the clinical story of their health. Despite many advances in making health records digital, it is still painful for consumers to collect a complete set of records. They often have to call or write to multiple providers, cover the cost of printing and mailing records, or log in to multiple portals, hoping that each allows them to download a complete record of care. If they succeed in that effort, they then must hope that the records are actually consulted when care is provided.

Surescripts announced a study in September of 2015 highlighting that patients often feel that their doctors don't have the information to treat them appropriately, as shown in Figure 4.2.[34] This is the clear consequence of a lack of true interoperability. Consumers also are impatient with the

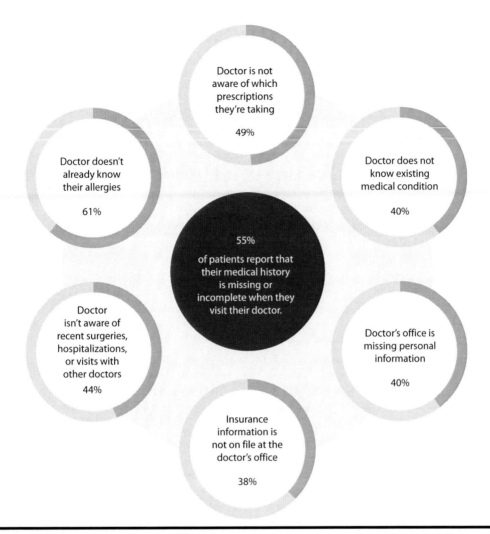

Figure 4.2 Study highlighting patient concerns that doctors don't have the information to treat them appropriately. (From Surescripts Connected Care and the Patient Experience Survey, September 2015. With permission of Surescripts.)

need to log onto multiple portals to get access to their clinical record and frustrated by the amount of paperwork needed in interactions with the medical system.

The Office of the National Coordinator for Health Information Technology is attempting to address these issues in the meaningful use stage 3 regulations, published in September 2015, by requiring providers and electronic health record systems to support application programming interfaces (APIs). In the rule it notes, "Patients would be able to collect their health information from multiple providers and potentially incorporate all of their health information into a single portal, application, program, or other software."[35] The rule goes on to support providing access to authorized patient representatives as well as patients themselves. These rules are set to take effect in 2018. They aim to "free the data" and allow patients to choose an app that would gather all their health data and help them make use of it more effectively than they may be able to do with a current patient portal.

In-Person Visits

Technology is being used to make in-person visits more convenient and effective. Some clinics enable patients to fill out forms and update medical histories online before the visit. ZocDoc (www.zocdoc.com), Practice Fusion (www.practicefusion.com), and NoMoreClipboard (www.nomoreclipboard.com), for example, enable clinics to offer this capability online.

Providence Health has eliminated waiting rooms by introducing technology that tracks the patient and assigns him or her a room—as well providing alerts to staff if the patient has been waiting more than 10 minutes to see a provider.[36] UCLA tracks when patients are due to arrive via the valet sticker they receive when they arrive at the parking lot. UCLA knows that the time from valet parking to arrival in the office is approximately 6 minutes and uses that time to have the doctors waiting for the patient.[37]

Virginia Mason Medical Center has been working to eliminate patient waiting rooms—and the waste that goes along with them—since a visit to Toyota helped leaders think differently about efficiency. An efficiency guru at Toyota looked at the Virginia Mason team's drawing of a patient journey and asked the meaning of the waiting rooms. Until that moment, Dr. Mecklenburg, one of the Virginia Mason leaders, had not made the connection that "this cost of waits and delays and these rooms with the Internet access and the fish tanks and the coffee machines, and the cubes of office staff keeping people waiting and trying to get them in for new appointments were all unnecessary costs which are ultimately paid by that patient."[38]

Other systems are focusing on the way patient–physician interaction is handled by training physicians not to interrupt patients, allowing patients to tell their stories in a coherent manner. Physicians using this practice have been surprised to find that most patients are quite coherent and brief. The outcomes are better because "when patients have been given the chance to say everything they want during the visit, they are more receptive to hearing our assessment and recommendations for managing their problems. After all, patients are in charge of their care. Our job is to serve them, respectfully and without interruption."[39]

Empowered by technology that aids workflow and provides just-in-time analysis, it is possible to envision clinic visits of the future where technology simplifies the tasks of medicine in ways that allow patients and doctors to spend more time together developing care plans that fit with the patient's lifestyle and goals.

End-of-Life Care

It seems likely that, in the future, more counseling about end-of-life care will take place in primary care settings of all kinds. A Kaiser tracking poll in September of 2015 found that 89 percent of consumers thought doctors should discuss end-of-life issues with their patients, despite the fact that relatively few reported having had such conversations. The same poll found that large majorities felt that such conversations should be covered by insurance, as shown in Figure 4.3.[40]

In January of 2016, Medicare began to cover end-of-life planning conversations between patients and physicians, and it seems likely that other insurance providers will follow.[41]

Other resources help people make end-of-life decisions, such as the Advance Care Planning Toolkit from the American Bar Association[42] to help a person build a legal advance directive, CareConversation.org's planning tools and resources,[43] Common Practice's MyGiftofGrace.com toolkit and game for engaging in family and community conversations about dying, and Engage with Grace.[44] These and many other resources can help individuals think through their wishes about end-of-life care and discuss them more easily with physicians and family.

**Large majorities say Medicare, private insurance should cover
discussions between doctors and patients on end-of-life care**

■ Percent who say Medicare should cover discussion between doctors and patients about end-of-life
   treatment options
■ Percent who say private health insurance should cover discussions between doctors and patients
   about end-of-life treatment options

Total   81%
                                                                             83%

**Figure 4.3   Bianca DiJulio, Jamie Firth, MollyAnn Brodie, Kaiser Health Tracking Poll, The
Henry J Kaiser Family Foundation, September 30, 2015 tracking poll showing consumer per-
spectives on whether end-of-life care discussions with physicians should be a covered benefit.
(From B. DiJulio et al., Kaiser Health Tracking Poll: September 2015, The Henry J. Kaiser Family
Foundation, September 30, 2015. With permission.)**

Staying Connected outside the Clinic

The current focus on population health, preventive care, and "fee for value" medicine means
that healthcare organizations of all sorts are focused on what happens to a patient's health in
the time when he or she is not actively in a physician's office or another care setting. This is not
an entirely new phenomenon, as wellness and chronic disease management programs have tried
to impact patient behavior outside the office using a variety of tools, from letters to reward systems to telephone-based coaching. Chapter 8, "Programs That Work to Promote Partnership and
Engagement," explores various approaches that are working today to engage patients and consumers in their own health and Chapter 3, "The Science and Practice of Health Behavior Change,"
highlights what we know about effective behavior change programs.

There is controversy about how well previous care management programs have worked. A
recent study suggests that in-person care management done in the context of a physician's office
is much more effective than are management provided via telephone through a third party, likely
because the first situation takes place in the context of a trusted relationship.[45,46]

The efficacy of wellness programs has also been called into question. A recent metastudy by
the California Health Benefits Review program suggested that wellness programs did not lower
blood pressure, blood sugar, or cholesterol—all risk factors for disease,[47] despite the fact that more
than 50 percent of large employers offer them.[48] In addition, questions about privacy abound in
many of these programs, as they may require people to report details about their health that may
be available to their employers or third-party vendors.[49,50]

But there is hope in new innovations around managing chronic illness. It is becoming far
more common for a clinical visit itself to feature not just the vital signs or lab test results gathered
by the physician's staff moments before he or she enters the room, but also to include patient-
generated health data (PGHD) from connected devices ranging from fitness trackers to connected
blood pressure cuffs, blood glucose and peak flow meters the patient uses to track his or her health
and symptoms between visits. Information may be stored on an app, presented in a spreadsheet or
graph, or be made available to the physician, with the patient's permission, through partnerships
such as Apple's HealthKit or Samsung's Digital Health platform.

Increasingly, programs offer connected options that help build relationship and trust between
visits, while also supporting people in their efforts to stay healthy at home. Predictive models

currently highlight patients who are at risk for adverse health events, and they are beginning to identify intervention approaches that are likely to work for individuals based on their preferences and inferred from their behaviors. The result will be more effective outreach that will support people with coaching supported by sensors and devices.

Mobiquity released a study in November 2015 showing that 85 percent of patients with chronic conditions wanted digital tools that would help them manage their condition. Patients with chronic conditions hoped that mobile tools could help them stay healthier, reduce the burden of self-monitoring, and make them feel less alone.[51] These findings highlight the role that well-designed apps, wearables, and connected health devices could have in helping people with chronic conditions take charge of their own health.

A program for remotely monitoring individuals with heart failure at Brigham and Women's Hospital highlights some of the characteristics of these future programs.[52] The program uses an implanted device called the CardioMEMS HF System in conjunction with rhythm data from implantable cardioverter defibrilators (ICDs). Both transmit data to the heart failure team. Analytic engines correlate the two sources of data and help predict the need for early interventions in the form of medication adjustments.

Other illustrations of how connected care might work in the future come from innovations on the patient side. Patients with diabetes and their loved ones, frustrated with the slow pace of change in medical devices and capabilities to support people living with diabetes, have found ways to put data from their continuous glucose monitoring (CGM) machines into the cloud, where it can be accessed and used to monitor the status of loved ones with diabetes, increase the loudness of blood sugar alarms, and predict "next best actions."[53] Under the banner of #WeAreNotWaiting, they are crowd-sourcing innovations, as illustrated by the story "Managing Diabetes with a DIY Pancreatic System."

This topic of patient activation is being studied, with Elsevier currently soliciting research on "self-evaluation in the frame of personalized health care and innovative strategies for disease prevention based on individual engagement."[54] Two recent studies used social media to explore how cancer patients made decisions about providers and care treatments.[55]

New devices, such as a portable device to count white blood cells through the skin,[56] offer the hope that coordinated care can be offered to patients who are able to stay in the privacy of their homes.

Right now, connected tools and devices seem to be optimized for use either by healthcare professionals or by individuals with a concern about their own health, but the fields are converging. Systems that allow doctors to view a patient's data remotely, whether from an ICD or from a blood glucose monitor, increasingly enable direct patient access to the same data, while devices optimized for patients increasingly support creation of visual charts that highlight trends and information for physicians.

Conclusion

In this environment, the challenge for patients, providers and health plans, entrepreneurs, and policy makers is to carefully consider how to build a healthcare system that best enables creation of healing relationships while supporting convenience, ease of access, and the ability to be "seen" virtually. It may be that each of us will end up with a trusted relationship with a personal health avatar at some future point—but if we envision it now, there's a version of the future that effectively merges high-tech convenience with trust, relationship, and empowerment.

Impact

To understand more about the impact of these issues in the lives of real people, please read the following patient and caregiver stories in Section II of this book:

Story 1   "A Cost-Conscious Consumer"
Story 2   "An e-Champion for Alexis"
Story 3   "You Must Have an Insanely High Pain Tolerance"
Story 4   "Give Me Autonomy, Not Engagement"
Story 6   "Concussion and Community"
Story 7   "Connected—But Not to My Doctors or Health System"
Story 10   "Grateful"
Story 15   "Living Well with Lupus"
Story 16   "Managing Diabetes with a Do-It-Yourself Pancreatic System (DIYPS)"
Story 19   "Prednisone and Misdiagnosis"
Story 20   "Standing Up for Myself through Many Medical Problems"
Story 21   "Staying Abreast: Cancer and Community"
Story 22   "Technology Can Make Pain Less Painful"
Story 25   "Visualizing Symptoms"
Story 26   "Wasting My Time"

Notes

1. http://well.blogs.nytimes.com/2013/05/30/for-new-doctors-8-minutes-per-patient/?_r=0
2. http://www.usatoday.com/story/news/nation/2014/04/20/doctor-visits-time-crunch-health -care/7822161/
3. http://humanism-in-medicine.org/anna-quindlen-advises-physicians/
4. http://www.annfammed.org/content/6/4/315.full
5. http://healthland.time.com/2010/12/27/placebos-work-even-if-you-know-theyre-fake-but-how/
6. https://www.google.com/url?sa=t&rct=j&q=&esrc=s&source=web&cd=3&ved=0CDcQFjACah UKEwjm0IX4jfXHAhVDmogKHbl4CsU&url=http%3A%2F%2Fmbr.journalhosting.ucalgary .ca%2Fmbr%2Findex.php%2Fmbr%2Farticle%2Fdownload%2F480%2F115&usg=AFQjCNFw8U AZ4usUGafq9DJV_suWxP3wuA&sig2=cMrOSV-aKxg1MVcfhAO6jA
7. http://thehealthcareblog.com/blog/2015/05/26/is-healthcare-designing-the-wrong-patient-experience/
8. http://sethgodin.typepad.com/seths_blog/2013/03/toward-zero-unemployment-.html
9. https://www.advisory.com/research/health-care-advisory-board/multimedia/video/2014 /medical-home-football-analogy
10. http://www.pewinternet.org/2013/01/15/health-online-2013/
11. http://www.bmj.com/content/351/bmj.h3480
12. http://www.clinicalcorrelations.org/?p=2356
13. http://www.pewtrusts.org/en/research-and-analysis/blogs/stateline/2015/2/24/states-strive-to -keep-medicaid-patients-out-of-the-emergency-department
14. http://www.azcentral.com/story/money/business/consumer/call%2012%20for%20 action/2014/04/26/health-net-target-consumer-complaints/8232663/
15. http://www.modernhealthcare.com/article/20140902/NEWS/309029816
16. http://www.latimes.com/business/la-fi-obamacare-network-probe-20141119-story.html#page=1
17. https://www.cms.gov/CCIIO/Resources/Regulations-and-Guidance/Downloads/2016-Letter-to -Issuers-2-20-2015-R.pdf and https://www.cms.gov/Medicare/Health-Plans/MedicareAdvtgSpecRate Stats/Downloads/Advance2016.pdf

18. http://www.futurity.org/doctors-patients-trust-emotions-890102/
19. https://books.google.com/books?id=eARU0-XQDHEC&pg=PA90&lpg=PA90&dq=match ing+to+the+right+doctor+for+care&source=bl&ots=skCqDaIUwM&sig=YimHfisE06-ZBVnj ZlNWJpdCES4&hl=en&sa=X&ei=_6N0VfPtIsyKsAXalICoCw&ved=0CGMQ6AEwCQ#v =onepage&q=matching%20to%20the%20right%20doctor%20for%20care&f=false
20. https://healthy.kaiserpermanente.org/health/care/!ut/p/a0/FcdBCoAgEAXQs3gA-YtKrF2nKN0N GiY0KiKFt6_e7sFih010x0At5kTXd8Nd-uxarovviTg6bLCw0cPMelJqHP6WSoEJJmXpyJ0H CrN-ViFekoIqcA!!/
21. http://aaucm.org/about/future/default.aspx
22. http://www.techrepublic.com/article/google-puts-doctors-on-call-experiments-with-telemedicine-in -search/
23. http://www.modernhealthcare.com/article/20141208/NEWS/312059944
24. https://www.advisory.com/daily-briefing/2014/11/17/target-partners-with-kaiser-permanente-to -offer-new-clinic-options
25. http://www.prohealthmd.com/wp-content/uploads/ProHealthCVSClinicalAffiliation.pdf
26. http://www.jmir.org/2011/2/e41/
27. http://searchhealthit.techtarget.com/feature/Telemedicine-clinics-make-inroads-into-primary-care
28. http://www.modernhealthcare.com/article/20141204/BLOG/312049976
29. http://www.clinical-innovation.com/topics/clinical-practice/saving-time-money-asynchronous -virtual-visits?page=0%2C0
30. http://telemedicine.arizona.edu/press-releases/Arizona%20is%20National%20Leader%20in%20 Telebehavioral%20Health
31. http://nationalpsychologist.com/2014/07/veterans-administration-is-leader-in-telemental -health/102562.html
32. http://ps.psychiatryonline.org/doi/ref/10.1176/appi.ps.201100206
33. http://www.ptsd.va.gov/professional/articles/article-pdf/id41831.pdf
34. http://surescripts.com/connectedpatient/default.html
35. https://www.federalregister.gov/articles/2015/03/30/2015-06685/medicare-and-medicaid-programs -electronic-health-record-incentive-program-stage-3#h-48
36. http://psqh.com/clinic-eliminates-waiting-rooms-with-rtls-technology
37. 2014 Interview with Dr. David Feinberg, former CEO of UCLA Health, now CEO of Geisinger Health.
38. http://www.pbs.org/newshour/rundown/should-hospitals-get-rid-of-waiting-rooms/
39. http://blog.stfm.org/2012/07/05/we-do-not-interrupt-our-patients/
40. http://kff.org/health-costs/poll-finding/kaiser-health-tracking-poll-september-2015/
41. http://kff.org/medicare/fact-sheet/10-faqs-medicares-role-in-end-of-life-care/
42. http://www.americanbar.org/groups/law_aging/resources/health_care_decision_making /consumer_s_toolkit_for_health_care_advance_planning.html
43. http://careconversations.org/planning-tools
44. http://www.engagewithgrace.org/About.aspx
45. http://jama.jamanetwork.com/article.aspx?articleid=2099528
46. https://www.camdenhealth.org/wp-content/uploads/2013/09/RCT_Telephonic_Care_Management .pdf
47. http://chbrp.ucop.edu/index.php?action=read&bill_id=149&doc_type=3
48. http://www.nytimes.com/2014/09/12/upshot/do-workplace-wellness-programs-work-usually-not .html
49. http://healthleadersmedia.com/page-3/HR-313233/The-Trouble-with-Wellness-Programs
50. http://vytm.in/A_19lw#http://ww2.kqed.org/stateofhealth/2015/09/30/employee-wellness-programs -often-not-bound-by-privacy-laws/
51. https://www.mobiquityinc.com/insights/blog/new-research-exposes-gap-mobile-healthcare

52. http://www.healthcare-informatics.com/blogs/david-raths/remote-patient-monitoring-heart-failure
    -grows-more-sophisticated?utm_source=SilverpopVG&utm_medium=eml&utm_campaign=HCI%20
    -%20Vertical%20-%20Top%20Blog%20Posts%20Update%20%282%29%2010/04/15%2011:00%20
    AM&utm_content=&spMailingID=49694724&spUserID=MTA4MjEzNjAzODMzS0&spJobID=780
    499768&spReportId=NzgwNDk5NzY4S0
53. http://sixuntilme.com/wp/2014/07/10/cgm-cloud-part/
54. http://www.journals.elsevier.com/computers-in-biology-and-medicine/call-for-papers/call-for
    -papers-self-monitoring-systems-for-personalized-hea/
55. https://www.linkedin.com/pulse/new-research-patient-voice-joan-justice?utm_content=buffer1936d
    &utm_medium=social&utm_source=twitter.com&utm_campaign=buffer
56. https://scicasts.com/bio-it/1844-bioinformatics/10108-new-portable-device-counts-white-blood
    -cells-through-the-skin/

Chapter 5

Acute Care and Hospitalizations

Jan Oldenburg, FHIMSS*

Introduction

Imagine waking up some morning to find yourself suddenly in a foreign country—you're not sure how you got there; you don't know the language or the local customs; you have neither a guide nor a reliable translator; and, worst of all, you are in pain. It would be disorienting and frightening. Travel can be wonderful and lead to great adventures, but most people are more comfortable when they are able to plan a trip, learn some of the language, and hire a guide or arrange accommodations and adventures in advance—and even the most well-planned trip can be disrupted by unexpected issues or getting sick. Figure 5.1 highlights the potential for multilingual confusion around hospital visits.

Entering a hospital, even for a long-planned procedure, is a bit like that trip to a foreign country (though you likely view it with less anticipation). You may have studied up on it, quizzed your doctor, chosen the surgical approach, planned the dates—yet often, especially when something doesn't go quite as planned, you end up feeling like that person in a foreign country whose attempts at communication are misunderstood and whose guides aren't available. Even people who work in healthcare, for whom the hospital is not a foreign country, experience some of this disorientation when they are on the other side of the invisible wall that separates patient or caregiver from doctor or nurse—suddenly "not in the know."

All of these factors are multiplied when you suddenly find yourself in the foreign world of the hospital, due to an accident, heart attack, or other acute episode—your own or that of someone you love. In these situations, you have no chance to learn the language in advance, choose your guide, know the terrain. You're suddenly plunged into a foreign world with an unknown future, an unfamiliar culture, a lot of fear, and loss of control over things you used to take for granted, often while you are in pain and disoriented from medications and the fog of illness. If you are lucky, you have someone with you to be your advocate, to ask the questions you cannot, to stand

---

* @janoldenburg

Figure 5.1 Opportunities for confusion when traveling. (Courtesy of Wikipedia, https://commons .wikimedia.org/wiki/File:Grace_trilingual_sign.jpg#filelinks, showing emergency and outpatient services in English, Chinese and Tamil.)

up for your needs, to translate, to help you navigate this territory. But your family or friends may also feel disoriented and confused both because they are learning new territory and because they are trying to process their own reactions to your illness. All too often, there is no one in the care system to fill that function for you either.

Confusion, Fear, Anxiety

Confusion, fear, anxiety, and a sense that you have lost control—they're not just discomforts associated with the experience of being hospitalized because it turns out that they actually contribute to poorer clinical outcomes. A study on patients hospitalized following acute myocardial infarctions (AMIs) showed first that those with high anxiety were at "increased risk for in-hospital arrhythmic and ischemic complications...independent of traditional sociodemographic and clinical risk factors." The study further showed that a *perceived sense of control* mitigated anxiety and resulted in better long-term clinical outcomes.[1] Perceived sense of control can be defined as "the belief that one can determine one's own internal states and behavior, influence one's environment, and/or bring about desired outcomes."[2] The association between anxiety and poorer clinical outcomes was also found in a study of chronic obstructive pulmonary disease (COPD) patients.[3] Another study of the effects on parents of having an infant hospitalized in the Neonatal Intensive Care Unit (NICU) shows that the stress to caregivers brings long-term health effects including depression, fatigue, and sleep interruptions.[4]

It is not surprising that perceived sense of control is eroded by the experience of being hospitalized or caring for someone who is. When that happens, your destiny is in the hands of the medical system and many aspects of daily life that you generally take for granted—simple things such as when you eat, go to the bathroom, or get up in the morning—are no longer under your control.

And yet, it is not very hard to create that "perceived sense of control" for patients and family members.[1] Education helps; framing the illness as a temporary setback and stressing the ways the patient can control long-term outcomes is helpful. In addition, there are many opportunities to make minor changes in hospital processes to restore a sense of engagement and control to the patient and his or her family and many opportunities to help both patients and family members understand what is going on, give back control where possible, ease their way, and, in the process, improve health outcomes and reduce stress. In this chapter, we'll explore some of the ways institutions and individuals are instituting such changes as well as the opportunities to do more.

Factors Contributing to Anxiety

It's important to begin by describing some of the things that make the hospitalization experience so disorienting. For both patients and family members, one of the most upsetting elements is the relative lack of information about what is going on. Nurses and doctors are often rushed and don't have time to answer all of the questions the family or patient may have—about prognosis, about why tests are being ordered and what the outcomes are, when doctors will be available on the floor, when discharge can be expected, and, perhaps above all, what the future holds. The anxiety lying behind all of those questions is compounded if the situation includes the worry that you or the person you love won't survive.

In addition, there are minor discomforts—a too hot or too cold room; a meal delivered late, cold, or for the wrong patient; or delayed help going to the bathroom, alleviating pain, or managing a new symptom. It can also be frustrating and anxiety producing for a caregiver to leave his or her family member's bedside to get food, take a shower, or let the dog out—only to miss the chance to ask questions when the doctor arrives to see the patient or to get lost in the confusing hospital corridors.

Patients and family members alike may feel as if they are labeled as "difficult" or "disruptive" if they push for information or try to get the patient's needs met. For the most part, all of this anxiety happens in a hospital environment where staff members genuinely want to do the right thing for patients and family members, but are often rushed, distracted, or not supported with the right tools.

In reimagining the patient and family experience of inpatient care, we will focus primarily, but not exclusively, on ways that technology could improve the experience. As you read through the next sections, you may be struck by the twin themes of communication and information distribution that underlie many of the techniques that can help change the dynamics of the inpatient stay.

How Long Will I Have to Wait?

For patients who need emergency care, there are key questions: (1) Where will I get the best care and (2) how long will I need to wait? Answers to the second question are easier to get now than they have been in the past. The Centers for Medicare and Medicaid Services (CMS) have begun posting average Emergency Department (ED) wait times by hospital and comparing them to local and national norms. Some hospitals post wait times for ED visits and there are a variety of applications that display comparative wait times for emergency care, including iTriage (www.itriagehealth.com), ZocDoc (www.zocdoc.com), and ER Wait Watcher (https://projects.propublica.org/emergency/). Some apps even allow users to make a "reservation" for an ED visit, similar

Figure 5.2   Example of freeway billboard showing emergency room wait times.

to being able to schedule a reservation at an upscale restaurant.[5-7] Wait times, whether available through applications or posted on freeway billboards, as shown in Figure 5.2, allow patients to "shop" for the closest care with the lowest wait times. This may have the effect of better distributing emergency care throughout the community.

There is some controversy in the industry about whether posting wait times is a good practice or one that might lead patients who truly need care to wait because they perceive the waiting times to be too long—or, conversely, might lead patients whose need is not urgent to go to the ED because knowing the wait time makes it seem as if emergency care will be more convenient than seeing a doctor in another setting. Studies on this issue are emerging, but the jury is still out on the full impact of this innovation[8]; what is clear is that if ED wait times are posted, patients want them to be credible.[9]

"Wayfinding"

The experience of being a patient begins before you walk in the door of a hospital. Unless you come in through the Emergency Department or by ambulance, it probably starts when you try to find the way to the hospital or when you enter the parking garage. Hospitals are beginning to think about these aspects of the patient experience by ensuring directions are clear on their websites, offering valet parking services, and considering how and when they charge patients and/or visitors for parking.

Once you walk in the door of a hospital, whether for an emergency visit, a scheduled procedure, an outpatient clinical appointment, or as a visitor, finding your way becomes a concern. Who has not wandered through hospital corridors with opaque signage, trying to find a department? Some caregivers use parking applications to "drop a pin" before leaving a loved one's room in order to increase the likelihood of finding their way back. Hospitals are responding to this need as well. There's a new science of "wayfinding" that incorporates things like color coding, signage, and visitor information desks.[10]

Hospitals are also adding digital tools to help people find their way. Castle Rock Adventist Hospital, for example, is using interactive kiosks throughout the hospital that allow consumers to map the route from one location to another—and then scan the results into a smartphone for step-by-step directions.[11] A system from Connexient called MediNav gives hospitals a way to address a number of dimensions of the wayfinding aspect of patient experience, from a digital parking planner to indoor maps, location-based content, and step-by-step directions—including after-the-fact surveys about the experience.[12] Ideally, wayfinding systems operate across multiple channels (phone, tablet, PC, in person) and modes, depending on the location and needs of the person who is searching for something or somewhere.

These kinds of tools help reduce the confusion of finding one's way through the hospital and reduce stress at an already stressful time.

Education before a Planned Procedure

Shared decision-making programs have the aim of helping patients participate with their physicians about what treatments will best fit their goals, values, and lifestyles. This admirable goal is often handicapped by lack of readily available information about patient outcomes and satisfaction levels with the treatment received. In a recent *Harvard Business Review* posting, two physicians recommended better collection of patient-generated data about outcomes to use in shared decision making.[13] They reported results from the Spine Patient Outcomes Research Trial (SPORT), saying:

> This large national study, conducted from March 2000 to February 2005, enrolled 2505 patients with disc herniation, spinal stenosis, or degenerative spondylosis. Today, thanks to the huge bolus of data from SPORT, patients with back pain related to those same underlying conditions can enter personal, demographic, and clinical information into an online calculator on Dartmouth's website. The calculator generates information, from SPORT-derived outcome models, comparing the anticipated outcomes of surgical versus nonsurgical interventions for patients with characteristics similar to their own. They can see projections with respect to post-treatment physical activity, severity of pain, and overall health. The doctor introduces the SPORT tool to the patient during an office visit, and the two of them view the automatically generated results together in real time. In effect, the patient, in direct consultation with his or her physician, gets to answer that crucial question: "How will this treatment decision affect someone like me?"

Poor communication between doctor and patient is cited as the root cause of 22 percent of malpractice claims and 78 percent of malpractice lawsuit situations where patients charge that physicians failed to disclose risks ahead of time.[14,15] Malpractice claims are but one measure of a common failure to make sure patients really understand the procedure they're about to undergo and the associated risks.[15] This issue is often addressed as part of the consent process. The starting point to rectifying these problems may be applying simple rules of effective communications to consent documents: Use larger type, shorter sentences, and smaller words to reduced reading levels; use pictures to describe procedures; and check for understanding.[16]

In addition, a number of companies are working to provide more effective communication about clinical information prior to scheduled inpatient stays—especially surgical procedures. EMMI Solutions is one example. EMMI has been assertive in using videos—and tracking whether or not patients watch and sign off on them—to improve patient understanding and informed consent. At least one insurer will rebate malpractice premiums to the healthcare organization if EMMI is used for consent.[17]

Another innovative approach to managing communications comes from HealthLoop which enables healthcare providers to deliver timely and bite-sized pieces of education and guidance to patients at home, and to remotely monitor patient clinical status through electronic check-ins that span the pre- and postoperative periods. Before a patient goes to surgery, patients receive automated HIPAA-compliant emails from their physicians with preoperative checklists, patient education resources, multimedia, and guidance, with added functions such as secure messaging and photo sharing. Postoperatively, the system enables daily remote monitoring of clinical signs and symptoms. According to Ben Rosner, MD, PhD and HealthLoop CMIO:

> HealthLoop measures engagement in real time, treating it much like a vital sign. If it dips too low, it represents both an opportunity and a call to action for the care team to reach out to the patient and re-engage him or her. As a first order description, if, as of today, a patient had 10 check-ins scheduled as part of his or her care plan, and completed eight of them, the patient is 80% engaged.[18]

Clinical studies are underway to validate outcomes, but HealthLoop reports that 81 percent of patients activate their HealthLoop account (more if the physician specifically recommends it); over the lifetime of a HealthLoop encounter, patients on average have 72 percent rates of engagement, meaning that they complete 7 of 10 check-in requests over the weeks or months of the experience; 86 percent of patients on HealthLoop answered "yes" to a question about how likely they are to recommend their doctor to family and friends.

Another approach for education and engagement involves a new approach to presurgery planning that improves outcomes. At the University of Michigan, surgeons use deep analytics on data from CT scans, something they call "analytical morphomics," to estimate each individual's surgical risk. The data generated are used to engage patients in training and toning before surgery to reduce the likelihood of adverse consequences afterward. This technique is promising not just because it actively reduces surgical risk, but also because it enables new thinking about helping people recover from surgery.[19]

What Is Happening? Communication in the Hospital

All the way through a hospital stay, patients and family members wonder how the person is doing, what plans are underway to address the person's condition, how doctors are collaborating, and what the patient's prognosis is. These information needs can be addressed with a variety of techniques that involve people, process, and technology. Just knowing the plan for a patient or even when doctors will be making rounds can relieve anxiety. When combined with techniques that enable families to initiate communications or manage some of the patient's needs themselves, these factors can have a positive impact on the experience of care as well as the perceived sense of control.

Who Is on My Care Team?

Patients and family members often have difficulty keeping track of the people caring for them during a hospital stay. There's a continuous stream of people coming into the room, introducing themselves briefly, checking the chart or the patient, and then disappearing. Nurses generally introduce themselves and write their names on the whiteboard in the patient's room at the start of each shift, but it can be difficult to track everyone else. A 2009 study found that 75 percent of 2500 patients were unable to name even one physician involved in their inpatient care.[20]

Cerner is addressing this by creating a system that can link each provider's name badge to a screen in the patient's room to create a record of every hospital employee who has been in the room. Other approaches include that noted by Todd Folkenberg, CEO of Castle Rock Adventist Hospital, who reports that his hospital is using radio frequency identification (RFID) chips in name badges that interact with light boards in patient rooms to provide a record of every staff member who has visited the room.[21]

Knowing the names and roles of your care team is such an important part of care we can expect to see additional technologies emerge in this category.

What Are the Treatment Plans?

Family members are often concerned that the moment they finally step out of the room—to get food, to find a restroom, to go home and let the dog out—will be the moment the patient's doctor shows up on the floor, and they'll miss that opportunity to ask questions and understand the patient's status. For both patients and family members, anxiety rises when questions go unanswered and even when it is not clear when doctors will be making their rounds or available to discharge the patient.

Hospitals are responding to this need in various ways. One hospital, DePaul Health Center in St. Louis, addressed this issue with interdisciplinary rounds, where patients and caregivers were notified ahead of time when the patient would be seen by the doctors, and during the designated time the whole care team was present to discuss the patient's condition.[22] The effect is a better opportunity to get questions about the patient's status answered.

Other hospitals are experimenting with shift turnovers at the patient bedside so that patients and family members can be a part of the process.[23]

At Radboud University Hospital in the Netherlands, patients *and* family members are included in collaborative care consultations with the physicians and staff. This is accomplished using a new technology called FaceTime that is both secure and Health Insurance Portability and Accountability Act (HIPAA) compliant. It's only one way that this hospital attempts to put patients at the center with efforts that include care councils staffed by patients, appointment of a chief listening officer, and a host of other initiatives to address full participation by "the people formerly known as patients."[24]

It also seems as if it should be relatively simple to notify patients or family members of physician rounding schedules through text messages. Some hospitals use family pagers, devices similar to those handed out in restaurant waiting lines, to notify family members when a patient comes out of surgery so that they can feel comfortable taking a short break.

These tactics make patients and family members feel more involved in the care that's being delivered and give them an opportunity to address new symptoms, ask questions about prognosis, or correct any inaccuracies—giving patients and caregivers alike more sense of control and helping to relieve anxiety.

Inpatient Access to a Patient Portal

Patient portals have been used more in ambulatory care than inpatient care, although meaningful use (MU) stage 2,[25] part of a US government program to increase usage of electronic health records, requires that hospitals achieve portal usage targets—generally, however, after the hospital visit concludes. Many of the components of access to a record that are useful on an ambulatory basis are also useful for patients and caregivers during an inpatient episode. These include access to lab test results and medication lists, ability to send a secure message to members of the care team, and the ability to view physician notes as well as discharge summaries.

An inpatient stay provides an excellent opportunity to help patients and caregivers to get registered for the patient portal and connect them with resources available through the portal. New studies support what has been intuitive knowledge for years. People are more likely to sign up for portal access if they are invited by physicians they trust, and portal usage may even enhance trust relationships. One recent study found that diabetic patients who reported high trust in their physicians were also more likely to register for the patient portal, a correlation that the study showed was true among white, Latino, and older patients.[26] Anecdotally, providers who use portals, open notes, and secure messaging report that when patients use the tools, it increases their trust in physicians.[27]

Electronic health record (EHR) vendors are adding portal features geared to supporting inpatient stays. Epic's MyChart Bedside offers a host of features to make a patient stay less stressful. It has been launched at Catholic Health Partners of Ohio, which reports,

> MyChart Bedside ties directly to each patient's electronic health record, providing information on test results, medicine, and upcoming procedures. It also provides educational information related to a patient's condition and treatment, and allows patients to access web-based programs like Facebook, and e-mail, to stay in contact with family members during their hospital stay. Patients may view medication instructions, learn about upcoming procedures, view photos and bios of caregivers, request blankets…and perform other tasks to make their stays more productive and enjoyable.[28]

MyChart is available as a tablet app and can be used either on a patient's own tablet or on a hospital-supplied device. It has also been launched at Ohio State University Medical Center, where it includes the ability to send secure messages to the care team at the hospital.[29]

Cerner offers similar features through CareAware, which can be delivered through the television in the patient's room. Cerner says that CareAware offers the following: "For example, when a care provider enters the room the patient can immediately see the person's name and role. The system also allows the patient to control room temperature, lighting, order a meal and control other environmental factors easily from their bed."[30]

Other types of tools can make it easier for patients to communicate about their needs to the nursing staff. The classic call button is one dimensional, and patients may not use it for fear of asking busy nursing staff to pay attention to relatively unimportant needs—despite the fact that addressing those needs may be important for the person's comfort. Some hospitals, such as New York Presbyterian, are experimenting with tablet applications that allow patients to specify the kind of support they need: "I am in pain. I need help going to the bathroom. My room needs servicing. I have a question." The tablets, equipped with custom-built applications, enable patients to seamlessly communicate with their care team and quickly access their health information on the MyNYP.org portal, built on Microsoft's HealthVault platform.[31]

It is a little more difficult to provide meaningful in-the-moment data to inpatients than to outpatients, as one of the characteristics of an inpatient stay is the sheer volume of clinical data generated. If these clinical data are released to patients, special care must be paid to ensure that they are useful rather than overwhelming. This makes design especially important and may mean things like highlighting trends in clinical tests rather than discrete results. It also means providing clear information about why tests are ordered and what results mean, easily accessible in the context of the data themselves. The same thing is true about inpatient medications and procedures. In all cases, it is important to provide not just the clinical information, but also an explanation—in context—for the information.

It's easy to see why features such as these can improve an inpatient stay for both patients and caregivers—providing more control over the environment, more information about clinical outcomes, and convenient ways to communicate with the care team. By addressing the information needs of patients and caregivers, as well as providing some control over the external environment, these types of features restore the "perceived sense of control" and help reduce anxiety.

This is rather new territory for both patients and providers, as one study from the University of Colorado Hospital highlights.[32] In the study, a patient's wife used online lab results available through the patient portal to carefully monitor her husband's inpatient care. Medical opinions differed on whether it helped with his care by enabling the wife to catch an issue his care team had missed or whether it was a distraction requiring time away from direct care to explain the meaning of tests to the man's wife. It emphasizes how important it is to provide contextual education when such information is available to patients and family members in an inpatient setting.

An article about inpatient medical record access in *Today's Hospitalist* published in January 2014 noted:

> Already, all patients in the VA system have online access to their hospital's EMR. The same is true at Houston's MD Anderson Cancer Center, while other facilities, including Beth Israel Deaconess and Cleveland Clinic, are planning rollouts this year. Other health systems around the country are exploring the expanded use of their patient web portals, which are now mostly used to access only labs, x-rays and medication lists and to communicate with outpatient offices.[33]

Making OpenNotes Available

In ambulatory care, access to clinical data and physician notes has been shown to increase patient engagement and relieve anxiety.[34] The OpenNotes program has been pioneering in providing patients with direct access to ambulatory and mental health notes written by physicians. Open-Notes is also championing doing the same in hospital settings, by creating a white paper, published in June 2013, suggesting how inpatient open notes access could be handled.[35]

Since that article was written, several hospitals, among them the University of Minnesota clinics and hospitals, have begun experimenting with providing access to physician notes while the patient is still in the hospital, where it can help as a communication tool between patients and the care system. An early pilot at the University of Minnesota showed that the results were similar to outpatient tests of open notes. After getting online medical progress notes for at least three days:

> Patients and families at the University of Minnesota Medical Center felt the notes allowed them to understand their care better (85%) and this was done with little to no disruption to provider workflow (in fact, 28% of providers actually felt delivering these notes made care more efficient).[36]

Others are opening hospital notes, but not necessarily while the patient is still in the hospital. The VA system posts both ambulatory and inpatient notes in the chart 3 days after they are signed as completed by the doctor, which may be after the patient is discharged.[33]

As more hospitals open inpatient notes to patients and families, additional best practices will emerge, and such access will begin to be an expectation on the part of patients and caregivers.

Inpatient Education

Access to the clinical record is one way of educating patients and family members about care. Hospitals are investing in other forms of education as well, since an inpatient stay offers opportunities to help individuals understand their condition, learn about how to deal with it, and begin preparing for life after discharge. The role of a hospital stay is changing, as Joan Saba, an architect who designs hospitals for the innovative architectural firm NBBJ Design (http://www.nbbj.com /about/), noted in a speech at Medicine X in 2015, "Now we are thinking about it being a place for learning and information exchange."[37] Interactive tools like tablets and bedside computing offer a forum for high-quality education and also enable providers to track whether patients have processed information relevant to their condition prior to discharge. This can offload the burden on nursing staff of providing one-to-one education, potentially offer a higher quality of education, and provide a resource that patients can return to after the visit.

There's a standard for providing context-sensitive patient education materials called the HL7 "Infobutton."[38] EHR systems are required to implement the Infobutton as a tool to enable doctors and staff to meet the MU requirement to "identify patient-specific education resources and provide those resources to the patient." Right now the standard is on the EHR side and requires provision of information in any form. Vendors such as Krames Staywell, and Healthwise, among others, marry their content to the InfoButton within the EHR as a way to provide contextually appropriate education. The Infobutton could certainly be added as an option on the patient side to ensure that patient portals easily provide patients with access to meaningful in-context education at the point they are reviewing their records.

Another innovative approach tested providing patients with education via their own cell phones while they are in the emergency department.[39] When field tested with a small group of prospective patients, the study found a positive impact on patient experience in the emergency room. This approach could be extended to education throughout the hospital stay. At a minimum, it would help patients and family members ask more intelligent and informed questions.

Some hospitals are using tools like *i*Engage to help elderly patients learn about fall prevention and become active in relation to their own health using their own tablets or hospital-issued systems while they are admitted for an inpatient stay.[40] Other patient education systems require the patient to view certain videos before discharge and record the outcome in the EHR as documentation.

Project RED at the Boston Medical Center tested interventions at discharge where nurses reviewed instructions in detail with patients to discuss what they should be doing after they leave the hospital.[41]

> When the discharge protocol is carried out solely by human nurses, it cuts costs by about $123 per patient (based on a 30% decrease in hospital and emergency department utilization). Although this process saves money, it costs nurses about 81 minutes of their time.

In an effort to further reduce the cost of the program and the burden on nurses, researchers developed on-screen conversational agents to talk about care planning and educate patients as a replacement for the in person nurses. The agents are able to compose responses in real time, based on what the patient says and indicate empathy in tone and expression. Evidence from several clinical trials shows this is an effective technique for educating patients about their conditions, especially for those with low health literacy. The virtual discharge system replaced 30 of the 81 minutes of nursing time with the virtual agent, which achieved additional savings: a total [additional] savings of $145 per patient. There were over 38 million hospital discharges in the US in 2003 alone—the virtual discharge system could save our health care system over $5 billion per year.

Such tools serve a dual role. They address information needs for patients and families who are in the hospital, while also preparing them to understand and manage care at home. They also may reduce inpatient hospital costs for nursing staff and reduce the risk of readmissions.

Designing a Quieter, Kinder Experience

People have come to expect that a hospital stay includes interrupted sleep, because the patient is awakened either to have vitals checked or to have blood drawn so that results can be available when the shift changes at 7 a.m. But interrupted sleep has adverse effects on healing and actually produces suffering for patients. Hospitals are increasingly doing something about suffering created by the way medicine is practiced. This is illustrated by Dr. Michael Bennick, the medical director for patient experience at Yale-New Haven Hospital, who began revamping procedures and routines with the goal of not waking patients up at night unless it was a medical imperative. As he said in a 2015 *New York Times* article, "I told the resident doctors in training: 'If you are waking patients at 4 in the morning for a blood test, there obviously is a clinical need. So I want to be woken, too, so I can find out what it is.'" No one, he said, ever called him. "Those … blood draws vanished."[42]

Other hospitals are focusing on noise reduction as a way to increase the peacefulness and healing quality of a hospital stay. The Hospital Consumer Assessment of Healthcare Providers and Systems (HCAHPS) surveys probably raised attention to this issue by beginning to ask, "Is it quiet in your room at night?" in 2007—and the question has consistently been among the lowest performing of any of the survey questions. Massachusetts General Hospital set out to address this issue with a set of best practices for addressing quietness on unit floors that helped the organization focus on the mantra that "a quiet environment is a healing environment."[43] Among the suggestions were that units purchase "yacker trackers,"

Figure 5.3 Yacker tracker can keep staff aware of noise levels in an inpatient unit. (From Fran Rebello, CEO and Inventor of the Yacker Tracker. Reprinted with permission.)

shown in Figure 5.3,[44] a noise meter designed like a traffic light to keep staff alert as to the level of noise on the unit. Reducing suffering from undue noise is an issue of architecture, practice, habit, and even equipment design. An increasing number of hospitals are making this a key initiative and there is much opportunity for improvement to redesign hospital environments to actively facilitate patient healing and reduce stress.

How Can I Keep My Extended Family and Community Informed?

It is clear that community support can make a significant difference in helping people recover from a severe illness—and it can also help family members cope with the stress of having a loved one in the hospital. At the same time, it can be a strain to keep everyone informed. The volume of calls and e-mails checking on status and offering support can be wonderful—and can add stress if you have neither the time nor the energy to respond appropriately. Increasingly, hospitals are providing access to tools such as CaringBridge (caringbridge.org) or Carepages (www.carepages .com) that can enable patients and/or family members to post updates and information to a dedicated site that helps them manage privacy and exposure while keeping a community updated and getting support. Increasingly, these sites are adding specialized services such as enabling people to sign up to bring a meal or provide transportation—often a significant relief to the family both during and after a hospitalization. Facebook is also experimenting with a special kind of social community to support people during an illness.

Discharge and Discharge Planning

Discharge. The moment the patient and family have been waiting for. And yet, it is also fraught with concern, as patients and family members may fear their ability to manage on their own. There are a number of ways that discharge can be simplified for patients and family members and anxiety reduced.

Many hospitals are beginning discharge planning early in a patient's hospitalization. Not only does this focus everyone on the goal of discharge, but it can also provide additional time to ensure that the patient has the right kinds of options available at discharge—a bed in a skilled nursing facility close to home or a home nurse scheduled to visit the first day.[45]

As a part of meaningful use, many hospitals are providing patients with access to discharge summaries and discharge instructions online—required within 36 hours of the discharge. Others provide medications for home use as part of hospital discharge, to reduce the added stress of figuring out where and how soon medications can be filled. Connecting patients with their first post-discharge appointments while still in the hospital and ensuring that they have transportation provided to that first appointment can also reduce the stress of a discharge while helping to ensure that patients have a satisfactory recovery.

MEANINGFUL USE DEFINED
Meaningful use is using certified EHR technology to

- Improve quality, safety, efficiency, and reduce health disparities
- Engage patients and family
- Improve care coordination and population and public health
- Maintain privacy and security of patient health information

Ultimately, it is hoped that the meaningful use compliance will result in

- Better clinical outcomes
- Improved population health outcomes
- Increased transparency and efficiency
- Empowered individuals
- More robust research data on health systems

Meaningful use sets specific objectives that eligible professionals (EPs) and hospitals must achieve to qualify for Centers for Medicare and Medicaid Services (CMS) Incentive Programs.[46]

New tools are enabling hospitals and clinicians to keep patients informed about their recovery and to check on them regularly after discharge. This is especially important in an era where success for hospitals includes reduced readmission rates, and follow-up care can be an important component of the solution. A study published in the *Journal of the American Medical Association* (JAMA) found that more than 60 percent of patients discharged from a hospital do not receive a follow-up visit with a physician within 7 days, despite the fact that hospitals providing the best follow-up care for heart failure patients within the 7-day discharge window had a 15 percent lower 30-day readmission rate.[47]

But follow-up care needs to go beyond ensuring that the first appointment is made and attended. Innovative approaches are focusing on how to keep patients and their caregivers aware of and informed about key steps in recovery, while keeping clinicians aware of any untoward issues in recovery. We mentioned HealthLoop earlier as an example of an approach that extends daily communication past discharge to catch red flags that might signal that the person needs closer management. Qualcomm's HealthyCircles program offers a similar set of capabilities by enabling patients (or caregivers) to answer questions as well as get educational information as needed. The answers to the questions then help case managers identify who in a panel of patients may need further follow-up to address problems that could otherwise lead to readmissions.[48]

Remote monitoring tools and telemedicine hold the promise of making it easier to check in on a discharged or chronically ill patient and intervene before symptoms are exacerbated and a hospitalization is necessary. These innovations are important because approaches using telephone-based questions and telephonic interventions have not been as effective as hoped.[49]

It is possible to imagine home monitoring, enabled by data from multiple sensors incorporated into devices, wearables, and the Internet of Things in the home, to enable patients to be discharged from the hospital earlier. The safety net of home monitoring could enable issues to be identified as they arise and physicians and caregivers to be alerted to the problem. Like remote ICU monitoring, such systems could make better use of sparse resources.[50] Remote home monitoring would need to be supported by home nursing and two-way communications, as well as accurate and robust sensors, but it is possible to envision all of these capabilities coming together to allow patients to return home more quickly, with a safety net that ensures they are recovering as desired.

Who Do I Pay and How Much?

Alexandra Drane has called cost one of the "unmentionables" in healthcare—present in every interaction a person has with the healthcare system, but rarely acknowledged. In an emergency, you or your family member may have time to check which hospital is "in plan" with your insurance, but you're unlikely to take the time to compare costs before you arrive. It's a little different when you are going to the hospital for a surgical procedure. In situations where preplanning is possible, you generally have time up front to understand the cost of your procedure and discuss coverage with your health plan. As discussed in Chapter 2, "The New DIY Health Consumer," patients have an increasing number of resources available to help them project costs ahead of time and manage payment for services rendered.

Worry about paying for the bills being accumulated during a hospital stay may contribute an underlayer of anxiety for both the patient and caregiver, a worry that may impact health and outcomes. Better insurance coverage, cost transparency, the ability to predict the cost of care, and enhanced payment options are part of addressing this issue; we still need to do more to manage and address the cost of inpatient care and to help people understand better how to predict and manage it.

Conclusions

It is clear that there are a host of available innovations that can make the experience of hospitalization—whether for an acute illness or a planned procedure—much less like a visit to a foreign country. Hospitals that focus on patient experience are putting in place a multitude of changes in process, policy, and attitude, along with digital innovations that support the transformation. Paul Keckley describes these as "second curve" hospitals. He suggests that "second curve hospitals see the future differently. Their clinical model is holistic and individualized. Technology is digital and shared, and the preferences and values of individuals are just as important as their signs and symptoms. They focus on persons, not patients."[51]

These new approaches are much welcomed by patients and their families, who are already voting with their feet for experiences where they are educated and cared for both during and after a hospitalization in ways that are empowering and help them understand and manage their health.

Impact

To understand more about the impact of these issues in the lives of real people, please read the following patient and caregiver stories in Section II of this book:

Story 2	"An e-Champion for Alexis"
Story 3	"You Must Have an Insanely High Pain Tolerance"
Story 5	"Becoming My Mother's Voice"
Story 8	"Ineffectual Transitions of Care Can Contribute to Death"
Story 9	"Do I Really Have to Do the Follow-Up? My Eight-Week Breast Cancer Journey"
Story 10	"Grateful"
Story 11	"Great Expectations"
Story 12	"Healing with Faith, Food, Friends, Family, and Laughter"
Story 13	"I Suggest You Check Yourself into the Hospital"
Story 14	"Learning from Others' Mistakes"
Story 17	"You Have a Mass the Size of an Eggplant in Your Abdomen"
Story 20	"Standing Up for Myself through Many Medical Problems"

Notes

1. http://citeseerx.ist.psu.edu/viewdoc/download;jsessionid=8653A6FFC7E3BDE1D8ADFCF20F2C1 F8F?doi=10.1.1.495.970&rep=rep1&type=pdf
2. http://www.nursing.vanderbilt.edu/faculty/kwallston/perceived%20control%20and%20health.pdf
3. http://thorax.bmj.com/content/65/3/229.full.html
4. http://www.aacn.org/wd/Cetests/media/C1343.pdf
5. http://www.reviewjournal.com/life/health/smartphone-apps-let-patients-gauge-entry-times-emergency -rooms
6. https://www.google.com/search?q=applications+that+show+ED+wait+times&ie=utf-8&oe=utf-8
7. http://patch.com/california/pasadena-ca/new-app-ids-which-hospital-er-has-the-shortest-wait-time
8. http://www.acep.org/workarea/DownloadAsset.aspx?id=86983
9. https://www.hugeinc.com/ideas/report/how-long-is-the-wait
10. http://www.wsj.com/news/articles/SB10001424052702303743604579355202979035492?autologin=y
11. https://www.youtube.com/watch?v=VLqiAZP2Cho
12. http://www.connexient.com/news/192-norwalk-hospital-selects-connexient-s-digital-wayfinding -solution
13. HBR Blog. "Patient-Reported Data Can Help People Make Better HealthCare Choices" by William B. Weeks, MD and James N. Weinstein, DO. September 21, 2015. https://hbr.org/2015/09/patient -reported-data-can-help-people-make-better-health-care-choices. With permission. https://hbr.org /2015/09/patient-reported-data-can-help-people-make-better-health-care-choices
14. http://medicaleconomics.modernmedicine.com/medical-economics/content/tags/injury/six-ways -physicians-can-prevent-patient-injury-and-avoid-lawsu?page=full
15. http://www.dialogmedical.com/2012/11/07/using-the-informed-consent-process-to-reduce-malpractice -challenges/
16. http://www.amednews.com/article/20130605/profession/130609995/8/
17. https://www.beazley.com/specialty_lines/professional_liability/healthcare_/hospitals/emmi.html
18. E-mail exchange with Ben Rosner, MD, CMIO of HealthLoop
19. http://www.morphomicanalysisgroup.com/sites/morphomics.drupalgardens.com/files/Medicineat Michigan_fall12_Inside_Out.pdf
20. http://archinte.jamanetwork.com/article.aspx?articleid=414715&resultClick=3
21. https://getwellnetwork.cld.bz/Patient-Engagement-Beyond-the-Buzz#10/z
22. http://www.todayshospitalist.com/index.php?b=articles_read&cnt=1596
23. http://www.ncbi.nlm.nih.gov/pubmed/21469417
24. https://joconnect.files.wordpress.com/2012/09/radboud20in20the20bmj20full20paper202014.pdf
25. https://www.healthit.gov/providers-professionals/meaningful-use-definition-objectives
26. http://www.medscape.com/viewarticle/812916
27. http://www.consumerreports.org/cro/magazine/2014/01/the-doctor-will-email-you-now/index.htm
28. Mercy Health. January 6, 2014. Reprinted with permission. http://www.mercy.com/corporate/news _show.aspx?mode=local&id=4322
29. http://mobihealthnews.com/30334/ohio-medical-center-discusses-mobile-first-strategy-and-epics -mychart-bedside-ipad-app/
30. http://www.cerner.com/solutions/medical_devices/interactive_patient_system/
31. http://www.nyp.org/news/hospital/2014-infoweek-elite100.html

32. http://www.jopm.org/evidence/case-studies/2013/06/12/divergent-care-team-opinions-about-online-release-of-test-results-to-an-icu-patient/

33. Deborah Gesensway. "Is it time to open up your notes?" January 2014 Issue of *Today's Hospitalist*. With permission. http://www.todayshospitalist.com/index.php?b=articles_read&cnt=1817

34. http://www.ncbi.nlm.nih.gov/pmc/articles/PMC3908866/

35. http://www.ncbi.nlm.nih.gov/pubmed/23813756

36. http://www.datuit.com/blog/entry/sharing_inpatient_progress_notes_with_patients_and_families

37. http://scopeblog.stanford.edu/2015/09/27/at-medicine-x-designers-offer-their-take-on-why-patient-centered-design-is-top-priority/#sthash.7nFnGwYa.dpuf

38. http://www.openinfobutton.org/hl7-infobutton-standard

39. http://research.microsoft.com/pubs/163349/paper789.pdf

40. http://www.ncbi.nlm.nih.gov/pmc/articles/PMC4027936/pdf/ppa-8-693.pdf

41. Brian Jack, MD and Timothy Bickmore, PhD. "A Reengineered Hospital Discharge Program to Decrease Rehospitalization: A Randomized Trial." *Annals of Internal Medicine*. February 3, 2009. With permission. http://annals.org/article.aspx?articleid=744252

42. http://www.nytimes.com/2015/02/18/health/doctors-strive-to-do-less-harm-by-inattentive-care.html

43. http://www.mghpcs.org/eed_portal/Documents/PatExp/ADDRESSING-QUIETNESS.pdf

44. http://www.amazon.com/Yacker-Tracker-Noise-Detector-5-5/dp/B001AZ2O2Q/ref=sr_1_1?ie=UTF8&qid=1448818439&sr=8-1&keywords=yakker+tracker

45. http://www.lifelinesys.com/content/blog/healthcare-professionals/care-coordination/what-is-good-hospital-discharge-planning

46. https://www.healthit.gov/providers-professionals/meaningful-use-definition-objectives

47. http://www.thinkdcs.com/2014/01/27/revolving-door-solutions-hospital-readmission/#sthash.hUZCzZAC.dpuf

48. http://www.healthycircles.com/solutions-expert-services/solutions-reducing-hospital-readmissions

49. http://circ.ahajournals.org/content/125/6/828.full

50. http://mhealthintelligence.com/news/how-could-remote-monitoring-serve-the-intensive-care-unit

51. http://www.hhnmag.com/articles/3775-the-differences-between-first-and-second-curve-hospitals

Chapter 6

Achieving Whole Health

Mary P. Griskewicz, MS, FHIMSS

A warrior's spirit needs a warrior's body.

Unknown

Introduction

When Sara was diagnosed with thyroid cancer, she resolved to do everything she could to manage her health during her treatment. In addition to the surgery and radiation her doctor recommended, she began a program of yoga and meditation. She also changed her eating habits to include more raw vegetables, fruit, green tea, and soy milk. The hospital where she received treatment offered both acupuncture and healing touch therapies, and Sara found that they helped her manage some of the side effects of treatment. Now, several years later, Sara has continued with most of the lifestyle changes she made during therapy, and she feels sure they have played a part in her recovery and continuing good health.

The components that Sara added to her thyroid cancer treatments exemplify a whole health or integrated approach to medical treatments and to managing health. Whole health is an approach to healthcare that takes into account the whole individual, the individual's responsibility for his or her well-being, and all the influences—social, psychological, environmental—that affect health, including nutrition, exercise, and mental relaxation. The most frequently used definition of whole health was created by the World Health Organization (WHO) more than 50 years ago: "Health is a state of complete physical, mental and social well-being and not merely the absence of disease or infirmity."[1] This definition encompasses mental and emotional health, balanced and nutritious diet, active and fit lifestyles, healthy weight, functioning body, sound financial health, physical appearance, and energy.

Today, the full definition of whole health includes not just the healthcare and health insurance systems' definition of health but also an expanded definition that includes complementary and alternative medicine services. In the United States, the market for complementary and alternative medicine therapies is approximately $9 billion annually, equal to 3 percent of national ambulatory healthcare expenditures.[2]

What Is Alternative and Complementary Medicine?

"Alternative medicine" is generally agreed to refer to therapies that are not taught in Western medical schools and are used *in place of* traditional medical care. "Complementary medicine" refers to nontraditional therapies that are used together with traditional medical care. When healthcare providers and facilities offer both traditional and nontraditional therapies, it is called integrative medicine.[3]

Dr. Andrew Weil is generally considered to be the father of the integrative medicine movement. He is a proponent of teaching clinicians that integrative medicine is not an option but a necessity to achieve true population health. Dr. Weil defined integrative medicine as "healing-oriented medicine that takes account of the whole person (body, mind, and spirit), including all aspects of lifestyle. It emphasizes the therapeutic relationship and makes use of all appropriate therapies, both conventional and alternative."[4] The illustration in Figure 6.1 highlights the many elements of integrative medicine.

Weil suggests that patients take conventional medicine as prescribed to them by physicians and then incorporate complementary therapies and remedies into their treatment plans, including meditation and spiritual strategies. Weil is not without critics, as some in the traditional medical model have criticized his inclusion of therapies that haven't been fully proven.

The concept is getting a lot of attention of late, however. Several major academic medical centers are incorporating integrative medicine programs including Vanderbilt University's Osher Center for Integrative Medicine; Cleveland Clinic's Center for Functional Medicine, the result of a collaboration with the Institute for Functional Medicine; MD Anderson's Integrative Medicine Center; and the Osher Center for Integrative Medicine, a collaboration between Harvard Medical School and Brigham and Women's Hospital, to name a few. The US Department of Health and Human Services created the National Center for Complementary and Integrated Health (NCCIH) in 1998 to study complementary health approaches.[5] The center's role is to provide resources and conduct education and research focused on these new therapies. Researchers today are exploring the potential benefits of integrative health in diverse situations, including pain management for military personnel and veterans, relief of symptoms in cancer patients and survivors, and programs to promote healthy behaviors.[6]

Many patients and consumers use complementary medicine as part of their integrated care daily. Yoga, chiropractic and osteopathic manipulation, meditation, acupuncture, and massage

Figure 6.1   Illustration of the many dimensions of integrative medicine.

therapy are all examples of complementary health approaches.[7] Some patients integrate apps into their approach to managing these aspects of their health. For example, the MindBody app enables yoga students to access a schedule of exercises whenever and wherever they need to, from a desktop, tablet, or phone.[8] Yoga.com allows users to access information on meditation and yoga poses from people across the world and hosts an online yoga community.[9] Memorial Sloan Kettering's integrative medicine clinic offers an app, "About Herbs," to help cancer patients understand what herbs might help them manage their treatments.

Whole Health Landscape and Key Components

Around the world, there's a growing perception that health is more than the absence of illness. For example, Australian aboriginal people generally view and define health in the following way: "Health does not just mean the physical well-being of the individual but refers to the social, emotional, spiritual and cultural well-being of the whole community. This is a whole of life view and includes the cyclical concept of life–death–life."[10] The Edelman Health Barometer, originally published in 2011, examines public opinions about health around the world, what drives health-related behavior, and how business stands to benefit from the unique role it plays in advancing health. Edelman Health Barometer results indicated that 80 percent of the public consider "being healthy" to be more than being free from disease. The survey also explored the specific factors that motivate individuals to make and sustain changes to their behavior in the context of health behavior change (Figure 6.1).[11]

While the general perception is that people turn to alternative medicine when conventional medicine has failed them, often it is because they see therapies that have value in addition to more traditional options. An old African proverb says, "It takes a whole village to raise a child." This saying applies to our healthcare system today. Patients and their families engage in a variety of activities to manage health and illness. We need one another to help us achieve our health goals: the person becoming an active participant in his or her health, family, friends and community supporting the person's heath goals, and clinicians functioning as supportive partners.

The reality today is that people have a new attitude about health and wellness; we are in a new paradigm where we acknowledge diverse factors that contribute to being healthy. This chapter will explore many of these components and the way they are impacting individuals' lifestyle choices as well as the way the healthcare system views and approaches the broader topic of health.

Physical Health and Wellness

Patients define physical health differently depending on their current health status. Physical health, we can all agree, relates to the amount of energy one has, which is often contingent on access to clean water, healthy food, adequate sleep, and exercise. Patients, consumers, and employers alike use a variety of strategies and tools—some helpful and some not—in their efforts to achieve or maintain physical health and reduce the cost of healthcare.

Optimal weight is often included as a factor in physical health due to the obesity epidemic that contributes to and often causes chronic diseases. Weight management is a big business. More than one-third of US adults, or 78 million people, today are obese. The annual medical cost for someone who is obese is $1429 higher than for someone who is of normal weight.[12] American consumers are spending a lot of money to manage their weight; in 2013, it was estimated that US consumers spent $2.4 billion out of pocket on weight-loss products and services.[13] Services range from the scientifically validated, such as Weight Watchers and Jenny Craig, to a wide variety of fad programs, pills, and services. Googling the term "weight loss" brings up (as of this writing) nearly 234,000,000 results in 0.69 seconds—a quick measure of our obsession with weight loss.

The media industry has created entire programming around weight loss and fitness with reality TV shows like "The Biggest Loser," "Extreme Weight Loss," "Heavy," and "Celebrity Fit Club." Many diet and fitness experts disagree with the weight loss methods showcased on reality TV programs and believe the promised outcomes cannot apply to the general public.

In the effort to manage diet and weight, consumers also turn to social media, which can help people lose weight and stick with an exercise plan through a virtual buddy system.[14] A recent meta-analysis by researchers from Imperial College, London, reviewed the results of 12 previous studies. The meta-analysis showed programs that included social media elements achieved modest but significant results in helping participants lose weight.[15] Health policy researcher and surgeon Dr. Hutan Ashrafian, the lead author of the study, noted that social media can be more cost effective than more traditional programs and has other advantages as well:

> The feeling of being part of a community allows patients to draw on the support of their peers as well as clinicians. ... The use of social media to treat obesity encourages patients to be more proactive and empowers them to contribute towards their own treatment.[16]

As reviewed in Chapter 2, "The New DIY Health Consumer," consumers are purchasing wearable devices in droves in order to track activity and motivate themselves to do more of it, and wearables increasingly track more than exercise. The wearables movement is notable for demonstrating ways consumers are taking action to manage health on their own, including an increasing number who are betting money on weight loss at sites such as Healthy Wage (www.healthywage.com), DietBetter (www.dietbetter.com), and StickK (www.stickK.com). Others are finding success by competing with friends and family through their wearable devices or apps like Matchup (www.matchup.com) that allow them to compete with others across devices. The high drop-off rate of wearables usage, however, indicates that on their own they are not yet compelling for helping people maintain use over time. This may be because they don't incorporate enough of the science of behavior change, as described in Chapter 3, "The Science and Practice of Health Behavior Change: A Consumer-Centric, Technology-Supported Approach"; it may also be due to the fact that consumers may want to combine and trend information from multiple sources—wearables, wireless scales, connected medical devices, and clinical records—to create an overall picture of their health and understand trends and correlations or some combination of these factors.

Employers' Role

More than 70 percent of employers offer their employees wellness and fitness programs today.[17] For example, Fallon Health's "It Fits!" is a fitness reimbursement program that gives employees up to $400 per family ($200 for an individual plan) to use toward everything from gym memberships and yoga classes to ski passes and race fees.[17] SAS, an international software company located in North Carolina, offers its employees a wellness program built around its recreation and fitness center (RFC). The RFC is open to SAS employees, retirees, and family members. The wellness program includes health checks, smoking cessation, and rewards for fitness accomplishments, participation in leisure-time activities, and completion of the six-month "Your Way to Wellness" program. The on-site healthcare center provides primary healthcare and preventive services to employees and covered dependents.[18]

Achieving physical health will continue to be a major contributing factor to reducing the cost of healthcare. It's important for employers to develop and offer a variety of programs and tools because one approach does not fit all; people gravitate to solutions that best fit their lifestyles, needs, and interests. Wellness programs are being held to a higher standard as employers look for proof they are spending their money wisely.

Environmental Health

Environmental health refers to aspects of our health and disease determined by factors in the environment. It also addresses the theory and practice of assessing and controlling these environmental factors. The WHO defines environmental health in the following way:

> Environmental health addresses all the physical, chemical, and biological factors external to a person, and all the related factors impacting behaviors. It encompasses the assessment and control of those environmental factors that can potentially affect health. It is targeted towards preventing disease and creating health-supportive environments. This definition excludes behavior not related to environment, as well as behavior related to the social and cultural environment, as well as genetic.[19]

People depend upon clean air, water, and a safe food-supply chain, and the consequences of not being able to depend on these resources can be dire. The lack of clean and safe drinking water, for example, was the number one global risk identified in the 2015 World Economic Forum.[20] In recent news we have had several instances where tainted food has resulted in cases of *Escherichia coli* (*E. coli*) or where a toxic spill has contaminated water supplies. Concerns about these types of consequences drive the focus on environmental health, which is changing how nations develop sustainable energy systems, green energy policies, safe food and water, and compliance standards that impact whole health.

There are hundreds of tests for conditions of air, water, and food. Individuals may be able to take action themselves to prevent some of the impacts of environmental triggers. One of the conditions with a direct link to environmental factors is asthma, one of our most common chronic health conditions. Patients with asthma can help control their illness by diligently monitoring their own environment to understand pollution, pollen, or mold levels that might trigger asthma attacks. They can get help from a variety of Internet sites that provide educational information,[21] including the Centers for Disease Control and Prevention.[22] Broader government regulations have a role in managing and controlling the irritants that can increase the severity of asthma symptoms, affecting overall population health in positive ways.

Technology aids in developing strategies used to test, treat, remediate, and dispose of environmental contaminants. Using detailed research and analysis, it is possible to assess the impact of ecological disasters and gauge their influence on public health, safety, and social and economic welfare. Today we have the ability to use technology to test the air, water, climate, and food supply chain in an effort to achieve whole health; sophisticated analytics can allow us to use data gained to predict and model the impact of potential disasters, changes in air, water, and climate on the health of millions.

Spiritual Health

Spiritual health is a component of whole health and integrated medicine. The definition of spiritual health varies. Many believe that spiritual health begins with an individual's desire to give life purpose and meaning through thoughtful reflection on the world. It is believed that someone's spiritual health can be gauged by the person's overall level of peace, harmony, and joy.

According to the editors of the *World Christian Encyclopedia: A Comparative Survey of Churches and Religions—AD 30 to 2200*, there are 19 major world religions that are subdivided into a total of 270 large religious groups, and many smaller ones. About 34,000 separate Christian groups have been identified in the world. Over half are independent churches that are not interested in linking with the big denominations.[23] Many people belong to some form of organized religion, while others practice mindfulness and harmony with the environment and others. All of these represent ways that people seek to incorporate a spiritual dimension into their lives and health.

Information technology and new media also play a role in assisting people in achieving spiritual health. We have seen the development of websites, videos, movies, and apps to promote spiritual health in recent years. Dr. Wayne Dyer, an internationally renowned author and speaker in the fields of self-development and spiritual growth, developed an entire tool set for people throughout his life (www.drwaynedyer.com).[24] Other examples include Vivid Life (www.VividLife.me), which assists people in practicing meditation techniques to achieve greater spiritual health.[25] The Mayo Clinic has a site dedicated to reducing stress by achieving spirituality[26] while Kaiser Permanente offers its members access to meditation classes and a series of guided imagery meditations through a partnership with Health Journeys (www.healthjourneys.com).

Deepak Chopra, MD—the guru on achieving well-being and spiritual health—uses social media tools to expand his message to others. He has achieved over 2.6 million followers on Twitter.[27] He also uses Google+ and has his own YouTube Channel, ChopraWell, "dedicated to inspiring, fun, and thought-provoking videos about healthy living, wellness, and spirituality" (www.deepakchopra.com).[28] Pope Francis is the first pope to use social media to spread his message. The pope app available on iTunes today provides all of his speeches, as well as photos and the full texts of his homilies.[29] The Dalai Lama is active on Twitter, with 12 million followers. There are also apps to help you meditate, focus your spiritual practices, and get wisdom from teachers from nearly every religion.[30] People are seeking spiritual growth, and look they for support in convenient tools such as apps. What is not as clear is how effective these sites are in providing spiritual support for people when compared to more traditional approaches such as classes or church memberships. It may be that in part people are hungry for community and relationship, a hunger that is unlikely to be fed by applications alone.

Social and Behavioral Health

Individuals with mental health and substance use conditions are in dire need of care coordination and other support, especially because mental health conditions may contribute to up to 70 percent of primary care visits.[31] In addition, as we address in Chapter 3, "The Science and Practice of Health Behavior Change: A Consumer-Centric, Technology-Supported Approach," people are looking for support with behavior change approaches and tools. We also need to support policies and funding that widen the adoption of and incentives for mental health providers to use health technologies. A white paper created by Third Way, called, "Treating the Whole Person: Integrating Behavioral and Physical Health Care," offers a wealth of examples of current practices that work and can be brought to scale.[32] Solutions such as those highlighted in the Third Way report will allow us to improve the health status of our most vulnerable populations. Continued innovation on models and tools that effectively support behavior changes, both those that individuals undertake on their own and those offered in conjunction with the healthcare system, will result in a healthier population.

Financial Health

Health is wealth. People worry about the cost of care, and that concern is present—though often unvoiced—in nearly every encounter in the healthcare system. As discussed in Chapter 2, "The New DIY Health Consumer," in the United States, consumers are bearing a larger share of the cost of healthcare today than in the past. Whether they receive health insurance from their employers or purchase it on their own, many have seen a substantial increase in the amount of money they pay when they go to a doctor or fill a prescription due to the prevalence of high-deductible plans. As we continue to move toward value-based healthcare, we see the continued need to provide patients and consumers with the best care at the best price for the best results. Patients need better tools to understand the real cost of care, how cost and quality intersect, and what they can do to ensure they are getting the best care possible at a price they can afford. Both patients and providers need and deserve price transparency in healthcare as well as continued efforts to reduce the overall cost of care.

Conclusion

To achieve whole health, consumers must understand what whole health is and feel empowered to take action to achieve it or move on the path toward it. When patients and their providers partner to develop a holistic plan that fits with the person's lifestyle and needs, the health outcomes are impressive. Connected health technologies can contribute appropriate tools and play an important role in helping people achieve whole health.[33]

We need to support policies that provide consumers, patients, and providers alike with access to connected health tools. The right tools, embedded in the right support system, can assist patients and families in achieving whole health goals. These technologies can include internet knowledge, mobile apps, personal health records, patient portals, connected medical devices, and wearable devices. The potential for using information technology to manage health and health management is far reaching. Health technologies are an important tool to achieving whole health as long as they are developed with both the patient and healthcare provider in mind.

Impact

To understand more about the impact of these issues in the lives of real people, please read the following patient and caregiver stories in Section II of this book:

Story 2	"An e-Champion for Alexis"
Story 6	"Concussion and Community"
Story 7	"Connected—But Not to My Doctors or Health System"
Story 9	"Do I Really Have to Do the Follow Up? My Eight-Week Breast Cancer Journey"
Story 12	"Healing with Faith, Food, Friends, Family, and Laughter"
Story 15	"Living Well with Lupus"
Story 17	"You Have a Mass the Size of an Eggplant in Your Abdomen"
Story 20	"Standing Up for Myself through Many Medical Problems"
Story 21	"Staying Abreast: Cancer and Community"
Story 22	"Technology Can Make Pain Less Painful"
Story 24	"Very Bad Genes and Very Bad Luck"
Story 25	"Visualizing Symptoms"

Notes

1. WHO. Preamble to the Constitution of the World Health Organization as adopted by the International Health Conference, New York, 19–22 June 1946, and entered into force on April 7, 1948.
2. http://www.ncbi.nlm.nih.gov/pmc/articles/PMC3644505/
3. https://www.nlm.nih.gov/medlineplus/complementaryandintegrativemedicine.html
4. http://www.drweil.com/drw/u/ART02054/Andrew-Weil-Integrative-Medicine.html
5. https://nccih.nih.gov/
6. https://nccih.nih.gov/health/integrative-health
7. https://nccih.nih.gov/health/massage
8. https://yoga.mindbodyonline.com/yoga-studio-scheduling-software/welcome-90UD-28257S
   .html?campaignID=70160000000PmPb&utm_adgroup=yoga_-_general&utm_term=yoga
   +software&utm_campaign=Yoga&utm_source=Bing&utm_medium=PPC
9. https://yoga.com/
10. National Health and Medical Research Council. "Promoting the health of indigenous Australians. A review of infrastructure support for aboriginal and Torres Strait Islander health advancement." Final report and recommendations. Canberra: NHMRC, 1996: part 2: 4.
11. http://www.slideshare.net/EdelmanInsights/edelman-health-barometer-2011-global-press-release
12. http://www.cdc.gov/obesity/data/adult.html
13. http://www.prweb.com/releases/2013/7/prweb10948232.htm/
14. http://www.sciencedirect.com/science/article/pii/S2211335515001072
15. http://content.healthaffairs.org/content/33/9/1641.abstract
16. http://www.eurekalert.org/pub_releases/2014-09/icl-snc090514.php
17. http://www.businessinsurance.com/article/20150630/NEWS03/150639987
18. http://www.livestrong.com/article/344920-examples-of-companies-wellness-programs/
19. World Health Organization Definition of Environmental Health. With permission. http://www.who
    .int/topics/environmental_health/en/
20. http://reports.weforum.org/global-risks-2015/#frame/20ad6
21. http://www.webmd.com/asthma/lung-function-tests-diagnosing-monitoring-asthma
22. http://www.cdc.gov/asthma/faqs.htm
23. David B. et al. 2001. *World Christian Encyclopedia : A Comparative Survey of Churches and Religions in the Modern World*. New York: Oxford University Press.
24. http://www.drwaynedyer.com/blog/
25. http://vividlife.me/ultimate/27902/practice-meditation-for-achieving-great-spiritual-health/
26. http://www.mayoclinic.org/healthy-lifestyle/stress-management/in-depth/stress-relief/art-20044464
27. https://twitter.com/DeepakChopra
28. https://www.youtube.com/user/TheChopraWell/about
29. https://itunes.apple.com/us/app/pope-app-official-pope-francis/id593468235?mt=8
30. http://www.elephantjournal.com/2012/02/10-apps-to-propel-your-spiritual-practice/
31. http://www.milbank.org/uploads/documents/10430EvolvingCare/10430EvolvingCare.html
32. http://www.thirdway.org/report/treating-the-whole-person-integrating-behavioral-and-physical
    -health-care
33. Davis, Matthew, Brook I. Martin, Ian D. Coulter, and William B. Weeks. "US Spending on Complementary and Alternative Medicine during 2002–08 Plateaued, Suggesting Role in Reformed Health System." *Health Affairs* 32 (1): 45–52.

Chapter 7

Family Caregivers, Health Information Technology, and Culture Change*

MaryAnne Sterling, CEA[†]

Introduction

What do family caregivers need from our healthcare system and from health information technology? What tools would make them more effective partners in caring for their loved ones? Until recently, these were questions that few had taken the time to ask. And yet, there are 93 million[1] family caregivers today in the United States who will provide an estimated $522 billion[2] in care for their loved ones (and that's just for eldercare!). Imagine the economic impact to our healthcare system if dedicated family caregivers did not exist. And imagine the cost to family caregivers who don't have the tools they need to manage their loved ones' care.

I am one of them. We are the perfect team of experts to help develop the health information technology tools that would support our caregiving needs. This emerging technology must satisfy our unique information requirements in order to become a permanent component of our caregiving toolbox, and it must be accompanied by a collaborative healthcare ecosystem in which the family caregiver is acknowledged as a key member of the patient's care team.

Background

We have a new normal in the United States: 39 percent of adults provide care for a loved one.[1] That number equates to roughly 93 million people, many of whom find themselves in the middle of the

---

* This chapter was originally published as a white paper (http://www.connectedhealthresources.com/What
  _Family_Caregivers_Need_from_Health_IT_and_the_Healthcare_System_to_be_Effective_Health
  _Managers_Sterling_December_2014_v2.pdf).
† @SterlingHIT

caregiving sandwich, often caring for children as well as a parent or spouse with a life-threatening illness or chronic condition (or simply struggling with advanced age)—many while trying to balance a career.

In 2013, the Pew Research Center quantified the family caregiver demographic in a groundbreaking report, "Family Caregivers Are Wired for Health,"[1] reflected in Figure 7.1.

Although we know that family caregivers are using online resources in greater numbers than noncaregivers and a sea of start-ups are beginning to develop caregiver-facing technology, there is a gap in understanding and addressing the real-time data and information needs of caregivers. The purpose of information technology is to put the right information into the hands of the right person at the right time—if developers don't understand family caregivers' pain points and information needs, they are unlikely to develop the right tools. Family caregivers are infrequently asked what information they need and when. The purpose of this chapter is to provide an information framework for technology developers to use as guidance.

Once family caregivers have the information they need to be effective health managers, they also need a healthcare system that is prepared and willing to collaborate with them as they support a loved one's treatment or recovery. Our current healthcare system falls short. This chapter will also address the elements of culture change necessary to create a healthcare ecosystem that empowers family caregivers, including opportunities for providers to partner with family caregivers to enhance care.

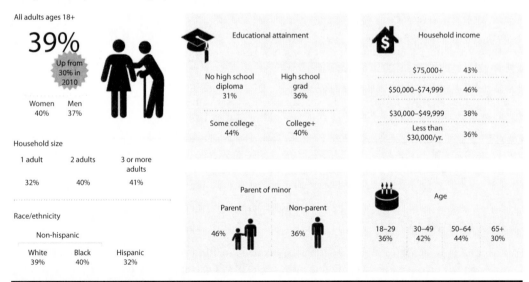

Figure 7.1 Illustration showing the demographic profile of family caregivers created by Pew Research Center. (From Pew Research Center, "Family Caregivers Are Wired for Health," Pew Research Center, Washington, DC, June 2013. http://www.pewinternet.org/2013/06/20/family -caregivers-are-wired-for-health/. With permission.)

Challenges Facing the Family Caregiver Today

Every discussion about technology solutions needs to begin with an analysis of the problem being addressed. Let's begin by level-setting how the family caregiver and the healthcare system interact today. This can best be illustrated by exploring the experiences of real family caregivers as a starting point, which we will do at the beginning of each section in the remainder of the chapter.

INADEQUATE COLLABORATION

Frances: "I am *not* getting good medical care!" This is how a conversation began with my 84-year-old mother, a retired nurse, 2 years ago. Issue #1 was lack of response from both her primary care doctor and cardiologist after she called each of them to report an allergic reaction to medication; issue #2 was a complete breakdown in communication between primary care doctor and pharmacy. The pharmacy could not refill critical medications for almost a week, including heart medication, until they were reauthorized by the nonresponsive primary care doctor. I became the middleman. The idea that Mom's primary care doctor, cardiologist, and pharmacy are even close to working as a team and exchanging information to improve her healthcare is still not a reality.

ACCESS TO INFORMATION

In Kathy's case, the frustration revolved around access to data:

I've struggled with the healthcare system as a family caregiver…to get access to information I need to manage my mother's low [blood] sodium—specifically, inability to get lab results electronically and in a timely manner. For months before my mother spent 4 days in the ICU because of low sodium, I had been trying to get Mom's lab results electronically. The geriatrician we use is part of a large group practice that has an electronic patient portal. However, unbelievably to me, the blood drawn at the residence where my parents live went to a lab that *faxed* the results back to the physician, where it was put in a paper record, which was then not accessible to me, clinicians in other locations, or the hospital.

There are a number of forward-thinking organizations within the healthcare system working to partner with patients *and* their family caregivers. For example, United Hospital Fund's Transitions in Care Quality Improvement Collaborative (TC-QuIC) brought together family caregivers and hospitals to discuss and pilot ways of including family caregivers in transitions of care.[3] The Family Caregiver Alliance (www.caregiver.org), the National Alliance for Caregiving (www.caregiving.org), and the Caregiver Action Network (www.caregiveraction.org) are all examples of foundations working to raise the visibility of issues facing family caregivers and advocating on their behalf at the community, state, and national level. But we still have a long way to go.

In general, the following problems persist, challenging the family caregiver at every step:

■ Lack of recognition of the family caregiver role and its importance, including listing in the medical record

■ Missing or inadequate dialogue between providers and the family caregiver

- Use of complex medical terminology and insurance jargon
- Lack of training/education to familiarize the family caregiver with next steps in recovery or how to perform caregiving tasks
- Inadequate access to the caregiver's loved one's medical information
- Misinterpretation of the Health Insurance Portability and Accountability Act (HIPAA) that further impedes family caregivers' access to information
- Clinical work flows/processes that don't incorporate the family caregiver
- Absence of a care plan created in partnership with the family caregiver
- Lack of coordination between healthcare and social services
- Inadequate collaboration between providers
- Poor care transitions between settings of care, especially to the home
- Woeful lack of reimbursement to cover long-term home care needs, home modifications, sensor technology, respite care, etc. to support keeping family members in the home setting

Many of these are problems faced by individual patients as well. We need a robust national dialogue to develop strategies for overcoming these issues. At the same time, we need to explore ways in which technology could better support family caregivers in this challenging environment.

The Caregiving Information Cycle

INFORMATION GAPS

My husband and I recently navigated the tricky waters of Medicaid eligibility on behalf of my mother. As part of that process, one of the aging and disability resource centers (ADRCs) in our state offered to assist us in our search for an assisted living facility with an empty bed. They e-mailed us a spreadsheet that contained the contact information for 314 assisted living facilities and informed us that we had to call each of them to find out if they accepted the Medicaid auxiliary grant (a Medicaid waiver program in Virginia) and if they had a bed available. Given the potential of technology, why is it that I can drive down the interstate and see the nearest emergency room wait-time on a billboard, but nobody has a database with the availability of a bed across my state's assisted living facilities?

This story highlights just one example of the many gaps across the healthcare ecosystem that information technology could fill. But before we go any further, we need to look at the information that family caregivers need in order to navigate their caregiving journey.

Family Caregiver Information Needs

Healthcare and social services information is the currency of the family caregiver. As it turns out, we need different information at different points in time, depending on the phase of caregiving we find ourselves in. I refer to this as the *caregiving information cycle*, shown in Figure 7.2.

Typically, a caregiver is dealing with a **crisis**, assisting a loved one through a **care transition**, or in **maintenance** mode—just trying to navigate day-to-day challenges.

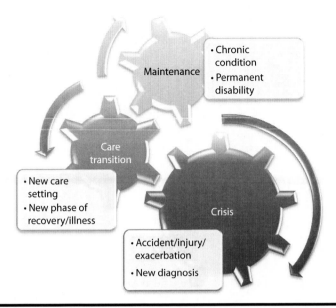

Figure 7.2 Illustration of the caregiving information cycle.

Family caregivers may find themselves in each phase of the caregiving information cycle many times over the course of their caregiving experience. Our information needs change as we move between phases, sometimes quickly and unpredictably. In addition, our information needs fall into two distinct categories: **gathering** information to act upon and **providing** information to others.

In the caregiving information cycle, a **crisis** refers to an accident, injury, or new diagnosis. During a crisis, caregivers may need to provide information to healthcare professionals, including the patient's

- Allergies and health history
- Family health history
- Medications
- Immunizations
- Test results/labs/films
- Health insurance

During a crisis, caregivers need to gather information, including

- Diagnosis or injury details
- Disease-specific information
- Prognosis and treatment plan
- Care options
- Next steps

Care transition refers to a new care setting or new phase of recovery/illness. During care transition, caregivers may need to gather information about

- The patient's care plan
- Housing/caregiving options (i.e., rehab, home health, nursing home, hospice)

- Social services and community resources (i.e., Meals on Wheels, transportation)
- Instructions for performing caregiving activities
- Medical equipment

Maintenance refers to a chronic condition or permanent disability. During the maintenance phase, caregivers may need to gather information about

- Long-term care support
- Financial options
- Assistive devices
- Medication regimens
- Respite care
- Support groups

The family caregiver often becomes an information expert, having compiled knowledge from the healthcare, social services, insurance, legal, and pharmaceutical domains, and is often the only person who can tell a coherent story about the patient's journey through the healthcare system.

Family Caregiver Technology Needs

Technology can be used in a variety of ways to support the information needs of family caregivers. In many caregiving situations, technology can be a lifeline to information, if it is intuitive and easy to access. The tech-savvy family caregiver generally has technology needs that fall into six categories: access, track, manage, coordinate, connect, and learn, described in Figure 7.3.

Category	Information Needed
Access	Allergies, individual and family health histories, medical records, test results, medication lists, legal documents such as healthcare proxy
Track	Immunizations, vital signs, blood sugar, weight, food intake, mood, rest, patient location
Manage	Medication administration, refills, care plans, insurance, finances
Coordinate	Doctor appointments and referrals, in-home care and services, other family caregivers, transportation, meals-on-wheels, medical equipment
Connect	With other caregivers, providers, family members, friends, support groups
Learn	About a diagnosis, disease, treatment, or the latest research, community supports, social services, housing options

Figure 7.3 Categories of family caregiver technology needs.

Figure 7.4   Family caregiver needs during the maintenance phase of caregiving.

When the technology needs of family caregivers are aligned with the caregiving information cycle, we see the following:

During a **crisis**, family caregivers may need to **access** allergy information, individual and family health histories, medication lists, and legal documents. They may need to **connect** with family members and **learn** about a diagnosis or disease.

During **care transition**, we may need to **access** medical records; **manage** insurance and care plans; **coordinate** in-home care and services, transportation, and medical equipment; **connect** with providers; and **learn** about a particular treatment, community supports, and housing options.

During **maintenance**, we may need to **access** test results and insurance statements; **track** a patient's blood sugar or weight; **manage** medication administration and refills, along with finances; **coordinate** doctor appointments and referrals; **connect** with other caregivers and support groups; and **learn** about the latest research on a particular course of treatment or social services that the patient may qualify for, as highlighted in Figure 7.4.

In summary, understanding the information and technology needs of family caregivers is imperative when developing information systems and tools that address these needs.

Reality Check. We Have Technology. Now What?

Family caregivers are already using a variety of technologies, but success is largely dependent on the comfort level of the user and the complexity of the problem he or she is trying to solve.

EXAMPLES OF CURRENT TECHNOLOGY SOLUTIONS

The Nelson family relies on spreadsheets:

I used Excel to create records that captured the data I needed over time, to keep up with all of Dad's medications (ordering them, making sure the prescriptions were right and up to date, and keeping track of what I gave him). I even used Excel to make a spreadsheet that helped me fill up the weekly dispenser in a way that was more accurate and made the task faster to do.

For the Connors family, e-mail plays a role: "We use e-mail with home healthcare providers so Mom has a steady team of companion caregivers."

The Mazza family turned to simple technology, generally used to monitor a much younger generation:

A few years ago, we cared for my mother, who was in an apartment across the street from my music store. We couldn't leave her alone because of Alzheimer's, but after she went to bed I had a wireless baby monitor system that allowed me to see if she got up. I could watch from my instrument repair workbench across the street and get my work done.

EMERGING TECHNOLOGY

Lynn is applying new technology in novel ways to document "a day in the life" of a family caregiver. She is using a GoPro to "capture as much as I can of our day and what we do" in order to share what they've learned "so others can have a better quality of life."

Apps are beginning to appear in the daily routines of caregivers. I recently met Loretta, an Alzheimer's caregiver, who uses three apps to help care for her mother. Each has a unique focus:

1. Ideas for the caregiver on how to deal with difficult behavior
2. Music to soothe sun-downing behavior (People with Alzheimer's often get more agitated when the sun goes down)
3. Reminiscing about days gone by (to engage her mom)

Technology Available Now

There is a vast array of technology that family caregivers can turn to in support of their information needs. This ranges from patient portals to wireless sensors, to devices that determine whether or not a patient has taken his or her medication, to online appointment scheduling and support communities. If we look at these tools using our technology categories, we discover ways current technology aligns with family caregiver needs, as illustrated in Figure 7.5.

At first glance, it may appear that a wealth of information technology tools exist to support family caregivers. However, a deeper dive reveals a more lackluster picture. Very few tools are designed specifically for family caregivers and their information needs nor are they readily adaptable. Many of these tools are "point" solutions that address one issue in isolation. Conversely, the availability of these tools does not guarantee access to information. Electronic access to personal health data is spotty and may require gathering data individually from separate patient portals with different logon and password requirements. Blue Button, designed to help aggregate medical information, is still in its infancy. Bottom-line: it is difficult to obtain and aggregate medical records, especially as a family caregiver.

Category	Information Needed	Types of Tools Represented
Access	Allergies, individual and family health histories, medical records, test results, medication lists, legal documents such as healthcare proxy	Personal health records, patient portals, Blue Button, Surgeon General's "My Family Health Portrait"
Track	Immunizations, vital signs, blood sugar, weight, food intake, mood, rest, patient location	Wireless sensors, i.e., mats in the bathroom and kitchen that indicate if someone has fallen or their weight has changed; GPS safety devices, health and exercise apps, spreadsheets
Manage	Medication administration, refills, care plans, insurance, finances	Medication reminders, online prescription refills, devices that determine whether or not patient has taken their medication (and provide the correct dose), care planning tools, insurance portals
Coordinate	Doctor appointments and referrals, in-home care and services, other family caregivers, transportation, meals-on-wheels, medical equipment	Online appointment scheduling, group calendars, apps to help coordinate multiple family caregivers
Connect	With other caregivers, providers, family members, friends, support groups	On-line support communities, secure messaging, email, blogging tools
Learn	About a diagnosis, disease, treatment, or the latest research, community supports, social services, housing options	Countless health and medical information sources, service directories, blogs

Figure 7.5   Current technology capabilities aligned to family caregiver needs.

From the caregiver's perspective, incorporating new technology into daily routines is often time prohibitive, and the applicability of technology to real-life caregiving scenarios is often questionable. In addition, uncoordinated technology, from multiple patient portals to unconnected apps, may simply create more silos. Overall, trying to keep track of multiple technology tools and the data they generate is sometimes more trouble than it's worth. Each of these challenges could be overcome by developers and a healthcare system that was more focused on the needs of family caregivers.

Not all caregiving challenges can be solved with technology, however. Caregiving is a complex web of tasks that turn everyday people into care coordinators, medical record keepers, medical decision makers, insurance navigators, medication administrators, and deliverers of complex medical care.

Technology can assist in making some of these tasks easier, but it's not enough. Just navigating the healthcare system is a monumental task that would be much easier if caregivers had access to care navigators or similar resources who could assist them through the maze of services, jargon, and red tape: people who understand the healthcare system and people who speak in the same way they do because the language of healthcare is not the language of the average American.[4]

And there are other barriers…

- Widespread adoption of existing family caregiver technology is painfully slow. Getting the word out to 93 million people is challenging and, right now, not being done in a coordinated fashion. Family caregivers simply don't know what tools are available to them.
- Information on the web is not curated and is often written at an advanced literacy level. It becomes a minefield for caregivers to find, sift through, and comprehend medical information.
- Connectivity and monitoring do not imply "action." They must be coupled with people in the community (in addition to first-responders) who can take action when red flags arise. For example, if sensor technology indicates that an elderly patient has not taken her medication or has gained three pounds this week, who is responsible for acting on this information?
- Patient (and caregiver)-generated health data are not widely accepted and no framework exists for receipt/review/response of this information by providers. In 2013, the Patient Generated Health Data Technical Expert Panel convened by the Office of the National Coordinator for Health Information Technology (ONC) and the National eHealth Collaborative[5] laid groundwork that will guide organizations in incorporating patient-generated heath data. Now we need to put those recommendations[6] into practice!

How Do We Move Forward?

We are early in the evolution of technology support for the family caregiver. We have an opportunity to lay the foundation to improve the quality of life for 93 million people and those they care for.

But we have to be realistic about this if we are going to be successful. It's one thing to search for information online (which 72 percent of family caregivers do[1]), but another to actually find meaningful, relevant information technology that can be used interactively in support of care planning, treatment, and recovery.

We need people involved in this process. The emerging workforce of navigators and care and case managers is a great place to start. Why? "Because data does not mean action and technology does not mean connected care" (Gail Embt at Kinergy Health). We need the ability to communicate with our loved ones' providers, to organize and interpret information, to monitor our loved ones' conditions (even when we are not with them!), to coordinate care and services. A few specifics include:

- Established resources in every community for healthcare, services, and technology coordination
- Education for family caregivers on tools and technologies that can support their caregiving needs
- Retooling of existing medical information into plain language and multilingual resources that family caregivers can easily understand
- Widespread use of secure messaging technology between patients and their health community, including their family caregivers, healthcare providers, and social services/community support resources
- Blue Button capability across providers so family caregivers can aggregate the patients' medical records and test results in one place as well as interoperable medical record systems to make a complete record of a patient's care standard practice rather than an anomaly
- Comprehensive care planning that is actionable and tailored to the needs of patients and family caregivers

---

Care plan redefined: An actionable plan to assist caregivers in providing and/or coordinating care for their family members that links the healthcare, social services, and community supports needed to support them in healthcare transition, medication management, treatment, and recovery.

Let us aspire to get to a place where family caregivers are respected, integral members of the care team, supported by advanced health information technology. We will discuss how providers can collaborate with family caregivers to accomplish this vision in the next section.

Culture Change: The Path Forward

Culture gaps: For Sarah, who was suddenly thrust into the role of caregiver for her husband, the blurred lines of communication were frightening:

Our biggest challenge was when the neurologist gave us the diagnosis and walked out of the room telling [us], as an afterthought, to make an appointment for another test that afternoon. I was in shock. I did not know whether to start crying or screaming. My children were young and I was pretty sure that would be Ernie's last day of work. I felt afraid and terribly alone. There were no words of encouragement about gleaning help or time for asking questions and getting answers about Alzheimer's disease. In Stan's case, the importance of two-way communication with his mom's providers was driven by a language barrier. "…sometimes I had difficulty convincing my mom's doctors/nurses that I need[ed] to accompany her on all her appointments due to her limited English proficiency."

A staggering amount of culture change is needed to reinvent our current "sick care system" and replace it with a collaborative health ecosystem that is patient- and family-caregiver-centric. We will soon have mountains of technology in place, just waiting for information to begin flowing.

But if we do not address the necessary culture change in parallel with the implementation of technology, family caregivers and patients alike will be left behind.

Providers are at the epicenter of this shift in culture and thus the focus of the following recommendations for moving forward.

Key Recommendations

Identify the Family Caregiver in the Medical Record

One of the recommendations of the Commission on Long-Term Care[7] is to identify the family caregiver in the patient's medical record. When you consider the many hats that caregivers wear—care coordinators, medical record keepers, medical decision makers, insurance navigators, medication administrators, and deliverers of complex medical care—who better to have as a partner in the patient's care? Allow the patient to identify his or her active family caregiver in the record, when applicable. This is the individual the patient relies on to help sort out health-related issues. If the individual is not competent to identify the caregiver, enable the person who holds the medical power of attorney (if there is one) to be named in the medical record.

COMMISSION ON LONG-TERM CARE RECOMMENDATION

"Family caregivers should be identified in the individual's EHR, especially when they are a part of the care plan. With the individual's permission, family caregivers should have full access to the patient's records and care plan."

Let's take this idea a few steps further and consider the workflow, process, and orientation changes required to make it a reality:

■ Capture the family caregiver's name and role in caring for the patient, along with contact information.
■ Make this the first step in developing a collaborative care plan in which the family caregiver is a key contributor and participant.
■ Participate in Blue Button and help make medical information useable and accessible.
■ Build training about collaborative, respectful engagement of patients and family caregivers into medical school curriculums.
■ Make sure technology and process are sensitive to special legal rules regarding adolescents, especially teenagers or foster children.
■ Make sure the family caregiver has access to the patient's online medical record and knows how to navigate and use the technology.

Include Family Caregivers in the Conversations and Treat Them as Key Members of the Patient's Care Team

Family caregivers often are the people doing the "heavy lifting" behind the scenes. You likely know the engaged family caregivers in your community. They frequently call to make medical appointments and accompany their loved one to those visits or show up in the ER when a family member is in need. Are they comfortable with the care they are being asked to provide? Do they

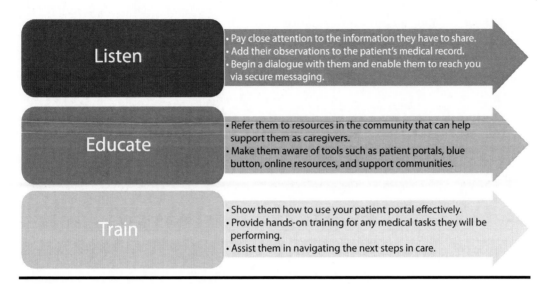

Figure 7.6 How the healthcare system can help family caregivers be successful in their roles.

know where to find support services? Ask them. Figure 7.6 illustrates how the healthcare system can help family caregivers to be successful in their roles.

Family caregivers can be your greatest asset if you take the time to engage them and share information with them. For example, be proactive—don't assume that family caregivers know about your patient portal, how to use it effectively, or how to navigate the next steps in their loved ones' care. This does not come naturally to most people, but it *must* be a skill set that we teach our population moving forward.

Redefine Care Coordination and Break Down the Silos of Healthcare, Social Services, and Community Supports

The family caregiver definition of "care coordination" differs significantly from the traditional version, which focuses on coordination between providers.

Care coordination, in the eyes of the family caregiver, is a collaborative process that happens at the intersection of healthcare, social services, and community supports. Without all three components working seamlessly together, our jobs become much more difficult, if not impossible. In fact, social services and community supports (meals, respite care, transportation) are often critically important to both the patient and the family during healthcare transitions, medication management, treatment, and recovery. Moving forward,

- Identify care coordination champions in your organization.
- Actively engage and partner with local organizations that can assist family caregivers (i.e., area agencies on aging, foster care agencies, faith-based groups, social services, adult day centers, respite care, and many more).
- Take advantage of the knowledge of your existing partners in home health or long-term care about local service providers.
- Assist family caregivers in finding resources in the community that can help support them.

Care coordination is truly a "community sport"! Organizations that provide these support services are eager to partner with healthcare providers. Identify a care coordination champion in your organization and start connecting the dots in your community. Leverage the knowledge of existing partners who know the social services and community supports landscape well.

Help Change Attitudes

Make it everyone's responsibility to assist the family caregiver in coordinating both healthcare and support services.

- Raise awareness with your staff.
- Establish key person(s) within your organization to take the lead in a caregiver initiative.
- Actively engage and partner with local organizations that can assist family caregivers.
- Be proactive: Learn about—and support development and use of—new technologies (including mobile apps) that can support family caregivers.

Changing attitudes is about changing culture and attitudes across the healthcare continuum. Start by identifying a champion in your organization to spearhead a family caregiver initiative. Learn about organizations and new technologies that can support family caregivers. Encourage your colleagues to do the same. Consider this an extension of patient experience initiatives.

Technology Needs a Little Help

Technology alone cannot address these challenges. It needs help from a realigned health workforce that includes patient educators, navigators, local care and services coordinators, and care/case managers to reengineered work flows that include:

- Capture of family caregiver information
- Collaborative health and care planning
- Education and training of the family caregiver
- Seamlessly coordinated care (including social services and community supports)
- Partnership with the community

Health information technology, in order to deliver on the promise of better healthcare, must be accompanied by people and process changes. Simply introducing the technology component and assuming that the problem will be solved is not realistic. Healthcare is complicated. We need to insert those who can help navigate, those who can educate, and those who can coordinate into the healthcare workforce. We need collaboration among healthcare professionals, service providers, and communities on a whole new level. Building Blocks. Technology must be a component of robust programs and policies that are designed to integrate and support family caregivers. Programs such as the Patient and Family Centered Care Methodology and Practice, pioneered at UPMC; and family caregiver philosophies integral to organizations like the Patient Centered Outcomes Research Institute (PCORI) are leading the way. In addition, a new law passed in several states, the CARE Act, requires hospitals to

1. Record the name of the family caregiver on the medical record of your loved one.
2. Inform the family caregivers when the patient is to be discharged.
3. Provide the family caregiver with education and instruction of the medical tasks he or she will need to perform for the patient at home.

Our ability to scale these programs and policy initiatives will set the tone for the successful adoption of health information technology that is tailored to the information needs of family caregivers.

Conclusion

We are at a critical juncture when it comes to the family caregiver, an indispensable and frequently underused member of the healthcare team. Caregivers need the right information at the right time in order to be effective health managers. How we enable technology to support and empower them will define the transformation of healthcare moving forward.

In addition to focusing on supportive technology, we need to embrace the culture change needed to shift the emphasis from the 10 to 15 percent of health that is determined by medical care delivery to the 85 to 90 percent of health that is determined by other factors,[8] where the family caregiver often plays a key role in patient outcomes. Let's celebrate the care they provide and give them the tools that enable them to be even more effective.

Impact

To understand more about the impact of these issues in the lives of real people, please read the following patient and caregiver stories in Section II of this book:

Story 2	"An e-Champion for Alexis"
Story 3	"You Must Have an Insanely High Pain Tolerance"
Story 5	"Becoming My Mother's Voice"
Story 7	"Connected—But Not to My Doctors or Health System"
Story 8	"Ineffectual Transitions of Care Can Contribute to Death"
Story 13	"I Suggest You Check Yourself into the Hospital"
Story 16	"Managing Diabetes with a Do-It-Yourself Pancreatic System (DIYPS)"
Story 19	"Prednisone and Misdiagnosis"
Story 21	"Staying Abreast: Cancer and Community"
Story 24	"Very Bad Genes and Very Bad Luck"
Story 27	"When Lightning Strikes"

Acknowledgments

Ms. Sterling gratefully acknowledges contributors and reviewers Gail Embt, Shannah Koss, Erin Mackay, Danny van Leeuwen, and the HIMSS Patient and Family Caregiver Advisory Council. Special thanks to both HIMSS and the National Partnership for Women & Families for their support.

Notes

1. Fox, Susannah, Maeve Duggan, and Kristin Purcell. "Family Caregivers Are Wired for Health." Report from Pew Research Center, June 20, 2013. Web. Nov. 16, 2014 (http://www.pewinternet .org/2013/06/20/family-caregivers-are-wired-for-health/).
2. Chari, Amalavoyal V., John Engberg, Kristin N. Ray, and Ateev Mehrotra. "The Opportunity Costs of Informal Elder-Care in the United States: New Estimates from the American Time Use Survey." Article first published online: Oct. 7, 2014, Wiley Online Library.
3. https://www.uhfnyc.org/assets/1111
4. http://www.tedmed.com/talks/show?id=47020
5. http://www.himss.org/library/NEHC
6. http://www.healthit.gov/sites/default/files/pghi_tep_finalreport121713.pdf
7. Commission on Long-Term Care. Report to the Congress, no. Y 3.2:L 85/R 29. US Senate Commission on Long-Term Care, Sept. 30, 2013. Web. Nov. 17, 2014.
8. Robert Wood Johnson Foundation. 2010. "Frequently Asked Questions about the Social Determinants of Health." Available at http://www.rwjf.org/content/dam/files/rwjfwebfiles/Research/2010/faqsocial determinants20101029.pdf.

Chapter 8

Programs That Work to Promote Partnership and Engagement

John Sharp, MA, MSSA, PMP, FHIMSS*

Introduction

Patient engagement has frequently been treated as something that payers and providers "do to" patients. Increasingly, however, it is clear that engagement is not a one-way street. Consumers and patients are looking for health systems that are more engaging: more convenient, more interactive, more digital, more personable, and more partnership oriented. Healthcare organizations are figuring out that if they want to build loyalty and appeal to consumers who are motivated about their health, they need to create two-way communications where individuals can interact with them in the setting and channel the person chooses.

As part of building partnerships with patients, providers are implementing digital capabilities that provide new ways of interaction. These capabilities are an outgrowth of the implementation of electronic health records (EHRs) that began in the late 1990s with early patient portal implementations of MyChart at the Palo Alto Medical Foundation and Indivo at Boston Children's Hospital.[1]

Activated patients are capturing personal health data about wellness and illness from a variety of devices, trackers, and applications to help them manage their health. Healthcare organizations are beginning to integrate these kinds of data into clinical records and determine how they can use them to collaborate with patients around their health. Payers and providers alike are experimenting with mobile and social applications to enhance patient and family experiences and participation.

Payers are working with claims and cost data to provide more transparency about pricing and payment. They are also experimenting with population health analytics to understand which patients are at highest risk and what is engaging for different individuals. For instance,

---

* @JohnSharp

some patients may prefer to be contacted by text messaging while others prefer a secure e-mail. After identifying those patients who are most likely to need intervention, payers or providers may communicate with patients using the channel that works best for that person or provide higher risk patients with remote patient monitoring devices to detect and prevent an emergency room visit or hospitalization. Healthcare organizations are increasingly using tools developed in the domain of marketing to deliver ever more customized, tailored, and interesting interventions.

Personal health technology is a key enabler for this changing landscape. A broad array of personal health engagement technologies is now available. But how do these technologies interact with patients in managing their health? What are the best practices in using these technologies? The opportunities to expand healthcare capabilities using approaches from other industries such as marketing, personal finance, and gaming offer endless promise. So, too, does the use of sensors and trackers to interact more fully with people inside their environments and to integrate with clinical records when appropriate. This chapter will discuss ways that technology is changing the healthcare dynamic and bringing better, more efficient, and empowering care.

Convenience

Healthcare consumers expect convenience from the healthcare system—they are used to the convenience of using websites and apps for managing travel reservations, conducting banking transactions, and finding repair services. Those expectations carry into their healthcare experiences. No longer do people assume that a long wait to see a doctor is normal; now they expect same-day appointments, online scheduling, and virtual visits. Some providers are responding to this new level of expectations with competitive solutions including the ability to make appointments online, register and complete paperwork before getting to the office, check in at a kiosk or by phone, participate in clinical decision making, and check out automatically.[2]

Consumers strongly prefer using web and mobile means to pay healthcare bills rather than sending checks by snail mail.[3] Consumers' desire for convenient healthcare extends to the desire to easily share data with all of their providers, get historical data, and coordinate care across different providers and locations.

Access to Your Own Clinical Data

Consumers increasingly consider *electronic* access to their own clinical data to be their right. The legal right to get a copy of your healthcare information has existed since the Health Insurance Portability and Accountability Act (HIPAA) was signed in 1996; as health systems install electronic medical records (EMRs), consumers expect that right to extend to digital access.

Many health systems began to provide patients with access to their clinical data through web and mobile portals as a part of the roll-out of electronic health records over the past 15 years. Patient portals typically provide a basic set of tools, including the capabilities required to address "meaningful use," (see inset): the ability to view, download, or transmit a copy of the patient's medical record and the ability to securely message a provider.

Meaningful Use Defined
Meaningful use is using certified electronic health record (EHR) technology to:

- Improve quality, safety, efficiency, and reduce health disparities
- Engage patients and family
- Improve care coordination, and population and public health
- Maintain privacy and security of patient health information

Ultimately, it is hoped that the meaningful use compliance will result in:

- Better clinical outcomes
- Improved population health outcomes
- Increased transparency and efficiency
- Empowered individuals
- More robust research data on health systems

Meaningful use sets specific objectives that eligible professionals (EPs) and hospitals must achieve to qualify for Centers for Medicare & Medicaid Services (CMS) Incentive Programs.[4]

Meaningful use has three stages, with the first stage starting in 2011. Stage three begins in 2016. Data that must be available online for patients according to meaningful use rules include:

> Patient name; provider's name and office contact information; current and past problem list; procedures; laboratory test results; current medication list and medication history; current medication allergy list and medication allergy history; vital signs (height, weight, blood pressure, BMI, growth charts); smoking status; demographic information (preferred language; sex, race, ethnicity, date of birth); care plan field(s) including goals and instructions; and any known care team members including the primary care provider (PCP) of record.[5]

Meaningful use stage 2 incentives were reduced in 2015 and now define patient portal success in the following way[6]:

- It is available to at least 50 percent of potential patients.
- One patient must use the portal to view, download, or transmit his or her records.
- The capability for one patient to send and receive a secure message must be enabled.

The Office of the National Coordinator for Health Information Technology (ONC) released a consumer survey about portal use in early 2015, "The 2013–2014 Consumer Survey of Attitudes toward the Privacy and Security Aspects of Electronic Health Records and Health Information Exchange."[7] In summarizing the results, ONC noted that in 2014, 40 percent of Americans were offered online access to their medical record, a significant increase from 2013. ONC also reported that 55 percent of Americans with access to their health information online

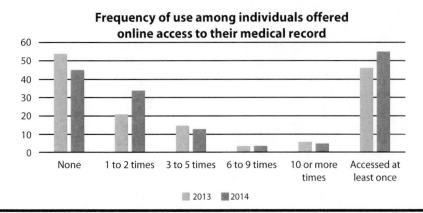

Figure 8.1   How often people access health data electronically from ONC survey of consumer portal use. ("The 2013–2014 Consumer Survey of Attitudes toward the Privacy and Security Aspects of Electronic Health Records and Health Information Exchange, with permission.")

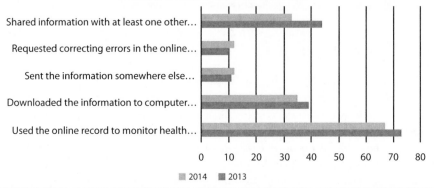

Figure 8.2   Trends in consumers' access to their online health data from ONC survey of consumer portal use. ("The 2013–2014 Consumer Survey of Attitudes toward the Privacy and Security Aspects of Electronic Health Records and Health Information Exchange, with permission.")

used that access at least once, with smaller percentages accessing their data multiple times, as shown in Figure 8.1. The same study showed how people used access to their online records, highlighted in Figure 8.2. The data showed that a full 81 percent of 2014 users felt the data they accessed was useful.

Similarly, a September 2015 study from Surescripts found that electronic access is quickly becoming a key issue in how people select new doctors, with more than 50 percent saying that if given a choice, they would select the doctor who would allow them to fill out paperwork online, receive tests results electronically, and schedule appointments online.[8]

While some providers are still struggling to implement basic portal tools, others are starting to implement more advanced capabilities that are more engaging and interactive. Some of these shifts are highlighted next:

- **Healthcare transactions**. Taking the mantra of convenience to heart, web and mobile portals increasingly offer transactional features that simplify healthcare tasks, such as the ability to make and change appointments, set up appointment reminders, refill prescriptions, complete forms, and pay bills online.
- **Clinical data**. The capacity to view aspects of your clinical health data from lab test results to medications, allergies, immunizations, procedures, and diagnoses is core to web and mobile portal functionality. Increasingly, data are being supported by links to education and action planning. In addition, clinical data collected in the healthcare system are being amplified by patient-generated data collected from trackers, sensors, connected medical devices, and even the Internet of Things (IoT). Health systems increasingly often are providing patients with access to physician notes—and sometimes the ability to comment on and annotate those notes.
- **Communication**. The ability to send and receive secure messages between providers and patients is being extended to include communications via texting, social media, and virtual visits using telemedicine resources. Patients and caregivers are also taking charge, using social media and online communities to connect with and learn from others who share the same conditions or struggle with the same issues.
- **Interaction and personalization**. As analytic capabilities become deeper, we can expect to see a more personalized experience created for individuals, as well as more integration of web, mobile, device, and social experiences to help individuals better manage their health and healthcare.

Next-generation portals promise to enhance consumer and patient experiences and improve outcomes: clinical, financial, and loyalty.

Implementation and Engagement Strategies That Work

Many providers have found it difficult to get the rates of adoption of their portals they would like or that are specified by meaningful use. Some patients are uncertain how to use a portal and what value it may have for them or for a family member. Organizations that are seeing successful adoption made extending portal use a community goal. They offer training to help patients understand what value is gained and how to use the portal. In addition to training, successful organizations make supporting the portal everyone's job, with scripts and role-based suggestions for encouraging patients to sign up and use the portal—and often those goals translate into new incentives for everyone in the clinic.

Healthcare organizations are using a variety of strategies to get better at engaging patients, ranging from strategies that better involve physicians and staff to strategies that enhance outreach to patients. The University of Iowa Health Care organization, for example, focused its patient engagement initiative on its accountable care organization (ACO).[9] The organization used messages delivered through the patient portal to promote preventive healthcare services. "With 40 percent of our current patients being active users of their [portal], we now use the portal for health maintenance cues." As a result of this program, the number of eligible patients who received screening mammograms grew. The portal has also been used to support sharing plans of care and enhance shared decision making.

Another example is highlighted in a study from Australia titled, "Diabetes Self-Management Smartphone Application for Adults with Type 1 Diabetes."[10] In this study the intervention group who used the mobile app and received text messages from a diabetes educator had lower HbA1c than the control group. In this study, medical outcomes were improved using patient engagement technology, although patient activation measures like self-efficacy, self-care activities, and quality of life were not affected.

A study of post-go-live results with patient portals found that patients who were more satisfied with their provider were also more likely to intend to use the personal health record. Also, those who found value in the portal and who believed the tool to be empowering "demonstrated higher intentions to use, which were further enhanced for highly activated patients."[11] In short, the more activated the person is and the better the person's relationship is with the provider, the more likely he or she is to use the portal.

Portal use is not just for already activated individuals; a study from Finland showed improvement in patient activation scores for those provided access to a patient portal.[12] The impact was especially high for those who started with lower scores. "Patients diagnosed with a severe diagnosis during the intervention showed greater positive change in patient activation compared to patients whose last severe diagnosis was made more than 2 years ago."

Virginia Mason Medical Center achieved high rates of portal adoption by promoting the portal on its website and in external communications as well as social media.[13] "The portal message was delivered in every office and at every discharge from its 336-bed hospital. Virginia Mason ensured every employee who interacted with a patient was an advocate and expert in the patient portal." By focusing on messages that highlighted the benefits to patients, Virginia Mason made it clear that the portal was an extension of its approach to patient-centered care. Its approach to marketing the portal summarizes the way Virginia Mason approaches everything: "thinking about the patient's needs first."

The 2015 version of "most wired" hospitals reports that one way Citizens Memorial Hospital, in Bolivar, Missouri, achieved significant rates of patient registration for the portal was that staff called patients to get them to sign up for the patient portal and use secure messaging. Chief Information Officer Denni McColm said, "We had to do some crazy things. If you signed up for the portal and sent a secure message, you were entered into a contest to win an iPad or a TV." She reports that most of those patients have remained active users of the portal.[14]

The 75 providers who are a part of St. Joseph Heritage Medical Group and 150 providers in St. Jude Heritage Medical Group achieved high rates of portal engagement by focusing on a portal that would allow them to share results, enable secure messaging, and allow direct scheduling, online bill pay, and two-way updating of problems, medications, allergies, and immunizations.[15] Dr. Michael Gilbert shared the most important factor driving engagement and use:

> When all was said and done, we determined the single most important factor in obtaining high patient registration and use of a patient portal was provider engagement. Despite all marketing efforts and staff engagement initiatives, it was the provider asking the patient to register, actively communicating results, responding to patient messages, and engaging the patient in their health care through the online portal tools that was the single most important factor in motivating patients to buy into the new system.

Focusing on the benefits to patients and getting providers involved in promoting it are the most effective ways to get patients actively involved in using your portal. While the meaningful use rules are a helpful initial benchmark, organizations are more likely to be successful if they view the portal as a way to become more patient centered and empowering, rather than just a numbers game to achieve meaningful use.

Engagement through the Use of Mobile Devices and Apps

The ways that patients and providers can engage digitally are expanding exponentially. IMS Health conducted a study in 2015 that found that the "number of mHealth apps available to consumers now exceeds 165,000, presenting an overwhelming amount of options" for consumers and doctors alike.[16] With new devices and mobile apps arriving on the scene regularly, sorting through them can be challenging. Providers are interested in what works and what can be easily implemented, sustained, and scaled. Remote patient monitoring has gone from a complex process using expensive equipment to relatively simple implementations using off-the-shelf products that can be implemented quickly. The explosion of capabilities and devices coming from the IoT is beginning to enable monitoring, management, and action that incorporate a wide variety of sensors in the home and "if this, then that" (ITTT) logic to care for an individual.

Incentives, such as penalties for hospital readmissions and upside potential for taking on the risk of caring for a population of people in accountable care organizations, give providers a new way to look at return on investment (ROI). If a small investment in monitoring equipment can prevent an emergency department visit or hospital readmission, the results may be worthwhile.

One pilot study used a Bluetooth-connected scale, a self-inflating blood pressure cuff, and a tablet computer to enable 20 patients with heart failure to do self-monitoring at home. While the pilot did not show significant differences in hospitalization rates, length of stay was briefer for those admitted. The study demonstrated the feasibility of this kind of home-monitoring approach.[17] Many other studies are in pilot stages, so more evidence on the value of this kind of approach will be forthcoming.

The use of apps for managing chronic conditions is also growing for both medical and mental health issues. A recent study by Manhattan Research showed that 32 percent of physicians in the United States had recommended a mobile health app to a patient.[18] Many applications show initially positive results in areas such as managing asthma and medication management for depression. Reminders built into applications are beginning to show improvements in outcomes.[19,20]

The Food and Drug Administration (FDA) has recently signaled a change in the regulations for applications that display health data, even data from clinical devices. Formerly, the FDA considered both the applications that displayed the data and the devices that gathered the data to be class III devices, requiring FDA regulation. With the approval of the DexCom Share device, which allows data from blood glucose meters to be sent to up to five smart devices, the FDA seems to be indicating that applications that display clinical data may be considered class II devices. Although manufacturers will still be required to register with the agency and follow certain controls, they may not need to get prior approval.[21] This shift seems to be connected to the advocacy from the NightScout Foundation,[22] which has advocated the need for blood glucose data to be more readily shared with patients.

Gamified applications have recently been released that help children and adolescents learn how to manage their diabetes, control asthma, and manage anger and grief.[23,24] The results show promise both in the engagement levels and outcomes. Some argue that the potential is much greater than has been displayed to date because many healthcare games are not yet entertaining enough. Games are also being used for diabetes prevention and management. One recent study demonstrated the feasibility of games in teaching adolescents to eat healthier. However, many of these studies have small sample sizes and need replication on a larger scale to demonstrate the effectiveness of games in diabetes and other aspects of health management.[25]

Patient-Generated Health Data (PGHD) and Wearables

PGHD offers another opportunity to use data exchange between provider and patient to enhance engagement. In this case, however, the data are created by the patient and sent to the provider. One of the advantages of this is that providers can be informed of changes in the patient's status between visits. This can include blood glucose levels for patients with diabetes, peak flow readings and inhaler use for monitoring asthmatic patients, or the amount of physical activity, such as steps, a heart disease patient completes daily.

The challenges of PGHD are twofold: (1) having a way to interface the data from devices to the provider's EMR (usually through a Bluetooth connection to a smartphone, which then transmits the data) and summarizing or presenting the data in a way that is meaningful to the provider. Many providers are worried about PGHD due to the sheer volume of data. But if the data are presented in an easy to interpret format, such as graphing trends or sending an alert when something is below or above a set threshold, then the PGHD becomes manageable and helpful in the care of the patient and promotes engagement. Graphic representation of patient-generated data is also helpful to patients themselves, as it helps them to see correlations and trends.

As described in more detail in Chapter 2, "The New DIY Health Consumer," many individuals are taking charge of their own health by using wearable devices and sensors and tracking outcomes of medical devices to understand their own health or how they can manage chronic disease. Although the devices may not be prescribed by a doctor, the data they generate have the promise to help everyone in the healthcare system understand correlations that might not be readily apparent simply from data collected in a clinic or hospital setting.

The industry is paying increasing attention to patient-generated health data with the advent of wearables and increasing accuracy of sensors. Apple came out with HealthKit in 2014; it provides a way of aggregating the data from multiple wearables and applications. EHR vendors such as Epic, Cerner, and AthenaHealth are creating interfaces to enable HealthKit data to be incorporated into EHRs. Samsung and Google are working on similar approaches to aggregate patient- and consumer-generated health data to provide a more comprehensive picture of an individual's health.

An example of successful incorporation of PGHD comes from Ochsner Health System, which was one of the first to integrate Apple HealthKit with its Epic® EMR. Its focus has been on gathering data to manage chronic illnesses such as congestive heart failure. Based on data about fluid accumulation, for instance, a nurse might call the patient and change his or her medication.[26] A study by Reuters in spring of 2015 showed that more than half of leading US hospitals are experimenting with using data from Apple's HealthKit,[27] and we can expect to see interesting and useful interventions and partnerships arising from this trend.

Communication with Providers through Secure Messaging, Texting, and Social Media

Smartphones and apps also enable provider–patient communication. Most web and mobile patient portals have a tool for sending and receiving secure messages, which then become a part of the permanent record in the EHR. EHRs can be set up to send automated appointment and health maintenance reminders. Providers can also use secure messaging to explain lab results. Patients can send a message asking a question they may have forgotten to ask at their last appointment or the team may use secure messaging to adjust medication dosages.

These uses extend the provider–patient relationship beyond episodic visits. While some providers are concerned that another layer of communication adds to their workday, others see it as a shift in communication modes from phone tag to asynchronous communication. Health systems like Kaiser Permanente and others have seen broad adoption beyond 50 percent among patients and convinced providers of its value. Some use secure messaging to create eVisits as well,[28] and the advent of telemedicine capabilities extends communications to true virtual visits.

According to a recent systematic review of secure messaging, the evidence supports "that the use of secure messaging can improve glucose outcomes in patients with diabetes and increase patient satisfaction."[29] A 2010 study from Kaiser Permanente showed improvements in HEDIS (Healthcare Effectiveness Data and Information Set) scores among chronically ill patients who used secure messaging.[30] A metastudy in the *Journal of Medical Internet Research* looking at studies published from 2011 to 2014[31] showed several studies that evaluated the benefits of secure messaging (SM) between patients and physicians. All the studies:

> …demonstrated a high level of patient satisfaction with the feature, and the users did not feel the process to exchange SMs was too complicated. Common to these studies was the perception of high-quality care, better patient-to-provider communication, greater levels of patient education, and a high level of patient engagement/empowerment.[31]

Technology enhancements also allow physician practices to incorporate HIPAA-compliant text messaging tools that encourage healthy behaviors. A review of current studies found evidence of the effectiveness of text messaging for diabetes self-management, weight loss, physical activity, smoking cessation, and medication adherence.[32] Texting can have advantages for lower income consumers who may not have a smartphone but have a mobile phone with texting. Texting is beginning to be used among the Medicaid population with indications of good effect.[33]

Two-way texting is the next stage in this technology. For example, ohMD.com has released the capability for HIPAA-compliant two-way texting, integrated with patient portals and EHRs so that messages to the provider drop into his or her inbox within the EHR.[34] This has the potential to increase convenience and the sense of immediacy for patients while still allowing physicians to respond within their EHR workflow.

Social media in healthcare is widely accepted by patients, despite the reservations of some providers. Providers who find value include a pediatrician who uses her blog and tweets to educate parents about common childhood conditions she frequently sees in her practice.[35] Hospitals and health systems also use social media (Facebook and Twitter, most commonly) to connect with patients about events, health and wellness content, and new discoveries and clinical trials.[36] Healthcare social media has traditionally originated from marketing, and concerns over privacy and risk limit its use for two-way communications.

Increasingly, comments are solicited from patients, as demonstrated by the memory project, where a health system piloted managing Alzheimer's disease using the hashtag #KeepMemoryAlive. Smaller providers may write disclaimers into their contracts with patients that enable them to use direct messages through Facebook and Twitter to communicate with patients. More examples can be found in *Applying Social Media Technologies in Healthcare Environments*[37] and in the social media chapter of *Engage! Transforming Healthcare through Digital Patient Engagement*.[38] Increasingly, healthcare organizations are using social listening as one of the ways to get real-time feedback from patients about their experiences and engage in "social care"—addressing problems and issues that surface in social media channels.

Communication with Other Patients through Online Communities and Social Media

Online communities for medical conditions evolved from listservs in the 1990s to fully social apps and disease-focused portals today. Hundreds of diseases have a social presence, with discussions from choosing a doctor to treatment choices and clinical trials. An Institute of Medicine study of the social network Patients Like Me discovered that a large majority of members wanted to share their health data to improve care, develop evidence, and help others.[39] Patients also use Twitter and Facebook to connect with others. Some with rare conditions only find that other patients with their illness exist when they become active on social media.

Online communities are generally not connected to clinical care and clinical data. One exception to this is a new partnership between Patients Like Me and a Boston hospital that will make the social network a resource on its patient portal, provide training classes on how to participate in an online community, and provide the community as a resource from clinical care websites related to specific conditions. Some medical practitioners have suggested prescribing patient communities to newly diagnosed patients with chronic or life-threatening conditions.

Communities are also becoming sources of activism for patients and families in areas such as crowdsourcing funding of treatments for their diseases. Michael J. Fox's Parkinson's community and Patients Like Me are examples of this phenomenon. Partnerships are also arising between communities and life sciences companies, which see patient communities as a way to collaborate with patients in development of new devices and drugs. Wego Health[40] has created a network of individuals who blog, tweet, and speak about their diseases as a way to raise the visibility of diseases through the voices of knowledgeable individuals and patient activists. Communities like #NightScout, #WeAreNotWaiting, and #DIYPS are arising to help individuals advance care of their diseases through collaborative coding. (See Story 16, "Managing Diabetes with a DIY Pancreatic System," for more details.)

Engagement in Patient Safety and Prevention

Patients are now becoming partners in initiatives to increase patient safety in hospitals and clinics.

The National Quality Forum is encouraging collaborative decision making that includes patient safety issues in their Patient Passport program. The program helps patients to be empowered to become their own patient safety advocates and engage in meaningful dialogues about their preferences for care.[41] If their preferences become part of their EHR, they can become part of care planning with their provider.

Other initiatives engage patients in asking providers if they have washed their hands when they enter patient rooms[42] and ensuring correct location of surgery.[43]

Evidence is emerging from the OpenNotes pilot that shows that individuals with access to their clinical notes catch inaccuracies in the record or identify necessary follow-up care identified in the notes. Several years ago, a study showed that even with EHRs in place, 7 percent of patients with problematic laboratory test results were never notified by their doctors; direct access to lab results through a patient portal can mitigate these concerns.[44]

Providers are also using technology to increase patient involvement in preventive care by providing preventive health reminders to patients based on age, gender, and health status. This can be accomplished by generating reports from the EMR of those lacking specific health screening or vaccines or who are past due for them and generating e-mail, text, or portal reminders or alerts.

Cost Transparency and Cost Estimation

Cost transparency is of growing importance in healthcare as consumers are more responsible for the cost of care, particularly through high-deductible plans. A study by the Kaiser Family Foundation found that 64 percent of workers had a deductible of $1000 or more.[45] Healthcare costs have traditionally been hidden from patients until they receive a bill. Even then, many patients are confused about what they are being charged for, especially when clinic and hospital bills seem to convey different information than health plan explanations of benefits (EOBs). Fortunately, new tools are becoming available to help patients understand their healthcare costs and reconcile provider bills with health plan EOBs. A study by the Leapfrog Group shows many hospitals becoming more transparent about cost and quality.[46] As mentioned in Chapter 2, "The New DIY Health Consumer," several companies offer apps to enable patients both to manage and estimate healthcare expenses, as well as simplify the payment process.[47,48]

Integration of Data and Tools

The good news is that patients are beginning to have broader access to their own health data through patient portals, devices and apps, and social media networks. The downside is that these platforms often lack integration across providers and systems. Many patients have multiple portals from different providers, each with different log-on conventions and each holding only a portion of the person's clinical data. This is a primary frustration for patients and it also impacts the quality of care providers can give.

It is important to note that the most successful organizations deploying patient engagement technologies and experiencing high adoption rates by patients are integrated delivery systems. Systems such as Kaiser Permanente, Geisinger Health System, and Group Health Northwest are successful because they are already managing populations and looking for opportunities to make patient participation part of their operational and clinical workflow. They recognize efficiencies brought by technology capabilities such as online registration, appointment scheduling, and electronic refill requests. They've also seen the benefits from providing patients with access to their healthcare data: Patients are more informed and more likely to work with their doctors to develop treatment approaches they can live with. Other healthcare organizations can learn from these examples.

What is the best platform to integrate data and what tools are necessary to accomplish it? For the provider, the EHR may be the preferred platform because much of the clinical data and decision making are based there. For the patient, the patient portal or a consumer-mediated exchange may be preferred if he or she has this tool available and knows how to use it. A consumer-mediated exchange is the "ability for patients to aggregate and control the use of their health information among providers."[49] Patients may also download data from multiple platforms via tools such as the Blue Button protocol, which is an ONC initiative to make it easier for patients to get direct access to their data. Currently, however, it is not simple for patients to aggregate and normalize their data to create a coherent overall picture of their health.

The ideal would be a solution where data would be able to freely and securely flow from wearables, EHRs, labs, hospitals, clinics, payers, and social media to be virtually aggregated and normalized. Such solutions must be considered if access to a complete record of patients' health history is to be as manageable as consolidating financial or travel histories. Applications that successfully integrate data across all of these platforms would also help physicians to provide more integrated and insightful care. The newest requirements for Meaningful Use stage three include requirements for vendors to provide Application Programming Interfaces (APIs), or means for other applications to access the data stored in an EHR, making it more likely that patients and providers will see aggregated sources of patient data.

We can also expect to see more advanced applications making clinical data more usable and actionable rather than the "lists" of information that currently make up most portals. Approaches that allow users to connect medications and symptoms to diseases would be useful, as would analytics that show an individual how he or she compares to a broader population with the same diseases or on the same medications. Increasing flexibility in integrating clinical observations and even genetic profiles into applications and wearables will enable tools that dispense personalized real-time advice, reminders, and observations, ushering in a new generation of precision medicine.[50]

Conclusion

We are in an early, dynamic stage of patient engagement technologies. The return on investment and value is beginning to be established as consumer demand escalates. Today's technology is often cumbersome and not well integrated, making it difficult for existing technology to reach its potential for engaging patients and consumers in their own care. This creates many challenges but also opportunity for innovation. Solutions must be patient centered and seamlessly integrated if they are to have an impact on the provider–patient relationship and health outcomes. There is reason for hope, however, as more organizations see the benefits of using technology to engage with consumers and patients in ways that create partnership and support individuals in managing their own health and healthcare.

Notes

1. http://www.childrenspartnership.org/storage/documents/OurWork/Technology_Enabled_Innovations/TechnologyProfilePHRs.pdf
2. http://s3.amazonaws.com/rdcms-himss/files/production/public/FileDownloads/Rethinking%20Revenue%20Cycle%20Management_April%202015.pdf
3. https://www.jpmorgan.com/cm/BlobServer/JPM-KeyTrends-in-HealthcarePatientPayments.pdf?blobkey=id&blobwhere=1320610345938&blobheader=application/pdf&blobheadername1=Cache-Control&blobheadervalue1=private&blobcol=urldata&blobtable=MungoBlobs
4. https://www.healthit.gov/providers-professionals/meaningful-use-definition-objectives
5. Stage 2 Data Elements Tipsheet for Eligible Professionals, January 2014. https://www.cms.gov/Regulations-and-Guidance/Legislation/EHRIncentivePrograms/downloads/Stage2_EPCore_7_PatientElectronicAccess.pdf.
6. https://www.cms.gov/eHealth/downloads/Webinar_eHealth_May5_ModificationsNPRMOverview-.pdf
7. https://www.healthit.gov/sites/default/files/briefs/oncdatabrief30_accesstrends_.pdf
8. http://surescripts.com/connectedpatient/default.html#information
9. http://www.himss.org/ResourceLibrary/ContentTabsDetail.aspx?ItemNumber=34981
10. http://www.jmir.org/2013/11/e235
11. http://www.jmir.org/2013/2/e43/
12. http://www.jmir.org/2014/11/e257/
13. https://www.cerner.com/blog/Virginia_Masons_Patient_Portal_Success/?langtype=1033
14. http://www.hhnmostwired.com

15. Gilbert, Michael, MD, "How to use a patient portal," http://www.healthit.gov/buzz-blog/consumer/patient-portal/].
16. http://www.imshealth.com/portal/site/imshealth/menuitem.762a961826aad98f53c753c71ad8c22a/?vgnextoid=365656f1603bf410VgnVCM1000000e2e2ca2RCRD&vgnextchannel=736de5fda6370410VgnVCM10000076192ca2RCRD&vgnextfmt=default
17. http://www.ncbi.nlm.nih.gov/pmc/articles/PMC4398882/
18. http://www.ihealthbeat.org/insight/2014/do-physicians-hold-the-key-to-consumer-mobile-health-app-adoption
19. http://blog.ginger.io/ginger-io-auch-and-cambia-health-foundation-launch-utah-smartcare-project-to-integrate-delivery-of-mental-and-physical-healthcare/
20. http://www.livescience.com/50543-asthma-patients-smartphones-inhalers-apps.html
21. http://www.cnet.com/news/apple-watch-app-will-track-your-glucose-levels/] [http://www.healthline.com/diabetesmine/newsflash-dexcom-share-gets-fda-clearance#1
22. http://www.nightscout.org
23. http://news.yahoo.com/correction-educational-apps-help-kids-control-health-164251227.html
24. http://www.imedicalapps.com/2012/02/results-from-a-study-of-kids-use-of-smartphone-in-juvenile-diabetes/
25. http://online.liebertpub.com/doi/pdfplus/10.1089/g4h.2015.0055
26. http://news.ochsner.org/news-releases/ochsner-health-system-first-epic-client-to-fully-integrate-with-apple-healthkit/
27. http://www.reuters.com/article/2015/02/05/us-apple-hospitals-exclusive-idUSKBN0L90G920150205
28. http://content.healthaffairs.org/content/33/2/251.abstract
29. http://www.ncbi.nlm.nih.gov/pubmedhealth/PMH0048536/
30. http://content.healthaffairs.org/content/29/7/1370.full
31. http://www.jmir.org/2015/2/e44/
32. http://www.ncbi.nlm.nih.gov/pubmed/25785892
33. http://kff.org/medicaid/issue-brief/profiles-of-medicaid-outreach-and-enrollment-strategies-using-text-messaging-to-reach-and-enroll-uninsured-individuals-into-medicaid-and-chip/
34. Personal communication with Ethan Bechtel, CEO, ohMD.com.
35. http://seattlemamadoc.seattlechildrens.org/about-this-blog/
36. http://www.jmir.org/2014/11/e264
37. Thielst, Christina Beach, ed. 2014. *Applying Social Media Technologies in Healthcare Environments.* Chicago: HIMSS Publishing.
38. Oldenburg, Jan, Dave Chase, Kate T. Christensen, and Brad Tritle. 2013. *Engage! Transforming Healthcare through Digital Patient Engagement.* Chicago: HIMSS Publishing.
39. http://news.patientslikeme.com/press-release/patientslikeme-and-partners-healthcare-collaborate-improve-patient-outcomes
40. http://www.qualityforum.org/Patient_Passport.aspx
41. http://www.infectioncontroltoday.com/articles/2013/01/patient-empowerment-as-a-hand-hygiene-strategy.aspx
42. http://patientsafetyauthority.org/ADVISORIES/AdvisoryLibrary/2007/jun4(2)/Pages/29b.aspx
43. http://www.rwjf.org/en/library/research/2012/10/inviting-patients-to-read-their-doctors--notes.html
44. http://www.castlighthealth.com/resources/healthcare-transparency/]
45. http://www.leapfroggroup.org/HospitalSurveyReport
46. http://mobihealthnews.com/29400/8-companies-working-on-price-transparency/]
47. http://www.healthdatamanagement.com/conferences/1_6/data-driven-population-health-management-50315-1.html
48. http://blog.himss.org/2015/05/20/how-close-are-we-to-consumer-mediated-exchange/
49. http://www.eurekalert.org/pub_releases/2015-08/bidm-rab081215.php
50. http://www.forbes.com/sites/davidshaywitz/2015/02/07/wearables-as-tools-for-precision-medicine-a-promise-insearch-of-evidence/

PATIENT AND CAREGIVER STORIES

Jan Oldenburg, FHIMSS

Introduction

Illnesses unfold as stories, and physicians need to learn how to listen to those stories.[1]

Furthermore, listening carefully to individual stories acknowledges personal engagement and fosters motivation...[2]

The Experience of Illness

There is nothing glamorous about being sick, nor about being the caregiver for someone who is. Illness leaves a mark: It can change a person's perception of vulnerability and sense of control over his or her body and the world. Studies have shown that the experience of illness—as well as the social stigma we attach to it—can have long-term negative effects on an individual's sense of self and body image.[3,4]

Being sick interrupts the expectations and beliefs people have about themselves and their lives. Even a relatively minor illness can result in rumination about the experience as the person tries to understand what happened and the ways life has changed because his or her health status has changed. Mike Bury suggests that "under conditions of adversity, individuals often feel a pressing need to reexamine and refashion their personal narratives in an attempt to maintain a sense of identity."[5]

Being sick, especially over the long term, can reduce a person's overall sense of hope about the future. People with chronic illnesses are more susceptible to depression than the general population,[6] and depression can compound the difficulty of coping with illness. Illness, especially something with a sudden onset, can be traumatic. There is evidence that severe illness can result in posttraumatic stress disorder (PTSD),[7] and nearly one in eight people who have had a heart attack go on to develop PTSD symptoms.[8] The impact of illness does not just affect the sick person, but may impact the whole family, especially spouses or caregivers such as parents or children who take on the bulk of caregiving. Multiple studies have found higher rates of depression among caregivers than among peers who are not responsible for caregiving.

In her story "An e-Champion for Alexis," Catherine Rose discusses the need for respite when you are the ones responsible for the long-term care of a disabled child. In "Living Well with Lupus" Amanda talks about the stress of knowing that another flare might happen at any moment, and the impact that's had on her life and career. Even more temporary illnesses leave both psychic and physical scars, as coping with pain and managing acute or chronic illness takes time, energy, and attention away from other, more pleasurable or fulfilling activities.

The Healing Power of Compassionate Listening

We know that having the opportunity to tell their stories can be an effective part of treatment for patients. A recent study showed that hypertension patients who had the opportunity to tell their own stories and listen to the stories of others with the same condition actually experienced lowered blood pressures.[9] A variety of studies have shown that healing benefits result from an empathetic encounter between a physician and patient, including improved patient satisfaction, enhanced clinical outcomes, increased likelihood patients will follow an agreed-upon treatment approach, and fewer malpractice complaints.[10–12]

Perhaps equally importantly, several studies have shown that empathetic physician–patient encounters also lead to increased physician health, decreased burnout, and enhanced professional satisfaction.[13]

This book is enriched by the courage of those who shared their stories because the stories are powerful in their own right and offer important insights into ways we can change systems, processes, and training to improve the experience of illness.

Patient and Caregiver Stories

The patient and caregiver stories in this book bring the experience of being sick to life. Some stories center around an acute event or illness; others record the long-term experience of living with one or more chronic diseases. The people who shared them were willing to reveal the intimate and messy experience of illness and recovery; their interactions with doctors, nurses, insurers, and the healthcare system overall; how their encounters felt in the moment; and how they have interpreted the experience over time.

Some of the stories included here are about people who are quite public about their illness or caregiving experiences and speak, write, or tweet about them often. Other stories are told by those for whom illness has been a more private and personal experience; for some, this is the first time they have talked publicly about their disease or experience. Together, they spotlight the many faces of sickness, the individuality of reactions, and the opportunities to bring innovation and change to the way care is imagined and delivered.

Some of you may ask, "But are these stories true? Are they medically accurate? Do they really describe what happened?" There are no simple answers to those questions. We have tried to provide context about the diseases and conditions they describe, but we did not interview these patient's doctors or review their patient records to ensure medical accuracy. Some situations, as recounted, may lead medical professionals to say, "It can't possibly have happened quite like that." But that is not a reason for discounting the stories told here. These stories describe the impact of illness on the lives of real people. These stories highlight the way specific care experiences either support recovery or detract from it. They help us understand how we could redesign the healthcare system to better serve these individuals and others like them as patients, as individuals, as family members.

Oliver Sacks, the famous neuroscientist and writer, talked about memory and narrative truth in a *New York Review of Books* essay, entitled "Speak, Memory," published shortly before his death in 2015:

> There is, it seems, no mechanism in the mind or the brain for ensuring the truth, or at least the veridical character, of our recollections. We have no direct access to historical truth, and what we feel or assert to be true (as Helen Keller was in a very good position to note) depends as much on our imagination as our senses.... Frequently, our only truth is narrative truth, the stories we tell each other, and ourselves—the stories we continually recategorize and refine. Such subjectivity is built into the very nature of memory, and follows from its basis and mechanisms in the human brain. The wonder is that aberrations of a gross sort are relatively rare, and that, for the most part, our memories are relatively solid and reliable.[14]

These stories represent "narrative truth" for their tellers: They explain the way the experience of illness and the care received has been processed, internalized, and understood by real people. Listening to the lived experiences of individuals, whether in the context of this book, a case consultation, or a patient council requires stepping out of defensiveness and distancing ourselves from our truth to listen to someone else's truth. The act of listening, truly listening, to a patient is healing for the person by bringing their reality into focus. The true story of illness is a collaboration between the person, his or her physicians, and the family and friends who help interpret the story and determine the meaning of the experience.

This idea is reinforced by Dr. Arthur Kleinman, a medical practitioner writing in the 1980s, who said:

> Illness has meaning; and to understand how it obtains meaning is to understand something fundamental about illness, about care and perhaps about life generally... an interpretation of illness is something that patients, families and practitioners need to undertake together. For there is a dialectic at the heart of healing that brings the care giver into the uncertain, fearful world of pain and disability and that reciprocally introduces patient and family into the equally uncertain world of therapeutic actions...One unintended outcome of the modern transformation of the medical care system is that it does just about everything to drive the practitioner's attention away from the experience of illness.[15]

Conclusion

These stories highlight the things we still need to change in the culture and practice of American medicine. Each story contains a set of "observations for policy and practice" that discuss key ideas and issues raised by the story. The stories illustrate that there is a long distance to travel to make the experience of being a patient consistently compassionate, convenient, connected, and healing. Further, there are enormous opportunities for us to be more creative in the tools and technologies we offer patients—both when they are in the purview of the medical system and in the daily tasks of living with illness or caring for someone who is ill.

We do not want to romanticize illness or the sacrifices that caregivers make when taking care of a sick family member or friend. Yet there is a compelling theme in these stories. People make meaning from the experience of being sick, sometimes through the way they incorporate illness into the narrative of their lives, sometimes by imbuing it with a spiritual meaning, or by turning the experience of illness into a mission and a part of their life's work. This ability to make meaning out of the suffering of illness surely speaks of resilience and the triumph of the human spirit.

We hope you find this book helpful as you contemplate your healthcare experiences as patient, caregiver, provider, or system designer. The experience of illness is one of the things that leads us to encounter our humanity. Only by listening to the experiences of others, discussing them, contemplating how we'd like to be cared for, can we together design the kind of healthcare system that we'd all like to experience.

Notes

1. http://www.huffingtonpost.com/richard-c-senelick-md/patient-care_b_1410115.html
2. http://munich.thechanger.org/blog/telling-stories-impact-storytelling-contributes-organizational-development-social-enterprises-non-profits/
3. http://www.bradley.edu/sites/bodyproject/disability/illness/
4. http://www.jblearning.com/samples/0763744611/4461_ch02_pass3.pdf
5. http://onlinelibrary.wiley.com/doi/10.1111/1467-9566.00252/pdf
6. http://www.webmd.com/depression/guide/chronic-illnesses-depression
7. http://www.healthcommunities.com/posttraumatic-stress-disorder-ptsd/serious-illness-ptsd.shtml
8. http://www.health.harvard.edu/blog/heart-attack-can-trigger-ptsd-201206254939
9. http://annals.org/article.aspx?articleid=746718
10. http://www.ncbi.nlm.nih.gov/pmc/articles/PMC4294163/
11. http://www.ncbi.nlm.nih.gov/pubmed/19150199
12. http://www.sciencedirect.com/science/article/pii/S0738399113005211
13. http://www.ncbi.nlm.nih.gov/pubmed/19773563
14. "Speak, Memory" by Oliver Sacks, originally published in *The New York Review of Books*. Copyright © 2013 by Oliver Sacks, used by permission of The Wylie Agency LLC. http://www.nybooks.com/articles/archives/2013/feb/21/speak-memory/
15. *The Illness Narratives: Suffering, Healing, and The Human Condition* by Arthur Kleinman, MD, copyright© 1988. Reprinted by permission of Basic Books, a member of the Perseus Books Group. https://books.google.com/books?id=dPN5N2qKGCwC

Story 1: A Cost-Conscious Consumer: "And What Will That Cost Me?"

Jan Oldenburg, FHIMSS with Kelly

Introduction

Kelly has been self-employed for years and is used to buying coverage on the individual market—has done so since 1995, in fact—but in order to keep the same price, he has had to raise his deductible each year. Since 2013 he has bought coverage on the Affordable Care Act (ACA) exchange market—without drama and without hassle. The price for his coverage was $238.59 a month and he received a subsidy of $219 a month, meaning his premium payment was $19.69 a month, with a $6500 deductible. By almost anyone's definition, Kelly's coverage is primarily catastrophic. It enabled him to get some preventive services, but for the most part, he must pay out of pocket for every prescription, every visit, and every medical service that falls outside the very narrow definition of preventive care in his policy, although prices are sometimes discounted based on rates his insurer has negotiated. This story describes what it's like to try to be a cost-conscious consumer with a high deductible in a system that still assumes insurance will pay the bulk of any health care bill.

What's That Ultrasound Going to Cost Me?

Last year, Kelly found a small nodule on his testicle. His primary care doctor recommended that he get an ultrasound. He sent Kelly out to the receptionist who told him they'd make an appointment for him and tell him when and where it would be. He asked, "Don't I get to make the appointment?" She replied, "Oh, no, we do that, and then you tell us if you're available." Kelly mentioned that it might be more straightforward if he could make the appointment himself at a time when he was available, but that wasn't a part of their procedure.

He then asked what the price would be. The receptionist suggested he call the billing department and gave him a phone number. Kelly asked if he needed to know the procedure code and the receptionist said no. When he called billing, however, they told him they needed the procedure code to give him an estimate. He called the office to get the code, then called the billing department back to give them the correct procedure code. They didn't have direct access to the price, so they called Kelly the following day to tell him that the billed amount would be about $800—but that the actual cost to him would depend on his insurer and the contracted rate. He asked the billing specialist what the contracted rate with his insurer was. She said she couldn't give it to him because it was "confidential" between the insurer and clinic. She said, "But don't worry—your insurance will cover the cost of this procedure." Kelly responded, "Actually, it won't because I have a huge deductible." He added, "Don't you think it's odd that the rate is confidential up until I see it show up on *my* bill?" but she didn't respond.

Is There an Alternative?

Kelly then sent a note to his doctor via MyChart, his patient portal, and asked whether the procedure was really necessary, given the $800 cost, or if there was an alternative to the ultrasound. His doctor responded by saying he didn't realize how expensive the ultrasound was and he could give Kelly a referral to a urologist instead. When Kelly called the urologist's office, however, they told him, "Given your age, it's likely there is nothing to be concerned about since the age range for testicular cancer is much younger, but we'd recommend an ultrasound to be sure." At that point they also told him that when he got the ultrasound there would be a bill for the radiologist to read it—but they couldn't tell what it would be. Depending on where he had the ultrasound done, there might also be a facility fee for hospital use. Kelly called three different radiology offices checking on the prices for the radiologist to read the scan and for the facility fee.

Is There Some Way to Find the Price I'll Be Charged?

He also checked on his insurance company website, where he found a cost estimation tool—but the procedure he needed was not listed on the tool. He called his insurer, where the representative suggested he use the cost estimation tool. When he explained he'd already tried that, the person told Kelly it really wasn't a very robust tool. In the meantime, his partner said, "We have a website from my insurer that allows us to look up the amount charged at various local facilities; how about if we use that?" When they put the procedure code into that tool, they could see the range of prices for the service in his area. It allowed Kelly to see that smaller hospitals in the communities around Madison were less expensive than in Madison proper.

Then he began using his insurance site to determine which locations in outlying communities were contracted with his insurance company. Kelly called two hospitals and a clinic, as well as several "private providers" of ultrasound services (which turned out to be maternity services) to find out what the cost for the procedure would be at their site. He included hospitals within an hour's range of his house that were covered by his insurance. He also called two radiology clinics to find out the cost for reading the ultrasound. Everyone he called needed to check the cost of the procedure but only one called him back with the cost. That cost was just over half the price of the original estimate, $442. Kelly sent a note to his doctor via his patient portal to verify that his doctor could get results from that hospital and that his doctor would trust the quality of their work. It turned out to be a hospital at which his doctor had admitting privileges, so it would work smoothly for his doctor to get the results. In the process of making the calls, Kelly learned that there would be an added radiology charge for reading the ultrasound, so he also called two radiologist offices to find the cost of the radiologist reading.

Having the Ultrasound

After all of this, Kelly went for the ultrasound. The technician he saw didn't seem particularly focused on her work, and when Kelly engaged her in conversation to distract himself from the fact that he was naked from the waist down and she was performing a procedure on his testicles, she actually said, "I'd rather be somewhere else right now."

A week later, his doctor called him with the test results. Because he'd gone to the outlying clinic, the results were not available to him via MyChart, although they mailed him a copy of the scan later. The good news: It was just a cluster of blood vessels and nothing to worry about.

But We Agreed on the Price

Then he got the bill from the hospital, which you can see in Figure S1.1. The rate for the scan was $442, as promised, but there was an extra $139 fee charged on top of that. The wording associated with the fee was confusing, so Kelly called the hospital billing department to ask about the extra charge.

The person who answered the phone said she'd research it and call him back. When the billing clerk called back, she explained that the extra charge was for an extra scan around the abdominal area to make sure there were no other issues. Kelly said, "I didn't notice her scanning my whole abdomen—she kept the wand in the same place," and, "She didn't ask me if I wanted the additional procedure, and I think I should have been asked." The clerk responded by saying, "We don't really ask patients because usually they don't know how to answer or aren't able to answer—and anyway, you wouldn't notice because she just has to push an extra button. Don't worry, though, your insurance

```
Patient Name:        ████████KELLY ●      Admission Date:   02/26/2013
Account Class:       Outpatient           Discharge Date:   02/26/2013
Primary Coverage:    ANTHEM BCBS

Charges
=====================================================================================
 Service   Cost    Rev.    Proc.   Description                        Qty.     Amount
 Date      Ctr.    Code    Code
=====================================================================================
 02/26/13  4206    0402    802946  US SCROTUM WITH DOPPLER             1        441.98
 02/26/13  4206    0921    802888  US ART DOPPLER ABDOMEN COM          1        139.13

       Total for 2 Charges                                                     581.11

Payments
=====================================================================================
 Post Date                           Recd. From                                Amount
=====================================================================================
 03/20/13                            BLUE CROSS BLUE SHIELD                       0.00

       Total for 1 Payments                                                      0.00

Adjustments
=====================================================================================
 Post Date                           Adj. For                                  Amount
=====================================================================================
 03/20/13                            BLUE CROSS BLUE SHIELD                     -57.46

       Total for 1 Adjustments                                                 -57.46

Balance
                                                                               523.65
```

Figure S1.1   Bill received from hospital after completed ultrasound, showing additional $139 charge for extra abdomen scan.

will cover it." Kelly said, "Look, I was lucid and I should have been made aware that there would be an extra charge if she did this procedure. In this case, my insurance won't cover it, but because most people's will shouldn't change the fact that you should ask." The clerk told him she'd call him back. Three days later, she called back saying they would just remove the charge from the bill.

At that point, Kelly paid the bill online. It cost him just a bit more than half of the original estimate. But it took *more than* 15 phone calls, two MyChart messages, several hours spent on web searches and phone calls—on Kelly's part and various clerks' part, and a great deal of persistence to get that result.

Does Asking a Question Mean It Isn't Preventive Care?

In 2015, covered by a policy purchased through the exchange, Kelly went to see his doctor for a preventive exam. This was a new doctor because his old one wasn't in the narrow network provided by his policy. Despite the fact that Kelly had been seeing his old doctor for 5 years, really liked him, and had developed a working alliance with him, he was forced to find a new physician by the plan network.

Preventive testing for his visit was covered by the plan. This was good news. In past years, Kelly would forgo testing every other year because of the cost. This year, his policy covered the tests as preventive services. As his visit was coming to a close, the doctor asked him if there was anything else about his health Kelly wanted to discuss. "Actually, doctor, there is one thing, but I'm a little afraid to ask you about it because I think I'll be charged extra for it." His doctor didn't think it would generate an extra charge as Kelly was already in the office, and asking/answering a question should be preventive. Thus reassured, Kelly asked about the weakness he was experiencing in one arm. His doctor checked the arm and shoulder functioning and where Kelly had pain, and wrote a referral for physical therapy.

You Were Charged Extra Because Your Doctor Gave You a Referral

Several weeks later, Kelly received a bill from his doctor's office (see Figure S1.2). Instead of the free preventive visit he expected, he was charged an "office visit" charge of $179 minus a $99 credit

Please detach and return top portion of statement with your payment.

ACCOUNT NUMBER	ACCOUNT NAME	PLEASE PAY	DUE DATE
▓▓▓▓	▓▓▓▓▓▓▓	$79.80	07/27/14

Date	Description	Provider	Charges	Credits	Patient Balance
	Detail for Patient: ▓▓▓▓▓▓▓				79.80
04/07/14	OFFICE/OUTPT VISIT,NEW,LEVL II	SOSMAN	179.00		
05/07/14	INSURANCE PAYMENT-UNITY AL			0.00	
05/07/14	UNITY CONTRACTUAL ADJ-UNITY AL			-99.20	

Figure S1.2 Bill received from doctor's office after "free" preventive service exam in which shoulder pain was discussed.

as the contracted rate with his provider was lower; he was charged $79.80 out of pocket, as shown in Figure S1.2. When Kelly called to inquire about the charge and explain the context, the clerk on the phone responded by saying, "Well, the doctor wouldn't be aware of this, but since he referred you, you'd be charged extra. But don't worry, your insurance will cover it." Kelly challenged the charge, saying that just because they'd had a conversation about something that resulted in a referral recommendation, he shouldn't be charged. The clerk told him they were required to do that by the "coding regulators" and that because all of their coding is audited, they would be noncompliant if they didn't charge the referral as an office visit. Kelly filed a dispute, but after 2 weeks was told that the charge would stand.

But I Never Even Used the Referral

The ironic part? In the end, he did not go to physical therapy because of what it would cost him. So an unfilled referral, the result of a 2-minute conversation in his preventive care exam cost him an additional $80—and made him deeply uneasy about having a "real" conversation with his doctor in the context of a preventive care visit.

Later in the year—likely because others were also challenging their charges—Kelly received the letter in Figure S1.3 explaining and justifying the policy on the basis that it was "required by national billing and coding guidelines."

It seems likely in this case that the physician coded the exam as "preventive" but during code review the referral was noted and it became the basis for the additional office visit charge. When Kelly went in for his next visit with his PCP, he took the letter along with him and explained what happened. His physician was upset that Kelly had been charged for an extra visit and clearly had not been aware that would happen.

Observations for Policy and Practice

Kelly's experiences provide some key insights into opportunities to improve the healthcare system, especially in the area of cost transparency:

- We need true cost transparency that makes it easy for consumers to compare the cost of services between physicians and sites, including any rate differentials negotiated by insurers—and perhaps including the "cash price" if someone elects to forgo insurance and pay directly. Contract clauses that prohibit doctors from sharing contracted rates with consumers—until they see the bill—need to be eliminated.
- Physicians and other providers need to incorporate cost as a dimension of discussion with patients about treatment options, as it is a trade-off for patients in the same way as treatment efficacy and patient values. This will require that doctors, too, have new tools to track, look up, and compare the costs of different procedures.
- Our opaque and counterintuitive approach to preventive care—whether supported by government policy or not—actually works against the expansion of preventive services as well as potentially disrupts the trust relationship between physicians and patients. True preventive visits should allow for wide-ranging discussions between patients and doctors about health issues and would only need to be coded differently if they spawn additional testing or procedures that are actually completed. It is far more likely that Kelly's encounter fell into a gray area that

Office Visit Billed with an Annual Preventive Medicine Visit

You are scheduled for a preventive health care visit which focuses on preventing illness, maintaining your health and screening for health issues common for your age and gender. During the preventive health care visit, your care provider may address a new or existing health issue, for example, your current treatment of high blood pressure or new lab work that shows a risk for diabetes.

When a new or existing health problem is identified and addressed during a preventive health care visit, a separate office visit will be billed as required by national coding and billing guidelines. UW Health follows these guidelines and bills for one preventive health care visit and a second office visit for the new or existing health problem. As a result, your insurance company may charge you for two separate visits.

How does UW Health decide that two services have been provided and should be billed as two separate visits?
- Preventive care services include a comprehensive exam and services to prevent or screen for illness, such as immunizations and lab tests.
- A preventive health care visit does not include treatment of a new or existing condition.
- If your health care provider spends time during your preventive care visit on a new or existing health care problem, two separate office visits will be billed.

Does this mean I will have to pay for two visits?
Yes and no. While you are billed separately for two different visits, adjustments to the cost of each visit may be reduced depending on the time spent on each health care issue. If the cost for the new or existing health care issue is more than the cost of the preventive care visit, the preventive care visit may be reduced or billed at no cost.

Will my insurance cover the bills for the two visits?
It is important for you to know what services are covered by your policy. If you are unsure what your policy covers, please check with your insurer prior to your visit with UW Health. Tell your insurer why you are seeing your health care provider. Ask your insurance provider the following questions:
- What is covered when your office visit is primarily a preventive health care visit?
- What does your policy cover if you are seeing your health care provider about a new or existing health care issue?
- If you are seeing your care provider for preventive health care, but during the visit the focus changes to a specific health issue, will your insurance policy cover both portions of the visit?
- What are your out-of-pocket costs for co-pays, coinsurance, or deductibles for each different kind of visit?

Will I have to pay two co-pays?
- Because two different services occurred during one office visit, you should have only one co-pay.
- If you are charged for two, please contact UW Health Customer Service at 608-829-5217 or 1-877-565-0505. We will appeal these with your insurer so that you are not charged for two co-pays.

This pricing policy is intended to limit your out-of-pocket expense and reduces the need for additional appointments.

Figure S1.3   Health system letter justifying policy for charging an office visit with a free preventive visit.

might be upcoded as an office visit rather than that it actually was required to be coded as an office visit. Was the $79.60 that the system gained worth the erosion of patient trust?
- Insurance approaches that focus on narrow networks disrupt trusted relationships between doctors and patients. We should be wary of this disruption because research shows that having a trusted relationship with your doctor matters to outcomes, and that one of the factors that engenders trust is that the patient can trust that the physician will "abide with him or her" across time and through trauma.[1]

Conclusion—What's Wrong with This Picture?

Kelly is in an advanced medical system associated with a major academic medical system. He has access to his medical record and test results through the system, and he uses it actively (where he can) to schedule appointments, manage prescriptions, and communicate with his doctors.

He also has access to a cost-comparison tool via his insurer as well as a physician and facility finder that allows him to determine who is an "in network" doctor or facility and who is not.

He is a cost-conscious consumer who has gone out of his way to manage his medical costs appropriately, asking all the right questions about medical necessity and the cost of treatment. He reviews his bills and challenges costs that don't seem appropriate. As you can tell, Kelly does all the things we encourage people to do in order to help manage the cost of treatment, driven in part by the high deductible that looms over his head.

And yet, he has been unable to get straight information about costs without extraordinary effort. It is clear that everyone in the system has gotten complaisant about "it's covered by your insurance," which has meant that they don't need to have simple solutions for cost transparency and cost comparisons. In addition, the fact that physicians and technicians are generally oblivious to the costs of the procedures they recommend or the cost impacts of the way they charge means that patients are unable to get a true understanding of financial impact as a part of assessing treatment options. Alexandra Drane has called cost one of the "unmentionables" in healthcare, as it is a concern that is present in nearly every interaction in the medical system, but generally too uncomfortable to talk about.[2] As we see in this example, often the people in the room don't have the facts about cost to have a meaningful discussion.

In addition, the complex contracted rates with various insurance companies make it difficult to find what a visit or procedure will actually cost any particular individual—especially if the situation happens to include something outside the standard list of cost-comparison situations. The "gag clause" in insurance contracts that prohibits health systems from discussing contracted rates with consumers until after they get a bill is outmoded and contradictory, especially if the same insurer provides a cost estimation tool that reveals the rates for at least some services.

Our approved definition of what is "preventive" is very narrow and is counterintuitive to a layperson, causing financial peril and leading people away from the very preventive services we want to encourage as a part of a wellness and "fee for value" strategy.

Kelly is healthy, and although price shopping is frustrating and painful, he has the tools and wherewithal to do it. Imagine if you were a single parent, working multiple jobs, juggling childcare responsibilities, in a job without time to make or take phone calls during the day, with every extra penny spent on healthcare putting you at risk for financial ruin: How would you navigate this complex world to get necessary care for yourself or a loved one?

Notes

1. http://www.annfammed.org/content/6/4/315.full
2. http://www.oandp.com/articles/2015-07_03.asp

Story 2: An e-Champion for Alexis

Jan Oldenburg, FHIMSS with Catherine Rose, MBA, PhD*

Introduction

Dr. Catherine Rose earned her PhD from Stanford in mechanical engineering, an MBA in finance, and has a wide-ranging professional life, but all of that recedes in importance compared to her role as Alexis's mom and caregiver. During the early stages of Catherine's pregnancy with twins, everything seemed normal, although she was monitored as a high-risk pregnancy, with ultrasounds every 2 weeks. At the 20-week ultrasound the doctor saw a thickening of the nuchal fold, which can be a sign of genetic abnormalities, and a potential problem in one of the twin's hearts, so he suggested an immediate amniocentesis. When the results came back, however, both twins seemed to be fine.

At 29 weeks, however, Catherine felt ill and was hospitalized for fatigue and dehydration. At the hospital, the doctors could only find one heartbeat and eventually told Catherine and her husband that one of the twins had died. Catherine continued the pregnancy on bed rest, carrying her dead daughter another 8 weeks for the sake of her living daughter. Both were delivered at 37 weeks. While Catherine and her husband were cradling their dead daughter, Kaitlyn, a doctor came in to tell them that Alexis, the living twin, would probably not live to see her first birthday. In their grief, it was hard to imagine how to move forward.

Diagnosis and Moving Forward

Yet move forward they did—because they had a daughter to care for. Over the next months they learned that Alexis had a variety of serious genetic abnormalities, including breathing problems (right side choanal atresia), cleft of soft palate, bilateral severe profound hearing loss, small right eye, low vision, narrowed arteries (peripheral pulmonary stenosis—PPS murmur), a hole in her heart that didn't close (atrial septal defect—ASD), fusions of the cervical spine, microcephaly, clenched hands, kidney problems (pseudohypoaldosteronism type II), abnormal brain spikes, and obstructive sleep apnea. They also learned that if their daughter was going to survive, they needed to be her champions, her advocates, the ones responsible for keeping the medical record correct. It meant being the communication hub and the watchdogs to ensure that she received the right care at the right time.

---

* @drcatherinerose

Access to Resources

Catherine has been lucky to have resources available to help her navigate the system. One sister is an ER doctor, the other a plant geneticist. Her mother is on the school board in North Carolina. Each of them provided perspective, helped her put the puzzle pieces together, and advised her what to do.

Catherine and her husband eventually found the CHARGE Syndrome Foundation and, with it, social support from other parents whose children were experiencing similar symptoms. CHARGE stands for Coloboma (a congenital abnormality of the eye), Heart defect, Atresia choanae (congenital disorder where the back of the nasal passage—the choana—is blocked), Retarded growth and development, Genital abnormality, and Ear abnormality:

CHARGE syndrome is a recognizable (genetic) pattern of birth defects that occurs in about one in every 9000 or 10,000 births worldwide. It is an extremely complex syndrome, involving extensive medical and physical difficulties that differ from child to child. The vast majority of the time, there is no history of CHARGE syndrome or any other similar conditions in the family. Babies with CHARGE syndrome are often born with life-threatening birth defects, including complex heart defects and breathing problems. They spend many months in the hospital and undergo many surgeries and other treatments. Swallowing and breathing problems make life difficult even when they come home. Most have hearing loss, vision loss, and balance problems, which delay their development and communication.[1]

While it helped to find common ground with other parents, CHARGE syndrome didn't really answer the questions about Alexis. Although she had many of the issues that children with CHARGE syndrome experience, the syndrome was not confirmed in genetic testing of her CHD7 gene. Like about a third of the children who have symptoms in common with the syndrome, commonality does not provide a definitive diagnosis.

Carepages (www.Carepages.com) has been a great help to them in keeping family and friends informed about Alexis's health. It was especially useful when Alexis was a newborn and they were trying to figure out what was going on and keep everyone in the loop. Catherine started Alexis's CarePages journal when she was 2 days old. In addition, she kept a private journal that gave her a space to voice her fears and doubts and frustrations. She tries hard to be supportive and positive in public and to voice her frustrations with individuals and the system individually and privately. Part of it is good emotional intelligence; part of it is to make sure that Alexis isn't punished by poorer care if Catherine voices her frustrations.

Managing Daily Care

Alexis is limited to eating purees and liquids of a specific consistency so that she will not aspirate her food into her lungs. It took a long period of trial and error to find a commercial solution with just the right consistency. On a daily basis, Alexis must be fed through a feeding tube to maintain her growth. She sleeps with a continuous positive airway pressure (CPAP) machine to help her breathe, and it needs to be monitored to ensure that it hasn't slipped off as she moves in her sleep. Each day, Alexis gets a probiotic, as Catherine figured out through painful experience that it mitigates the systemic diarrhea that affects Alexis every time she takes antibiotics.

At the beginning, Catherine and her husband were determined to care for Alexis themselves. She now wishes that the doctors or nurses had told her before they took Alexis home the first time,

"You will need private nursing at home." Because they started without private nursing, it is now virtually impossible to get it—and they now bear the long-term cost of interrupted sleep, constant vigilance, and little respite. Other children with problems similar to Alexis's have at-home nursing care, and it is deeply frustrating to realize their situation could easily have been prevented from the start.

The Communication Hub

The physician team supporting Alexis includes at least 15 different doctors in different specialties and different health systems. Just keeping up with the appointments, prescriptions, therapies, insurance, and communication required to keep everything synchronized is a major task. Alexis is in school, and Catherine also acts as the primary link between the teachers and aides and the medical system. Catherine sits in on 97 percent of the doctors' appointments and manages all of the communications to doctors, insurance, and school. E-mail—with attachments—is the primary tool she has to manage all of it. At the heart of it is a five-page document she developed to tell Alexis's story. It contains:

- Some elements of Alexis's history and diagnoses
- Her doctors' names, phone numbers, e-mail addresses, and why each doctor is involved with Alexis's care
- Insurance coverages and contact points
- What therapy she goes to and the schedule
- Her food schedule
- Past surgeries and complications

Catherine has found that keeping and sharing this proactive record "all about Alexis" functions like preventive medicine. It allows her to ensure that the right information is available to people who need it and helps to keep Alexis's medical record clear and error free.

Another Baby

When Alexis was just 8 months old, Catherine realized she was pregnant again—an "oopsy" baby. When people asked her and her husband if they weren't afraid the baby would have the same genetic abnormalities as Alexis, they answered, "If that happens, we know all of the RIGHT decisions, already have the best doctors available, and will support this baby as necessary." They were confident that Alexis could overcome her challenges and felt they were well equipped to handle similar challenges in a new baby—which didn't stop them from being concerned. They had chorionic villus sampling testing done at 10 weeks, which didn't show any genetic abnormalities. When Jessica was born, they breathed a sigh of relief that there were no obvious genetic defects. They have since discovered that Jessica, too, has some issues, including an ASD that didn't close, attention deficit hyperactivity disorder (ADHD), auditory processing disorder, sensory deficiencies, learning disabilities related to reading and acquiring knowledge, and some issues with social interactions. Nonetheless, as they predicted, they were already well equipped to address whatever issues arose based on their experience with Alexis.

Being a Parent and an Employee

All of this takes both energy and time, and Catherine has learned to be open about that at work. When she moved to Philips, she talked about it at the initial interviews and with her team. She knows that she can't be a 24-hour player at work anymore and can't live as if she has two personalities, one as worker and one as Alexis and Jessica's mom and caregiver. She no longer gets really upset about work deadlines, as she's clear they pale in comparison to her main mission: keeping Alexis and Jessica alive and thriving. Catherine and her husband had a housewarming party shortly after moving into a new home and a co-worker spilled red wine on the white carpet in the living room. As Catherine went to clean it up, a co-worker asked, "Why are you so calm about this? I'd be freaking out." Catherine was clear in her response, "Proportionally, this is a small thing compared to what really matters."

The things Catherine has learned from her parenting journey have also enabled her to make an impact at work. Her perspective as a caregiver has enabled her to push Philips to look at benefits, advantages, and design from the perspective of patients, and to add features that make a difference in the patient's experience of care. She was working in the Finance Department when she had the opportunity to visit Philips's lighting department, where she saw engineers working with commercial products using brightly colored LEDs. Catherine realized that Alexis would be really attracted to the lights, and she immediately saw the potential to use them as a teaching tool. She went to the CEO at Philips Healthcare and asked for funding to make one of the products a reality. He gave her a million dollars to make it happen, along with permission to work on the product 2 days a week (while managing her full-time job in finance the other 3 days). Engineers signed up to help in their "innovation time"—the 5 percent of their time that Philips allows them to work on "just for fun" projects. She pulled in teachers from Perkins School for the Blind, where her daughter attended school. They eagerly worked with the engineers to suggest applications and uses.

The work was promising, and in 2014 she began working full time in the Lighting Division, her job paid for by the Healthcare Division. In 2014 the Lighting Division fully funded her work on LightAide. "LightAide™ creates a variety of interactive displays of color that support core learning goals and help instill the building blocks of literacy and mathematical concepts in learners with low vision, cognitive disabilities and other special needs."[2] Since being launched in 2013, the product is available in 32 states and eight countries, even winning the prestigious Edison Award for innovation. It is deeply rewarding to her that she is able to merge support for her daughter's needs and her work in such a seamless way. (Catherine is no longer working for Philips, although LightAide™ is on the market.)

Empathy and Bureaucracy

Although Catherine and her husband are doing an exceptional job of managing their children's health and healthcare, she is very clear that all of it could have been and would be far easier if the healthcare system was interconnected and focused on convenience and simplicity. Often, the same things that would make it more convenient would also make it safer for her children and herself.

Catherine and her husband have experienced some wonderful physicians and caregivers on this journey—but they've also experienced examples of caregivers and organizations who were insensitive, unempathetic, inept, or didn't take the time to communicate clearly or understand the full situation. This was especially difficult when Alexis was an infant and they were still trying to process what was happening, but it takes an emotional toll at any point.

For example, we noted earlier that Alexis is nourished through a feeding tube and needs just the right consistency of liquid to prevent aspiration of fluid into her lungs. Catherine had a legendary battle to get the right formula for Alexis's feeding tube when her insurance company, after authorizing it for the previous 2 years, abruptly stopped authorizing it in January of 2014. After endless phone calls to the insurer and to the supplier and after faxing and refaxing new prescriptions to both the insurer and supplier with no movement, Catherine finally threw the equivalent of a tantrum and tweeted about her experience, copying the relevant company twitter accounts. She also sent e-mails to the executive teams at all of the companies. Only then did she get action—though not without hiccups—and was able to finally resolve a problem that had been going on for nearly 6 months. As she wrote, "I do not like having to resort to a temper-tantrum to get services covered— but when a saga continues for 6 months with constant circles—I saw no other method." You can read more about this particular adventure at http://drcatherinerose.com/2013/06/18/the-circles -for-my-childs-survival/ and http://drcatherinerose.com/2013/06/19/the-journey-to-resolution/.

What is particularly ironic about the story is that the alternative to getting the right formula to Alexis was a costly hospitalization—the very thing that all the rules were put in place to avoid. Experiences like this have made Catherine, against her will, a connoisseur of on-hold music and on-hold messages. More importantly, they suggest that the rules that govern care, even though well intentioned, serve as roadblocks and frustration points for the very people and functions they were designed to serve.

Early in Alexis's life, she was assigned a case manager who would call monthly to find out if anything new was going on or if they needed help with anything. She was wonderful, and having a knowledgeable navigator was immensely helpful to Catherine and her husband in resolving issues, payment snafus, and just getting services aligned. It was the case manager who suggested that they sign up for MassHealth, which has been wonderful. It serves as secondary insurance for Alexis and covers all copayments as well as things like her hearing aids, glasses, and dental care. Although Alexis doesn't have a case manager at the moment, there's a nurse at Alexis's primary care provider's office who serves that role. It is helpful that Catherine can work with her through e-mail.

Convenient Tools

Scheduling doctors' appointments is an "adventure" that could be vastly improved with technology. Catherine points to a blog post by Dr. Paul Levy, where he compares what it takes for him to schedule an appointment with his doctor to what it takes to schedule a checkup for his Subaru. It is perhaps needless to say that the comparison is unfavorable.[3] Catherine's experience of appointment scheduling has been exponentially more difficult due to the fact that she is trying to schedule appointments with 15 different doctors, dealing with front-desk call-backs at inconvenient times, and finding herself repeating things like, "Alexis has diarrhea" multiple times a day amid co-workers while at work. Alexis's augmentative communication physician sees her once a year; getting that accomplished requires them to schedule the next year's appointment at the time they check out of the previous year's appointment, or they will never get on the schedule. Even though Catherine can schedule some appointments online, too often even that results in someone calling her back for more details or to confirm a date.

Keeping track of everything is also complex. Catherine's need for tracking tools was once the topic of a Hackathon, where all of the teams competed to build an app that would help Catherine and her family. So far, nothing works better than the complex Excel calendar she has created. Everything is color-coded by topic, person, and issue. Her husband is a scientist and the calendar is complex enough to confuse him. They tried a family Google calendar for a while, but it was hard to keep it updated and her husband didn't check it regularly enough. Now Catherine ends up sending e-mail updates to him about the schedule.

Catherine also notes how helpful it would have been to have everyone who saw her daughter in the NICU to write their names and roles on a whiteboard. It also would have helped to have access to the record and physician notes while Alexis was in the NICU (see Chapter 5, Acute Care and Hospitalizations, for example of some of these ideas in action). She learned to carry a notebook all the time to write down what was said and by whom, but she would really like to have access to the full record and open notes, not just in retrospect, but also during the hospital encounter.

As we noted earlier, Catherine has always been the communication hub for information that needs to be passed between doctors and care systems, as well as between doctors and the school system. She can see how useful it would be if doctors had simple means of integrating Alexis's records, highlighting new information and prescriptions. She also envisions a system that would allow a sort of round-robin of communication with rich discussion between her and all of Alexis's doctors and care team members, rather than having be treatment dependent on her to remember and convey what is important.

Parental Advocacy Improves Safety and Reduces Costs

Often Catherine's advocacy has resulted in safety improvements for her daughter, shorter lengths of stay, and lower costs. Because Alexis requires a CPAP to sleep, when she has a surgical procedure, the hospital insists that she stay in the Cardiac ICU afterward to be monitored. At one point, Alexis needed both an MRI to make sure that the fusions in her neck were stable and a cardiac catheterization procedure. Both needed to be done under general anesthesia, and the hospital wanted to do two separate procedures. Catherine was clear that two procedures would increase the risks to Alexis as well as the cost of both. It took multiple phone calls and e-mails to get everyone to agree to coordinate the procedures. In the end, Alexis was put under general anesthesia in the cardiac catheterization lab, escorted down to have the MRI, and then escorted back to the cath lab for the cardiac procedure. Alexis had one general anesthesia, one overnight stay, and two procedures—but only as a result of Catherine's advocacy.

Another example of Catherine's impact occurred when Alexis was 3 years old. Alexis was hospitalized for an eye surgery and was being monitored in the Cardiac ICU afterward because of her cardiac history. She couldn't be discharged because the ophthalmologist wasn't in the discharge drop-down menu in the cardiac unit. No one seemed to know what to do. Catherine paged the ophthalmologist from her cell phone. When the doctor called her back, Catherine asked if she could come to discharge Alexis before she started morning clinic. The ophthalmologist showed up, wrote a paper discharge for Alexis, and left for morning clinic. All the nurses asked Catherine and each other, "How did the doctor know to come?" Catherine noted that generally nurses want to focus on caring for patients, so they aren't best at maneuvering through the system.

Observations for Policy and Practice

Catherine's experiences navigating through the system on behalf of Alexis illustrate a number of lessons for improving care, coordination, and the experience of patients and caregivers.

- Focus on convenience when building tools for patients and caregivers.
- Share records and information with patients and/or their caregivers including notes, communications, and data *in the moment*—not just after the fact.

- Find ways to integrate records and communications to make it easier to understand a patient's journey.
- Listen to patients and caregivers—often what makes things better for them actually may save you money.
- Encourage parents to find and join support groups, either virtual or in person, which can provide education, information, and social support.
- Develop ways to increase coordination and collaboration within and across systems and roles.
- Review your policies and procedures with an eye toward empathetic interactions and procedures that reduce friction and hassles.

Conclusion

After years of treatment and following Alexis through one challenging diagnosis after another, one of Alexis's doctors recently watched her walk out of her annual checkup, hand-in-hand with her dad. The pediatrician was so moved by all Alexis has overcome she started to cry. She told Catherine later that the tears started flowing because she was proud of Alexis, proud of Catherine and her husband as parents, and proud of herself and her staff for helping everyone get so far. At that moment, Catherine knew Alexis had a team behind her, supporting her and her parents along the journey, wherever it may take her.

Catherine, in her journey with Alexis and Jessica, is truly an example of an empowered caregiver. She has made a significant difference in the lives of her children as well as the lives of others. Through her advocacy, Catherine is changing healthcare one interaction at a time. She remarks, however, that you shouldn't need both an MBA and a PhD to navigate the health system on behalf of your child.

Notes

1. http://www.chargesyndrome.org/about-charge.asp
2. http://www.LightAide.com
3. http://runningahospital.blogspot.com/2014/10/still-using-horses-and-buggies.html

Story 3: You Must Have an Insanely High Pain Tolerance

Jan Oldenburg, FHIMSS with Brittany Draper

Introduction

Brittany's experience highlights how difficult it can be to get appropriate care when you are not displaying the symptoms that doctors expect—and how that can increase the risk of long-term complications.

A Growing Crack

Brittany was skiing at Lake Tahoe in March of 2014. She hit an icy patch of snow, lost her balance, and fell hard on her hip, with her legs askew because her skis didn't pop off as they should have. She heard a huge snap as she landed and thought, "Oh, no, that must be my ACL…" When she managed to stand, she didn't feel pain in her knee and didn't notice hip pain until later in the day. At 29 years old, it didn't even seem possible to her that the fall put a crack in her right femoral neck (the area just below the ball of the hip's ball-and-socket joint). Who breaks their hip in their twenties during a casual day of skiing? Even though she was shaken up from the fall, Brittany continued to ski the rest of the day. She felt pain in her hip for a few days, but gradually forgot about it and went back to her life in San Francisco, interrupted by frequent travel for her consulting job.

Nearly a year later, in February of 2015, she was on a marathon trip: traveling all week, stopping by her parents' house in Ohio, and then attending a wedding. Her suitcase was heavy because she needed to carry clothes for business, a wedding, and casual occasions. As she walked down the stairs to her childhood room, lugging her bag, her socks slipped. She lost her balance and fell down the stairs, landing again on her right hip, her big suitcase ending up on top of her. Afterward, she was a bit sore, but didn't think it was anything major. Unbeknown to her, this fall increased the crack in the neck of her right femur, which had never healed from the previous year's fall while skiing.

Several days later, after attending her friend's wedding in Washington, DC, Brittany was jogging on the treadmill at her hotel on February 15. She was a marathon runner, so this jog wasn't anything out of the ordinary. After 45 minutes of running, she stopped her run because it felt as

127

if she had pulled a groin muscle. Something felt off—she had pulled muscles before and this was much more painful.

She limped on it for a day and by the time she left for the airport the next afternoon, she couldn't put any weight on her leg. She was alone and knew she needed to get home to San Francisco. She hopped on her left leg to a cab and had to be pushed in a wheelchair to the plane. The flight was delayed repeatedly, and Brittany couldn't get comfortable. She was anxious about her injury, the 6-hour flight that had stretched to 8 hours after delays, and how she was going to get home by herself. Wishing she had crutches or someone to help, she hopped to the bathroom on the plane and hoped not to fall.

Brittany was relieved when she landed in San Francisco, and asked for a wheelchair to take her to the taxi stand. She hopped and stumbled into the taxi and texted her roommate, Alison, hoping she could help her up the 40 stairs to their flat. Her cell phone was about to die, but she was able to contact Alison before it did. The driver delivered Brittany and her bags to her apartment. She stood with her weight on her left leg trying to figure out how to get up the stairs. Alison's boyfriend Karl suggested he carry her—though between the time he took her upstairs and went back to get her suitcase and her purse, someone had stolen her purse from the sidewalk. Exhausted from the events of the day, Brittany went straight to bed.

A Visit to the ED

When she woke up the next morning, February 17, Brittany still couldn't walk. She hobbled around the apartment using a stool to support her body weight. Knowing that something was really wrong, she asked her friend Jack to carry her down the apartment stairs so she could take an Uber to the nearest emergency department. Jack put her in the car and sternly said to the driver, "Make sure she gets there safely." The driver looked horrified by the situation, and Brittany tried to lighten the moment by saying, "Hey, it's cheaper than calling an ambulance."

When she arrived at the ED, Brittany used her arms to pull herself out of the Uber as the driver drove away as quickly as possible. She was standing on the sidewalk outside the ED unable to move, waving frantically to the people inside for help, but no one came. Her distress mounting, she continued to try to flag someone down, struggling not to cry, hurting a lot, and feeling very alone and helpless. Eventually, a man walking by asked if she needed help, went in, got a wheelchair, and wheeled her in. She was later told that California ED workers aren't allowed to help someone until they are actually in the ED.

Brittany eventually saw an ED doctor, who barely examined her, didn't do an x-ray, and told her that she had pulled a muscle. The doctor explained that rest, ice, ibuprofen, and crutches would get her through it. Brittany said, "But I've pulled muscles before and this feels much worse than that. Do you need to do a more thorough exam or take an x-ray?" Despite her assertiveness, her doctor insisted that it was a pulled muscle, or, worst case scenario, she had partially torn the muscle. Brittany was frustrated that the exam was not more thorough, but she felt helpless. What was she supposed to do if the doctor kept downplaying her injury and trying to rush on to the next patient? She sat alone in the exam room and waited for the crutches to arrive. Eventually a nurse popped in to tell her that they hadn't forgotten her, but could only find one crutch. Finally they found a second crutch and then sent Brittany to the pharmacy for industrial strength Ibuprofen and instructions to rest.

I'm Sure I'm Fine…

Thinking that she had a strained muscle, Brittany took a business trip to LA the next day. She took a taxi to the airport, then asked for a wheelchair to get to and from the plane. She sat through long business meetings with a broken hip and no painkillers. When she was ready to fly home to San Francisco on Friday, an airport worker pushed her wheelchair through security while her crutches went through the scanner. The armpit pad on one crutch fell off and was lost. Brittany patiently asked an airport worker about the missing armpit pad. "Miss, are you sure you brought the entire crutch to the airport?" was the response. With a missing armpit pad for one of the crutches, Brittany unevenly and uncomfortably made her way to the plane.

…But This Seems Off

The injury still wasn't getting any better, and she had a gut feeling that something was really wrong. She tried to get an appointment to see an orthopedic surgeon, but they were scheduled weeks in advance. She called every day to see if there were any openings or cancellations. Each time she explained that she was in a lot of pain and asked "Aren't there any emergency appointments available?" Finally, on Wednesday, February 25, 10 days after the injury, she got an appointment with an orthopedic doctor.

"It's Far Worse than I Thought"

After assessing the hip, the orthopedic surgeon told Brittany it was probably a tear in her muscle, but sent her for an x-ray just to make sure there was nothing wrong with the bones. When he came into the room with the x-rays, he was emotional. "It's a lot worse than I thought," he told her. "You broke your hip at the femur neck. When did you last eat? We need to rush you into emergency surgery. I've already called the orthopedic surgeon who specializes in hips to do the repairs, and he's on his way here right now." Brittany was in shock, wondering, "How can this be happening?" She thought she'd pulled a muscle…and she'd broken her hip?! The orthopedic surgeon continued:

> Usually with this type of injury, we do emergency surgery within 48 hours. It's been 10 days, so it's possible that the blood flow to the area has been compromised, the bone may have died, and you may need a total hip replacement. There's also a possibility that the break was caused by a tumor, so there may be a serious underlying condition we have to deal with. We're very sorry we didn't see you sooner. We don't know how you have coped with this—you must have an insanely high pain tolerance.

He showed her the x-ray, which clearly displayed the femoral neck snapped in half and the rest of the bone displaced into the middle of her pelvis. In disbelief, Brittany asked "Are you sure that's my x-ray? Could it have been mixed up with another patient's?" He confirmed that it was indeed her x-ray and asked her if she had noticed her right leg was an inch shorter (from the displacement). He had her wait in the room until the orthopedic surgeon who would be performing her surgery arrived.

The femoral neck is the most common site of hip fractures, accounting for 45 to 53 percent of cases. People with this type of injury are at high risk of complications, because the blood supply to the fractured portion of the bone is often disrupted. The concern is that the decreased blood supply will lead to nonhealing or the death of bone cells, known as osteonecrosis. As noted earlier, Brittany was at especially high risk for this complication because of the 10-day delay in getting treatment.[1]

Brittany sat in the room waiting for the surgeon, terrified that she might need a total hip replacement or have cancer. She was 30 years old. She'd never had so much as a set of stitches before, never took painkillers, was always in perfect health. Sitting alone in that small exam room crying, she felt very alone and very afraid. Her life had just been turned upside down. Over and over again, she thought, "I broke my hip?!?!"

She was also angry. Angry about the care she'd received in the Emergency Department 8 days earlier. She presented to the ED within 48 hours of her injury, within the preferred time frame for an optimal surgical repair, but the ED doctor didn't do a thorough examination, take an x-ray, or consider the seriousness of the injury even though Brittany insisted that it felt a lot worse than an ordinary pulled muscle.

"I'm Getting Her a Bed and an Operating Room"

Trying to prepare the best she could for her first surgery, Brittany quickly researched the surgeon on her cell phone. He was well educated with fellowships in both hip and spine surgery and he received almost perfect patient satisfaction scores on HealthGrades. She hoped he was as good as he sounded.

Eventually, the surgeon arrived. He was not much older than Brittany, but she instantly trusted him. He explained that they could either go straight to a hip replacement, which would last about 20 years and require a second revision surgery at that time, or they could try to fix her hip with screws and a rod, technically called a "closed reduction of the femoral neck with internal fixation."[2] He recommended the latter since she was so young, but it also meant a longer recovery. If all went well with the procedure, it could mean that she would be 100 percent back to normal. However, there were a variety of potential complications that could result in a second surgery and a total hip replacement. She told him she wanted to try the closed reduction of the femoral neck.

Still at the physician's office, she needed to get across the street to the hospital. An office worker brought Brittany a wheelchair, but it didn't have a footrest. With a broken hip, unable to support her leg, Brittany patiently asked for a wheelchair with a footrest. But the staff left her sitting in the hall; no one seemed to be planning on a way to get her to the hospital. Eventually, her surgeon saw her sitting in the wheelchair in the hall, took it by the handles and rolled her across the street to the hospital himself. At the registration desk, the clerks wouldn't let him admit Brittany because they said they didn't have a room available. Impatient, he started rolling her toward the elevator. One of the clerks tried to stop him, saying, "Who are you and where are you going?" "I'm her surgeon and I'm getting her a bed and an operating room," he replied.

In the orthopedic department, where they knew him well, he was able to get Brittany admitted, get her a room, and schedule the surgery. A nurse arrived to draw blood for blood tests and insert the IV line. By this time, Brittany was pretty dehydrated, as she hadn't been allowed to drink water most of the day as preparation for surgery. The nurse attempted to draw blood and collapsed Brittany's vein. Brittany, in pain, asked, "Did you get all the blood you needed?" and the nurse responded, "No, none, sorry, I'll have to try the other arm," as she smacked the vein trying to draw it to the surface. After several attempts, the blood draw was completed and Brittany was left alone in the room waiting anxiously for surgery. She was dreading calling her parents; she knew they would panic because they didn't even know she had injured herself in the first place. Trying to be casual, she explained that she had broken her hip and was getting emergency surgery, "But I'm OK." Her father told her he was finding a plane flight and would be there as soon as possible.

Pre-Op Preparation

After she had waited 2 more hours, a nurse arrived to roll Brittany to a room outside pre-op. The anesthesiologist explained the anesthesia options: either general anesthesia, which would require inserting a breathing tube, or twilight sleep, essentially an epidural to numb the body from the waist down combined with light sedation that includes an amnesiac so the patient doesn't remember any surgery details. The surgeon's preference was twilight sleep, because it causes fewer complications than general anesthesia, so Brittany opted for that. As they discussed the options, sirens went off in the hallway. Brittany asked the anesthesiologist, "Is everything OK? There are a lot of sirens going off." He responded, "Oh yeah, that's no big deal."

Eventually her surgeon arrived and explained that they'd do the surgery as soon as the hospital put out the fire. She said, "Really, there's a fire in the hospital? No wonder sirens were going off in the hall."

Brittany was anxious and wanted to get the operation over with. She was also concerned about the potential lack of blood flow to her hip. She couldn't bear the thought of a total hip replacement. The surgeon waited by her side and consoled her. He even offered to call her parents, but Brittany declined, thinking it would scare her mother too much to know the details of the surgery beforehand.

Her surgeon also mentioned that one of his partners, who specialized in reconstructive orthopedics, was coming in to help with the surgery rather than the surgical assistant he normally would use. By this time, Brittany could tell that the surgical team was excited about her surgery, because it was complex and novel to be doing it on someone so young. "I read your case. Wow!" was the response of each team member—nurses, anesthesiologist, surgeons—all of whom were about Brittany's age.

Aiming for Perfection

As Brittany was rolled into pre-op, the anesthesiologist told her that if she was nervous, he could give her Valium to relax her. She eagerly nodded and was instantly relaxed by the Valium. She asked the surgical team, "So what's on our music playlist for the surgery? I want you to be focused." They asked her what she would like to listen to and she suggested Coldplay—just the right degree of mellow. Brittany bent over in bed to receive the spinal epidural to numb her from the waist down, and the next thing she remembered was waking up in the recovery room with a body-warming bag surrounding her. Brittany's immediate questions in recovery were, "Is my bone dead?" and "Do I have a tumor?" The answer to both was "no," so her prognosis was very good.

Surgery had taken 3 hours, ending around midnight. Her leg was placed in a robotic traction machine during surgery. The surgeon used the machine to adjust the position of her leg 1/1000 of an inch at a time and take an x-ray during each manipulation. After hundreds of manipulations, the leg and hip were correctly realigned and two titanium screws were placed in the femoral neck (one screw was spring-loaded) and a nine-inch titanium rod was inserted into the femur for additional stability. An additional titanium screw was placed perpendicular to the bottom of the rod for additional support. After the surgery, the surgeon said that he could have inserted all the hardware in 15 minutes, but he spent 3 hours operating because he was aiming for perfection. "I wanted to put you back together exactly the way you were before," he said.

Discharge: Don't Forget the Blood Thinners!

Brittany's surgeon was already making rounds by 7 a.m. the next morning. Between morphine and Oxycodone for pain, she tried to comprehend and remember all the information that he provided. There was potential that she could be discharged that day, but when she nearly collapsed during her first physical therapy session, they kept her an additional night.

With her dedicated and hardworking personality, Brittany opened her business laptop and attempted to respond to business e-mails, but the strong painkillers made her fall asleep in the middle of typing the first one. She insisted that she was fine and would be back to work on Monday. Little did she know at the time how intense and challenging the recovery process really would be—essentially requiring her to take disability for 6 months.

Before being discharged the next day, she met with the physical and occupational therapy staff and had another round of blood work. She was discharged with Oxycodone for pain. Reviewing her discharge instructions, she remembered talking to the surgeon about self-administering a blood thinner shot into her stomach each morning for 1 month during recovery to minimize the risk of blood clots. Blood thinners are a standard medication protocol for hip patients. She noticed it wasn't on the list of discharge medications and asked about it. The nurse who was discharging her went back to the notes and said, "Oh, you're right; the surgeon did write that down." Only then did she get the blood thinner prescription and instructions on how to self-administer the shot.

Brittany's father hadn't arrived in town yet, so she called a friend to help her get home safely. She was still very weak and needed someone who could carry her, if needed. Her friend Paul was more than happy to help. He arrived at the hospital and picked up her prescriptions at the pharmacy across the street. He took her insurance card and driver's license to ensure that he would be able to pick up a prescription written for someone else. To lighten the heavy mood, he arrived back to the hospital room and joked, "I have your narcotics and syringes…let's go!" Paul helped Brittany into a cab and up her apartment stairs, and her dad arrived shortly after from Ohio.

The First 6 Weeks of Recovery

For 6 weeks, Brittany couldn't put any weight on her right leg. The first 2 weeks were the most challenging: Her leg was swollen, she was on heavy painkillers, and she slept a lot. Her father stayed in San Francisco to support her the first few weeks. In the warm afternoons, he would help her down the stairs and use a rented wheelchair to wheel her out to a nearby park where she could enjoy the bay view, watch the cyclists and walkers, and get fresh air and sunshine—the highlight of each day.

Brittany had never taken medications for anything and had mixed emotions about the Oxycodone. When she saw her surgeon for a follow-up at 2 weeks, he told her, "It's probably time to wean yourself off the Oxycodone." In a sign that he really understood her, he added, "Use this for motivation—once you're completely off Oxycodone, you can drink wine." With that encouragement and yearning to be off the heavy pain medication, Brittany just stopped taking the Oxycodone cold turkey, even though she still had shooting pains in her leg, sometimes so bad that it would wake her up in the middle of the night. She would lie awake for hours wishing the pain would go away and that she could peacefully fall back asleep.

As the 6 weeks progressed, Brittany would use her crutches to get to the park and sit on the same bench waiting patiently to heal and move forward with her life. One day a cyclist stopped and said, "Oh look, you're healing! You've gone from wheelchair to crutches." He had ridden past her many times as she was sitting on that same bench with her father.

Before Brittany went to her 6-week appointment, she was instructed to get a new set of x-rays. The paperwork would be faxed in ahead of time by the surgeon's office staff. When she showed up to radiology, they didn't have her paperwork and had never received the fax. Radiology staff asked her to go get it from her doctor's office. She navigated her way to her surgeon's office on crutches, only to find them closed for lunch. She waited an hour for them to open, got the paperwork, and "crutched" back to radiology. In radiology, despite the paperwork right in front of them, they asked if she was there for an ultrasound—just a small example of the way patients often bear the brunt of the inefficiencies in our healthcare system.

Finally, she presented back to her surgeon with x-rays on a disc. The goal of the first 6 weeks was to make sure the placement of the rod and screws had not shifted; the x-rays were fine. At this point, Brittany would be able to begin putting weight gradually on her leg and begin physical therapy.

Brittany also saw an endocrinologist to ensure her calcium and vitamin D levels were optimal and that there was no underlying issue with bone development. She received both blood and urine tests as well as a DEXA bone density scan. All results were normal.

Learning to Walk Again

In the 6 weeks since her surgery, Brittany had lost 15 pounds of muscle mass. Not only do the muscles atrophy during an event like this, they also forget how and when to trigger and the muscle memory is lost. In recovery and physical therapy, Brittany had to regrow muscles, retrain them to trigger, and rebuild the muscle memory. Simple muscle memory movements, such as sitting down and walking, had to be relearned. Brittany had to slowly wean her body off the crutches by starting to bear 25 percent body weight. She gradually progressed to 50 percent body weight and then 75 percent body weight. At this point, she used one crutch until her body would tolerate 100 percent body weight. Her first steps without the crutch were extremely painful, and her muscles were still very weak. As a result, her body compensated by limping. Her physical therapy clinic had a weightless treadmill that allowed her to adjust the amount of weight her legs needed to bear when practicing walking.

In the 6 months since her surgery, Brittany has healed slowly. She still uses one crutch occasionally, because her muscles are still weak. Her body is gradually rebuilding muscle and is compensating less than before, but a slight limp is still noticeable and will diminish in time. She is able to swim and ride a stationary bike.

Brittany currently sees two different physical therapists, who work in harmony but still give slightly different exercises, stretches, and instructions. If she wasn't diligent and attuned, it would be very confusing. Brittany has learned to trust her body. When exercises hurt badly, she is vocal about it, and her therapists are clear that it's a signal that she isn't ready to progress yet. Her muscles tighten up around the injured areas resulting in pain and knots. The therapists have taught her techniques to massage her hip flexor and IT band to reduce the muscle tightness and the pain of getting out of bed in the morning. The full healing process will take 12 to 18 months with the potential of a 100 percent recovery.

Returning to Work Too Soon

Brittany returned to work at the 3-month mark, but unfortunately the return was too soon in her healing process. She plateaued on her recovery and remained on one crutch much longer than the expected amount of time. Additionally, sitting was a challenge. If she sat for more than 5 to 10 minutes, her muscles tightened up around the hip, causing additional pain and difficulty walking. Brittany took additional time off work to recover and heal.

People stared a lot, and asked silly questions: "You broke your hip? But where's your cast?" "Is the rod outside the bone?" "Will you limp forever?"

Insurance

Brittany's been lucky about insurance—except for the fact that her plan didn't cover a wheelchair for a broken hip, leading her to wonder, if a wheelchair isn't covered for a broken hip, in what situations insurance would consider one as medically necessary. Her surgery cost $68,000, and that's without additional fees for the surgeons, anesthesiologists, endocrinologist, prescriptions, physical therapy, and some laboratory and radiology work. Her insurance plan is a high-deductible PPO with a deductible of $2500 and then patient responsibility of 20 percent after reaching the deductible. Her out-of-pocket limit was $4000, which she quickly reached and put on her credit card.

Brittany's provider has a "My Health Online" patient portal that she used to get test results and e-mail with her doctors. The limitations were that not all physicians used the system and she could only request appointments, not schedule them directly (and you couldn't do that as a new patient). The bill payment site had a different interface that didn't connect to the patient portal and required a different username and password.

Observations for Policy and Practice

Brittany learned a number of lessons from this experience; all of them can help other patients and help us design a system that supports patients in getting the care they need:

- She had to be her own advocate. Because she was functional despite the pain of the broken hip, doctors didn't take her seriously, even when she said it felt much worse than a strained muscle. She had to be persistent in order to get the care she needed—from seeing an orthopedic surgeon to getting discharged from the hospital with the correct medication.
- Always get a second opinion. There are lots of mistakes in healthcare, and getting a second opinion is a key part of being your own advocate.
- Write everything down, especially if you're on painkillers, so you can remember everything what you need to know.
- Hospital food is actually good.

- Brittany has also needed to be assertive in her recovery—finding a physical therapy office that had access to the antigravity treadmill and being attuned to her body so that the physical therapists didn't push her beyond what she was capable of.
- Navigating a complex and disconnected health system is frustrating and difficult.
- Many facilities are not as handicapped accessible as they should be: The parking garage for the orthopedic surgeon's office is eight stories high and has no elevator. The front entrance of the hospital only had stairs; the ramp was on the other side of the building. That's not helpful when you can't navigate the stairs.
- High-deductible insurance plans seem like a good idea until you actually have a serious illness; then, paying off the deductible can be daunting.
- She's learned to ask for help. No matter how independent you are, there are things you simply can't navigate with a broken hip. Help came in the form of roommates, friends, family, and random strangers. It's been a good lesson in interdependence.
- Injuries give you a new perspective on life and help you put what is really important in perspective.
- Being disabled helps you learn who your true friends are. Who stops by? Who keeps you company? Who sends flowers?

Conclusions

Brittany was lucky enough to find a set of people to be her champions in the medical system: the surgeon who took charge, rolling her across the street to the hospital, getting her admitted, finding her a bed, and aiming for perfection in the surgery; and the physical therapists who worked with her three times a week helping her learn to walk again. Her father stepped in during the most difficult parts to help her manage, and friends supported her in ways large and small. Nonetheless, Brittany's experience highlights the difficulty of being your own advocate in a medical system that lacks many support systems that would make it easier to navigate.

Notes

1. http://www.hss.edu/newsroom_mri-see-through-metal-screws.asp#.VU-tCRd33-8
2. http://www.aaos.org/news/aaosnow/dec12/clinical12.asp

Story 4: Give Me Autonomy, Not Engagement

Jan Oldenburg, FHIMSS with Hugo Campos*

Introduction

By any measure, Hugo Campos is engaged, empowered, and activated about his health. He wants to manage his health as much as possible on his own and is frustrated by a health system that doesn't release the data or provide the tools to enable him to be autonomous. For Hugo, the term "patient engagement" as defined by the healthcare system is inherently paternalistic, implying that engagement can be bestowed by the system rather than that it arises from the person's intrinsic motivations. He believes what he tweeted recently:

> #**PatientEngagement** should not be required for #**patient** #**activation**. Not everyone wants #**engagement**. #**Autonomy** must be taught and encouraged.

The system must change to recognize patients who, like Hugo, want to be autonomous by empowering them with the tools and technology they need to be successful.

A New Reality

In 2007, Hugo was living an active life. By any definition, he was "well." Until he wasn't. He was on his way to visit his parents in San Francisco on an ordinary Saturday morning and was planning to take BART, the local commuter train. He ran up the stairs to the platform and when he got to the top of the stairs, his heart racing from the run, his heart continued to beat faster and faster, and he fainted. He came back to consciousness lying on the platform, reborn into a new reality.

It took nearly 3 years to determine what was amiss, but eventually he was diagnosed with hypertrophic cardiomyopathy (HCM), a relatively common genetic heart disease in which the heart muscle (myocardium) becomes abnormally thick (hypertrophied). HCM can cause problems in the heart's electrical system, resulting in life-threatening abnormal heart rhythms (arrhythmias), which was what Hugo was experiencing.[1] For many people with HCM, the first symptom is sudden cardiac death. In

---

* @hugooc

that way, Hugo was lucky to have fainted on the BART platform. Soon after the diagnosis, he received an implantable cardioverter defibrillator (ICD) to help control the potentially life-threatening arrhythmias he was experiencing. This small device was implanted in his chest and connected to the heart with wires or leads. When the ICD senses a dangerous change in heart rhythm, it sends an electric shock to the heart to restore a normal heartbeat. Hugo's life has been saved several times by his ICD.

Defective by Design

And yet, despite the fact that the device is life saving, Hugo considers it to be defective. Not just defective, but defective by design. The reason? His ICD collects massive amounts of data about his heart—literally, his life—on a daily basis. The data are generated by *his* heart in combination with a device implanted in *his* body, paid for by *his* insurance. And yet, he has no access to it. The data are transmitted regularly to the medical device manufacturer, in this case Medtronic. Medtronic, in turn, provides reports and alerts to Hugo's cardiologist or electrophysiologist, highlighting abnormal patterns, tracking when and why the ICD administers shocks, and notifying the physician when significant issues arise that require action. The physician, in turn, has the responsibility to call Hugo when there are issues that require him to be seen. Hugo relies on that process to work. When he experiences an issue or receives a shock, he has no direct access to information that would help him understand what just happened and how serious it is. Quite often, this information is only shared with him during a visit to the clinic, months after the event was logged by the ICD. He asks: "Is it right that I, the person whose life is at stake, am the last person in the chain to know what happened? And then only if my doctor deems it important enough to notify me?"

"Defective by Design" is the mantra of a group of activists who are trying to raise awareness about technology that intentionally restricts its users. They note:

> Digital restrictions management is the practice of imposing technological restrictions that control what users can do with digital media. When a program is designed to prevent you from copying or sharing a song, reading an ebook on another device, or playing a single-player game without an Internet connection, you are being restricted by Digital Restrictions Management (DRM). In other words, DRM creates a damaged good; it prevents you from doing what would be possible without it. This concentrates control over production and distribution of media, giving DRM peddlers the power to carry out massive digital book burnings and conduct large-scale surveillance over people's media viewing habits.

Hugo's ICD is an example of digital restrictions management. You can read more about this movement at www.defectivebydesign.org.

In May 2008, shortly after his ICD was implanted, Hugo met a Medtronic public relations person. He followed up in June, trying to cultivate a relationship, but it wasn't until the head of communication for Medtronic's cardiac rhythm management (CRDM) unit contacted him in early 2009 that he was able to begin a conversation about remote monitoring. Although the Medtronic staff has always been cordial and open to discussions, after 7 years it has become clear to Hugo that providing remote monitoring data to patients is simply not their priority. They consider their customer to be Hugo's physician, not Hugo, despite the fact that it is Hugo whose life is dependent on the ICD. Hugo is frustrated by the fact that 7 years later, very little has changed for him and other ICD patients, as this is an overall issue in the medical device industry, not an issue with one manufacturer.

Autonomy

Hugo notes that we live in a free society with systems that help individuals to be accountable. He can choose to gamble all his money, buy a gun, or vote without asking someone's permission, but he can't refill a prescription for a beta blocker without a doctor's signature. Hugo notes that certain behaviors are expected of every citizen, and—unless they stray into illegal behaviors—individuals are trusted to manage their lives; only when it comes to healthcare are people not trusted to manage their own lives and their own data. Although the term autonomy makes everyone in the healthcare system nervous because it implies self-prescribing and self-diagnosis, it appropriately describes a setting in which individuals have the data, tools, and technology to manage their own care—if they so choose.

Hugo explains that people choose to engage in their lives with the people that matter to them, doing things that bring them joy and pleasure—they are engaged in their lives. He sees engagement as the path to autonomy and empowerment and feels that as long as control is in the hands of providers, there may be engagement but there won't be autonomy. This encourages patients to be passive recipients of whatever the healthcare system has to offer rather than active partners in the process.

To explain how uncomfortable it still makes the healthcare system to have an activated patient, Hugo mentions going to the ER during an episode of atrial fibrillation, an abnormally fast heart rhythm. The physician ordered a chest x-ray. Hugo questioned why she would order an x-ray for a bout of atrial fibrillation, saying, "I don't want any unnecessary tests." At that, the doctor threw up her hands and said, "We have a dangerous one here."

Hugo has philosophically refused remote monitoring of his ICD, because the reports are provided to his doctor, not directly to him. Hugo tracks his arrhythmias so he can understand trends and correlations in his data, and it has been a continuing issue to get information regularly, in readable format, and at the level of detail that he needs—and when he does, he needs to transcribe it from PDFs because he doesn't get the actual data in usable form. He doesn't want to be a "difficult patient," as that label could impact his care, but there seems to be no other choice for him to get the data that enable him to manage his condition, learn more about his arrhythmias, and remain engaged with his health and healthcare.

Currently there are no incentives for medical device manufacturers to give patients access to the data—in fact, there are disincentives. Doctors and manufacturers seem to fear that if patients had the data they might take inappropriate action and put doctors and the manufacturer at increased risk of liability. In a fee-for-service system, doctors don't have incentives to provide these kinds of data to patients either, as the pattern of monitoring every 3 months means that review of the data is a billable event.

Managing without Insurance

Hugo was receiving insurance through his spouse, and when his spouse decided to become a freelancer, Hugo realized he wouldn't have access to insurance. They went on COBRA (Consolidated Omnibus Budget Reconciliation Act of 1985) for 18 months, but Hugo began preparing to go without insurance, especially after he was turned down for individual insurance due to his ICD. In 2012, it was still legal to refuse coverage to someone because of a preexisting condition, and his ICD signaled the existence of his condition, loud and clear. Hugo went without insurance until the Affordable Care Act took effect and he was able to purchase an insurance policy on the Affordable Care Act (ACA) exchange in January of 2014.

In preparation for this period without insurance, Hugo watched online auctions for a Medtronic 2090 programmer, a device used at the clinic to interrogate ICDs and pacemakers. Hugo believes that a person has a right to defend himself or herself if no one else does. He thinks of his action as an extension of his Second Amendment rights. Even if the rest of the system breaks down, he wants to be able to defend himself by having the tools that allow him to manage his own health and healthcare. The 2090 programmers are hard to find, but Hugo was lucky. He also took a course to understand how the device worked and how to read the reports, and he considered it a safety valve while he didn't have insurance.

Hugo also acquired an AliveCor device in January of 2012. The AliveCor is a smartphone case that takes a one-lead electrocardiogram, or ECG (http://www.alivecor.com). Paired with the AliveCor app, it allows individuals to understand what is happening with their hearts' electrical rhythm. It is comparable to a reading from lead 1 of a standard EKG machine and is especially appropriate for monitoring episodes of atrial fibrillation.[2] Hugo received his very soon after AliveCor's invention by connecting with the inventor, Dave Albert (MD), who was in Mountain View, California, for FutureMed in January of 2012. He gave Hugo one of the AliveCor devices.

The AliveCor is not fast enough to catch all ventricular arrhythmias—by the time Hugo is ready to record them, they are gone. It does show arrhythmias that take place in both the upper and lower chambers of the heart, including ventricular tachycardia (VTs) and premature ventricular contractions (PVCs) in the lower chambers and atrial fibrillation (AFib) in the upper chambers. It gives Hugo peace of mind to know what is happening with his heart rhythms in the moment. Now the FDA has approved the algorithms the device uses to detect atrial fibrillation, Hugo can send a reading to AliveCor for interpretation and send the record to his doctor. He can also easily track the data from all the readings he takes using the AliveCor. Although his doctors have not fully embraced the AliveCor, it has been a great step for Hugo on his journey of autonomy.

Designing the Future

Hugo envisions an interface with his ICD that would enable him to do the following things to better manage and communicate about his health:

- Set alerts to notify him, as well as designated family members or friends, when the ICD detects a potential issue. This is more important to Hugo than having the device alert his doctor, because the doctor isn't always available to take immediate action or know what is going on with the patient at any given time.
- Track arrhythmias so that he can correlate them with events and activities in his life. For example, Hugo has noticed several emerging patterns: (1) when he drinks hard liquor he is more likely to have atrial arrhythmias, and (2) abstaining from coffee seems to create more rather than fewer arrhythmias. Providing Hugo with direct access to the data would give him more ability to correlate the symptoms recorded by his ICD with other events in his life. When data from other data sources were added—pollution levels, pollen levels, temperature—he could also see if there was any connection between his arrhythmias and other external factors.
- Finally, he would like to be able to connect to other patients who have arrhythmia patterns similar to his to find out what works for them and what their triggers are. He envisions an ability to find patients like him by virtue of diagnosis, age, and similarities in lifestyle and arrhythmia patterns so that successful treatments could be crowdsourced.

One of the reasons Hugo is such a champion for getting people access to their own data is stories about patients who receive shocks from their ICD, but then are not able to reach physicians or the device manufacturers due to holidays, creating risks that would be more manageable if they had direct access to alerts. It would also enable patients to make better decisions about when to visit emergency rooms.

In the fall of 2009, when Hugo visited Medtronic, he told his audience, "The good news is that, for all of you here, this is a job and a career and you will retire some day. For me, it is not. It is a matter of life and death. I will stop talking about it when they put me in the ground."

Heroes of the Autonomy and Participatory Medicine Movement

Hugo notes that there are many heroes of this movement, including Dave deBronkart, "Doc Tom" Ferguson, Susannah Fox, Gilles Frydman, Regina Holliday, and so many others who have shared their stories, challenged the system, and helped to change attitudes and beliefs. In addition, he calls out:

- Karen Sandler is a software lawyer who wanted access to the source code of the computer running her heart and who, in *Killed by Code: Software Transparency in Implantable Medical Devices*, addressed the potentially fatal risk of source code defects in implantable medical devices. She advocates for transparent and open-source software and says, "Clearly, we need mandatory, public, and broad safety review of code that runs these devices. At the very least, the US Food and Drug Administration must require device manufacturers to submit software to the agency for review and safekeeping."
- Ben West wanted to reverse engineer his diabetes pump because he felt patients should be able to independently verify the safety and efficacy of their medical devices—an approach that could be extended to ICDs. Ben noted, "There's no way to cross-check to make sure your pump or meter is operating correctly, or merge with other devices; it's just weird that you can't do that. My point is that safety is not a feature, especially not with medical records. Safety is public—a public good."
- Patients with diabetes who have hacked their continuous blood glucose meters in order to have more access to data about their health give hope that the same opportunity will become available to patients with ICDs. See Story 16, "Managing Diabetes with a DIY Pancreatic System," about one of these patients.

Observations for Policy and Practice

Hugo's story and his approach to managing his illness gives us many lessons for policy and practice:

- One of the revolutions in healthcare is the shift from health-system-centered care to patient- and consumer-centered care. Part of that revolution means that medical device manufacturers—like all other entities in the healthcare ecosystem—need to begin treating patients as customers, not just physicians. Providing consumers with access to their own data is a key piece of this revolution. Incentives may need to be provided to push medical device manufacturers to provide patients with access to their data.
- While doctors and health systems can encourage consumers to engage with their own health, they cannot bestow engagement on someone; engagement comes from within.

Policies about data ownership and direct access to one's own data can encourage consumers to take action on their own behalf.

■ One of the likely outcomes of the "big data" revolution is personalized analytics. This is where large sources of data, including data generated by implanted and wearable devices, is merged with external data sources to develop personal data analytics. This would mean that an individual could understand and manage his or her disease at a very granular level—either with or without doctors. This is the path to personalized or precision medicine, and making the data generated by devices such as ICDs available to patients is a critical underpinning.

■ Determined patients are already making it their business to get access to their own data, as Hugo's story and the DIY diabetes group are making clear. There is an opportunity for medical device manufacturers to support this effort, working directly with patients and consumers to design and build systems that will help them live better and more autonomous lives. A change that recognizes that people have a right to the data generated by their bodies is coming, though more slowly than many of us would like.

Conclusion

Hugo believes that for healthcare to be truly patient centric, it needs to be designed around individuals and patients. Designs should enable patients to control their own data and health, choosing what they share and with whom they share it.

Recently, Hugo was recognized by the White House as one of nine Champions of Change in Precision Medicine. The White House defines precision medicine as the right care at the right time for the right person.[3] In addition, Hugo and 3 others supported by students at Harvard Law School won a copyright exemption that grants them access to the data from their implanted devices for study in October of 2015.[4] The recognition from the White House and the copyright exemption win have given Hugo hope that progress is being made in changing attitudes toward these issues, and that patients will eventually have the autonomy, tools, and data that he craves.

Hugo's story is a part of a sea change in the field of medicine: from patients as passive consumer's of their doctors' instructions to patients who are partners in their own treatment and care, choosing when and how they interact with the healthcare system and taking responsibility for their own health.

Notes

1. http://www.mayoclinic.org/diseases-conditions/hypertrophic-cardiomyopathy/home/ovc-20122102
2. http://www.empr.com/medical-news/do-smartphone-ecgs-have-similar-accuracy-to-standard-ecgs/article/397148/
3. http://susannahfox.com/2015/07/10/champions-of-change/
4. http://cyberlawclinic.berkman.harvard.edu/2015/10/27/dmca-exception-granted-for-medical-device-research-patient-access-to-data/

Story 5: Becoming My Mother's Voice*

Mary P. Griskewicz, MS, FHIMSS[†]

Introduction

On Friday, March 8, 2013, I landed at Bradley International Airport in Windsor Locks, Connecticut, returning from HIMSS13 in New Orleans. As soon as I landed, my husband called me (he tracked my flight) telling me he would be at the airport, waiting to take me to a famous academic medical center. My mom, Patricia—or Patty, as she liked to be called—was in an ambulance on the way to there.

When I arrived in the emergency room, I met my cousin Mary Kay, my mom, and the attending physician. It soon became clear to me that Mom could not represent herself, as she couldn't explain what was wrong or express herself clearly.

I later learned that Mom had what clinicians called aphasia, a condition that robs one of the ability to communicate[1]; as a result, she could no longer express her wishes to others. I took on a new persona as the "voice of the patient," becoming my mom's legally appointed healthcare representative.

Patient Representative

As the minutes, days, and weeks passed, my mom did not get better. I became the patient advocate, addressing providers and healthcare industry representatives, trying to ensure I represented my mom and her wishes to the best of my ability. As clinicians administered medications and ordered tests and procedures, I had to think about:

- What would my mom want?
- Would the test hurt her?
- Is she or will she be in pain?

---

* Modified from a September 15, 2014, blog post on the HIMSS website. The original can be found at: http://blog.himss.org/2014/09/15/representing-the-voice-of-the-patient-why-patient-and-family-engagement-matters/
[†] @mgriskewicz

- What are these medications, what are they for, and will they help? What are the potential side effects? Will they interact badly with other medications?
- Will this provide her with the best quality of life?
- What does the rest of my family think?
- What do I think?
- What are the chances this treatment will allow her to recover?

Mom's Data

The health system had recently installed a new electronic health record (EHR) system—thank goodness! My mom had been a patient in this hospital about a month previously, which meant the EHR had her updated health information, medical history, medication list, and other vital data. I did not have access to this information as the hospital did not have a personal health record for patients, their families, or referring providers to access.

The biggest and most important questions to me were "Could her doctors help her recover and identify the cause of her illness and the aphasia?" "Could they make her better?"

Test after test, day after day went by with no clarity. We had many medical opinions and theories from teams of the physicians at this renowned teaching hospital, but no official diagnosis.

My mom did not have an advance directive in place, which made many of my decisions even more difficult. I had to make all of the decisions related to her care, based on what I thought was best, with no guidance from my mother about her wishes. I was lucky to have the support of family and friends as I made crucial decisions.

The nursing staff, clinical technicians, and physicians at the hospital took good care of my mom and my family. They tried their best to keep us informed on her condition and worked with me every second of every day to try to heal Mom and make her comfortable. She did not improve, however, and became progressively worse over the days and weeks that followed.

After two MRIs, two CAT scans, and a PET scan that was performed at my request, we finally received a diagnosis. Mom had inoperable small-cell lung cancer. After consultations with family, friends, and the support of many great colleagues at HIMSS (Health Information and Management Systems Society), we acknowledged that treatment for the cancer was not going to provide my mom with a positive outcome or an improved quality of life. With the support of family and friends, I made the difficult decision to remove Mom from life support. She passed on the very same day, April 13, 2013.

Observations for Policy and Practice

My experience as my mother's representative highlights opportunities for system change:

- Anyone who reaches my mother's age (she was 72) should have an advance directive. The question should be asked by health systems, doctors, and family members. If you don't know a family member's wishes, ask! Make it a topic at Sunday dinners or holiday afternoons, especially with those you truly love. You'll be glad later not to have to guess. For more about how to have these conversations, watch Alexandra Drane talk about Engage with Grace[2] or visit its Facebook page (https://www.facebook.com/engagewithgrace). The Conversation Project (http://theconversationproject.org/) also has wonderful tools as does Common Practice with their game for discussing end of life wishes (www.mygiftofgrace.com).

■ If you are a doctor or a nurse, begin asking questions about dying wishes as a routine part of medical care and care planning conversations. A recent Kaiser Family Foundation tracking poll showed that about 8 in 10 Americans support the idea that Medicare and private insurance should reimburse doctors for end-of-life conversations. Fully 9 in 10 people surveyed felt their doctors should have those conversations with patients, though a far lower percentage had actually had such conversations.[3]

■ Although everyone in the system supported me and my family, we would have loved to have had one consistent team of physicians in charge of care for my mom. We also wish the opinions of other specialists would have been brought in much sooner. Because Mom had aphasia, they were treating her from a neurology perspective, but it turned out the root cause was elsewhere. Had the hospital performed the PET scan earlier, we would have known about the lung cancer much sooner. Having a diagnosis would have made some of my decisions as a healthcare representative much easier.

■ When you are suddenly thrust into the role of patient representative, trying to do the right thing in the midst of noise, confusion, and sometimes conflict, it can be easy to forget that you need to take care of yourself. Getting enough sleep, eating well, and having the support of friends and family are crucial to be able to perform the role.

Conclusion

Through the privilege of being my mom's healthcare representative, I have to agree with Leonard Kish's equation: "The blockbuster drug of the century = engaged patient." In addition, I now know that the "voice of the healthcare representative" and family caregiver, as described in Chapter 7 is equally important. I thank all of the providers and healthcare representatives for listening to me as "Mom's voice." I ask you, and all healthcare providers, to keep engaging with and listening to the "voice of the patient" and the patient's caregivers and representatives.

Are you listening to the patient's voice? If not, find ways to engage with your patients and invite their participation.

Notes

1. http://www.mayoclinic.org/diseases-conditions/aphasia/basics/definition/con-20027061
2. https://www.youtube.com/watch?v=6JB-5O0ArZQ
3. http://kff.org/health-costs/poll-finding/kaiser-health-tracking-poll-september-2015/

Story 6: Concussion and Community

Jan Oldenburg, FHIMSS with Kay

Introduction

Kay is an artist who lives and works in Boise where she teaches and collaborates other artists. Early in 2014, she was in Arizona with friends, going on a rock-hunting expedition on a two-lane road. Kay was driving her car with her dog and a friend riding along, following friends in another car. A pickup coming from the other direction veered into Kay's car, hitting it near the driver's side window, smashing the whole left side of the car and knocking the rear wheel out. Kay's car spun around while the car that had hit her veered back across the road and landed in the ditch on the other side.

Her friends in the car ahead saw the accident in their rearview mirror. They came back to help and called paramedics. Kay's friends got her and her passenger out of Kay's car, then checked on the driver who had hit them. He was unconscious when they got to the car but began rousing as they talked to him. He said that something bad had happened two days before and that he had been feeling dizzy and had fainted a couple times since, and had a pounding headache.

The paramedics came, told Kay and her passenger to go to the hospital when they refused a ride in the ambulance, and took the other driver in the ambulance. Kay's friends took her and her passenger to the hospital and took the dog to an emergency vet. At the hospital Kay had x-rays and the doctors checked out her body. Her whole left side was sore, and the diagnosis was "contusions." The doctor mentioned that he'd treated the driver of the pickup before seeing Kay. He said that the pickup's driver told him "something" had happened two days before and he'd had a headache, fainting, and dizziness since. The doctor also said the other driver had been moved to a hospital in Phoenix.

Concussion

Kay went back home to Boise and her soreness lessened gradually. Although the fact that she didn't have a car to drive served as a constant reminder of the accident, the worst seemed to be behind her.

Two weeks later, however, she began having severe headaches and dizziness. The doctor she saw in Boise diagnosed her with a concussion and told her it was not unusual for symptoms to begin several weeks after the precipitating event. He sent Kay to a rehab clinic, where she saw several physical therapists. The first physical therapist treated her dizziness with movement therapy. When that didn't help, she sent Kay to someone who did more massage and muscle work. After six or seven treatments that didn't resolve the headaches, he sent her to someone who worked on her shoulder and the muscles in her neck. None of them felt their treatment was helping very much, and Kay continued to experience dizziness and severe headaches that were exacerbated by noise and movement.

In the meantime, Kay saw two additional doctors. Each recommended a variety of medications, but none seemed to help Kay's symptoms. She even seemed to suffer a paradoxical effect from several, experiencing even more intense headaches when on the medications. Kay pushed for an MRI to see if something else might be wrong, but when she finally got one it showed nothing new. Each time one of the doctors or a therapist wanted to refer Kay for additional therapy or diagnostics such as the MRI, she needed to get approval from her doctor and insurance. In each case, several weeks elapsed before she could begin the next phase of her treatment.

More than a year after treatment Kay continues to suffer from some of the concussion symptoms. It is likely that she has **postconcussion syndrome**, or **PCS**, a set of symptoms that may continue for weeks, months, or a year or more after a concussion—a minor form of traumatic brain injury (TBI). Because the symptoms can indicate other conditions or psychological factors, the diagnosis is somewhat controversial. Generally, PCS is diagnosed when at least three of the following symptoms persist more than three months after the injury: headache, dizziness, fatigue, irritability, impaired memory and concentration, insomnia, and lowered tolerance for noise and light. The reported rates of PCS vary because the inclusion criteria have not been firmly established. A diagnosis may be made when symptoms resulting from concussion last for more than three to six months after the injury.[1] Risk factors for PCS include:

- Age: the older you are, the more likely you are to experience PCS after an injury.
- Sex: women are more susceptible to PCS than men.
- Trauma: concussions that are the result of car collisions, falls, assaults, and sports injuries are often associated with postconcussion syndrome.

The likelihood of developing PCS does not seem to be associated with the intensity of the injury, nor are there any generally accepted ways to avoid it or treat it, other than rest and time. The first doctor Kay saw told her she had PCS, but since then her injury has been designated as whiplash and migraines.

Insurance

At the time of the accident, Kay had no health insurance. She became eligible for Medicare in a week and she was playing the odds. Her car had liability insurance, but it was old enough that she wasn't carrying collision insurance. She ended up with a bill of nearly $5000 from the emergency room and the full cost of buying a replacement car.

The pickup's driver was covered by a Canadian insurance company. For negotiations with Kay, they used an Arizona insurance company to represent them. A month after the accident, Kay was informed that the pickup driver's insurance would not pay any of her expenses. They had determined that the accident was caused by an aneurism, which they classified as an "act of God."

Kay challenged this because she knew that the other driver had been experiencing symptoms for at least two days and understood he had seen a doctor during that time.

Kay's subsequent treatment has been covered by Medicare, and she feels lucky not to have any prohibitions about "preexisting conditions" prohibiting her from getting coverage. The issues associated with payment for the original bill and replacement of her car are winding their way through the legal system. More than a year later, she is still exchanging letters with the pickup driver's insurance company. Her attorney originally said the insurance company would rather settle than go to court, so Kay compiled all the costs (the amount Medicare needed to be reimbursed, attorney fees and expenses, and Kay's own expenses for the car and downtime from work). Her attorney packaged that information in a letter and recently sent it to the Canadian insurance company. The company then changed its mind, and said they would go to court. Kay was able to find a firm that took her case on contingency, and she is is now waiting for resolution.

Healing and Recovery

None of Kay's providers offered an understanding of how long the symptoms might last or what she might expect during recovery. One of them suggested tracking her symptoms, but did not suggest a tool or approach. No one suggested finding a support group of others who had had concussions.

What did help was Kay's community: She has a cousin who's had a concussion and suggested ways of coping. She suggested the best earplugs to use and ways to have her community come to her so that she could control the noise level when socializing. A nurse explained how long the symptoms might last and what Kay could expect over time. A group of artist friends organized a jewelry sale to raise money for a replacement car (with lots of car-shaped and car-oriented jewelry to sell). They raised almost exactly the amount she needed—and brought fun to the process. Friends took her places, picked up groceries, and kept her company. Other friends came with information or resources to help her deal with the financial and emotional stress of the long drawn-out legal and financial issues.

Kay has learned patience in dealing with her symptoms. More than a year after the accident, she is still careful about exposing herself to too much noise and stimulation, as well as limiting TV and screen time and getting sufficient rest, as all of them—in excess—exacerbate her headaches.

Observations for Policy and Practice

When Kay thinks about the experience she had versus the one she would have liked to have had, a number of things would be different. Those issues represent opportunities for change in the system:

- Early in her treatment, Kay would have been referred to a doctor with expertise in concussions. Even if the course of treatment was not different, this would have helped Kay to feel more cared for and cared about, especially if she had received education about concussions early on.
- Someone would have recommended an app to enable her to track her symptoms and share them with doctors and physical therapists. Ideally, the app would have helped Kay recognize

patterns in her symptoms and associate them with activities that could help her address triggers.

- Kay would have received a referral to a community on the Internet that might have helped her with coping mechanisms and suggestions on how to ease her symptoms.
- Within the system, the referral process would have been streamlined so that Kay would have experienced a continuous care experience rather than one that progressed in fits and starts with long delays at each transition of care.
- At the beginning and with each new doctor, Kay would have been asked her treatment preferences, so she wouldn't have had to reiterate her desire not to be heavily medicated and to search for natural remedies. Ideally, her preferences would have been recorded and stored somewhere so each new doctor would have understood without a need for repetition.

Conclusion

The lack of coordinated care and helpful support has made Kay realize that she has to be her own advocate to understand her condition, get care that works for her, and keep the ball rolling. The financial worries, the fight with the Canadian insurer, and the ongoing disruption of her life from the symptoms have made recovery slower and more fraught with anxiety than it needed to be. Through it all, she has been deeply grateful to have the benefits of good friends, a supportive community, and a job with the flexibility to enable her to recover at her own pace.

Note

1. http://www.mayoclinic.org/diseases-conditions/post-concussion-syndrome/basics/definition/con -20032705

Story 7: Connected— But Not to My Doctors or Health System

Jan Oldenburg, FHIMSS with Elizabeth, JD

Introduction

Elizabeth is definitely a connected consumer. She lives near Washington, DC. She's at the intersection of Gen X and Gen Y and uses technology in nearly every aspect of her life as a part of the first generation to grow up with ubiquitous technology.

Living Digital

Elizabeth and her husband found each other online, using one of the early social networking sites, MySpace. When they were planning their wedding, they used "TheKnot.com" to plan the details, organize the guests, and make sure nothing was forgotten.

Hooked, when they decided it was time to buy a house, they searched for homes using Redfin.com and Trulia.com, eventually finding their home through a listing their realtor had not shown them. They also used a companion app to TheKnot.com called TheNest.com, which offers a host of useful advice on home buying, providing "expert tips and advice on finding the perfect neighborhood, agreeing on a home with your spouse, hiring a real estate agent, and getting home inspections." The site also offered them checklists, tools, and articles to help plan their married life.

It only made sense, then, that when Elizabeth and her husband contemplated pregnancy, she downloaded "TheBump.com." It offers everything baby, from advice on getting pregnant to social support and education during pregnancy, and even updates on baby developmental milestones during the first year of life. (Elizabeth used the web versions of these tools, though they've now been updated to mobile versions as well.) It helped Elizabeth predict ovulation and then track what was happening each day of her pregnancy. She even used the Q&A to check out things like what cheeses she could eat during pregnancy, and she used the app to track her weight and research questions to ask her doctor. With her first child, she also signed up to receive BabyCenter's weekly e-mails about child development and searched the site for answers to questions she was too embarrassed to ask her doctor.

Elizabeth wears a Fitbit to track her steps and exercise levels, making sure she's staying up to date on exercise and activity. She also uses Couch-to-5K and RunKeeper to track and pace her runs, and she continued to use these tracking tools throughout pregnancy and to recover her shape afterwards.

After her second child was born, she found another app, TotalBaby, to track her son's sleep, when he ate, the length of his feedings, and his diaper changes. It gave her the ability to chart at the end of each day how many times he ate, length of feedings, diaper changes, wet and bowel movements, and sleep. Those features were primarily useful during her son's first 3 months. Two years earlier, when her daughter was born, she had used a baby book to track developmental milestones, but TotalBaby made tracking much easier. After the first few months, she used TotalBaby primarily to track milestones at each doctor's visit: weight, height, length, head circumference, vaccinations, growth charts.

Her children's photographer is online, and Elizabeth and her husband downloaded pictures from the site, sent digital birth announcements, and provided access to the pictures for friends and family.

Online privacy is important to Elizabeth. Unlike many of us, she pays attention to her Facebook privacy settings. Only friends—and sometimes only specific friends—can see her posts/photos and she's only searchable to friends of friends. She is careful about when and where she shares her e-mail address and salient facts, like her due date. Most sites, however, require such information in exchange for access and tailoring. She gives it, reluctantly, when the perceived benefits of the information are high enough, but she has been dismayed at the way tailored advertising for infant and toddler products haunts her inbox—clearly the consequence of the data she shared with some of these sites. She finds it deeply dismaying to think that the small digital pieces of herself and her children that she gave up to individual sites could be combined into a metapicture of their lives and used to harm them.

Tracking Health

Clearly, Elizabeth is a connected consumer. She lives in a high-tech part of the country. She uses digital tools as part of both her home and work lives. And yet, she does not yet have a way to connect with her doctors or her children's pediatrician via secure messaging, nor does she have access to their medical records online. In turn, none of the data that she collected about her own or her children's health were accessible to her physicians. Elizabeth has found this frustrating in many ways—partly she resented the lack of convenience but she also worried about whether her family would get optimal care in an emergency.

She would like to be able to ask her children's pediatrician questions online, rather than playing telephone tag or storing her questions up for a visit—all the more true now that she has gone back to work. She would like to download the stats from her children's medical visits into her tracking tool, rather than entering them during the visit or writing them down for later entry—and her pediatrician might be interested in some of the statistics she has tracked, especially when something is amiss with one of her children.

A New Diagnosis

This issue also hit close to home in relation to Elizabeth's own health. She was recently diagnosed in the early stages of multiple sclerosis (MS).[1] Her doctors initially thought the disease might have been triggered by an adverse reaction to a vaccine, so she tried to collect her detailed medical history. She called all her former clinics to find out how to get her records, then filled out forms and sent self-addressed, stamped envelopes along with checks to each of the clinics she'd visited in her journey from childhood to adulthood: at least six doctors' offices: two neurologists, one neuro-ophthalmologist, two PCPs, one international travel clinic, and at least three MRI providers. Even with that effort, when she received the files she was still missing appropriate detail on two vaccines. It would have been extraordinarily helpful—not to mention much faster and less expensive—to have had an easy, electronic way to request and accumulate her records—or better yet, a historical record that traced her history. (This experience has made her especially careful to keep track of the details of her children's vaccinations.)

Integrated Medicine

The fragmented nature of the US healthcare system adds complexity in dealing with a multifaceted systemic illness like Elizabeth's. She is cared for by four doctors, a neurologist, a PCP and OB/GYN, and an ophthalmologist, and each doctor looks at different body systems. To her neurologist, she is a brain and a spinal cord; to her OB-GYN, she is primarily her reproductive system; to her ophthalmologist, she is an optic nerve; to her PCP, she is the result of her comprehensive metabolic panel—yet everything about her health is related. She is a very skinny person and has always worked out extensively, though sporadically, so she was shocked when her annual physical showed a high triglyceride count. This can be an early indication of a metabolic disorder, but her primary care doctor wasn't watching for that.[2] She's careful about nutrition and what her family eats, yet none of her doctors seem particularly interested in the correlations between diet and health—or autoimmune disease and the consumption of sugar.

As a result of her fragmented experience in the traditional medical system, Elizabeth has become *very* interested in functional, integrative medicine. The doctors practicing that kind of care, however, tend not to participate in insurance plans. With a tight budget and little free time, submitting her own claims and hoping for—at best—60 percent reimbursement doesn't make sense right now. When her children are older and they have more free time and more wiggle room in their budget, Elizabeth plans to start seeing a functional medicine practitioner as her PCP. She also became interested in acupuncture, essential oils, and other forms of "alternative" medicine, primarily because of their holistic approach to health; each views a person as a whole system, not as independent, compartmentalized organs and parts.

Partnership

Elizabeth has worked hard to find a team of doctors she could trust. Getting her doctors to work together was hard enough—the problem was compounded by the fact that they don't share a medical record system and Elizabeth did not have easy access to her records. She has to be a health information exchange (HIE) of one, hand-carrying medical records and test results to each of her many doctors. It also took searching to find doctors who were willing to partner with her as an informed consumer who is reading the most recent scientific studies and asking sophisticated questions. Too many of the physicians she saw dismissed her and her questions. Her current neurologist views her as a partner. For example, Elizabeth took in an article that described a controlled study in which MS patients who took beta serums were compared to those who did not—with no clinical difference in the outcomes. Her doctor had read the study and walked through the implications with her.

Last year, Elizabeth went to a well-known multispecialty clinic in the Midwest. It was before her second episode, so she had not yet been officially diagnosed with MS. She walked in with the unwieldy stack of medical records that she had collected. Her doctor was fabulous. She took the time to read all of her medical records and review them with her, take a detailed medical history, and ask questions throughout. The doctor spoke with Elizabeth's neurologist and followed up with Elizabeth afterward. Unfortunately, diagnosis was hindered by the fact that Elizabeth's records were again incomplete. Despite her efforts to gather her records, at the time she was missing what turned out to be a crucial MRI scan of her thoracic spine from 2008. This multispecialty clinic was the only place where Elizabeth had access to her records online through the MyChart application. It has been really helpful to have access to those records, but, unfortunately, that isn't where she gets regular care and their records aren't connected to any of the physicians she sees regularly.

Elizabeth had been conscientious about tracking her MS symptoms from the very beginning, before they even had a name or a diagnosis that linked them together. She has kept a journal in which she tracked every symptom, recorded what happened at every doctor's visit, and documented each exacerbation. It's filled with medications, quantities, medical journal articles, questions to ask her doctor—all the things familiar to those of us who have wrestled with an illness. She hasn't found any digital tools that simplify the tracking process or help her correlate symptoms and activities.

MS is an odd illness. Doctors treat you for it before you have an official diagnosis—usually because it takes time for the distinctive changes that definitively signal MS has shown up. It wasn't until Elizabeth's second acute episode, 5 years after her first, and an MRI showing changes distinctive to MS that she received an official diagnosis. She's now admitted to herself that she has MS and has begun adjusting to that new reality.

Current Reality

In the 6 months since the initial interview, Elizabeth and her husband decided to switch to a new, concierge PCP practice that better fits into their connected lives. In exchange for an annual membership fee of $300 each, they now have 24/7 access to a doctor or nurse practitioner via messaging and e-mail, an app to refill prescriptions and make appointments, and access to Google Hangouts with their doctor. The first experience in scheduling an appointment was great—they had next-day access for new member appointments. A friend recommended the practice to them and it offers the kind of connected access that they want, though at this stage of their lives the membership fee feels like a luxury they can ill afford; however, they would pay that amount in a heartbeat for more connected access to their children's pediatrician. Through the portal, Elizabeth has access to the record of all care at the clinic.

In the intervening months, her children's pediatrician has also begun offering online access. Elizabeth and her husband find that the online tools are great, but it is still frustrating that they don't include any historical information, nor are they interconnected with any specialty care.

Observations for Policy and Practice

Elizabeth's experience of being very connected in the rest of her life and being impatient with the healthcare system is increasingly common. We can find a number of lessons for improvement from the experience and expectations of a connected consumer like Elizabeth:

- Consumers are impatient with the slow pace of the healthcare system in providing convenience and connection. Like Elizabeth online access as well as integrated care.
- Far too few people have access to electronic versions of their current records, much less access to historical records and the ability to transfer digital versions from one physician and care system to another.
- Few good symptom/activity tracking applications exist—and those that are developed tend—like our Western medical system—to focus on one body system at a time. Increasingly, we are growing to understand the connections between body and mind, nutrition and health, as well as the interconnected nature of body systems. Tools for tracking health need to figure out how to build connections between symptoms in diverse organ systems, as well as ways to link behaviors, symptoms, and environmental factors.
- Consumers like Elizabeth also need far more ability to understand what data are being stored and shared about them, and with whom—and the ability to control that sharing at a granular level, even if it means paying a price for otherwise "free" services in order to manage and control their privacy and access to data stored about them.

Conclusion

As a twenty-first-century consumer who is managing a complex health condition as well as monitoring the health and development of her children, Elizabeth would like the healthcare system to catch up to her. She would like to be treated in a system that is as digital, connected, and convenient as the rest of her life: one where portable and interconnected electronic records follow you from birth, where physicians and patients can all communicate as a care team with access to the same data and the comments of others, where she has control over access and privacy, and where there are tools to help her correlate her symptoms to other things in her environment—and easily share those correlations with her doctors. She would also like to be treated in a system that takes for granted that she is a partner and a savvy member of her own care team.

Notes

1. http://www.webmd.com/multiple-sclerosis/guide/multiple-sclerosis-symptoms
2. http://www.medscape.com/viewarticle/754979

Story 8: Ineffectual Transitions of Care Can Contribute to Death

In loving memory of Betty Volm

Introduction

Several months ago my family and I buried my mother. She was 85, and she died from an acute—but treatable—infectious disease. The circumstances leading to her death spanned several weeks from when she was ill at home to the time she was in the hospital. Her death was untimely, as she did not have cancer or an end-stage chronic disease. There was a delay in treatment from when my mother presented to the ER and was sent home to when she was started on intravenous antibiotics during her subsequent hospitalization. The delay in treatment most likely contributed to her death. In the end, when it became clear that the situation was futile, life support measures were withdrawn and she died peacefully in a hospice facility. My family eulogized our mother in a very moving ceremony.

Being a physician, I was not allowed downtime for grieving or exhaustion. I returned to work on Monday after the Friday funeral and immediately tried to catch up on patient care activities and running the business of my medical practice. All the while, I was sorely missing my mother, fooling myself into believing that I was at peace with her death. Finally, it came to me in a reflective moment on Easter Sunday that there was more that I needed to share about my mother's death that I hadn't said at her memorial service.

A Tech-Savvy Consumer

My mother believed in the power of the electronic medical record (EMR) and was hoping to live to see the day when healthcare providers shared information electronically as a matter of routine. She died before this vision became a reality. My mother was very well educated on the topic of electronic medical records and health information exchange because, like most mothers, she was

---

* @EMRSurvival

interested in my career and wanted to support me. About 12 years ago when my previous practice went live on our first EMR, my mom came to visit and watched the children so that I could stay late at the office each night during that first week and not have to worry about getting home. Ever since that day, most of our phone conversations included her query about how the medical records business was going. She didn't use the terms "EMR" or "health information exchange," but she would cut out articles and send them to me in the mail about both of these topics, as she knew that I was an early adopter of EMR and a pioneer in the field of health information exchange.

I have been sharing a summary of care records electronically with other providers since 2005. I also had an early interest in personal health records and I created a Consumer Empowerment National Demonstration (CEND) personal health record for my mother 7 years ago. She kept it up for a bit, but over time her medications and health conditions changed, and since it was an untethered personal health record, it was difficult for her to maintain.

She was very happy when her primary care doctor, of whom she was very fond, started using an EMR. When he referred my mom to a new specialist, she would ask the specialist if he or she was able to look up her information in the computer system and it perplexed her that sometimes they had access to her electronic medical record and sometimes not. She was very frustrated that her specialists didn't routinely share information about her care with her primary care provider. Sometimes when her medical conditions were not responding to her treatment plan, her primary care doctor would call her other physicians to discuss her case. She was very appreciative of these telephone communications.

Failed Transition of Care

A contributing factor to my mother's death was that she had an ineffectual transition of care. Her death could just as easily have been the untimely death of one of my own patients. My hope is that, by sharing this story, other deaths might be prevented. My mom and I lived in different states, but the failures that contributed to her untimely death are the same issues that could lead to adverse events when my own patients experience a transition of care from their home to an acute care facility.

Failure to Deliver Tests Results to Primary Care Office

An initial communication error was the ineffectual data sharing of test results between the emergency room and my mother's primary care physician. Let's face it: One of the negative consequence of hospitals moving from paper records to an electronic medical record is that emergency room test results are no longer faxed or mailed to the primary care physician. For my mother this meant that the negative stool culture and the lack of testing for *Clostridium difficile* by the emergency room, both critical pieces of information, were not delivered to her primary care physician. If he had been alerted to these test results, he would most likely have ordered further testing and, ultimately, lifesaving antibiotics could have been started sooner.

I encounter this same issue with my own patients when crucial lab tests from treatment in the ER are not delivered to me. The majority of my patients go to a hospital that is on a different EMR than my practice. My office staff must log in to the hospital EMR several times each day to print out labs on our patients seen in the emergency room. My staff is not allowed to route test results electronically for two of the three hospitals where I am on staff, and for this reason emergency room labs are printed and handed to the physician.

Failure to Exchange Office Notes with Hospitalist

A second communication lapse occurred when my mother's condition deteriorated and she returned a second time to the hospital emergency room and was admitted to the hospital. She was admitted on a Sunday and her primary care provider's office was not open. It is possible that if she had been admitted during the week that a transition of care record could have been created by her primary care provider and shared with the hospitalist who was caring for my mother. My mother's mental status and her physical exam findings were very different on admission than at the time of her last encounter with her primary care provider. If the hospitalist had been aware of these critical changes in her status, perhaps the impending sepsis could have been identified and treated sooner.

Inaccurate Medication Reconciliation

The third error was inaccurate medication reconciliation at the time of my mother's second hospitalization. My mother had an up-to-date list of her medications that she brought with her to the hospital ER on her first encounter with the emergency room, but at the time of the second encounter her condition had declined and she was less clear about her medications. In the days leading up to her hospitalization, her primary care physician had made some changes to her medications. The lack of a concise listing of medications was unfortunate as her mental status changes were initially attributed to drug interactions rather than impending sepsis. If an up-to-date medication list had been requested from her primary care office, it is possible that the correct diagnosis would have been made sooner. It is very important that ambulatory and acute care facilities share information during transitions of care. Increasingly across the United States, hospitalists are caring for patients on behalf of primary care providers. I use the services of hospitalists, as does my mother's primary care physician. I have implemented the following practices to ensure that my patients receive the best possible transition of care.

Best Practices for Optimal Transitions of Care

When a patient contacts the office by telephone or my cell phone after hours and it is deemed that going to the emergency room is the best plan of action, I complete the following steps:

- Create a telephone encounter in the EMR, explaining the present illness.
- Create a transition of care referral.
- EMR generates a summary of care record.
- Fax all of the files to the hospital emergency room.
- Call the emergency room and speak to the staff to alert them to expect a fax on my patient and to call me back if they do not receive the fax.

This last step is very important because frequently the fax will fail and the files will have to be resent to a different fax number.

There are times when my patients will present to the hospital without my knowledge. I have requested that the hospitalist service contact me when my patients are admitted, but sometimes this does not happen.

When a patient is seen in the office and it is deemed that the patient needs to go to the emergency room, the same steps are followed. In addition, I also call the hospital and request to be transferred to the clinical staff in the ER to give my impression of the situation.

When a patient is seen in the office and it is clear that the patient needs to be admitted to the hospital, I complete the following steps:

- Complete the office encounter, print it out, and hand it to the patient to bring to the hospital to give it to the nurse on admission.
- Contact the hospitalist service by phone and determine which provider will be responsible for admitting my patient.
- Discuss the case on the phone with the hospitalist.

The Potential for Health Information Exchange to Improve Transitions of Care

A more optimal situation to deal with transitions of care between ambulatory and acute care facilities includes implementation of health information exchange service provider (HISP)-to-HISP exchanges between ambulatory EMRs and hospital information systems. Unfortunately, HISP-to-HISP exchanges are in limited use across the country. Widespread participation in health information exchanges that allow for the sharing of ambulatory EMR-generated files with emergency rooms or hospitalist services and emergency room test results with the patient's primary care physician would be an additional way to improve transitions of care. Currently in my medical practice, we continue to utilize multiple media to capture the necessary data to ensure that our patients' transitions of care are as effective as possible. The additional effort is worth it to ensure our patients' safety, but it costs time and money that would better be spent on care.

Observations for Policy and Practice

- Patient safety dictates that we find ways to simplify the process and increase the number of electronic record transfers between clinics and hospitals to minimize the opportunity for errors due to incomplete information. These include both hospitals and physicians participating in local and regional health information exchanges (HIEs), ensuring that EHR-to-EHR transfers are priorities, and encouraging patients to take ownership of their own records by downloading copies.
- While we wait, physicians can improve this process for their patients by being hypervigilant to ensure that hospitals receive up-to-date records on their patients upon admission and ensuring that they receive discharge summaries as soon as possible, as well as by following the best practices outlined here previously.
- Hospitals must adopt procedures that include requesting records electronically or by fax on every patient to maximize the likelihood that they will receive up-to-date records.
- Patients, family members, and caregivers can sign up for portals, download copies of their records frequently, and bring all paperwork with them upon admission to the hospital, as well as medication lists and actual pill bottles. This story also highlights additional questions for family members and caregivers to ask hospitalists: Have you talked to the primary care doctor? Do you have an up-to-date list of medications? Are you aware of the previous hospitalization? Has anyone reconciled the medications?

Conclusion

In closing, I have learned much in life and now in death from my mother. I will continue to be ever vigilant for my patients who have a change in their medical condition that requires them to seek care in a hospital. I will make sure that I review information in a timely fashion and communicate effectively with the emergency room physicians and hospitalists who care for my patients. I will continue to advocate for the advancement of health information exchange in the United States to ensure that the most up-to-date information is available at transitions of care and hopefully prevent other untimely deaths. In addition, I hope this provides caregivers with some additional questions to ask to help protect a loved one who may be experiencing an ineffective transition of care.

Story 9: Do I Really Have to Do the Follow-Up? My Eight-Week Breast Cancer Journey

Anna-Lisa Silvestre, MPH*

Introduction

When I got the call that my biopsy showed a malignant tumor, my knees actually buckled. My mind went blank, then I screamed inside my head. The words "breast cancer" appeared in my mind like a glaring neon sign.

I've always gotten my mammograms on schedule, but this time I put it off. I had a funny feeling in my stomach every time I thought about it. In early January, not wanting to face my primary care physician without having it done, I scheduled it for a Friday morning prior to my afternoon appointment with her. My registration slip that afternoon did not show the next scheduled mammogram, but I didn't think anything of it. I figured the data hadn't transferred yet and felt smug about my knowledge of clinical systems.

I was very wrong; the data were withheld since the result was in question.

"Please Come in for a Recheck of Your Mammogram"

On Monday afternoon I was in the car with my husband returning from a long weekend away. My phone rang, and it was the scheduling clerk in the mammography unit. She let me know I needed to return because "Your mammogram isn't clear and the doctor wants to recheck it." Recheck it? Didn't they know I had dense breasts? Did they look at the previous mammograms I'd had in the same department? Was it a new radiologist? These questions ran through my head and I told my husband, "This is a waste of 2 hours; they won't find anything." He calmly told me, "I think they just want to be safe." OK, I thought, I'll do it for them.

It never occurred to me that there was anything to worry about.

When I returned just 4 days later, I knew something was up when the technician turned left down the hall instead of the usual right turn to the mammography room. The room we entered had two

* @ALSilvestre

pieces of x-ray equipment, not just one. The first x-ray machine took a picture of my right breast from a very specific angle. Hmmm, that's not the usual mammogram, I thought. The technician said she would have the radiologist take a look at the film and left the room. A couple minutes later, she stationed me at the second machine, and this time I felt more pressure on my breast than in any previous mammogram. Again the technician went to check with the radiologist and returned with, "She'd like you to get an ultrasound." I started to feel a bit unsteady as she walked me across the hall to yet another exam room. The ultrasound took just a couple of minutes, and again the technician trotted down the hall to confer with the mysterious radiologist. A couple of tears ran down the side of my face as I waited.

An Architectural Distortion

After a bit of waiting, the radiologist walked into the room. She radiated competence and was beautifully composed, which was slight comfort given why she came. My first thought was, "I'm hosed. She's not coming in to tell me to come back in a year." I didn't hear another word until she said "Your mammogram showed what we call an architectural distortion. It is not a cyst, since it has no fluid. I strongly advise you to have a (needle) biopsy, which I can do in about an hour."

Tears streaming down my face, I asked her "Do I have time to go home and take some medication?" I don't remember what happened next but apparently I drove home, took a sedative and a pain killer (approved by the radiologist), and texted my friend Rose for a ride to and from the appointment. Rose is the very person you want to be with in an uncertain medical situation. She doesn't wring her hands or over-react. "Step at a time," she always says.

Back in the exam room I was shown the first needle, containing a local anesthetic, which was deceptively tiny. The radiologist told me the shot would sting like crazy for about 10 seconds, then not at all. She was right; it felt like fire inside my breast that was quickly doused. The second needle didn't cause any pain, and then my breast was fully numb. The radiologist told me the biopsy needle would feel like a quick punch inside my breast. It felt just like getting your ears pierced, only in the wrong location. She inserted a small tag, called a radio opaque clip, at the location of the tumor so it could be easily found if needed for surgery.

Researching to Alleviate Stress

It was then Friday afternoon, and the results weren't expected for 3 or 4 days. The weekend was difficult. I alternated between feeling strident, "Get the damn thing out!" and being in denial, "No way this is real." I spent hours online, viewing photos of tumors, reading breast cancer message boards, learning about breast cancer stages and grades—interspersed with intermittently crying. I just couldn't believe it was happening to *me*—I don't have any cancer in my family. I exercised and ate fairly healthy foods (OK, the occasional chips and dip). Uh, oh, could it be the hormone replacement therapy I had been taking for over 10 years? Was I supposed to have just one glass of red wine, or was that for heart disease? Didn't all the blueberries I ate count for something? I felt sick.

On Monday, I was in San Francisco at a high-profile healthcare investment conference. The room was a sea of men in dark suits, talking practically nose to nose. The few women at the conference appeared to be wearing Manolo Blahnik-like high heels and tight skirts—the whole scene looked like a surreal episode of *Mad Men*. As a 59-year-old woman, I definitely felt like a fish out of water.

Diagnosis

As I stood in a line, my cell phone rang. It was the nurse from the clinic. She quickly got to the point, "The biopsy results are back. As we suspected, the tumor is malignant." That's when my knees buckled. I numbly confirmed an appointment to return in a few days and then turned to my boss and with a sob blurted out, "I have breast cancer." He gave me a hug and whispered the right words, "Let's get you out of here. There's a restaurant across the street." I remember hoping it had a good bar.

Feeling a need to dull the shock, I ordered a Bloody Mary and some French fries. This was a good excuse to blatantly ignore nutritional guidelines. My "diagnosis diet" helped me during certain points along my journey, but I eventually returned to my (mostly) plant-based diet. But that day I ate, drank, and sobbed. I called my husband to share the news as I walked around Union Square in a daze. My makeup was ruined, which in most cases doesn't matter, but this time, I felt a need to "chin up" and return to the conference. The Chanel counter at Saks Fifth Avenue beckoned. I planted myself on a stool and dramatically announced, "I just got diagnosed with breast cancer; can you fix me?" Ironically, I bought bright pink lipstick for the first time. By midafternoon, I felt better and waded back into the sea of suits. Denial and pink lipstick worked hand in hand for a few hours.

During an early evening reception my new health status caught up to me and the neon sign was glaring brightly. The party was packed with the same sea of suits. Everyone was talking loudly about topics that no longer seemed to matter. I quickly found the stairs and descended with tears pouring down my face. No one seemed to notice until I literally ran into a female colleague. I blurted, "I have breast cancer and have to leave now." She gave me the kind of big hug women give to each other when words aren't sufficient.

By Friday, my husband (who happens to be an internist) completed his own research on early stage breast cancer, treatment options, and various outcome studies. Without saying so, we were making a team decision (although I knew the final choice was really mine) on the treatment plan. Having him as my "wingman" turned out to be an essential part of my care experience. Just as we were included in the *care team*, I quickly realized I had an equally powerful *patient team*. While the neon sign kept flashing in my head, my patient team expanded with friends, neighbors, and family who offered support, food, and company.

My husband wanted to make sure the breast cancer had a zero chance of returning. He heavily favored—and I nearly did as well—a double mastectomy and surgical breast reconstruction. At one point, I even felt slightly giddy at the concept of getting a fat transfer for the reconstruction from my hips and buttocks. In my view, I'd end up with a double win: perkier breasts and smaller hips and buttocks. I shared my thinking with my walking friend, Debbie, and proclaimed, "What's not to like!"

I felt courageous and confident. The neon sign glared a bit less.

Consultation

Next up was a consultation at the Breast Care Clinic. Our clinic appointment followed a "tumor board" meeting earlier that morning. This is an interdisciplinary case conference that includes specialists in breast cancer, among other conditions. They review patients' relevant clinical information and determine treatment options and recommendations. That morning the meeting included my eventual oncologist, the surgical radiologist, a surgeon, and the breast care coordinator.

Afterward, it struck me that I wasn't invited. After all, it's my tumor they were talking about, right?

The opportunity for a shared decision arrived just hours later. My husband and I were ushered into an exam room and offered some refreshments. We could tell it would be a long morning. One by one, the breast care clinic providers came in and introduced themselves, told us what to expect, and then went over my results to date. The breast care coordinator set the stage and handed me a fat binder with a lot of information, including a simple paper log to track my progress, which helped me to focus on what is known now versus imagining worst-case scenarios. That damn neon sign kept flashing—I began to think it would never turn off.

The surgical radiologist came into the room, shared what he saw on the x-rays and ultrasound, and then did a breast exam. Next came the surgeon to discuss the treatment options and for good measure, I guessed, did another breast exam. The tumor board laid out two options: a partial mastectomy (just one breast) or a lumpectomy. If the cancer had not spread to my lymph nodes (indicating a spread of cancer), I was eligible for a relatively new procedure: intraoperative radiation therapy (IORT). We learned that IORT is given in a concentrated dose during surgery, directly into the cavity after the tumor is taken out. It can eliminate the need for further radiation while sparing healthy tissues. I imagined the radiation and neon sign in a futuristic sci-fi battle. I hoped radiation would win that round.

Our care experience followed an ideal script for what's called "patient engagement." We were given time to ask questions, probe "what if?" scenarios, and learn about clinical evidence for alternate treatment options. I remember cutting to the chase by asking, "Is the risk of recurring breast cancer greater than the risk of a double mastectomy and reconstruction?" The surgeon paused and stated, "A double mastectomy with reconstruction is a 10+ hour surgery. The lumpectomy is the minimal necessary surgery that I would recommend to a family member." That's all I needed to hear. Several days in the hospital would unnecessarily expose me to other risks. Lumpectomy and hopefully the intraoperative radiation it was.

Surgery was set for 2 weeks later, which provided me time to process the next wave of information and take care of obligations. I plunged into work—both to clear the decks for time away and as a way to escape from the neon sign that began flashing in my head as soon as I woke up in the morning. A week before surgery, I stopped drinking alcohol and also permanently stopped taking hormone replacement therapy (which had been a savior for wicked hot flashes during menopause). I rested and tried to meditate as much as I could before the big day. I wasn't nervous.

Surgery

My surgery was on January 30, just a few weeks from the initial diagnosis on January 9. I started in a department called Nuclear Medicine (a name ripe for becoming more patient friendly) to help identify the precise location of the tumor. They inserted a needle to pinpoint the location for the surgeon.

They didn't let me walk across the street to the hospital with a needle in my breast for safety reasons, so we were escorted by shuttle to the hospital entrance. The surgery was performed in a brand-new outpatient surgery center, which has beautiful nature murals on the walls instead of the usual off-white walls. As a pregnant nurse rolled me into the operating room, she held my hand and offered reassuring words. It's true what they say about the power of "hands-on care." That turned out to be the most important healing gesture of my care experience. I call her my nurse-angel.

Fortunately, the cancer had not spread to my lymph nodes, which allowed the radiologist to administer the IORT for 40 minutes directly into the breast cavity after the surgeon removed the tumor. It would be all the radiation that I required. I woke up in the recovery room to a nurse cracking not very funny jokes. I really wanted him to quiet down and hold my hand like my operating room nurse-angel, but he had other ideas. Maybe guys like jokes after getting ACL surgery, but those of us who wake up to a tender and deformed body part want some hand holding.

Treatment

I went home with a sizeable piece of my right breast missing. The surgeon told me it would "fill out" over time. Clearly that will take months, I thought. Oddly, I felt protective and tender toward this breast, despite the deformity. When the biopsy report came back, the news was positive. The cancer was smaller than two centimeters, stage 1A, and a grade 2 (the only subjective finding). Significantly, it was also 100 percent "estrogen-receptor-positive breast cancer," which measured a group of my breast cancer genes. Estrogen-receptor-positive breast cancer means the risk of recurrence can be lowered through hormone therapy.

My care was then transferred to an oncologist who requested an "Oncotype dx" test, which helps determine the risk of recurrence and whether chemotherapy treatment is warranted. If the risk score is less than 18, chemotherapy is not recommended. If it's over 30, chemo is highly recommended. The numbers in between seem harder to judge. I was happy when my score was 19, since I think 19 is pretty much the same number as 18. My oncologist agreed with my numbering system and ruled out chemotherapy. It turned out, though, that I wasn't completely off the hook for more treatment.

Hormone therapy is a misnomer, since my prescription for an aromatase inhibitor suppresses the estrogen that can feed a tumor. I call it "antihormone therapy." I will take this for 5 years. After a few weeks I began to experience frequent hot flashes accompanied by sweating. "Just grand," my mother would say. I also was prescribed an infusion of *Zometa* every 6 months.

Studies show that Zometa can help reduce the risk of cancer recurrence when it's included from the start in treating hormone-receptor-positive early stage breast cancer in postmenopausal and older premenopausal women. So a couple times a year I become part of the cancer community in the infusion clinic, only I keep all my hair and I don't vomit afterward.

The combination of a lumpectomy, intraoperative radiation, medication, and the infusions shaves points off my recurrence score. "Go menopause!" became a new mantra for me, since treatment options available only for postmenopausal women were available to me.

While my treatment plan will extend for 5 years, after 6 months my neon sign, "I have breast cancer," flickers rarely. Now, "I *had* breast cancer."

Observations for Policy and Practice

My story illustrates some best practices that can be implemented more broadly to support patients in similar situations:

- Preventive reminders are effective. I didn't find the many reminders I got annoying and, in fact, they prompted me to finally get it scheduled. I didn't read all the words in each reminder; just seeing "you are due for your mammogram" worked.
- Providing access to resources, information, and support can help people cope with the emotional toll of the experience. For example, provide links to reputable websites that have more detailed information; I found a 44-page annotated bibliography on lifestyle and cancer risk

(http://radonc.ucsf.edu/patient_information/pdf/nutrition_breast.pdf). It illustrates that we still have a gap between what is considered "medical knowledge" and other disciplines that have powerful effects on our minds and bodies, but that are not considered "mainstream medicine." I didn't happen to find online or in-person support groups especially helpful, but others might.

■ Creating a coordinated experience from the patient perspective is critical to helping patients and families cope with a difficult diagnosis and feel a part of the process. To do this, involve patients as much as possible. Ask patients with breast cancer to share their end-to-end patient experience that goes across departments and time spans. There is no survey that asks questions like, "What was your experience in recovery?" or "Did you ever feel your care was unsafe?" I would have answered with, "Don't tell jokes" and, "The van driver should help the patient directly into the van instead of letting a woman with a needle in her breast bump her head on the way in." And asking the question, "What single experience mattered the most?" would have gotten my answer about nurse-angels.

■ Recognize that a patient team is as important as the care team. Family and friends are important resources for patients. It's simple to ask patients who is supporting them and then encourage them to let others know what they are going through.

■ Finally, remember that patients appreciate when you reach out. Think about sending cards or secure messages to patients a week after a surgery with a thank-you and "How are you doing?"

For Patients

■ Don't try to be tough. Ask your friends and family for help. A group of women in my neighborhood became amazing friend-angels. I often heard, "I want to bring you a meal; please let me bring you a meal." A friend from Orange County insisted on coming to help. Her humor and perspective made a big difference. I called a friend to ask, "Can you get me groceries and something to make for dinner? I can't bear to make decisions or be in a store." People can only help if they know what you are going through.

■ Jump in. It helps to look up every term you hear, and understand what is going on. I am still intrigued by the term "architectural distortion," which is what the radiologist saw on my first mammogram. It's your body and your care plan, and with some knowledge you will feel stronger and more in control. If you are visual, ask for a drawing or a picture. Ask which online references are credible and don't be afraid to bring up a treatment option you read about or heard from someone else. Not every physician will be on top of current treatment options; you can help out by scanning what is online. Physicians will help to put options into perspective. Write down your side effects as they occur and look for ways to make it easier on yourself. It's a great time to paint, draw, or even glue objects on paper that will help you express what's going on inside.

For Family and Friends

■ Don't ask, "What can I do?" Instead, be specific: "I'll bring you dinner on Thursday" is easier than "Can I cook for you?" Text or call when you are at a grocery store to find out if the person needs anything.

■ If you don't have words, send a card that expresses that you care.

■ Don't let your own discomfort get in the way of providing support.

Conclusion

My care experience was optimal and available today to patients at Kaiser Permanente. Every patient deserves to have physicians who communicate with each other without being prompted, appointments and prescriptions coordinated on their behalf, and the ability to view their records and e-mail care team members with questions. My care was timely: Only 8 weeks elapsed between my initial mammogram and the start of long-term treatment. Because I have excellent health insurance, I only had a copay of $5 for each 90-day prescription. The genome test costs ~$4000, but it was covered by my insurance, as it was clinically relevant to inform my treatment plan. While the clinic ended up with a lower cost, as I didn't have to undergo chemotherapy, it was my doctor who made the decision, not the health plan. I felt my care was safe and appropriate; I didn't worry whether one of the clinicians was making a decision to further his or her research or earn more money by recommending one option over another. My patient team formed organically and my loving wingman, Victor, helped me stay sane during a tough time. I am very grateful for the excellent care and service I received at Kaiser Permanente in Oakland, California.

Story 10: Grateful

Jan Oldenburg, FHIMSS with Kevin Fowler*

Introduction

Kevin always knew that it was possible he would end up with polycystic kidney disease (PKD). It is a genetic disease, after all, and his mother had had it. It's characterized by the formation of numerous cysts in the kidneys leading to reduced kidney function and, sometimes, kidney failure. So it wasn't a complete shock when he was diagnosed with it in 2001—but it didn't make it any less scary. At that time, his children were 10 months and 3 years old. Kevin was working for Pfizer and living in St. Louis. He had the advantages of good health insurance and a supportive employer.

Diagnosis

Going in for his first nephrology appointment, Kevin was nervous. He had watched his mother live with the disease, watched her go on dialysis, and watched her die at 52 of lung cancer. When you are on dialysis you are more susceptible to other illnesses, including cancer. His first appointment was on March 6, his mother's birthday. The nephrologist he saw was a really good teacher, with excellent interpersonal skills—exactly what you want when you are diagnosed with a life-altering condition. In Kevin's very first visit, his nephrologist explained a lot about kidney transplantation and how to avoid dialysis. He went on to discuss how a "preemptive" kidney transplant would allow Kevin to avoid dialysis completely. His nephrologist estimated it would be 5 to 7 years before he would need a kidney transplant, but when the time came, he thought Kevin would be an excellent candidate for this treatment option.

His doctor's positive perspective on Kevin's future was infectious. Kevin hadn't been aware that a preemptive transplant was even an option, and it was reassuring to know from the beginning that there would be an alternative to dialysis. He walked into the appointment feeling very afraid and walked out with a lot of hope and confidence.

---

* @gratefull080504

Getting Involved with Addressing His Condition

It was clear immediately that Kevin would have a role in keeping himself healthy. He understood that cardiovascular disease would be a potential issue after the kidney transplant. As a result, he began to exercise more frequently and monitor his blood pressure. He began experiencing persistent anemia soon after his diagnosis, so he started Epogen, a treatment for anemia, 6 months later. At that time, Kevin also made some modifications in his diet. Because unhealthy kidneys have difficulty removing excess phosphorus from the blood, he minimized intake of foods that were high in phosphorus, such as beer, milk products, and high-protein foods. He also began to drink a lot more water and avoided soft drinks.

His wife got them involved with the Polycystic Kidney Disease Foundation, and they began actively raising funds. His wife resurrected the local St. Louis PKD chapter and organized several fund-raising walks for the PKD Foundation.

With appropriate care, Kevin was able to maintain a demanding job, working with no limitations.

Renal Failure

Kevin's kidney function declined more rapidly than anticipated, however. The first sign was that the 24-hour kidney test that he received annually showed a marked decline in his kidney function from the previous year. He began to have back pain associated with the cysts, as well as pain from enlarged kidneys. With the decline in his kidney function he also began to experience chronic fatigue. He continued working, but it was definitely harder. However, he was able to maintain his level of energy and focus.

In January 2004, 3 years after his original diagnosis, his doctor told him that he was going into renal failure and would need a transplant in the next 6 to 12 months. Since Kevin had decided to have a preemptive kidney transplant, he needed to find a donor. His wife sent an e-mail notifying their friends about his condition and they began talking openly about Kevin's situation and his need for a kidney. They were astonished at the number of people who wanted to help. About 14 people volunteered to be tested—friends, work colleagues, acquaintances from church. Kevin and select volunteers went through tissue matching testing. Out of the four people tested, Kevin was blessed to find a match, a friend of the family. (As of June 2015, there were 101,367 people waiting for a donor kidney according to the United Network for Organ Sharing [UNOS] website.[1])

Transplant

By May of 2004, Kevin knew he had a donor and a match, and they could move forward with scheduling the surgery. Kevin's was scheduled for August 5, 2004. He was admitted the night before to begin some of the medications and preparation. His dad, sister, and wife were all with him. He remembers talking with both his doctor and his donor, and feeling at peace.

The surgery itself took 5 hours. He woke up after the transplant in a lot of pain, but already feeling better. His native kidneys were left in place and eventually would no longer function. The disease, PKD, does not recur in the new kidney, and patients with this disease tend to have better outcomes than other kidney transplant recipients.

Kevin had a very good experience at the hospital in St. Louis. He was in a lot of pain the first few days, but very motivated to do well. The staff got him on his feet immediately, so Kevin spent the 3 days before his discharge walking the halls with his IV. His donor was discharged before he was, also recovering well.

Two weeks after surgery, he was well enough to go to Mass. It was an exhilarating experience, where he could really feel the impact of all the people who had been praying for him and his family, as well as the joy of a new lease on life.

Each day, Kevin takes seven or eight medications as well as vitamins, some to suppress his immune system and prevent it from rejecting the kidney. That adds up to 16 pills a day. When he first got home from the hospital, the number of pills and getting used to how and when they needed to be taken felt overwhelming, though by now it is routine. One of the reasons that kidney transplants fail is that patients stop taking their medications as instructed, which underscores both the importance of the medications and the importance of medication adherence.[2] Tools to help patients understand and manage medications, especially during that overwhelming time when they first leave the hospital, are very helpful. Prior to his kidney transplant, his care team educated him on the importance of complying with his medication regimen. Resources are available to help patients stay aware that failure to take medications on schedule may result in loss of their transplanted kidney.

After almost 3 months of recovery, Kevin returned to work. The psychosocial adjustment after being confronted with his mortality at age 43 took some time. For the first year post-transplant, Kevin really struggled, asking himself questions like: How long will my transplanted kidney last? How long will I live? Emotionally, he was overwhelmed. When he went to his post-transplant team looking for help, he did not find the answers he was looking for. Through perseverance and experimentation, he found a path to help him adjust post-transplant. He began working out frequently. The physical exercise provided a nice antidote to the side effects he experienced with some of his medications. He practiced meditation and journal writing. By consistently applying this routine, Kevin began to feel better about his future and became stronger. In Kevin's opinion, this is an area that is critically important but is not well understood by most in the transplant community.

A New Life

It has now been over 11 years since Kevin's transplant, and his renal function has remained stable the entire time. He is very aware that not all patients experience this type of clinical experience. In fact, at 10 years, less than half of transplanted kidneys are still functioning.[3] His life is good. The woman who donated a kidney to him has become a part of their extended family. He has productive work, much of it connected to his transplant and his desire to "give back" in gratitude for his life. He has worked in transplant marketing and recently consulted for a company preparing to launch a post-transplant diagnostic test. He wants to stay in a field that is related to his mission. He continues to volunteer and was recently appointed to a 2-year term with the Kidney Health Initiative, serving on their Patient Family Partnership Council. His experience with the transplant has taught him the importance of self-care and self-management.

He has noted that the US healthcare system is focused upon 1-year patient and graft survival rather than long-term health and outcomes for kidney transplant recipients. The average cost of a kidney transplant in 2011 was $262,900.[4] It is expensive, but when you consider that the annual cost of keeping someone on dialysis is $80,000, it is a good return on investment, paying for itself within 2 years if there is no re-hospitalization in the first year.[5] About 75 percent of a transplant's cost is before or during the transplant, while about 25 percent of the costs are allocated for post-transplant care during the first year. Kevin is reliant on his insurance to pay the annual cost of medications, his monthly lab work, and checkups.

Kevin participated in online kidney disease forums for a while, but he did not find value from these communities. One of his coping strategies has been to be and stay positive, and he works hard to keep negative influences out of his life.

Observations for Policy and Practice

In an article written on the tenth anniversary of his transplant, Kevin made recommendations about the opportunities for change in transplantation policies and approaches. He notes that in July 2014 the American Society of Transplant launched the Transplantation Immunology Research Network to encourage research to achieve the goal of improving quality of life and outcomes for all transplant recipients. This action will hopefully result in additional transplant research to improve long-term outcomes and foster greater collaboration with the transplant community.

Kevin's recommendations for change follow[6]:

- Outcome incentives: As a starting point, the Centers for Medicare and Medicaid Services should add additional reimbursement incentives for 5-year outcomes and a phased plan for 10-year outcomes. While transplant centers are under tremendous pressure to expand the number of transplant recipients, which can have an adverse impact on outcomes, they should be rewarded for providing care and services that result in superior long-term outcomes.
- Health literacy and care management incentives: If you speak to any transplant professional, everyone will tell you that having patients conform to their immunosuppressant regimen is a challenge. Education and counseling about immunosuppressant medications should be a continual process rather than a 10-minute discussion while being discharged from the hospital. For example, after surgery, Kevin struggled with the side effects he experienced with his regimen. However, once his transplant team told him he could return to his exercise routine, his workouts offset the side effects, and he felt mentally stronger. Healthcare providers should be able to earn incentives for this educational service and be rewarded with additional reimbursement for effective outcomes and interventions.
- Comprehensive Immunosuppressive Drug Coverage for Kidney Transplant Patients Act of 2013 (H.R. 1428/S. 323): Currently, Medicare B provides coverage of immunosuppressant medications for 3 years. The comprehensive immunosuppressive bill would extend immunosuppressive coverage beyond 3 years. To Kevin, it is a no-brainer. On average, an annual immunosuppression regimen costs $25,000. If a patient does not have access to immunosuppressant medications because of cost, the lack of access will lead to graft loss and initiation of dialysis to maintain life. The annual cost of dialysis is $75,000.
- Clinical research into long-term outcomes: The Long Term Deterioration of Kidney Allograft Failure (DeKAF) Study was completed in April 2015. This decade-long study should provide insights into the causes of late graft dysfunction and guide the development of interventional clinical trials to prevent or reverse late graft dysfunction, but complete results have not yet been published. With diagnostic monitoring tools on the horizon, clinicians will be armed with additional clinical knowledge and opportunities to make intervention decisions.

Conclusion

What makes the difference for Kevin in staying on his medications and staying positive? He thinks a part of it is that he saw his mother and her sisters suffering from PKD, with no opportunity to get a transplant. He wants to live and feels that he has a lot to offer. His decision to celebrate by working in the field may also help him to stay positive—but it is a choice he makes daily.

Kevin is also aware that the way he dealt with his disease was an opportunity to be a role model for others. For one thing, his children were watching. He wanted to send a message to his children and others facing similar health challenges that it is possible to live a full, fulfilling, and grateful life. His life is a reminder of just what a gift good health is and how much suffering ill health brings. Kevin chooses to live in the spirit of gratitude and thankfulness. Each day is a reminder of the gifts, large and small, that good health brings.

Notes

1. https://www.unos.org/data/transplant-trends/#waitlists_by_organ
2. http://www.medscape.com/viewarticle/757852
3. http://us.milliman.com/insight/research/health/2014-U_S_-organ-and-tissue-transplant-cost-estimates-and-discussion/
4. http://www.transplantliving.org/before-the-transplant/financing-a-transplant/the-costs/
5. http://jama.jamanetwork.com/article.aspx?articleid=1839743
6. www.emmisolutions.com/blog/2014/10/10/now-is-the-time-to-improve-long-term-outcomes-for-kidney-transplant-recipients

Story 11: Great Expectations

Jan Oldenburg, FHIMSS with Paul, MD

Introduction

When you are a doctor, it can be hard to find yourself on the other side of the exam room table. That's especially true when you've been a physician champion for medical informatics, interoperability, and patient-centered care. You come to the experience with great expectations: an abiding belief in the way things can and should work for both patients and physicians, and an understanding of what is currently possible, as well as the knowledge that all too often the healthcare system and the people in it work imperfectly. It's one thing to know that intellectually; it's quite another to experience it firsthand as a patient in the system you're working to reform.

That's what happened to Paul. He is a primary care doctor and has always been interested in engaging his patients. He has been at the center of multiple electronic health record (EHR) implementations and sees healthcare IT as an important tool in changing medicine for the better. As a physician, he used the EHR as a teaching tool and loved patients who came in armed with challenging questions and information. As a medical informaticist and policy maker, Paul began working inside the system to make changes. He has been deeply involved in the systems and culture change created by EHR implementations and meaningful use certification. He carries his passion for patient-centered care into his interoperability and policy work, always keeping in mind that the end goal is better, more connected care for patients.

As someone deeply involved in the delivery of medical care, who looks at issues from the perspective of a systems thinker, Paul is a keen observer of the moments when things are just harder for patients than they need to be. He is outspoken about mentioning these hurdles to his doctors as well as to administrators. He knows they may be able to hear the critique more easily from a fellow doctor, and changes will make things easier for future patients.

Polycystic Kidney Disease

Paul has polycystic kidney disease (PKD), a condition that causes cysts to form in the kidneys, gradually reducing kidney function and leading to a host of complications up to and including kidney failure.[1] Paul's family has no known history of the disease, which is an anomaly given that it is usually inherited. Knowing that he has PKD, Paul has carefully managed his weight and blood pressure through healthy eating, exercise, and vigilance. Despite his vigilance, the disease has continued to progress in the 10 years since he was diagnosed, and recent tests showed that he is currently at stage 4 of PKD. There are generally considered to be five stages of PKD, followed by kidney failure.

Paul recently had a "get to know you" exam with a new primary care doctor who was supposed to test Paul's kidney function and assess the progression of his disease. Because the condition was serious, Paul made an appointment to get his results. He and his doctor spent the 10-minute visit in conversation about the likely course of his polycystic kidney disease and some social conversation. Paul left with a referral to a nephrologist. When he got the bill, he was surprised to find the follow-up had been billed as a level-4 exam. No physical examination had take place and that's a requirement for coding a level-4 exam.[2] Paul protested the coding, but the office reviewed it and told him that it had been appropriately billed based on the documentation submitted by the doctor. Paul couldn't see what the doctor had submitted, but based on what had actually happened at the visit he felt the documentation must have exaggerated the care provided.

Frustrations

Paul was also frustrated to find that his basic demographic information was recorded incorrectly in the system. Since he was a new patient to this provider, he filled out the information form (on paper!) and answered all the questions he was asked by the registration clerk. When he looked up what was recorded for his race and ethnicity in MyChart, the chart said "patient refused to answer." This kind of careless and inaccurate medical coding reduces the value of the electronic medical record. Paul finds it especially frustrating because bad, incomplete, and missing data are a significant contributor to the difficulty of understanding the social determinants of health and making sure care is equitable and culturally sensitive.

Paul keeps a complete copy of his medical record since his history is complex and he wants to have it available in case of emergency. At one location, he was able to download a copy of his medical record, but it came with a password generated by the system that he has to use each time he opens it on his PC. Adding insult to injury, it blocked him from being able to copy the record until the mandatory password requirement was removed—a level of security that is not required by the Health Insurance Portability and Accountability Act (HIPAA) and creates an unfortunate hurdle for him as a patient. Paul called the system administrator and suggested changing the password requirement. He also mentioned the "patient refused to answer" data that wasn't correct and suggested the clinic have a contest and give a pizza party to the clinic with the lowest "decline to answer" entries. The password lock on his downloaded data was corrected, but it is not clear that any improvements in data entry have occurred.

In at least one instance, Paul wasn't provided with an after-visit summary following his appointment. He asked for it, but was told he would need to sign a form before they could release it to him. Paul challenged the clerks, saying, "Do you know this is a meaningful use requirement? You should be providing after-visit summaries routinely." That finally broke the logjam for Paul, but illustrates the way systemic barriers are put between patients and their information—even when patients are savvy enough to ask for it.

The Things That Matter

Paul was interested in building a relationship with a doctor somewhere who would be able to handle a kidney transplant for him if or when the time comes for that. His options were a major academic medical center or a well-known center of excellence. When he called to set up an appointment at the major academic medical center, he was put on hold three times, then cut off midcall without a call-back. In contrast, when he called the center of excellence he was asked, "Oh, you're a doctor; do you want to talk to the head of the department?"

The new clinic not only provided Paul with access to the basics of his medical record—medications, allergies, diagnoses, immunizations, lab results, and procedures—but also provided open notes so Paul could see everything the physician recorded, including the questions he asked. Paul also appreciated having labs drawn early in the morning and then being able to review results on his iPhone by 10:30 a.m. before his appointment with the physician.

Even though—or perhaps because—Paul works in interoperability, he hand-carried his records to the new clinic. He's previously been seen in three health systems, all with Epic-based EHRs, but despite a common underlying system his data are not integrated. He has Continuity of Care Documents (CCDs) of his records from all of the health systems he's been seen in and also a spreadsheet where he tracks all of his labs, blood pressure, and kidney function tests so he can tell a coherent story across the multiple systems in which he's been seen over the past 10 years. That spreadsheet allowed his new clinic physician to see the progression of his polycystic kidney disease over time, rather than relying only on current data and anecdotal information to understand its course.

At this point, Paul and his doctors are in watchful waiting mode on his PKD. His lab results show his kidneys are still functioning too well for him to be a candidate for a transplant, so he continues to exercise, watch his diet and blood pressure, and take the best care of himself that he can.

Partial Bowel Resection

In addition to PKD, Paul had a history of colon polyps. During his first colonoscopy, his doctor found and removed quite a few polyps. During his next colonoscopy, 2 years later, there were a few more, which were also removed easily. During his most recent colonoscopy, however, his gastroenterologist had found a flat polyp in the transverse colon that he was unable to remove. Flat polyps, also known as sessile polyps, are not only more difficult to detect than raised polyps but also have a more aggressive pathology, so it is important to remove them as quickly as possible.[3] He saw a second gastroenterologist who was also unable to remove it. His colonoscopist recommended that he see a surgeon to discuss resection of the bowel, a procedure where the section of his colon containing the polyp would be removed. The surgeon was significantly late for Paul's first appointment and she did not address her lateness.

Paul elected to have the surgery done at the center of excellence, where he had existing relationships and they had his medical record. Before the surgery, Paul asked for the postoperative order set, so he'd know what to expect. The physician's assistant told him she couldn't give those to him. He followed up by asking for any special materials online. She wasn't aware of anything online but provided him with a generic handout on bowel surgery, which seemed a little old-school for an advanced center of excellence.

Hastening Recovery

The surgery went really well, though Paul had some cognitive dissonance about walking into the hospital feeling great but realizing he was going to walk out feeling lousy. Paul's surgery was written about in a popular news magazine, as his surgeon had used a new process called enhanced recovery protocols (ERPs). The approach is based on the theory that patients need to build resilience before surgery, starting with carbohydrate loading the day before, much the way an athlete would prepare his or her body for a marathon. In addition, rather than asking patients to avoid drinking anything after midnight the night before surgery, they are allowed to drink clear liquids up to 2 hours before surgery. Afterward, they are encouraged both to move and to eat much faster than is "normal"—especially following bowel surgery. Pain is rarely managed with opiates in ERP procedures; instead anti-inflammatories and steroids are generally used to manage pain. Paul did not have NSAIDs or steroids, however, due to his kidneys. The spinal block worked well to manage his pain and he used a few mild narcotics to add pain relief.

Paul was able to eat a roast beef sandwich several hours after surgery, and recorded 200 steps on his Fitbit that night. The next day, he started walking the corridors to hasten his recovery. Tennis shoes on, he walked six miles in the hospital each of the next 2 days. He was in the hospital for only 52 hours following surgery. The innovative surgical preparation approach is part of the reason Paul was able to recover so quickly.

While hospitalized, Paul saw several physicians and residents, who rounded to see how he was doing. The person he expected to see, but didn't until discharge, was his surgeon. At discharge Paul finally was able to hear what was actually removed during surgery, which was the end of his small intestine and the ascending colon. He expected more of the colon to be removed, so it was good news.

Great—But Areas to Improve

Paul felt he received tremendous care—and there's still room for improvement in his experience. He would have especially liked to see the plan of care before he entered the hospital so that he could understand the goals for him and how he was doing in meeting them. His surgery was done using a new tool and a new procedure, and it would have been helpful to see a video of it either before or after surgery; advance information about the procedure would have meant he knew what to expect. He would have liked to have had more time to ask questions of his providers—especially his surgeon. Every clinician who came into his room seemed to be in a hurry. If Paul had had access to a low-paid staff member who had recorded his questions, his visits with clinicians would have been more productive. It would also have been helpful to see both clinician notes and lab results while he was an inpatient.

When Paul needed a nurse, he would have liked to let them know whether his issue was urgent or not via text or an intercom. Instead, he had a call button, which made it seem equally urgent whether he was in pain or just needed more water. Paul had his iPad and great TV—but he would rather have listened to music than watched TV.

Once Paul was out of the hospital, he checked his patient portal for information about the procedure. The record showed that the anesthesiologist had noted that the treatment was for a malignant polyp in his colon, which was an error. Paul called the anesthesiologist and asked that the notation about malignancy be removed from his record, which it was. If he had not been vigilant and informed, however, the error would have stayed in his record.

Observations for Policy and Practice

Despite the fact that Paul's experience has been wonderful, not everything is seamless. Paul pointed out a few troublesome issues:

- The health system blocked caller ID on a number of incoming calls. As a result, it was impossible to tell the difference between a spam call and a "do not miss" call from his doctor when deciding whether or not to answer.

- His EKG was not available online and getting a copy of it turned out to be unduly complex.
- E-mail wasn't as integrated into the workflow as he would have liked it to have been. For example, when Paul's colonoscopy was approaching, he didn't have a prescription for the prep materials. He e-mailed his doctor with a request that he phone in a prescription for the prep materials. The next day, he got an e-mail back saying, "Call us," but without a phone number to get directly to the right department. He was in meetings and was very frustrated with playing e-mail tag as he had spelled out exactly what he needed in the e-mail.
- He could request an appointment and give some time parameters, but couldn't make the appointment directly.
- He was also a little frustrated by completing the entire previsit questionnaire online only to have all the same questions asked in the visit—not as verification, but as if they were new questions.
- His test results were online and he could view and graph them but there wa's no link between his test results and the wonderful content about medical issues. If he weren't a physician, he would really have needed that capability.
- The site had deep medical and clinical content, but the content has not been connected electronically to patients and diagnoses so patients have to hunt for the link between their clinical results and content that applies to them.
- It would be great to see health systems asking individuals how they want to communicate and then adapting communications to serve the individual's preferences.

Conclusion

Paul clearly has a number of significant advantages over most of us in negotiating the healthcare system: Not only is he a physician who can speak the medical language fluently, he also understands the systems and the data deeply. We took advantage of Paul's multiple roles as patient, physician, and medical informaticist to ask him how he would design the system if he were able to start from scratch. Policy makers, designers, developers, and physicians take note!

In Paul's ideal situation, there would be no silos of information. Everyone would contribute to a common record located somewhere in the cloud. As a patient, Paul would be able to input information into the system. Patient-generated data should trigger alarms if readings are out of whack and should be available to be examined in concert with the clinical data contained in the EHR. Physicians and patients alike should be alerted to trends in a visual way.

He would like to be able to make his own appointments—including estimating the time he requires for a visit and being able to see the associated cost and then pay accordingly, as he does in other aspects of his life. He'd also like to be able to send his questions to his physician in advance so that he and his provider could organize the visit according to his questions. It would be helpful to choose the level of security he's comfortable with to minimize the risks of information exchange. He wants his e-mails to be incorporated into the record and the care plan.

Convenience is key! Make messaging simple, as well as appointment scheduling and data aggregation. He likes that he gets an alert on his phone when he gets an e-mail from his provider but he would also like to be able to click on it to read the contents as opposed to opening a browser and going through several layers in order to read that the doctor will respond to his message within 2 days. It's his health, and it is urgent to him—he'd like the system to highlight it and give it the same respect.

Health systems, insurers, and individual clinicians would lead a culture change focusing on individuals as key partners in their care, and giving them the respect, courtesy, and partnership that they deserve.

Paul's "secret sauce" for patient engagement: Providers encourage patients to participate in online and electronic tools; in return, the online tools are convenient, easy, and contribute to education at every step.

Notes

1. http://www.mayoclinic.org/diseases-conditions/polycystic-kidney-disease/basics/definition/con -20028831
2. http://www.aafp.org/fpm/1999/0700/p32.html
3. http://www.sciencedirect.com/science/article/pii/S1590865814007038

Story 12: Healing with Faith, Food, Friends, Family, and Laughter

Mary P. Griskewicz, MS, FHIMSS with Roberta, MS, CISSP

Introduction

Roberta celebrated her fiftieth birthday this year—and she was deeply grateful to have the opportunity. When she was diagnosed with stage-3 breast cancer 12 years before, it had seemed like a very distant possibility that she would survive to see such a birthday, celebrated with friends and family.

During Roberta's initial year of treatment, from the moment of diagnosis on, she learned many things. Some were welcome and others were not; some were surprising and others mundane. Roberta's journey through breast cancer surgery and treatment taught her about things she thought she already knew. She learned that, in order to heal, you need the four Fs and one L: faith, food, family, friends, and laughter.

Faith and Food

She learned that you must have faith in something or someone greater than yourself in order to heal. Her faith and church family sustained her. She learned to use her energy to control the things she could, the foods she selected, the attitude she chose, and the friends she could lean on for help. She learned that food is fuel, and it soon became clear what foods were helpful or harmful during her healing process. It became very important to select foods that provided her with energy and stopped the nausea, like the comfort of a great pot roast (her favorite). Understanding that food was part of her treatment plan became just as important as the chemotherapy the doctors prescribed or the good friends who supported her. Friends planned and delivered food weekly for Roberta and her family (pot roasts, soup, meatloaf, casseroles, salads). She appreciated every morsel of every meal and was grateful for the way friends showed their love with food—though she still felt guilty she could not prepare the meals herself.

Friends and Family

Learning who you could choose to help you pick out a wig or watch a movie with became part of Roberta's healing process. Asking friends for their support was difficult but turned out to be life-giving. Every week her sister Gail drove an hour each way to clean the house for the family. Roberta learned that friends and family were there to pick her up (literally in her case, as she frequently collapsed for no apparent reason while undergoing her treatment) and clean her off (as hand–eye coordination was one of the first areas affected by the treatments, so missing her mouth was a common occurrence).

Laughter

Learning to laugh at herself and with others was also a key part in Roberta's recovery. Learning to laugh whenever she wanted (even when others thought it was not appropriate) was helpful and healing. She always felt better after she laughed, even though she did not understand why. She later learned from a health seminar that laughter releases endorphins that allow your body to heal and manage pain better. Laughing literally made her feel better. She came to understand that the saying "laughter makes the best medicine" is completely true.[1]

Information

Almost from the moment of diagnosis, the Internet became her friend and her enemy. She researched everything she could on inflammatory breast cancer (IBC): treatment options, what to expect with chemo, surgery, and radiation—the good, the bad, and the ugly. When she was diagnosed and underwent treatment, e-mail, text messages, and video technology were not used for communication between patients and their care team and phones were not "smart." The only communication vehicle used then was the telephone, and it was frustrating, as it is still is today, to leave clinicians messages and wait for them to call back. "Why can't providers simply e-mail me or use a patient portal," she thought. "It would be much more effective and efficient for us all."

Roberta used technology (blogs, and e-mail) to keep everyone in her circle of friends up to date on her treatment and progress—and remember, this was in the era before Facebook, Twitter, or Instagram. With one blog post or e-mail everyone in her circle of friends and family could be updated on what was happening. If she needed something or there was a new development in her treatment, her friends and family knew about it from her group e-mails. Most importantly, e-mail allowed friends and family to brighten her day when she wasn't feeling well, and she wondered why her clinicians couldn't do the same.

Observations for Policy and Practice

Roberta recognized the importance of the nonmedical parts of dealing with a serious diagnosis for herself, but others may not realize the importance of what Anna-Lisa Silvestre calls "the patient team":

- Encourage patients to reach out to family and friends for support and help getting their needs met. It may feel difficult to ask, but it is healing both for the patient and the circle of friends that are asked.
- Encourage family and friends to bring laughter into the mix by taking the patient on a fun outing, bringing over a silly movie or a new pet, telling funny stories. Yes, sometimes people want to talk about their deepest fears, but they may also just want to be silly for a while.
- Support patients in making use of their patient portals, ability to e-mail their doctors, view lab tests, and research their conditions.

For Family and Friends

- Make little things into celebrations. Candles at dinner, a pretty ribbon or plant, or beautifully prepared food can add a bit of cheer even in a hospital room.
- Your friendship and love matter more than anything you say or bring or do. Don't let finding the perfect gift or the perfect thing to say get in the way of just being there.

Conclusion

Using information technology for healthcare services like scheduling, prescription refills, secure communications with providers, web portals, remote monitoring devices, and social media all are steps in supporting and empowering patients in their care. Today Roberta sees the value of health IT and wishes it had been available to her. Her hope is that providers will educate themselves on the need and value of health IT along with the power of faith, food, friends, family, and laughter to achieve health. Roberta has been cancer free for more than 15 years and is still waiting for her providers to adopt a patient portal and other relevant technologies to support her health and wellness.

Note

1. http://www.scientificamerican.com/article/why-laughter-may-be-the-best-pain-medicine/

Story 13: I Suggest You Check Yourself into the Hospital

Jan Oldenburg, FHIMSS with Susan

Introduction

Several weeks after the worst sinus infection of her life, Susan started having some tingling and slight numbness and pain in her feet. It felt as if her feet were continually awakening from being asleep, but was more painful. Then the sensation began creeping up her legs. It was odd, but she powered on. She was busy: Her son was 18 months old, her husband was traveling for business, and she was working at a demanding job. She didn't have time to focus on the tingling. But then, 2 days after it started in her feet, her hands started tingling as well. When the feeling began creeping up her arms, it no longer was something she could ignore.

Diagnosis

Susan went to see her internist. He checked her eyes and her reflexes. Then he said, "You need to see a neurologist immediately. You have no reflexes and your affect is flat. I'm worried about this." He picked up the phone, called the office of a neurologist who happened to be located a block away and got Susan an immediate appointment. Susan left her car in his parking lot and walked to the neurologist's office. Never had a block seemed so long. By the time she arrived at the neurologist's office, she was exhausted and puzzled; she was young, in shape, and the degree of exhaustion she felt from walking a block was confusing.

The neurologist checked her reflexes, listened to her story, and said he believed she had Guillain-Barré syndrome (GBS).[1] He explained that the symptoms she was experiencing were common to its onset and that, while its cause is unknown, GBS can be triggered by a respiratory infection. He also explained that it mimicked some of the symptoms of polio (hence the nickname "French polio") and she would likely experience partial or complete paralysis. He said, "I advise you to check yourself into the hospital now." Susan told him that her husband was out of town, her child at daycare, and that she had no one to pick him up or take care of him if she checked herself in. The doctor sighed, and said, "All right, but you're eventually going to be in the hospital."

Guillain-Barré syndrome is an autoimmune disorder in which the body's immune system attacks parts of the nervous system. The immune system begins to destroy the myelin sheath surrounding the nerves, which in turn affects the signals the brain transmits to the muscles. Susan was lucky that both doctors identified the condition so quickly, as GBS can be hard to diagnose in its early stages. Weakness and tingling in the extremities are usually the first symptoms, but the sensations spread, eventually paralyzing the person completely. In its most severe form GBS can interfere with respiration, blood pressure, or heart rate and is considered to be a medical emergency requiring hospitalization.[1]

Susan is normally a very incisive and decisive person. At that moment, however, she was so tired and so shocked that all of her challenging, inquiring, take-charge personality traits deserted her. She asked few questions—not even about how soon she might become paralyzed. Instead, she left the office and trudged—so weary—the block back to her car, picked up her son at daycare, and made it home. She fed her son dinner but was too tired to eat herself. When she tried to carry her son upstairs to bed, she simply couldn't do it. She sat on the landing, halfway up the stairs and they cried together. Immediately after finally getting her son to bed, Susan called her sister-in-law and said, "I need help. Please come over and bring your pajamas." In bed that night, Susan had the persistent sensation that she was being inexorably pulled underwater, as she could feel her strength deserting her, swirling out of her body. In the middle of the night, she called a cab and went to the hospital.

Treatment

Immediately after being hospitalized, Susan was delirious for several days and doesn't remember much about that time. Her mother came and, when he returned from his trip, her husband. Her husband hadn't realized how serious the situation was until he returned home and found that Susan was still hospitalized, nearly immobile, delirious, and being checked every hour or two for respiratory distress. Susan's father, a doctor, also flew in several times during Susan's hospital stay. Susan was relatively lucky: She never experienced the most severe stage of GBS, which involves paralysis of the muscles that control respiration.

Dr. N, the neurologist who diagnosed Susan, was also overseeing her treatment and provided a reliable, stable, intelligent, and even humorous perspective throughout. He ordered plasmapheresis, in which whole blood is removed from the body and processed to separate the red and white blood cells from the plasma, or liquid portion of the blood. The blood cells are then returned to the patient without the plasma, which the body quickly replaces. Scientists still don't know exactly why plasma exchange works, but the technique seems to reduce the severity and duration of the GBS episode.[2] Plasmapheresis was begun using the veins of her arms, but her veins quickly wore out and the decision was made to insert a shunt on the right side of her chest wall.

Before the shunt procedure, Susan was asked to sign a form acknowledging the risk of a collapsed lung from the procedure by Dr. T, the nephrologist who was to insert the shunt. When she asked about the likelihood of this happening, Dr. T told her he had done "about a thousand shunt insertions" and had never collapsed someone's lung. Dr. T inserted the shunt, the treatment worked, and Susan began to get better quickly. The muscles in her face recovered first, and then she was able to stand and use her arms. After 3 weeks, they sent her home, though she was still weak and not eating very well.

Relapse

Susan was happy to be home, happy to see her son and husband, happy to feel better—but it didn't last. After a few days, she began feeling the same tingling, the same sense of progressive weakness, the same feeling of overwhelming tiredness that characterized the onset of GBS. Her husband took her back to the ER, where the examining doctor said, "You are having a relapse," and admitted her to the same ward she'd been in before.

GBS is rare, attacking one or two people in 100,000. Having a relapse is even more rare. It can occur as a result of "treatment-related fluctuation," which sometimes happens if therapy is initiated very early when the disease process is active. In these cases, it will only temporarily arrest the disease process and once treatment is complete, the disease can recur. In such instances repeat treatment improves the outcome.[3]

Since Susan responded well to the plasmapheresis treatment the first time, Dr. N decided to begin it again immediately. The shunt was inserted in her left chest wall, again by Dr. T. This time, the shunt didn't go in easily, and he had to push really hard on her chest to complete the procedure. Susan could tell immediately that something was wrong, and said, her voice weak because she was having trouble breathing, "It doesn't feel right." His nurse listened to Susan's chest sounds, and when she said there was air moving, the doctor sent Susan back to her room.

Back in her room, Susan continued struggling to breathe and also began throwing up. Dr. T came back to her room. He again delegated listening to her chest to his nurse, who still heard air moving, which can happen if the lung is partially but not fully collapsed. Dr. T and his nurse seemed satisfied that air was moving and left—leaving no instructions with the nurses about what to do if Susan's symptoms became worse and not saying anything to alleviate Susan's concerns.

Susan was very frightened as well as frustrated and angry that her distress was being ignored. She was well aware of the respiratory risks of GBS by then, and now she was struggling to breathe—and her doctor had just walked out of the room without offering a word of comfort or reassurance. Her mother was frantic—Susan was clearly in trouble and no one else seemed concerned. One nurse told her mother, "We can't do anything without a doctor's orders." Her mother called Susan's husband, who called the hospital ombudsman and demanded someone help Susan immediately. The ombudsman called one of Susan's other physicians, who ordered an emergency x-ray that showed her lung had collapsed.

Susan was immediately put in intensive care with a chest tube inserted to reinflate her lung. A collapsed lung in addition to GBS put her at significantly elevated risk of being unable to breathe at all. Each day Susan was in the ICU, Dr. T would come by and look at her chart. He never looked her in the eye or spoke to her beyond a simple greeting. Finally, after several days of this, Susan said to him, "I know you feel badly about what happened." Then he said, "I do, I do. I feel terrible about what happened." Susan said, "I guess that's why you have us sign the disclaimers." Dr. T was silent. It would have been the perfect moment for an apology. Susan had the strong impression that he was embarrassed, but he seemed unable to voice his regret.

In the ICU, her shunt was removed and they restarted plasmapheresis through the veins in her arms. Her recovery was slow this time; the two conditions slowed recovery from both. Susan gradually recovered her strength and her lung function and was sent home at the 3-week mark. She had lost 15–20 pounds she could ill afford to lose and was still very weak. It was months before she could carry her son. It took a full 6–9 months for her to regain full muscle strength and, even now, 20 years later, she has residual tingling in her hands and feet.

Connections

There were a number of moments of wonderful human connection throughout Susan's illness, despite the discomfort of the incident with Dr. T. During Susan's time in the ICU, her father couldn't free time up to visit, so he asked a doctor who had trained under him to check on her. Her father's emissary sat with Susan in the ICU, comforting her and standing watch to correct any further errors. Dr. N, her neurologist, and the internist she'd seen initially stopped by almost daily during the 6 weeks total she was in the hospital—to check on her, joke with her, and make sure she was progressing. All these doctors were strong advocates for her, and Susan is grateful for both their instant recognition of her condition as well as their daily concern for her well-being.

The nurse who did Susan's plasmapheresis exuded briskness and confidence and seemed ultra-professional. During Susan's first stay, just as they were about to start plasmapheresis, Susan heard a child crying. She began crying, missing her child, feeling so sick. She couldn't cry normally because her face was frozen, so the tears were welling up and streaming down her face while Susan made a kind of gasping noise. The nurse heard and turned from her equipment to say, "What's wrong?" Susan said, "I haven't seen my baby for so long, and I miss him." Tears welled up in the nurse's eyes as she began the treatment; Susan treasured that moment of personal connection.

Observations for Policy and Practice

There are several lessons to be learned from Susan's experience:

- **How important it is to have someone to be your advocate when you are hospitalized**: Susan's mother and husband were available to jump into action and push for action when the medical system wasn't responding to her collapsed lung. They would have been able to be more effective advocates had they been notified when one of Susan's doctors was rounding. Often they missed the opportunity for an update because they had stepped out to make a phone call or get food. Not everyone has the benefit of family or friends who can support them in this way, so every hospital should have patient advocates who really can "take on" their own medical system to support patients, especially those who don't have family or friends available to help them.

- **Each patient should have a tablet or screen with their status information on it**: This would include the nurse assigned, your doctors, your medications schedules, estimated physician rounding schedules, planned procedures, and most current lab tests. Susan noted that often she had no idea who her nurse was, when her doctor was coming, or when her next plasmapheresis was scheduled. One day she was surprised to find that she was scheduled for a spinal tap that day! In a situation where you feel powerless and anxious, even knowing your schedule is significant. Knowledge is always power. See Chapter 5 for more ideas about how to increase patients' feelings of control over their situation and reduce anxiety.

- **The need for a medical culture where mistakes can be admitted and are viewed as opportunities to improve procedures and techniques rather than failures to be shoved under the rug**: A simple apology from Dr. T would have gone a long way toward alleviating Susan's anger—and studies show in general that this can reduce the risk of malpractice lawsuits.[4] More than that, however, the whole incident—especially when the doctor left her gasping for breath without providing any orders for the nurses—eroded Susan's sense of safety and her trust that she was being cared for appropriately. Trust is a precious commodity in healthcare; when present between doctor and patient, it actively aids healing. Anxiety, too, is correlated to slower healing.[5] We owe it to the patients we serve to use safety incidents to improve our operations. It is also important to remember that every patient deserves reassurance and comfort when in distress, and cultures that value following orders over patient comfort and safety are dangerous in a host of ways. Healthcare's embrace of patient safety increasingly means empowering nurses and other staff members to stand up to doctors for the sake of patient safety.[6]

■ **The nuances involved in shared decision making**: When Susan was in the neurologist's office and he encouraged her to check herself into the hospital, one could argue that he was using appropriate shared decision-making techniques, and Susan was exercising her prerogative in choosing not to follow his recommendation. But there are limits to shared decision making and patient choice, and doctors need to be trained to recognize the nuances so they can respond appropriately to patient cues in the moment. At that moment, Susan would have welcomed a "take charge" doctor despite the fact that it would normally have been a problem for her. This highlights that there are no simple formulas for shared decision making; even the same patient may have different needs at different times.[7]

Conclusion

Susan was lucky. Her medical team recognized her symptoms early. She was able to get herself to the hospital when it became clear that was what she needed. Her family was able to be her advocate when she wasn't able to create her voice heard. She recovered.

If, however, we are to create a medical system that promotes positive outcomes for everyone, we need to make systemic changes that empower staff members as advocates for patients, find better ways to listen to the patients and their advocates, build a medical culture in which mistakes are acknowledged and used to improve process and technique and, last but surely not least, find ways to promote empathy and caring across all members of the medical team. Some of the changes surely involve training all members of the medical team in active listening and shared decision-making so they can better support patients at all stages of illness and recovery.

Notes

1. http://www.ninds.nih.gov/disorders/gbs/detail_gbs.htm
2. http://www.healthcommunities.com/guillain-barre-syndrome/treatment.shtml
3. http://www.ncbi.nlm.nih.gov/pubmed/3341955
4. http://www.ncbi.nlm.nih.gov/pmc/articles/PMC2628492/
5. http://citeseerx.ist.psu.edu/viewdoc/download;jsessionid=8653A6FFC7E3BDE1D8ADFCF20F2C1F8F?doi=10.1.1.495.970&rep=rep1&type=pdf
6. http://www.rwjf.org/en/library/articles-and-news/2011/04/nurses-are-key-to-improving-patient-safety.html%2FDocuments%2FViewDocument.aspx%3FAddToLog%3D1%26DocumentID%3D372&usg=AFQjCNF45_X2T33t_KyFo2PxbCLycNyTuA&sig2=X14uRbqEykpbZF5WM8RoNA
7. http://www.healthtalk.org/peoples-experiences/improving-health-care/shared-decision-making/why-do-people-sometimes-not-want-decision-be-shared

Story 14: Learning from Others' Mistakes

Jan Oldenburg, FHIMSS and
Mary P. Griskewicz, MS, FHIMSS with Nancy

Introduction

In early November 2012, Nancy had hip replacement surgery. After surgery, she developed a serious MRSA (methicillin-resistant *Staphylococcus aureus*) infection and was readmitted to the hospital for treatment. MRSA infection is a significant risk associated with joint replacement therapy—it is significant because it is resistant to many commonly used antibiotics.[1] Nationally, it occurs in 1 to 3 percent of patients following total joint replacement surgery.[2] At the time of her readmittal, her surgeon stated the infection was "topical" and only required 2 weeks of antibiotics. After 4 weeks in rehab, Nancy returned home and received home health physical therapy (PT) treatment before starting outpatient PT in early February. Although she was going to three outpatient PT sessions a week, Nancy didn't see much improvement. She was able to transition from a walker to crutches, but wasn't able to progress further.

Slow Recovery

In mid-March, nearly five months after her surgery, she saw her surgeon. At that visit, she related her concerns and those of her physical therapist to him: She wasn't improving, her pain level was still high, her mobility was low, and she couldn't transition from crutches to a cane. The physician seemed angry that she was still using crutches and suggested that she wasn't working hard enough in physical therapy. He told her the x-rays of the implant looked fine and didn't change anything in her treatment plan. After that visit, Nancy's physical therapist contacted her surgeon twice to voice concerns over Nancy's lack of improvement and high pain level. He again stated that the x-rays were fine and dismissed the physical therapist's concerns about Nancy's pain.

By April of 2013, Nancy's pain and mobility were getting worse. She was in constant, extreme pain and walking was incredibly difficult—some days were nearly impossible to get through. Her quality of life was extremely poor: She was essentially housebound and even the smallest tasks were painful. On April 19, during a physical therapy session, she had strong, shooting pain from her hip radiating through her leg. The physical therapist stopped the session and said Nancy couldn't come back until she saw her surgeon again or got a second opinion and found out what was going on.

The following week, Nancy went to see her surgeon and again voiced concerns. The fact that the physical therapist discontinued her therapy program finally caught his attention. But once again, he maintained that the x-rays looked fine. He told Nancy that out of all his patients, she was doing the worst, and he didn't know why. He sent her for blood tests as well as a nerve test. Nancy never received any notice about the test outcomes, so she called his office to find out the results. She was very concerned about infection, given her earlier diagnosis of MRSA, but she never received a call back and had no way to look up her own results online.

Nancy again saw her surgeon in mid-May, when she finally received the results of her earlier tests. The nerve test had come back fine but the blood test results were abnormal. During this appointment, her final with this surgeon, he acknowledged that her blood test results were abnormal only after she pressed him to explain them. He said he was concerned about infection only after she brought up the possibility. He then examined x-rays that had been taken during a previous visit for quite a long time, finally saying that there seemed to be a problem with the implant—after telling Nancy for months that the implant was fine!

Second Opinion

With the help and encouragement of family and friends, Nancy went to see an orthopedic surgeon at a different hospital to get a second opinion on May 30. The results dismayed her. Not only did she still have the MRSA infection, the implant was "grossly loosened." The surgeons at the new practice listened to her concerns and explained very carefully and confidently what was going on and what needed to be done to fix her problems. They also reassured her that she could recover from this because she was young and the problems were fixable.

Nancy subsequently had two additional surgeries, performed by the new surgeon. The first surgery in early July was to treat the infection; tests during that surgery showed the level of infection to be five times higher than the level required to indicate infection is present. The loosened hip implant was removed and spacers with antibiotics were inserted. For 8 weeks following surgery, Nancy took oral antibiotics and administered IV antibiotics to herself twice a day. On August 29, 2013, she had the final surgery. With the infection finally cleared up, her surgeon was able to perform the revision hip replacement. The surgery went extremely well. Nancy recuperated on medical leave for 6 weeks, followed by 3 months of physical therapy. Finally, 15 months after her original surgery, she was fully recovered.

The Need for Information

Once things took a turn for the worse, Nancy realized that she couldn't rely on her surgeon to provide the information she needed—especially because she had stopped trusting what he told her. She began researching the problems related to her case online using search topics like "hip replacement complications" and "infections post hip replacement." The American Academy of Orthopaedic Surgeons website (http://www.aaos.org/home.asp) was a great resource for her. Nancy was knowledgeable about these complications by the time she went to get a second opinion. Because of her reading, she was ready with questions. Her research also prepared her for the possibility that she might need further surgeries. As a result, when the new surgeon told her that she would probably need two more surgeries (depending on whether there was infection or not, which they would determine once they were in surgery), Nancy wasn't as shocked or upset as she would have been had she not done so much reading on her own.

Nancy also used the Internet to learn about the new surgeon. She had never done this before. She had always just assumed that the doctor she was seeing was the "right one," especially if another doctor or a friend or family member had recommended the person. Since she was extremely unhappy with her first surgeon, the care she received from him, and the fact that he ignored and dismissed her concerns, Nancy realized she needed to see the best person possible. She searched for answers to a new set of questions: What is this doctor's biography and credentials? Where did he or she go to school? What does he or she specialize in? Has he or she been published or active in research? Has this doctor been censured? Will he or she treat me as a partner?

In conducting her online research, she found out that the surgeon she was seeing for a second opinion specialized in hip/knee replacements and postsurgical infections. That mattered a lot to Nancy, since she was convinced that she still had an infection. The surgeon who ultimately performed the second and third surgeries specialized in hip surgery revisions. Nancy was confident she was finally being treated by the right doctor.

Nancy also looked for feedback online about patients' experiences with the new surgeon. She wanted/needed a surgeon who recognized the importance of direct and straightforward communication, one who would listen to her concerns and respect the fact that she would be an active participant in her own care. When the surgeon she saw for the second opinion referred her to another partner within the practice, Nancy started her research all over again, focusing on the new surgeon.

Nancy understood that Internet searches would not give her a complete picture of her surgeon. But the information she was able to obtain, coupled with great interactions with the surgeons at the new practice, made her realize she was in the right place with the right surgeon to get her problems fixed. Because she was now an informed and activated patient, she was confident that her decisions were correct and appropriate.

The Need for Peer-to-Peer Sharing

Nancy had a difficult time dealing with her health issues both emotionally and mentally. At times she was overwhelmed with fear and anxiety about what was happening. In hindsight, she wishes she had looked online for blogs or other sites with patient stories. Hearing what others were experiencing in similar situations and how they coped—and knowing that she wasn't alone—would have really helped Nancy and might even have resulted in her taking action earlier.

When things were going badly in Nancy's recovery, she felt ashamed and didn't want anyone to know. But she had a wonderful support system of friends and family. They became concerned because they weren't hearing from her and reached out to find out how she was doing. If Nancy had used social media to keep people updated on what was happening with her recovery, it would have been easier for her family, especially her sister, to respond to people's inquiries. In addition, Nancy might have found that it would have given her an unexpected pool of support.

Supportive Technologies

Nancy's first surgeon used no information technology to communicate with patients. Her only options for getting in touch were phone calls for appointments or to leave word that she had concerns. When many of her calls were not returned, it was especially frustrating to feel as if she had no data and no additional support.

At the second practice the primary means of communication was also phone calls, though Nancy's new surgeon returned her calls in a timely way, no matter when Nancy left a message. Her second surgeon also used e-mail. When Nancy had questions that didn't need to be addressed immediately, she e-mailed them and the staff responded very quickly. When she had concerns about how her incision looked and whether the drainage was a cause for concern, her doctor's staff had her take photos of the incision and e-mail them so they could better assess what needed to be done.

Nancy also was able to pay her bills online, complete previsit forms and register to get test results and other information online through the hospital's MyChart patient portal.

Nancy found that using technology tools made it easier for her to be involved in her care and communicate with her providers. It gave her some measure of autonomy, allowing her to view her test results and electronic medical record, choose her own appointments, and communicate with her providers between appointments. Patients expect healthcare providers to have technology to make interactions convenient in the same way they expect convenient resources from their banks or travel companies.

Family Use of Technology

Nancy's family, especially her younger sister and close friends, took a very active role in her health. They did quite a bit of research online themselves. When she was seeing surgeons regularly, her sister and friends came along to the appointment armed with a list of questions just as Nancy did. One friend even took notes during the first postsurgery appointments to make sure they captured all the nuances of Nancy's treatment plan.

Nancy's experience has changed the way her whole family approaches their health. Now, anytime members of Nancy's immediate family have a health concern or are prescribed a new medication, they research it online. Nancy has begun to research the credentials of every doctor she sees, not just her surgeons. This information is useful and can be forwarded to others with a link to the physician's bio and videos about him or her. Nancy also encourages her family members to check out their doctors' patient portal, which usually has a lot of helpful information.

Having more tools and e-mail to communicate or get test results and health information electronically is now a necessity for Nancy, and she would think long and hard before seeing a physician that didn't provide such access. She also believes strongly in the power of social media to keep family and friends informed on her health status as well to use as a tool to interact with other patients.

Work Yet to Be Done

Providers still need to be educated on the importance of communicating with their patients. Nancy wonders if and how that is being taught in medical schools today. She said, "Sure, I wanted a surgeon who was at the 'top of his or her game,' so to speak, and extremely skilled/qualified. But I also needed providers who would listen to me—to my concerns, fears, and problems, and answer my questions—and not dismiss what I was experiencing." Doctors may see conditions/ health problems every day but patients don't, and treating patients as if their experiences don't matter invites medical errors.

Observations for Policy and Practice

Nancy's story illustrates the importance of patients taking action when they know something is not right with their care or recovery—and that a physician who does not listen to valid health concerns is a problem. It offers lessons for ways we can change the system to ensure these kinds of events don't happen to others.

- Educate patients and caregivers about how important it is to research both physicians and treatment options. Make it easy for them to get a second opinion and encourage it if they have any questions. This may be a topic worthy of a public service campaign.
- Provide more and better tools to enable patients to research prospective providers' history and experience; it will help them make better decisions about their treatment based on what matters to them.
- Patients want to believe that their doctors know best and have their best interests at heart—but there are danger signals when a physician seems defensive about the outcomes or simply doesn't listen to valid concerns. When that seems to be happening, don't wait to take action! Get a second opinion. If nothing else, enlist your health insurer to help you find someone reliable. It is your right to get the best care.
- Social support helps people recover from illness and surgery, and physicians should ask about what kind of social support the person has as a part of treatment. If you are a patient, or planning for a surgery, plan for social and physical support. If you are a friend or family member, step in to take action if someone you love or care for seems unduly isolated or is having difficulty recovering.
- Listening is such an important skill in the practice of medicine that we should build it into the medical curriculum and routinely audit physicians based on how well they practice this essential human—and medical—skill.

Conclusion

As a result of having a bad experience in the healthcare system, Nancy became an activated and engaged patient. To her, that means being someone who doesn't sit back and let medical professionals solely determine the kind of care she receives. Activated patients recognize the important role they need to play in their care. They research conditions, diseases, and related issues. They ask questions about test results, care plans, alternative treatments. They're open to using new technologies to aid in recovery and get the care they need/deserve. If they're not happy with the care they're getting, they speak up to let their providers know. And then they get a second opinion—or third or fourth—if needed. Having providers dismiss their concerns, not return phone calls, or not provide test results isn't acceptable to anyone—but activated patients do something about it!

Notes

1. http://www.ncbi.nlm.nih.gov/pmc/articles/PMC3032119/
2. http://healthcare.utah.edu/orthopaedics/jointreplacement/infection.php

Story 15: Living Well with Lupus

Jan Oldenburg, FHIMSS with Amanda*

Introduction

Amanda noticed that something was wrong the year she was 14. Her friends were all busy after school: doing drill team, running track, babysitting, cooking dinner—while she was going directly home to nap. It was a significant change for Amanda, and it began having an effect on her social life and her mood.

Diagnosis

Her mother took her to the doctor, who checked her for mononucleosis, "the kissing disease." Amanda wondered about that, as she hadn't kissed anyone, so she wasn't surprised when the test came back negative for mono. Two weeks later, she leaned against a wall. Shortly afterward, she had a small bruise the size of a quarter in the spot that had touched the wall. By nightfall it exploded into a bruise the size of her hand, and her parents had a hard time believing that it was from leaning against the wall. While that bruise was fading, she chased the dog and bumped her shin. This time, both her mother and brother saw the incident and were shocked when it turned into another bruise bigger than her hand. They took her back to the doctor, who again tested her for mono.

This kept happening all summer. Tiredness, bruising, difficulty sleeping, joint pains—and mono tests. By the fifth test, when she asked them to test for something other than mono, the nurses decided she'd grown an attitude. By the eighth test, they decided that she was depressed and sent her to therapy. It was LA in the early 1980s. One of the girls in her group was being abused by her father; one of the boys was being battered because he wasn't American enough. Amanda was being stigmatized in the group as a hypochondriac because her problem—being tired—seemed so minor. Her therapist told her, "You're cute enough—you should just get a nose job. Why don't you get one over spring break?"

Her parents agreed and found a plastic surgeon for her. She went in for her pre-op lab testing. The plastic surgeon came back into the exam room and said, "Sorry. This is an elective surgery

---

* @LAlupusLady

and your PTT test came back abnormal. Your blood doesn't appear to clot. We're not doing the surgery as you could bleed to death on the table." Amanda remembers wondering what a PTT test was, and thinking, "It's like the Michael Jackson song, 'PYT, Pretty Young Thing.'" She said, "I'm not going back to that doctor—he'll just test me for mono again." Her doctor told her he could guarantee that they wouldn't test her for mono. "It's something much worse." PTT stands for "partial thromboplastin time." It is a blood test that measures the time it takes your blood to clot.[1]

This time when she went back to her family doctor, he ordered a spinal tap—a bone marrow test—as well as a full blood workup. Finally, after the extensive testing, he came into the room to say, "It's not leukemia; it's not anemia; it's not cancer. We think we've figured it out. It's an autoimmune disease called lupus." Amanda and her mother were both relieved, although in the age of AIDS, hearing you had an autoimmune disorder was scary. Her mom said, "OK. Now we know what it is; how do we get rid of it?" The doctor subtly shook his head, "no." Amanda's first question was, "Will this affect my ability to have babies?" In a high school class, she'd just been learning about nonverbal communication and she noticed the doctor's reaction: his eye rolls, the shake of his head. He was saying a lot even though he wasn't speaking. The doctor said to her mother, "I'd like to talk to you alone." Amanda said, "What? You're going to tell my mother about *my* disease?" Her mother said, "I will tell you everything he says." Afterward, going home, her mother said, "He's the wrong doctor for us." Amanda found out later that the doctor told her mother that Amanda had, at best, seven or eight years to live. Her mother did not tell her that for many years.

Finding the Right Doctor

Amanda and her mother began looking for another doctor by asking people for recommendations. One doctor was on two lists, so they went to her. Dr. W put Amanda on 80 mg of prednisone: three pills, three times a day, with no taper up to the full dosage and no taper down from it. Amanda's whole body went crazy. She stopped sleeping and started eating. She was depressed and hungry and started having as much difficulty with the side effects of prednisone as she'd had with the disease itself.

Her grandmother found another doctor, a rheumatologist, at a major academic medical center in the area. Dr. M did an exam and said, "You are on way too much prednisone. I can't tell what is side effect and what is disease." Her mother kept her in the room and said to the doctor, "I don't think we should discuss life expectancy." The doctor took the time to explain lupus. He explained that Amanda needed to stay out of the sun—a hard message for a teenager in LA—as the cell walls are fragile in people with lupus, and the sun can trigger a breakdown of the cell walls, with cascading symptoms including joint pains, weakness, fatigue, and fever.[2] He also began tapering her prednisone from 80 down to 20 mg, as gradually and as safely as possible. After three months at 20 mg, she asked to go lower. Amanda and Dr. M were both Jewish, so they first agreed to taper her dose of prednisone to 18 mg, as the Hebrew word for life is "Chai," and has the same symbol as the number 18. Then they tried 17, and ever so gradually, Amanda got down to 10 mg. Dr. M said, "Let's stay at 10 mg for a while, because you remind me of Bo Derek." (The movie "10," starring Bo Derek, had previously been released, but he thought it would keep spirits up if he compared Amanda to Bo Derek.)

Amanda kept pushing to further reduce her prednisone dose. She was one of the four patients Dr. M had who were under the age of 57. Her mother kept saying to the doctor, "If you had a daughter Amanda's age, how would you treat her?" They agreed to continue to taper her off prednisone—she wanted to be off it by her birthday on August 3. They worked on the tapering from February to July 31. Dr. M told her, "I'm with you on this program as long as you follow my rules and as long as you are totally honest with me." As Amanda sees it now, she had to become the very queen of patient adherence. They tapered from 10 to 9 to 8 to 7 mg, and then started tapering one-half a milligram at a time. She was able to manage it and keep her condition stable.

Learning to Live with Lupus

A year later, someone asked her, "Whatever happened to that nose job of yours?" So Amanda asked about her PTT blood work. Dr. M told her, "They're good enough that if you wanted the nose job now, you could get it."

Her mother and her doctor talked. He told her mother, "Amanda's survived the worst, but we don't know if she will have another flare that could kill her. She's got a great support system. If she wants a nose job, let her get a nose job." Amanda was on prednisone for a flare at that point, but as soon as she tapered off she went in for lab tests that confirmed her PTT was fine and she got her nose job. The truth was that, in 1987, if you were a lupus patient, it was unlikely you were going to survive for long. There were no medications targeting lupus and no researchers working on it. However, the advent of AIDS meant that researchers had begun working on autoimmune disorders and there might be an associated breakthrough on lupus. Amanda's nose job became a signal for her that if lupus couldn't stop her from getting a nose job, it was not going to stop her from anything else in the world she wanted to accomplish!

At 18, Amanda planned to attend the University of California, Santa Barbara. After she applied and was accepted, she started realizing that it was a college culture where everyone was on the beach all the time. She couldn't do that. The culture was going to reinforce how different she was. She decided that UC, Santa Barbara, was the wrong place for her, so she took a year off and researched colleges. She finally decided on the University of Oregon. It was usually rainy there, and if it was sunny, Amanda could wear a hat. It turned out to be a good place for weather if you were a lupus patient, but not such a good place if you were a Jewish woman.

Finally, she ended up at San Francisco State, where she found her niche and her home—and could take quick flights back to LA if she had a health scare. She saw her rheumatologist every break. Dr. M would come in to see her on the Friday after Thanksgiving, and spring break, and over Christmas. She made it through college with a major in broadcasting communications.

While at school, she realized she was really good at writing. She began doing marketing and PR at school. When she graduated, she got in at Warner Bros. She was doing an assistant job, 40 hours a week paid and 10 hours a week unpaid. After about four months working full time for one of the producers—and loving it—she got the flu. She got it the way a person with lupus gets the flu, which is severely. She missed four days of work as a result. While she was out, the producer got a temp in, and when she came back to work, he told her, "I'm not discriminating against you because of your disease but because you can't do your job. I'm putting you back in the pool." She found the temp pool very stressful. Because she couldn't plan her work or take care of herself with temp work, she eventually ended up quitting.

Amanda had become politically active with the Young Democrats. The 2000 convention was being held in LA at the Staples Center, and Amanda, with the Young Democrats, was a part of it. *The West Wing*, produced by Warner Bros. and filming in LA, was at its height. At the last minute, Martin Sheen, star of *The West Wing*, suggested that there was an opportunity to make use of the contemporaneous events. Amanda was called into a production office at Warner Bros. Martin Sheen was sitting there with John Wells, the lead producer for *The West Wing*. He said, "So, Amanda," as if they had known each other for years. That was how she became the liaison between the Democratic Party and the Warner Bros./*West Wing* team. She choreographed most of the action, especially the planning for a party on Saturday/Sunday night of the convention. Some of the cast members wanted to help, and Amanda coordinated most of the action, especially the planning of the Young Democrats Convention Kick-Off Party that included a concert by The Goo Goo Dolls that was attended by Al Gore's daughters and Dulé Hill of *The West Wing*. Because of Secret Service protocols, they had to close the press list for the event 48 hours beforehand. Amanda, starstruck, thought, "Wow, I've hit the big time!"

After that, the Democratic National Committee, the Democratic Coordinating Committee, and the Warner Bros. special events team all wanted to hire her. She was thrilled, but knew she couldn't work 40 hours a week, so she started her own company where she could be a consultant and plan and manage her own schedule.

All of this happened in the context of repeated bouts of lupus complications. Episodically, set off by forces she couldn't control and couldn't predict, she would find herself in an acute exacerbation. The disease required her to be honest with clients. Public relations jobs require flexibility, not unpredictability. Many jobs went to other firms. Amanda's small but active clients kept her busy. Often the stress of planning a crucial product launch would trigger a lupus flare. Managing the disease was a full-time job and managing her small consulting firm was another. You may remember that one of Amanda's first questions was whether lupus would affect her ability to have children. In fact, it did. She experienced early onset menopause, so was not able to have children of her own. She and her husband pursued adoption, but after working extensively with an open adoption attorney, were not able to find a birth mother who was comfortable giving her baby to a mother with a chronic illness who might die young. It has been another adjustment to living with the disease—although Amanda notes that she is a fun and cool aunt and loving cat mom.

Flares and Complications

Amanda has developed irritable bowel syndrome (IBS) in the last few years. Although the pathways are not clear, IBS is often seen in conjunction with lupus. It took three months for her insurance to approve a capsule camera—essentially a small pill with a camera embedded in it to check the mechanisms of the disease. Amanda wanted to live stream the event, but couldn't get approval. The camera showed nothing wrong in her stomach but did show a small hiatal hernia in her bowel and a nodule on her left lung. IBS is complicated to treat under the best of circumstances, but especially in conjunction with lupus, as the normal treatments compromise the immune system and someone with lupus can ill afford that. IBS has become part of Amanda's "new normal"—one more thing to manage. Amanda has a growing knowledge of foods that can help lupus-specific issues and is combining that with IBS-sensitive diets to see what works for her. One of the things that makes lupus so difficult is that every patient is unique and requires a unique treatment approach.

In 2014 Amanda had health complications that were exacerbated by illness in her family. She was in a severe lupus flare and simply wasn't responding to any of the treatments that had worked in the past. Her insurance approved an experimental treatment that involved giving Amanda oral chemotherapy drugs. For most people, this would have required hospitalization, but with Amanda's compromised immune system, it was too risky to administer in the hospital, so she did the treatment at home. While she was struggling with the flare, her father-in-law went to the hospital for a chest x-ray, and turned out to have an infection so severe he was hospitalized immediately. After four months of alternating cycles of rehab and readmittance, he died in the hospital.

On the seventh day of Amanda's oral chemotherapy treatments, she flew to New Jersey for her father-in-law's funeral.

The day after they got back from the funeral, Amanda's mother took her 99-year-old grandmother in for a checkup, as she seemed to be failing. Her grandmother was one of the rocks in Amanda's life, always alert, cheerful, and upbeat. The doctors asked her grandmother several questions and felt she wasn't responsive. They performed a CAT scan that revealed an inoperable brain tumor. She was three weeks away from her hundredth birthday and died the day after she turned 100. The emotional stresses of both these events made it even more difficult for Amanda to recover from her flare. Amanda soldiered on through another funeral despite both emotional and physical pain.

Many Doctors; Many Versions of Her Medical Record

Many specialists are involved in managing Amanda's conditions. In a recent eight-week period, she saw the following doctors: Her internist gave her a general checkup. Her dermatologist (who still has paper files) checked on lupus-related skin conditions. She saw a GI doctor for IBS and her rheumatologist to adjust her medications. She saw her cardiologist because there are heart issues connected with lupus. Instead of a psychologist or psychiatrist, Amanda has a lupus support group. She just saw a dentist who specializes in lupus-related dental issues and has just made an appointment to see an ophthalmologist who specializes in lupus. She has a pain specialist but isn't going right now because she doesn't like the side effects of the pain medications. Amanda also sees a medical doctor who is focused on alternative medications and treatments. She takes vitamins and minerals, as lupus patients have difficulty absorbing nutrients. She takes olive oil pills and turmeric for pain, as well as a Lidocaine patch when the pain is severe.

Amanda chose a connected health system to get her care, as she wanted her complex medical record available to all of the specialists who treat her, and she wanted to be able to use an interconnected portal to manage her own health. Despite her care in choosing a system that would have those advantages, there are still situations where lack of immediate interoperability causes problems. For example, she's been asked to give blood for a CBC test when she's had the same test only days before, and the results simply aren't yet available in the system. Although her dentist and dermatologist are treating lupus-related issues, their records don't interconnect in the health system. She can see her record on the system, but can't make changes to it. Her internist recently implemented an EHR system that makes it simple for her to view her lab results on all of her devices using the patient-friendly Healow app.

Becoming an Advocate

Finding the balance of managing a small business and lupus was not easy and the advent of social media brought new PR issues to the fore—while giving Amanda a forum for her passion for advocacy and lupus awareness. Through it, she is able to connect with other patients and advocates in a new way and share some of the lessons she's learned through 34 years of coping with symptoms like joint pain and inflammation.

Over time, Amanda came to the realization that lupus was her defining issue. As she puts it, "I have been in lupus college for 34 years, and I'm not getting extra credit." She found mission and meaning in using her PR training and her speaking and writing ability to be a lupus advocate. She is making up for lost time, as she is acutely aware that she may not have another May to participate in Lupus Awareness Month, or may not be able to make it to various conferences next year or next month or even next week.

She is part of the WEGO Health advocates group and has hosted four chats. With Tiffany (@TiffanyandLupus), Amanda co-hosts the bimonthly Twitter chat through #LupusChat, which is one of the only patient-run health chats currently on Twitter. Several years ago, she did a blog post every day in April, but she's realized that she needs to make trade-offs between doing that and being effective for Lupus Awareness Month in May. Amanda isn't yet being paid for her advocacy, although she was sponsored by GSK to travel to the Lupus Blogger's Summit in 2015 and was awarded a scholarship from HISTalk to attend Healthcare Information Management Systems Society (HIMSS) 2015, with free passes to the actual conference from CTG Health and HIMSS. Amanda has two jackets that are part of Regina Holliday's Walking Gallery of Healthcare, and it was great at HIMSS to be among others wearing Walking Gallery jackets. While at HIMSS, she had the opportunity to meet Jack Barrette, the founder of WEGO Health, and to write a blog post for HISTalk. It has been exciting to see her advocacy making a difference, although the price is high; each event is draining and takes days to recover from, but she loves the role of advocate, ambassador, activist.

Amanda recently participated in a Flip the Clinic event in Phoenix (http://fliptheclinic.org/). Flip the Clinic events are an effort to bring community innovation and collaboration to healthcare. Amanda's contribution was to reimagine the waiting room experience. She'd like to see waiting rooms with coffee, tea, and water available for patients. Comfortable chairs are a must, as are WiFi and good lighting. She also suggests good art, up-to-date magazines, and good music. As a slightly disruptive patient advocate, Amanda often challenges doctors to spend 30 minutes sitting in their own waiting rooms to get an idea what it's really like. One of the doctors she challenged with that at HIMSS told her, "This is my takeaway from HIMSS—I'm going to go sit in my own waiting room!"

Implications for Policy and Practice

As an engaged and connected patient and advocate, Amanda would like to see several things different in the healthcare system:

- As noted before, the experience should be tuned to the patient from the parking lot to the waiting room to the gowns patients are dressed in.
- She would like to be able to see her records—all of them—from any device: her phone, tablet, and laptop, including the latest results. As you can imagine, Amanda has records located in many places, and today neither she nor her physicians can see her whole history—but it would be incredibly helpful to do so.
- It would be helpful to be able to review her record and the physician notes online and correct or annotate them on the spot.
- When she is in a flare, it would be great to be assured that her rheumatologist and internist are looped in, no matter where in the world she is when the flare occurs.
- Patient–physician communication needs to be improved. Secure messaging helps, but it would also be useful to be able to chat, text, and video-conference, depending on the situation and urgency.

Conclusion

Amanda teaches about lupus—and about what it means to be a connected patient—in every situation she can, but she is dismayed by the lack of knowledge in the general population about the importance of having your health record. She would like to see a public service campaign that educates everyone about their rights to get their health records electronically and how important it is to do so. As an embodiment of a connected patient and patient advocate, Amanda is hopeful about the future and her ability to make an impact.

Notes

1. http://www.webmd.com/a-to-z-guides/partial-thromboplastin-time
2. http://www.lupus.org/research-news/entry/new-light-shed-on-photosensitivity-among-people-with-lupus

Story 16: Managing Diabetes with a Do-It-Yourself Pancreas System (DIYPS)

Jan Oldenburg, FHIMSS with Dana M. Lewis*

Introduction

Dana Lewis was diagnosed with type 1 diabetes when she was 14 and shortly thereafter got an insulin pump. After college, she moved across the country to Seattle and lived by herself for the first time. That's a scary moment for most of us, but it was especially scary for Dana, who worried that without someone who could hear the alarms on her continuous glucose monitor and wake her up, she would die in her sleep. It was a significant worry—one with a very strong basis in probability because she is such a deep sleeper.

She asked her mother to call or text her every morning to make sure she was awake, alert, and alive. It was a safety net, and while it alleviated Dana's fears of dying in her sleep, it wasn't an optimal solution. She started wondering how things would be different if her continuous glucose monitor (CGM) had louder alarms, or if her mother could see her blood glucose readings from Alabama and know when she needed help.

While Dana may be an exceptionally sound sleeper, many people report similar concerns with CGM devices—the alarms just aren't loud enough to wake up some of the people with diabetes who wear them, much less alert loved ones who may sleep in another room.[1] Apparently the devices have a battery life problem, and the louder the alarm is, the more it drains the batteries. In the absence of a way to increase the loudness of the alarms, Dana worked with—and around—the imperfect situation by having her mother and other friends call to make sure she was OK.

Gaining Control and Reducing Cognitive Load

A few years after moving to Seattle, Dana began dating Scott, a network engineer. Scott soon took on the role her mother formerly played, texting or calling to make sure Dana woke each morning and was able to raise a red flag if she was unresponsive. (Luckily, this has never happened.) They

---

* @DanaMLewis; www.DIYPS.org; www.OpenAPS.org

began talking about ways to make the situation better and obsessing about how they could get the data from her CGM.

In November of 2013, they saw notes circulating online about a new approach. It was pioneered by John Costik, then a software engineer at a supermarket chain. He had found a way to upload his son Evan's CGM data to the Internet every 5 minutes.[2] Dana and Scott eagerly began exchanging messages with John, who was willing to share his uploader code, and a community formed around the capability of remote data uploading and monitoring. Many in the community are parents of children with diabetes who are frustrated by their inability to see what is happening with their children when they are at school, at a friend's house, or at a sleepover. Others are adults who live with diabetes themselves, like Dana, or loved ones, like Scott. The group primarily convenes on Facebook, growing from a few dozen original developers and users to more than 12,000 members in a year. Many people in the community are adding information or sharing stories, supporting others in using this community-developed tool, while others spend time fine-tuning the capabilities. The number of people involved illustrates a deep hunger and need for better tools for both people with diabetes and the people who care for and about them.

Once they had access to her CGM data in real time, Dana and Scott began experimenting with ways to send the CGM data to Dana's smartphone so she could set alarms at a level that would wake her up. Since Scott had a Pebble SmartWatch, they also added the capability for a quick-view display on his watch. It turned out to be the perfect tool for Scott to quickly view Dana's CGM readings. In the first month they were using the system, it woke Scott up twice. Each time Dana's blood sugar was down to 50. They set the system up so Scott would only get an alert if Dana wasn't responding to an alarm. Dana didn't want Scott to get constant alerts if she was one point over or under the alarm threshold, but only if she was truly not responding and needed an additional alert or support. They added additional buttons to their system, using a basic web interface, to allow Dana to enter what actions she was taking.

Making the System Intelligent

Gradually, they made the interface more specific—not just that she was eating something or taking insulin, but exactly how many carbs she was taking in and how much insulin she was injecting. Figure S16.1 shows Dana's Pebble SmartWatch showing her blood glucose readings, the amount of insulin and carbohydrates she has in her body, and that no action is required.

Soon they began wondering how they could make the system better, perhaps in a way that enabled it to anticipate or predict what Dana would need to do next. Each insulin pump has a proprietary way of managing the timeline of insulin decay in the body. Dana and Scott began to reverse engineer the insulin activity curve using basic calculus.

By closely watching Dana's data, they also realized there seemed to be a constant rate at which carbohydrates are used by her body and thus how they impact blood glucose levels. They decided it was also ideal to treat to a range rather than a specific number as a blood glucose target, as a certain amount of the insulin won't be used and a certain percentage of the carbs won't be appropriately absorbed. And, in diabetes, there are many more factors than insulin and food that impact blood glucose. Temperature, activity levels, hormones, etc. all impact blood glucose levels and are hard to measure! Gradually, the algorithms Dana and Scott were using got better and better. The system can make three kinds of real-time predictive alerts: more insulin needed (X.X units of bolus insulin); less insulin needed (temp basal to zero insulin for X minutes); or carbohydrates (sugar) needed. They call the system DIYPS—the Do-It-Yourself Pancreas System.

Figure S16.1   Dana's Pebble SmartWatch, showing blood glucose readings, the amount of insulin and carbohydrates in her body, and that no action is required.

One of the advantages of this approach—and using DIYPS—is that it reduces the amount of mental energy that Dana has to spend managing her diabetes. The cognitive load of doing background calculations about how much insulin she needs and when she needs to ingest carbohydrates is significant and means she doesn't have as much mental energy for other pursuits. DIYPS does most of these background calculations and pushes alerts and notifications when Dana needs to take action. It also provides alerts, usually well in advance, of any pending dips or surges in blood glucose.

Outcomes

Using this algorithm and Dana's entries tracking insulin taken or reduced and carbs ingested, she has been able to significantly impact her diabetes outcomes in positive ways. After a year of using the DIYPS, she has reduced her average glucose (eAG) and hemoglobin A1C, which have been significantly modulated with both fewer lows and fewer highs. Both eAG and HBA1C are measures of how well controlled blood glucose levels have been over the past time period. This is a very positive sign, as it means that her time in the correct blood glucose range improved from 50 percent to regularly 80+ percent, which helps improve quality of life. Figure S16.2 shows the way the DIYPS has helped Dana control her average glucose readings over time.

Although Dana is an "*n* of one" in this pilot and is a highly motivated patient, she has been able to compare her months of results using the DIYPS to a controlled study of another artificial pancreas system called the "bionic pancreas." While DIYPS is "single hormone" and Dana only uses insulin, the bionic pancreas is a bihormonal artificial pancreas system that also uses glucagon to help treat low blood glucose levels. Dana's DIYPS performed as well as the bionic pancreas, even though DIYPS was not automatically adjusting her insulin levels at that time.

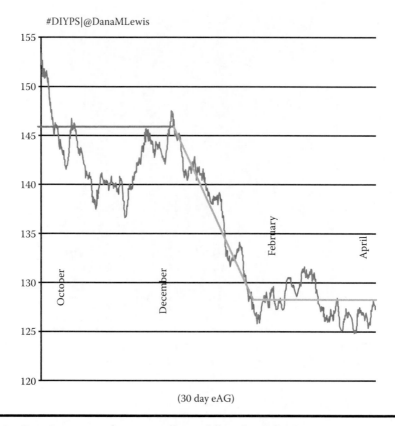

Figure S16.2   Dana's average glucose readings while using DIYPS.

In December of 2014, Dana and Scott engineered a way to "close the loop" so that the DIYPS could move from advising Dana how she should be dosing her insulin to actually adjusting the levels of insulin itself. She initially used the closed loop version of the system at night because it is cumbersome to cart around all of the components, but it works so well and so significantly reduces the cognitive requirements of living with diabetes that she is increasingly using it during the day as well.

Highly Activated

Dana is highly motivated to manage her diabetes, and her work on DIYPS helps her to stay active and engaged in managing it better. The work makes her feel empowered as well, now that she has more control with self-designed tools that ease some of the biggest burdens of living with diabetes. It is still hard to stay motivated all the time, though.

Dana has been a patient with diabetes for 14 years. For the first 10 or so years, she used the same style of insulin pump insertion sites, which eventually became painful to use. However, as she moved across the country and changed doctors, her doctors never asked her about the specific types of supplies she used, nor did the medical device manufacturer ever suggest there were other types of insertion sites that she could use. She realizes that despite being highly engaged, there are still numerous ways a person with diabetes or another chronic illness can fall through gaps in the system.

Dana would love to feel more supported by the healthcare community. Her doctor is pleased with her outcomes, but not especially interested in how she has achieved them. She thinks her doctor should be more interested in DIYPS, especially because the information it generates could help the medical community learn new ways to manage and help people treat diabetes.

Managing a disease like diabetes requires ongoing support regarding the person's whole lifestyle; it is not just a matter of prescribing the right drugs and equipment once. People need support throughout their life—especially during different stages of life—to best manage their diabetes.

Looking Forward

Many people ask Dana and Scott if they can try her DIYPS, or they want her to share the algorithms. The FDA would view that as distributing a medical device, which is prohibited. Instead they have chosen to crowdsource and share as much information about their experiment as possible. They are actively contributing information to the #NightScout community (the original community that helped them upload CGM data to the cloud). They have also started a movement called #OpenAPS, which is an initiative to build on the DIYPS closed loop work and eventually make this type of technology available (faster than the market and traditional research are otherwise moving) for more people with diabetes. They hope to use OpenAPS to create a closed loop artificial pancreas system that can be self-built and used by multiple "*n* of ones" and for clinical trials to reach more people. They are partnering with other independent researchers to help them improve the design and move the effort forward even more quickly than they can do themselves.

All of this takes place under the banner of #WeAreNotWaiting—a rallying cry that the medical device community and the FDA should pay attention to as the diabetes community is impatient about the slow pace of change and adoption of new technologies. The FDA has actively met with representatives from the #NightScout community, and Dana and Scott have had additional meetings with the FDA to discuss various parts of their work around DIYPS and OpenAPS.

None of this would be possible without social media, and the way it has enabled connections, communication, sharing, and social support is noteworthy. Unfortunately, medical device interoperability has a long way to go to make data accessibility and sharing as seamless as the tools that patients are building themselves. It would be easier if medical device companies were listening better to the pool of activated users who can explain what else they need from their devices—and then build what they need in a reasonable time frame.

Observations for Policy and Practice

Dana's story—and indeed, the story of the whole night scout community—holds lessons for the way we think about patients and consider them as participants in innovation and development:

- Patients are increasingly impatient with the slow pace of innovation and change in the medical device market and pharmaceutical and are demonstrating that they are not waiting for the industry to catch up with them by experimenting on their own. It is time for the industry to respond with true partnerships with engaged patients and family members to codesign products that better fit people's lifestyles and needs.

■ Dana's story shows what a patient who is driven to have a better life and motivated to manage her illness can do to impact the course of her own disease. It also shows how patient-created tools can have a powerful ripple effect not only in the community but also in the industry.

■ Social media are a powerful force for helping like-minded individuals to connect and collaborate in real time. Already established communities provide the opportunity for industry to engage and participate with committed individuals in exploring solutions.

■ Physicians have the opportunity to work with their patients and industry to design solutions that provide them with more effective ways of managing diabetes in partnership with their patients.

■ Every patient deserves the opportunity to be engaged and supported in managing his or her disease. Different approaches work for different individuals, so systems need to be able to support both the neophyte and the advanced patient.

Conclusion

Dana feels lucky that she has her CGM data on her phone and that Scott is always able to see her data, regardless of where they are. Even when there's no crisis that needs intervention, knowing that Scott can tell whether she had a good or bad night—or day—is reassuring. It means he doesn't have to ask her all the time how she is doing with regard to her blood glucose level and enables him to empathize with her. Dana realizes she is lucky on many levels; there are many in the diabetes community who don't have access to CGMs, or don't have someone to be their partner in receiving alerts, or who worry about whether they can trust the person they are relying on to know their data. Perhaps most of all, she is lucky that the improvements she has been able to make in stabilizing her own blood glucose levels provide a better quality of life and allow her to do more of the things she loves.

Scott asked Dana to marry him in the fall of 2014, and she was delighted to say yes. Shortly afterward, a happy adventure to try on wedding dresses was interrupted when Dana had low blood sugar. It was a reminder that her goal is not just to keep herself and others alive, but to allow all of them to live better: to be present for more of the events they want to remember, to live without extreme blood sugar events, and to cause less worry for the people who love them.

Dana and Scott originally had a simple goal: to help keep Dana alive. Their longer term goal was more complex: They wanted to reduce the cognitive load of managing her diabetes and allow her to keep her blood sugars better managed with less time, energy, and worry. Their joy is that the information they have uncovered and the algorithms they have created might keep not just Dana alive, but many others as well. The significance of Dana's work is being noticed, as she was honored in February of 2016 by being asked to participate in the White House Precision Medicine Event as a representative of patients taking action to improve their lives and the lives of other patients.

Notes

1. http://www.insulinpumpforums.com/lofiversion/index.php?t3715.html
2. http://www.healthline.com/diabetesmine/diabetes-data-all-with-a-quick-glance-at-your-wrist#3

Story 17: "You Have a Mass the Size of an Eggplant in Your Abdomen"

Jan Oldenburg, FHIMSS with Susan, MBA

Introduction

Susan embarked on a program of self-improvement after she retired from her teaching job. She began taking yoga classes, started a diet, and lost 15 pounds—though she noticed that she seemed to have lost more weight on her right side than her left. She'd also been having some difficulties with urinary incontinence, so she went to a physical therapist for help with that. The physical therapist palpitated her abdomen, then followed up with a sonogram. "There's a tumor," she said and showed it to Susan on the sonogram. The physical therapist called Susan's internist, who was dismissive. Susan thought it was because it was reported by a physical therapist rather than a doctor. When Susan called to get an appointment, armed with the knowledge there was a problem, her internist didn't have any openings for a month.

Diagnosis

When Susan finally got in to see her internist, and Dr. X had the opportunity to palpate her abdomen personally, things suddenly became urgent. Dr. X scheduled her for a CT scan the following day at the local hospital, on a Friday. Dr. X called Susan after the CT scan and said, rather abruptly, "You have a mass in your stomach the size of an eggplant. I've arranged for you to see a surgeon on Monday." Susan later learned that the tumor was watery and cystic and had probably been growing for at least 5 years. At 24 cm, it was at least eggplant sized.

Susan began doing research. Her friend, Bev, helped her find abdominal cancer sites to understand what it might be so that she could ask better questions of the surgeon. She initially understood it to be a gastric tumor, however, so some of the initial research pointed her in the wrong direction. Her tumor was pancreatic.

Susan was scheduled to depart on a long-awaited 2-week Alaskan cruise later that week. She seriously considered going anyway, thinking, "What's two more weeks if the tumor has been growing for 5 years?" Her family was very much against that plan, however, and wanted her to pursue treatment immediately, so Susan reluctantly cancelled the cruise and continued instead with doctors' visits and second opinions.

Choosing a Surgeon

The following Monday, she took Bev with her to see a surgeon, recommended by her internist, who practiced at her local hospital. He told them there was a mass in Susan's stomach, and they didn't yet know what it was. When she asked how many such surgeries he'd done, his response was, "I do a lot." He didn't review the CT scan with her or talk about what the options would be. Instead, he patted her on the shoulder and said, "Don't worry dear; I'll take care of you." Susan was annoyed at his condescending treatment and asked for several names in order to get a second opinion. He gave her the names of several surgeons in the region.

Bev also accompanied Susan to her second-opinion appointment with Dr. T at a teaching hospital 2 hours away from home in Evanston. It was really important to have another person along so that Susan could check her impressions with someone else, and someone else could take notes in case Susan became overwhelmed. Susan knew from her research that Dr. T was one of the authors of the protocol for abdominal cystic tumors. In her first visit with Dr. T, Susan was introduced to his team, including the nurse and chief resident. Dr. T told her, "I've done 1800 of these surgeries." He reviewed the CT scan with her in detail and told her that she would probably lose her spleen, pancreas, and part of her stomach—all issues that the first surgeon hadn't shared. He also shared his assessment that it was likely that the tumor was not cancerous. His team provided three things that were really important to Susan: they treated her as a partner, they made her felt cared for, and they gave her hope.

The Belly Blob Blog

Here's the e-mail Susan sent out to her immediate family and closest friends reporting on that visit:

> Hi, all,
>   Decided to update all of you en mass so I don't forget anything. Went to Evanston today to see Dr. T, he specializes in all kinds of stomach surgery and is very highly rated. He is also a very nice guy and a great teacher. He totally explained to me about my blob (friend Bev and I even got to see the CT scan pictures!) and what would happen during the surgery. First of all he doesn't think it is cancerous though, of course, he can't totally rule it out. He thinks this tumor has been growing for a long time but since I don't have any pain he feels my body has just accommodated it. The rest of the news isn't as good. He thinks the tumor is connected to my pancreas and that he might have to remove one-third to one-half of it. Long term he notes that this isn't a problem because there will still be enough pancreas to avert diabetes but I probably will have to be better about my diet. (Hence, eat fewer but better chocolates!) He also feels he might have to remove my spleen. Again, not a long-term worry. There is

a possibility that the tumor is attached to the stomach. If this is true he may have to remove part of my stomach and reattach the bowel. This, as you can guess, is a little more serious. This is basically the same surgery that people get for weight loss. It means smaller meals, more often. Of course a change but not impossible.

Anyway Dr. T says the operation will take 2 to 4 hours, and I will have to be in hospital for 3 to 5 days after that.

I still have to decide who is going to do the surgery but Dr. T is really looking good.
Susan/Mom

Susan named the e-mails she sent to family and friends "the belly blob blog." Her son helped her visualize the experience as a journey. As she explains, "We decided that this is a river journey. I like rivers and waters and the visualization worked/works because sometimes there are rapids ahead but often the river is slow and sluggish, just waiting. But like many rivers there's muck underneath." After he saw Susan's e-mail about her visit to Dr. T, her son responded with this:

Thank you very much for keeping me up on the situation. I see this as an excellent new addition/edition to the map: he's steering you away from Cancertown. Granted, it looks like he's taking a swerve into the CarveYaUp Strait, but you've weathered worse storms. You've got one more cartographer to meet and then you can set a course confident you've got a good lay of the land. It's a good day! Give me a call if you need anything, even if it's just to talk. Hope you have an excellent rest of the day!

Surgery

Susan decided to have Dr. T do the surgery and it was scheduled for 3 weeks later on a Thursday (1 week of the delay was caused by the disruption of the Labor Day holiday). In order to be cleared for surgery, Susan needed a physical. Her local internist, Dr. X, scheduled it for 9 days before the surgery and faxed the records of the physical over to Dr. T's office. The Friday before the surgery, Susan got a call from Dr. T's office telling her that her presurgery physical hadn't included an EKG, and she needed to get one along with a cardiology consultation before the surgery.

Her local hospital couldn't do the EKG until the day before the surgery, so Susan called Dr. X for help getting it scheduled earlier. Neither her internist nor her staff were helpful. By this point, Susan was frustrated and scared she wouldn't get the right prerequisites accomplished, so she called Dr. T's staff. Despite the fact that they were located 2 hours away, they got Susan in at her local hospital for both the EKG and cardiology consult the following day. The next hurdle was getting her internist to clear her for surgery. After calls from Dr. T's team to her internist, Susan was finally cleared for surgery at 3 p.m. on the day before surgery.

Here's the note Susan sent out to family and friends the night before surgery:

Hi, all,

It's finally official—I'll go into surgery tomorrow (Sept. 18) at 5 p.m. They expect the operation to last 3 to 4 hours and I will be separated (Hooray!) from my 8 inch "tummy tumor." Can't wait to lose the weight!!

I am so very blessed to be very healthy and without pain. This is one of the reasons why they think my tumor is noncancerous. Of course, we won't know for sure for several weeks because of lab tests but I am feeling very positive.

I am also feeling very supported. I truly believe in the power of prayer and I have a lot of prayer power going for me. I'm not just on the wings of prayer, I have muscles and shoulders supporting me! I feel God's grace. Thanks to all of you for helping me with this journey!

Susan

PS: Bev will send out an update. From what I understand I will be pretty out of it for a least 2 weeks and won't be able to respond to e-mails. Please know that your prayers are important!

Susan was relieved to have the waiting over when surgery day arrived. Her family was prepared for surgery to last 3 to 4 hours, but in the end, it took only a little more than 2 hours. Her surgical team was very positive—they'd removed the whole cystic tumor and didn't think it was cancerous. She went in expecting to lose her spleen, some or all of her pancreas, and some of her stomach. When she came out, however, they had taken the spleen and about a third of the pancreas that the tumor was attached to, but they hadn't needed to remove any of her stomach or intestines. Her incision went from her sternum to her pubic bones and removed 10 pounds of "stuff."

The nurses and licensed practical nurses (LPNs) who took care of Susan were wonderful. One LPN had just been admitted into a nursing program. He was wonderful about figuring out the bed, helping Susan learn how to sit up and how to move to minimize pain. He educated her about pain meds and how to manage pain but still be alert enough to sit up right after abdominal surgery. The phlebotomist was amusing—he would announce himself by saying, "The vampire is here" and had a never-ending stock of vampire jokes that made her laugh. Because she was at a teaching hospital, the residents always showed up at 6:04 in the morning, which was predictable if irritating.

Because the surgical team was pretty sure Susan's tumor was noncancerous, she didn't receive cancer education materials in the hospital or as part of discharge. She had received information about pancreatic cancer and www.pancan.org as part of her initial visit along with information about diet, because if they had needed to remove her pancreas she was at risk of becoming a type 1 diabetic.

Cancer

Susan was discharged 6 days after surgery without knowing the results of the pathology report. On this point, communication was imperfect. No one told her they had some questions about the pathology report and had sent it out for a second reading, so Susan was left wondering why it was taking so long. Then, a week after discharge, Dr. T called her and told her there was cancer. Susan said, "Frankly, I don't remember much about that call except the word cancer—and that he said he would explain more at my postoperative visit the following week."

Susan was lucky, however, as the cancer was still stage 1. This is unusual with pancreatic cancer; because there are often no symptoms, it is usually not caught until a very late stage. As the Mayo Clinic says in its definition of pancreatic cancer, "Pancreatic cancer typically spreads rapidly and is seldom detected in its early stages, which is a major reason why it's a leading cause of cancer death. Signs and symptoms may not appear until pancreatic cancer is quite advanced and complete surgical removal isn't possible."[1]

Dr. T developed Susan's chemotherapy treatment plan, but told her, "We have very good people here, but why would you want to drive so far? I have a wonderful colleague at your local hospital who can take care of you, and your quality of life will be improved if you don't have to drive 2 hours each way to get your chemo." His nurse called the medical oncologist at her local hospital, made the referral and her first appointment. The smooth transition of care made her feel very well taken care of.

Here's the belly blob blog e-mail Susan sent out at this stage of the process:

> Hi, all,
>
> Just finished with my post-op checkout and got the pathology report. It's very mixed. I do have stage 1 pancreatic cancer but it was caught very early, it is very slow growing and all my lymph nodes are clear. I will receive chemo but not radiation. I believe I will get through this. I am strong, I have great medical help and most of all I have the important support of my friends and church. All of you are truly blessings to me!
>
> Susan

Chemotherapy

Susan felt very good about the medical oncologist at her local hospital, saying, "He treats me as a person. He listens to me. I am not a script." Because her local hospital is on Epic, she could pull up her MyChart account and show him her EKG as well as the CT scan. Susan noted, "I am very thankful for electronic medical records because I can go anywhere within my local system and they have all my records at their fingertips." Dr. H, the medical oncologist, made arrangements for another woman with pancreatic cancer to call Susan, just so that she would know what to expect. Dr. H reminded her that she was very lucky because her cancer was caught early, but noted that it is a very aggressive form of cancer. The e-mail she sent out after this highlights some of the information about her chemo treatments:

> Hi, all,
>
> I'm beginning a new part of my journey—I'm starting preventative chemotherapy next Wednesday. Because my cancer was caught so early, the chemo will be pretty mild with the goal of killing any stray diseased cells that might be floating around in my much reduced belly. Everyone is different but generally people getting my prescription don't lose their hair or have a lot of nausea. Again, I am very lucky. Thanks again for all your prayers and support. I am strong.
>
> Susan

Susan started chemotherapy shortly after she first saw Dr. H. She developed a rhythm for the Tuesdays when she got chemo. In the morning, she walked 4000 to 5000 steps and then did yoga. Chemo began at two in the afternoon, starting with lab tests, which the doctor had to review before the start of chemo. The waiting for review of her labs was the hardest part. Although it was supposed to take less than 15 minutes, sometimes she had to remind the receptionist that she was still waiting. Depending on the treatment they were giving, each chemo treatment lasted between 90 minutes and 2 1/2 hours. Susan was always really tired after chemo was over. Although the hospital was close, each week she became more tired and eventually asked a friend to drive her to and from her treatments.

After each chemotherapy treatment, Susan slept a lot for 2 days. By Thursday afternoon, she generally felt like herself again. She allowed herself to catnap when she felt tired and that allowed her to keep going all through the treatment. Susan did not lose her hair, although it got very fragile;

she was relieved not to have baldness signal her health status to everyone. Another thing that helped her during this process was planning some sort of an expedition toward the end of every month. It gave her something to look forward to and something else to focus on beside her treatment.

Susan religiously used MyChart to monitor her lab tests and ate more bananas in response to seeing from her chart that her potassium levels were dropping from chemo. Each week all of her labs were available by the time she arrived home after chemo. Secure messaging and e-mail allowed her to get questions large and small answered—both with Dr. T's staff and with her medical oncologist. She is part of Dr. T's research database, and he has a certified data specialist to whom she can also send questions about prognosis and treatment.

Community

The strong community that Susan has been building for years helped her through this process. Her church, family, and friends all pitched in to offer support, to bring meals, to send prayers, and to keep her feeling connected and cared for. "I am strong" was her mantra through the experience, and she tried to stay perky and upbeat each day, but sometimes she was just tired. She found herself making the choice to stay upbeat every day—sometimes several times a day—but also learned to forgive herself on the days she just couldn't. Although going through chemotherapy was the perfect "get out of jail free" card to say no to things, Susan found herself using it carefully, as she didn't want to be isolated when chemo finally ended. She has learned the power of networking, of sharing, of asking for help.

Susan's experience with payments and billing was relatively painless. She was covered by a Blue Cross Blue Shield (BCBS) plan, and they were wonderful about covering all of the procedures. The only issue Susan encountered was with the bill for the CT scan. Because it was set up as a "rush," BCBS charged extra for the rush processing. She received that bill in January for a CT scan that occurred in August. Her chemo cost nearly $17,000 a month. Susan joked that because of chemo she met her deductible for the year on January 2.

Observations for Policy and Practice

Although Susan had a very good experience overall, there are things small and large that she would change if she could. Each represents an opportunity to ease the journey for cancer patients:

- In the hospital during recovery, when sleep is so important to healing, is it really crucial that residents wake you up at 6:04 for tests? In a February 15, 2015, article in the *New York Times* entitled, "Doctors Strive to Do Less Harm by Inattentive Care,"[2] Dr. Michael Bennick, medical director for patient experience at Yale-New Haven Hospital discusses how he stopped middle-of-the-night blood draws because they hurt patients' sleep and caused unneeded suffering.
- Susan's hospital discharge would have been easier if she had been provided with medications at discharge rather than having to stop to get the prescriptions filled on the way home. The trip home was 2 hours, and she needed pain medications every 4 hours, so it was complicated to endure the trip home and get medications in time for her next dose.
- Midway through her recovery, Susan realized she was going to run out of pain medication on a Sunday. It was hard to get through to the on-call physician, so she spent Saturday from nine to three on the phone trying to reach someone who could authorize her prescription extension.

- It is frustrating that each physician and hospital has a different portal with different rules, different password requirements, and different data. It would be nice to designate one site as your "home" portal, have all of the data from all of your medical care show up there, and be able to use it to send secure messages to all of your doctors.
- Susan still carries some anger at her former internist, Dr. X. She would have liked her to have responded more urgently to the call from the physical therapist, to have been more sensitive in announcing that Susan had a mass in her stomach, and to have been more responsive to the need to complete all the steps to clear Susan for surgery.
- The first oncologist that Susan saw was condescending and didn't understand that she wanted details and data, not just reassurance. She signaled her dissatisfaction with his paternalistic style of practice by voting with her feet, but he may never realize that his approach is outdated.
- When the teaching hospital where Dr. T practiced expanded, the city wouldn't allow them to build their own parking garage. Instead, the city built the garage adjoining the hospital so that it could get the revenue from the parking. The day a person is scheduled for surgery, family members get a 2-hour free parking certificate, but the rest of the time everyone pays every day for every hour. It's a small but continued annoyance.

Conclusion

During recovery, as Susan struggled to make sense of both the physical and emotional impact of cancer, she took heart from reading. It was especially helpful to read "Seasons of Survival,"[3] written by a doctor who was himself a cancer survivor, talking about the stages of illness and recovery. She also appreciated the definition of cancer survivorship from the National Coalition for Cancer Survivorship.[4] As a result of her reading and thinking, Susan has issues with the words we use to talk about cancer.

All the terminology about "fighting" cancer bothers her, because it implies that if cancer wins, it was because you failed to fight hard enough. She has similar issues with being a "cancer survivor" and all of the celebrations for cancer survivors, and the "count up" mentality of surviving 1 year, 2 years, 5 years. While "cancer survivor" is a better term than the one it was coined to replace, "cancer victim," Susan feels that there really isn't a bright line with cancer, where on one side of it you are still sick, and on the other you have survived. The word "survivor" suggests that if you have a recurrence, you have failed. She is hoping for a third-generation term, one that embraces the elements of survivorship but focuses less on the bright line between sickness and health. The perfect term, for her, would signal: You have come through a difficult journey that has marked you forever but, for now, you are doing well.

Notes

1. http://www.mayoclinic.org/diseases-conditions/pancreatic-cancer/basics/definition/con-20028153
2. http://www.nytimes.com/2015/02/18/health/doctors-strive-to-do-less-harm-by-inattentive-care.html?_r=0
3. http://www.canceradvocacy.org/wp-content/uploads/2013/01/Seasons-of-Survival.pdf
4. http://www.canceradvocacy.org/about-us/our-history/

Story 18: Overcoming Adverse Childhood Events

Jan Oldenburg, FHIMSS with Kait B. Roe*

Introduction

Kait wrestles each day with the fallout from her difficult childhood. It would be a cliché to say that she has "triumphed over it," as its legacy is still with her and creates struggle every day. And yet, both because and in spite of it, she has managed to create meaning, build expertise, and contribute her gifts as an advocate for others.

A Difficult Childhood

By any measure, Kait has had a difficult life journey. When she was 5, her mother went to the hospital to deliver another sister for Kait and never came home. She died of a heparin overdose given to her during the birth. Her mother lingered on for several weeks and Kait remembers a nurse smuggling her and her older sister into the hospital in a laundry basket in the hopes that seeing them would give her mother the will to live. Her mother died shortly after, and Kait felt the burden of "not being enough" for her mother to live for. After her mother died, her stepfather kidnapped Kait and her older sister and held them for several months until her sister let her real name slip at school. They were returned to their grandparents to live. Just a few months later, her stepfather died in a one-car accident. He was drunk and nearly killed two passengers as well as himself.

As a result of the trauma, Kait went mute for the better part of 6 months. The pediatrician said it was common in the loss of a parent and that Kait would likely snap out of it eventually. Her grandmother didn't feel psychiatry was a valid medical practice, so Kait didn't get the real help she needed at any point during her childhood, although she eventually began talking again.

---

* @fuse_kait

Adverse Childhood Events Survey

Kait has since used the Adverse Childhood Events Survey (ACES) score as a way to look at her history. Her scores on the 10-question quiz are off the charts. The ACE score matters, as a 10-year study on the topic found:

> [T]he key concept underlying the study is that stressful or traumatic childhood experiences such as abuse, neglect, witnessing domestic violence, or growing up with alcohol or other substance abuse, mental illness, parental discord, or crime in the home (which we termed adverse childhood experiences—or ACEs) are a common pathway to social, emotional, and cognitive impairments that lead to increased risk of unhealthy behaviors, risk of violence or re-victimization, disease, disability and premature mortality. We now know from breakthroughs in neurobiology that ACEs disrupt neurodevelopment and can have lasting effects on brain structure and function—the biologic pathways that likely explain the strength of the findings from the ACE study.[1]

Although it is cold comfort to Kait to understand that her childhood experiences are at the root of some of the things she struggles with as an adult, it is still helpful to know that there is causality.

Coming Out

At 15, Kait came out as a lesbian. She was madly in love with her English teacher, who rejected her. She drank extensively, trying to cope with the pain, and eventually tried to kill herself. She was sent to the hospital on a 72-two-hour hold. Although she got some counseling, it didn't really change her attitudes or beliefs.

Later in the year, still drinking, she wrecked her car and broke her back. Because of the car accident and its fallout—a DUI at 16 meant mandatory drug/alcohol therapy and 200 community service hours in the public library—shelving, organizing, cleaning, and working at the head librarian's behest. For Kait, it was a godsend. She was nurtured and cared for. Lenore Bright, the head librarian, saved her life, and books gave her an understanding of the world beyond her small town and its provincial ideologies.

During this tumultuous time, Kait was kicked out of her home Baptist church, apparently because she was gay—but no one told her the reason why. The church had been one of her refuges, so it was another blow to her sense of safety and community. She was so angry about the rejection by the church that her spiritual development was stunted for many years afterward.

The Desire to Die

Bouts of profound suicidality are the milestones in Kait's development, in the way that other people mark milestones with certificates or degrees. A constant undertone in her life is the deep and profound WANT to die: the desire to kill herself and be done with the struggle of survival. Poverty, depression, extreme feelings of alienation, failures at school and in relationships, and the feeling that she could never live up to others' expectations of her have repeatedly pushed her to the edge of suicide.

College and Early Adulthood

At that point in her late teens Kait was angry all the time, rejecting everyone who tried to help her. She tried to go to college but failed—miserably and dramatically. No one taught her money management and she had few skills in time management. She was socially isolated, in part because of her poverty. Eventually, deeply depressed and suicidal, Kait once more landed in the hospital.

She moved to Colorado and attended Colorado State University. When she ran out of money, she worked as an emergency medical technician (EMT) for several years. In 1989, a relationship ended and Kait moved to Aspen/Glenwood Springs. Shortly thereafter her right arm became paralyzed. It was diagnosed as psychosomatic, a "hysterical conversion." Conversion disorder is diagnosed when psychological stress manifests itself as a physical ailment.[2] Kait was hospitalized again for treatment.

When she recovered, she moved to San Francisco for several years. While in San Francisco, Kait met and became domestic partners with Amy. They had a child together (the baby was carried by Amy). They were together for five and a half years after their son's birth. Kait was the stay-at-home caretaker for most of that time. They moved to Maine together in 1996. Not long after the move, Kait and Amy broke up, which sent Kait into a tailspin leading to several hospitalizations. Kait got herself stable again, and their relationship and parenting stayed amiable for three years until Amy married a man, the biological father of their child. Amy and her new husband decided to cut Kait out of the child's life—primarily, it seems, because of the stigma of Kait's mental illness. Since Kait wasn't the birth mother, she had no parental rights, and no standing to fight for continued contact with her son. This remains a daily source of grief in her life.

In 2000, Kait entered a United Church of Christ (UCC) seminary in Bangor, Maine. She felt that someone had stolen God from her and she wanted to understand what had happened. She didn't have a bachelor's degree, but she was able to enroll in a program that allowed her to complete bachelor's and master's degrees at the same time. She was 32 or 33 at the time. She attended for two years and did really well. The experience allowed her to reclaim her spiritual life and realize her intellectual competence.

Incapable of Making Her Own Decisions

While at the seminary, Kait reinjured her back. She was treated with narcotics, which sent her into a deep depression and another suicide attempt. It's recently become clear that use of narcotics can increase the risk of depression, especially in those with an existing tendency for it.[3] That sent her into the hospital again and, because she was a student without money, she ended up in charity care.

For Kait, this suicide attempt was actually a happy accident, as she got some of the best care ever from the nurse practitioner assigned to her case. Her nurse practitioner saw her situation both with a nurse's eyes and the eyes of a mental health practitioner. She was helpful in enabling Kait to make sense of her situation. She also helped her apply for social security benefits, which have given her a base-level stream of revenue to tide her over during hard times.

On the other hand, Kait was also experiencing the mental health system firsthand, in a situation and hospital that were incredibly patriarchal and paternalistic. For the most part, the system seemed to be organized around the assumption that being a mental health patient meant that she was not capable of being her own agent or making her own decisions.

For Kait, intelligent, determined, and angry, this was incredibly frustrating. Her journey had made her well aware that although she needed the support of others, she was going to have to save herself. Being subject to a system in which people assumed that they knew what was best for her and that she was not capable of being a partner in the decision making fueled her determination to find a solution for herself—and help others in similar situations.

"But It's the Only Thing That Works"

One of Kait's hospital physicians gave her a pain prescription for Celebrex 200 instead of Celebrex 100—and it worked. Celebrex is a nonsteroidal anti-inflammatory medication, but one that is easier on the stomach than many others. The change to a stronger dosage was almost magical for Kait—it stopped her back pain in its tracks. In the hospital, there were no restrictions on the medications ordered for Medicaid patients.

When Kait was discharged, however, Maine's drug formulary took effect and Celebrex 200 was no longer allowed. Kait was back in a state of constant pain. Someone told her that she could challenge the ruling and her nurse practitioner told her she would go along with Kait to the hearing. The hearing was in Augusta, Maine, and, although the nurse lived more than an hour away in Bangor, she took the day off to accompany Kait. It was the very definition of patient-centered care.

Kait went to three hearings about her situation, each ending in a denial. She continued to challenge the denials, however, and ended up at the formulary committee of the state of Maine. She argued that the cost of a 200 mg Celebrex tablet was miniscule compared to the cost of an inpatient stay and, finally, that changed things. In January of 2002, her prescription was approved and the state formulary was changed.

Advocacy and Connections

Kait's advocacy made a difference and an impact. She was invited to sit on the Medicare Advisory Board, the only actual Medicaid patient in the room. Everyone else was a policy wonk. She participated for two years on a volunteer basis. As a result of the experience, people started to ask her to participate in other committees. By this time, she had been clean and sober for many years, but she still qualified for "dual diagnosis" status, meaning she had coexisting mental health and substance abuse disorders. People would say things like, "Hey, we know you have a substance abuse disorder; can you be on a state integration meeting?"

Other committee members began to realize how helpful it was to hear from someone who was actually subject to the policies they were debating. Kait began getting stipends for her participation, which, even though meager ($50 for 2 hours), helped her realize that it was legitimate work. Although Kait was eventually paid a stipend, payment for expertise continues to be an issue for many activated patients, who are expected to volunteer time to "help" systems make improvements or lecture on participatory medicine without appropriate compensation.

Kait eventually met someone from the Maine Quality Counts Patient Centered Medical Home (PCMH) pilot committee. Maine's pilot involved adding a PCMH option to 16 practices in Maine, organized and paid for by the state of Maine Medicaid Program, the Centers for Medicare & Medicaid Services (CMS), and the Robert Wood Johnson's Aligning Forces for Quality Program. Kait asked how many patients were on the committee. There were none. They hired her for a three-year contract helping them design truly patient-centered PCMH practices.

During that time, Kait began to be invited to speak about her experiences. She was in Boston at a meeting of the Institute for Healthcare Improvement, sitting on a panel, when she realized that the meeting overall had far too few actual patients present. At an Aligning Forces meeting in 2009, she met Dr. Ted Eytan, a tireless champion for patient voices and patient-centered care. Ted introduced her to Regina Holliday, who was just starting work as a professional patient advocate and speaker. She and Kait bonded and pledged to do patient advocacy work for a living.

Shortly after that, Kait was asked to be on a panel for the Patient-Centered Primary Care collaborative. Kait was the only patient in a room full of a thousand people—one of them Christine Bechtel, who was at the time a vice president in the National Partnership for Women and Families. She fell in love with Kait's story, her patient perspective, her pragmatism, and her ability to see all sides of the healthcare situation. She hired Kait to work on behalf of the National Partnership in Maine. The National Partnership told her they'd hire her if she moved to Washington, DC. She moved, leaving behind her beloved dog and the whole support system that had helped her find her roots. By the time she arrived, however, the National Partnership had changed its goals for the role and Kait was no longer a fit. Devastated, without a source of income, she lived with Regina and cared for her sons while she figured out her next move.

A Patient-Centered Medical Home (PCMH) Expert

Gradually, Kait began to rebuild her life and her connections. She moved to Baltimore. In the process, she met Steve Daviss, the chair of psychiatry at Baltimore Washington hospital and a self-described health information technology (HIT) geek. He wanted them to go into business together and loaned her the money to get content certified in PCMH. As far as she knows, she is the only patient who is content certified in PCMH. The National Committee for Quality Assurance (NCQA) hired her to help develop the 2014 PCMH standards. She and Steve began developing a consulting capability as Fuse Health Strategies, with a mission to help integrate behavioral health into primary care.

Observations for Policy and Practice

Kait's journey provides many opportunities for insights into new ways to approach healthcare. Key among them are the following points:

- Change the way we educate doctors to shift them from the assumption that patients are uneducated and passive toward an understanding of patients as true partners in their care.
- Use incentives to continue to shift practice and reimbursement from fee for services rendered to payment for outcomes generated.
- Involve patients in every part of healthcare, creating patient champions and bringing the voice of patients—patients who aren't tokens—into leadership conversations with hospital administrators, CEOs, and boards. Things won't change until patients are involved in every conversation from the exam room to the boardroom. As we do so, however, figure out appropriate strategies to compensate them for their time and expertise.
- Create experiences that allow those in leadership positions not just to hear patient voices, but also to experience their environments and processes as patients.

- Incorporate consideration of the social determinants of health into conversation and policy so that people can intervene early to prevent and address healthcare costs created by adverse childhood events such as those Kait lived through.
- Find ways to increase mental health parity in policy and also in access. Kait did the research to determine that today there are only four private psychiatrists in the state of Maryland that take insurance, and none of them take public insurance. Laws requiring mental health parity don't work if there is still no access and no availability of therapists.
- Finally, Kait notes that it is important to be sensitive in how patient advocates are chosen, as the need is for people who can articulate their experience, generalize it to the experience of others, and speak up despite the intimidation of being a layperson in a community of experts.

Conclusion

Kait is still not completely making it financially as a patient advocate, although she has begun to feel truly valued in the last few years. Her story highlights the culture change gradually occurring in healthcare: The industry has finally begun to understand that to be patient centered, it is necessary to find ways to listen to the real voices of patients.

Kait is truly a survivor, who has found ways to take her experiences and transform them into system change. As we consider how to effect long-term transformation in healthcare, it is important that we find ways to help other people like Kait get the help they need to make an impact transforming both their own lives and those of others.

Notes

1. http://acestudy.org/files/Review_of_ACE_Study_with_references_summary_table_2_.pdf. Note that the information is in the public domain.
2. http://www.mayoclinic.org/diseases-conditions/conversion-disorder/basics/definition/con-20029533
3. http://www.sciencedaily.com/releases/2013/10/131031124725.htm

Story 19: Prednisone and Misdiagnosis

Jan Oldenburg, FHIMSS with Joan

Introduction

Joan's story highlights the perils of having a rare disease. In the years that it took doctors to properly understand her condition, she was misdiagnosed as having asthma. The high levels of prednisone she was given for the asthma she doesn't have created a host of other health conditions that still plague her. Because she has a rare disease, the doctors in her small city struggle to understand how best to treat her condition.

You Have Asthma

Joan had been told she had asthma for years. Her family doctor sent her to a specialist, who confirmed the asthma diagnosis. She certainly wheezed like an asthmatic, to the point that she was nicknamed "Darth Vader" among one group of friends. Doctors gave her a standard mix of asthma medications including frequent high doses of prednisone, which seemed to help when nothing else did. She had such difficulty breathing that if she had to walk up a flight of 50 or 60 stairs, she would see black at the top from lack of oxygen. That same lack of oxygen made it difficult to exercise and created problems with memory and concentration.

In turn, Joan's inability to exercise and the high doses of prednisone caused her to gain weight. She developed type 2 diabetes although she has no family history of the disease; her clinical record from 2006 lists "steroid-induced hyperglycemia" as a condition. Diabetes is one of a great number of metabolic side effects that can occur from prednisone use.[1]

Without other options, Joan became a "frequent flyer" in the local emergency room as her inability to breathe scared her and those around her.

Diagnosis

One of the doctors Joan saw in the emergency room at her local hospital in 2001, years after the onset of her symptoms, realized that she was wheezing at the wrong time for an asthmatic.

Asthmatics wheeze or cough when they expel air; Joan wheezed when she breathed in. The doctor suspected that she had a condition called "subglottic stenosis," a significant constriction of her airway. The confirmation came from an endoscope procedure performed in her ear, nose, and throat (ENT) doctor's office after she was sent home from the emergency room. The procedure allowed Dr. S, her ENT specialist, to see that Joan's airway was significantly constricted in the lower part of her larynx. This specific blockage is referred to as subglottic, which refers to the region just below the vocal cords extending to the top of the trachea. It's an area surrounded by the cricoid cartilage, ring-shaped cartilage of the larynx.[2] A CT scan found that Joan's narrowing was at the level of the thyroid gland and thoracic inlet at the top of her ribs. For most people, the tube is about the size of a quarter; when she was diagnosed, Joan's was the size of a nickel.

Subglottic stenosis is on the National Institutes of Health rare disease list; it is considered challenging to treat because relapses are frequent. Although this blockage can involve both soft tissue and the cricoid cartilage, in Joan's case it is caused by the soft tissue, which narrowed the airway so much that it impeded air intake. There are a number of causes of subglottic stenosis. Sometimes the narrowing is present from birth, but it can also be acquired from external injuries or injuries due to treatments like endotracheal intubation, tracheotomy, or radiation. There's also some evidence it can be a consequence of an autoimmune disorder.[3] Subglottic stenosis is often misdiagnosed as other conditions, including asthma.[4]

Joan was finally correctly diagnosed in 2001, when she was 46. She had been experiencing wheezing since her twenties and had gone to a variety of specialists ranging from pulmonologists to ENT doctors. In hindsight, she actually had a number of the symptoms of subglottic stenosis all along: shortness of breath, coughing, wheezing, difficult or labored breathing (dyspnoea), and a breathing noise that was louder and harsher than a wheeze.

In Joan's case, it is not completely clear what caused the original condition. She has been tested for autoimmune disorders, which don't seem to be the cause; her condition does not seem to be congenital, because it started when Joan was in her twenties. She was intubated once during gall bladder surgery. Dr. S called the anesthesiologist from Joan's gall bladder surgery. The anesthesiologist said there was a small narrowing in her airway at the time but he didn't think it was bad enough to document. It is still unclear if the injury arose from that surgery or predates it. In any event, had she been correctly diagnosed earlier, she would have been on less prednisone and likely wouldn't have developed diabetes.

Treatment

Now that they knew what was really causing Joan's breathing problems, her doctors could offer her new treatment options. During the first biopsy of her airway, Dr. S used a laser to open the blocked area by removing the excess tissue. That restored the air passage to the size of a quarter and it was wonderful. Gradually, however, the area scarred over and the same problem occurred again. Over the course of 10 years, Joan had two more surgeries to open the blockage, but each time scar tissue gradually constricted it and the narrowing recurred.

While in college, Joan had a bicycle accident and damaged the right orbit and cheekbone. She may have damaged her nose at the same time, as her nose shows some damage and narrowing of the right side nasal turbinates, the nasal structures that carry air. Endoscopes always have to enter through her left nostril, as they can't be threaded through the right nasal passages. When Joan went in for the last laser surgery on her subglottic blockage, Dr. S planned to surgically open the turbinates in her nose as well. After Joan was anesthetized, her doctor halted the surgery as he feared one part of her trachea was too weak for another surgery and that surgery on her nose would constrain her ability to breathe too much.

Her local doctors referred her to the nearest academic teaching hospital, where they had concerns about trying to open the blockage as they also thought it was possible Joan's trachea could collapse entirely. They suggested she lose weight, hoping it would help her breathing and reduce the impact of the constriction. Joan lost 60 pounds, which helped the condition, though it didn't cure it. Losing weight, as well as being off prednisone, also eased Joan's diabetic symptoms.

Today the blockage has reduced Joan's airway to the size of a drinking straw due to the progression of the disease and excessive scarring. In February of 2014, Joan was hospitalized several times after 3 years with no hospitalizations. The first ER doctor told her that she had a cold and not to worry about it. The second time, a few days later, Joan was planning to take her brother to chemotherapy, but ended up being transported to the ER herself and admitted to intensive care because of her severe breathing problems. She had another endoscope and a CT scan. The next morning, her mother and a friend from church came to the hospital to tell Joan that her brother had died during the night.

After her brother's funeral, Joan followed up with the ENT doctor she'd seen in the hospital. The new ENT doctor told her that the CT scan looked no different from the previous one, performed in 2011, and suggested that much of the problem was now in Joan's head. Nonetheless, he suggested performing another dilation procedure to expand the blockage.

Several weeks later, Joan was again transported to the hospital by ambulance and again admitted to intensive care. At that point she was seen by a pulmonary specialist as well as by an associate of the ENT doctor she'd seen the previous time. They performed another endoscopy and told her that there was no way another dilation could be performed; they suggested that it was time for another kind of surgery.

The last resort is a very specialized surgery called a cricotracheal resection (CTR) or tracheal resection (TR) to fully remove the diseased portion of the trachea. Once a CTR or TR is performed, the trachea usually returns to normal.[5] In this procedure, the portion of the trachea with the blockage is removed. Joan has avoided this surgery so far because, during the time it takes to heal, her chin would be sewed to her chest and she would need to get all her nutrients through a feeding tube. None of Joan's local doctors can do the surgery, so she would need to travel to an academic medical center to have it performed. She is not yet seriously considering such a radical procedure.

Living with Limited Breathing Capacity

Joan has learned to cope with the limitations of the condition. She has learned how to pace herself, resting when she feels short of breath and planning out any walking she needs to do.

She sleeps with a bilevel positive airway pressure (BiPAP) machine, which is used to help people with sleep apnea. The BiPAP has two pressure settings: the prescribed pressure for inhalation (ipap) and a lower pressure for exhalation (epap). The dual settings allow Joan to get more air in and out of her lungs during sleep. Joan no longer uses oxygen, primarily because Medicare no longer pays for it.

She uses a pulse oximeter daily to measure her blood oxygen levels. Most people can function normally with a blood oxygen level above 89 percent. When Joan's tracheal stenosis is particularly bad, it can result in significant lowering of her blood oxygen levels and in carbon dioxide concentrations that are far too high. At one point, Joan said to her mother, "The walls are moving, Mom." It turned out that she was hallucinating because her oxygen level was only 60 percent. Too much carbon dioxide blocks Joan's oxygen receptors, so it can be hard to reverse the condition once the proportion of carbon dioxide in her bloodstream gets out of whack.

Community

Joan found others with the condition through a Facebook group. She started watching and listening to others rather than contributing directly. In the end, the group was so negative—about everything, including medical issues—that she stopped participating. In the meantime, she has found one other person in her hometown who also suffers from the condition.

Joan worked as a corrections officer in the local prison. Some of her co-workers were supportive of her struggles with the disease—others not so much. She decided it was time to retire when she realized that she enjoyed the inmates more than most of her co-workers.

Despite her daily struggles to breathe, Joan is an active member of her community. She's been involved in planning and preparing the Friends Thanksgiving Dinner for more than 45 years. She is the informal host of a Facebook group for current and alumni residents of her town. She and her mother set up a soup kitchen at their local food pantry 3 years ago and still manage its operation.

Joan is lucky to live in a supportive community. Her friends and church family rally around her in times of illness, bringing food and driving her when she can't drive herself.

Coping with the Medical Establishment

Nearly everyone gets a little cranky when they feel sick. For Joan, this reaction is compounded when her carbon dioxide levels are high. She gets very cranky, and it can be an issue when she is dealing with an uncooperative medical system. At those points when she can't breathe it is also difficult to explain what is wrong and provide her history, and the frustration of not being able to explain herself can exacerbate the situation, and the perception that she is a difficult patient.

Joan's original ENT doctor, Dr. S, was wonderful. He treated her as a partner in her care and worked closely with her in managing her symptoms and the disease. Unfortunately, he left town to practice in a larger community. Since then, she has had difficulty finding a local ENT doctor who is willing to treat her as a partner. Some of the relationships have been frustrating; others have been downright unprofessional.

At one point Joan was hospitalized with breathing problems and out-of-control diabetes. Her blood sugar was in the six hundreds—far above the 140 milligrams per deciliter (mg/dL) that indicates diabetes that is under control.[6] She wanted to have someone teach her to use insulin so that she could go home. It was late on a Friday, however, and no one was available to teach her. The doctor said to her, "You want to leave? You can just go out on your front porch and die!"

Another ENT doctor suggested that Joan see someone at a well-known Midwestern center of excellence. When Joan voiced concern about how she would get there, the doctor suggested that social services could handle it for her. When Joan asked how she would qualify for social services, the doctor turned to Joan's mother and said, "Is she always so stubborn?" Her mother is hard of hearing and didn't understand what the doctor said. Joan responded, "It's lucky she can't hear you, because if you think I'm stubborn, you've clearly never dealt with my mom!"

One of the perils of living in a smaller community is that you can't always avoid doctors with whom you've had a bad interaction, so Joan often sees physicians she has concerns about in the ER or when she is hospitalized.

Those difficult interactions are the exception, however, as most of the time the doctors and nurses have been wonderful—patient, willing to explain what is going on, teaching her techniques for coping, and educating her about the progression of her disease. It has been hard for Joan to deal with her brother's death, and her family physician has been very supportive in helping her figure out coping strategies.

She has a patient portal that she uses primarily for e-mail exchanges with her doctors and to view laboratory results. It is much easier than playing phone tag to get questions answered.

Family Caregiver

Despite Joan's own illness, she has also been the family caregiver for her aging mother and for her older brother, who has myelodysplastic syndrome (MDS). In MDS, the blood-forming cells in the bone marrow are damaged, resulting in production of abnormal blood cells that leave the person short of functioning blood cells of one type or another. MDS is considered to be a form of cancer, but in about a third of MDS patients it turns into a very fast growing cancer of bone marrow cells called acute myeloid leukemia.

Her brother was nearly deaf, which made it difficult to communicate with doctors and other medical professionals. Joan witnessed firsthand how easy it is to get lost in the medical system if you don't have an advocate—so she became his, finding him a more caring oncologist and getting him out of a bad nursing home situation. Once her brother had an oncologist who treated him as a partner, he was able to make decisions about how he wanted to be cared for and what course of treatment made sense for him. He decided not to get a bone marrow transplant, as his doctors were unsure he would survive it; instead, he chose maintenance chemotherapy. This is the brother who later died, but Joan had the comfort of knowing that he died on terms he chose.

Observations for Policy and Practice

There are a number of important lessons from Joan's experience:

■ It is really important to be persistent in pursuing solutions to medical problems. When the standard treatments for a diagnosis aren't working, it may be because there is a different root cause. Doctors as well as patients can become resigned to a nonresponsive condition rather than continuing to pursue an alternate diagnosis.

■ It is important to be your own advocate or have someone to be your advocate in dealing with the healthcare system. When you are constrained from speaking up for yourself because you are breathless or frustrated or cranky because you don't feel well, it can be difficult to state your case clearly and reasonably. Patients justifiably worry about being labeled as "difficult" when they push to get the services or treatments they need—healthcare staffers need to be trained to deal with the underlying need being expressed rather than reacting to the patients' frustration with the system. The labels "disruptive," "difficult," or "stubborn" may provide an excuse to ignore the patient's trenchant observations about his or her condition or treatment.

■ Treatments can sometimes exacerbate conditions rather than solving them and need to be used sparingly. In Joan's case, the prescribed steroids resulted in weight gain and diabetes and were of limited efficacy in treating her real condition. In addition, the attempts to relieve her constriction probably exacerbated the scarring that has resulted in her airway narrowing to the size of a drinking straw. There's no easy solution for these kinds of problems, but they act as warnings to patients and doctors alike not to rush into interventions.

Conclusion

Joan is not bitter about her condition or the time wasted with inappropriate treatments. She has learned to say that she has "good days and better days" rather than "good days and bad days," as the phrasing helps her stay upbeat and optimistic. She soldiers on, making a life of meaning, recognizing that all of her doctors were doing their best trying to help her, though with a limited toolset.

Notes

1. http://www.ncbi.nlm.nih.gov/pmc/articles/PMC4112077/
2. http://emedicine.medscape.com/article/865437-overview#a12
3. http://ucneurofunctionalcenter.com/types-of-neurosensory-disorders/adult-airway-disorders/
4. http://emedicine.medscape.com/article/865437-overview
5. http://ucneurofunctionalcenter.com/types-of-neurosensory-disorders/adult-airway-disorders/
6. https://www.virginiamason.org/whatarenormalbloodglucoselevels

Story 20: Standing Up for Myself through Many Medical Problems

Jan Oldenburg, FHIMSS with Janie

Introduction

Janie is a determined, successful businesswoman, CEO of her own company, and forceful about getting her needs met. Nonetheless, it took a series of medical problems, procedures and complications for her to realize how important it was not just to listen to her body, but also to make sure her doctors were listening to her.

Vertigo

In April 2006, Janie was at home with a slight cold. Going to the bathroom, bearing down a bit, she got very dizzy. That was the start of a period of intense vertigo. Her ears felt blocked, despite having them candled. She began hearing her own voice as if she were underwater. The vertigo came and went, triggered by things like the lights in a Target store, or turning her head to talk to people beside her in a restaurant. She couldn't wait to work out every day, because it was the only time she didn't feel dizzy, probably because when she was working out the fluid in her ear moved with her and reduced the sensation of dizziness.

Janie finally went to an ear, nose, and throat (ENT) doctor that September who told Janie there was nothing wrong with her ears and suggested she see a neurotologist, a branch of clinical medicine that studies and treats neurological disorders of the ear. The neurotologist did a CAT scan and reviewed the results with Janie. He pulled up a scan of one side of Janie's brain in one computer and the other side in another computer so they could look at both together. Janie said, "Look, you can see that there's something on the right side that isn't on the left." The neurotologist told her she was exactly right, and said, "I think it's a dehiscence of the left superior semi-circular canal." He went on to explain that it is a rare condition, but not life threatening. It was discovered in 1997, because that's when CAT scans became precise enough to view it. The mean age of onset is 45. The core cause seems to be a developmental anomaly that causes an abnormally thin bone plate over the superior semicircular canal, a part of the inner ear. The *semicircular canals* are lined with cilia (microscopic hairs) and filled with a liquid substance, known as endolymph. Every time the head moves, the endolymph moves the cilia. This works as a type of motion sensor, as the movements of the cilia are communicated to the brain.[1] Over time, the bone wears away due to exercise or trauma. This creates a third window into the inner ear, which disrupts the fluid mechanics. Diagnosis is made by a combination of CAT scans and exploration of symptoms. Several of Janie's symptoms were classic: increased resonance of one's own voice and vestibular dysfunction and dizziness.[2]

Janie now had a name for her condition, but still found it debilitating. The neurotologist who diagnosed her condition had only done one surgery to repair it. Surgery generally relieves the symptoms with minimal hearing loss. Janie asked to talk to that patient, who was somewhat frustrated with the outcome. Janie began searching for experts in the condition. She eventually found the doctor who discovered the disorder in 1997. At the time Janie met with him he had seen 150 patients with the condition and performed 50 surgeries. Janie talked to several of his patients who had good outcomes to report. She had surgery in June 2007, more than a year after the onset of symptoms. Janie was firm that she didn't want her head shaved, so her doctor made a pencil line shaving to do the surgery. In Janie's case, the surgery consisted of removing a square of the cranium and making a new bridge over the superior canal. The scar tissue creates a hard mass that mimics the original bone. During the surgery her doctor realized Janie also had a hole in her dura, the covering of the brain, so he repaired that as well.

During recovery, Janie was in the neurosurgery intensive care unit (ICU) for 2 days—not because of the complexity of her condition, but because they couldn't find a standard room for her after the first night in the ICU. Standard practice requires a catheter for everyone while they are in the neurosurgery ICU. Janie again stood up for herself and said, "You aren't keeping a catheter in me for 2 days just because you can't find me a room. I don't need it." As a result of her advocacy they removed the catheter after the first night.

Her doctor told her to expect to be out of work for 6 weeks. Janie told him that was nuts and she'd be back at work in 2–3 weeks. Her doctor told her, "You can try, but you won't want to go back earlier." He was right. It took Janie 7 weeks. She was rigorous about physical therapy. At the beginning, it felt as if she had 2000 cotton balls in her head. Each day, she got slightly less foggy, as if one or two cotton balls were gone. Janie's surgery effectively removed one of the three balance canals in her left ear, so she now has three in her right ear and two in her left.

Her only residual effect is that she can't do certain motions/exercises at the gym because they make her dizzy. For her, it was the right procedure with the right surgeon. She was covered by United Healthcare through her employer and received no bills and had no insurance hassles. A year after the surgery, she was 95 percent recovered. She will always have a slight echo when she hears her own voice, but she is so used to it at this point that it rarely bothers her.

Breast Cancer Diagnosis

Janie has always had very dense breasts. In 1994, coming home from a fishing trip with her husband, listening to *Portnoy's Complaint* on the car's tape player, she was struck by the thought, "Oh my God, I am going to get breast cancer." The feeling paralyzed her. Her mammograms frequently showed cysts, which her surgeon would aspirate to test the fluid for cancer. Although none of the cysts showed evidence of cancer, the process fed her underlying fear, compounded by the feeling that her doctor wasn't a good listener. Although they went to the same synagogue and he had delivered both of her children, whenever they talked, it was all about him and his family; he asked nothing about Janie or her children.

In January of 2008, Janie felt a lump on the side of her left breast. She went to see her OB/GYN, but he said, "That's the same lump we always see; don't worry about it." In April, however, Janie also felt a lump under her left arm. When she went back to her OB/GYN this time, he sent her to a breast surgeon immediately. The breast surgeon had an interventional radiologist do a biopsy that day. The interventional radiologist told her that it was an odd shape that looked as if it had been there a long time and she didn't think it was cancer. She also did an ultrasound, which showed cysts, but otherwise appeared clear. A mammogram performed the same day showed no malignancy and no lump. They sent her home to await the results of the biopsy. Fearful, Janie called her mother and sister in New York at 10 that morning. They arrived in Minneapolis by three that afternoon to be with her. Shortly after they arrived, her radiologist called with the news that the biopsy showed cancer and she would need to find an oncologist.

The next few weeks passed in a blur. She had an MRI of her breast and armpit, which showed that there was a 4.3 cm lump in her breast and a 2.5 cm lump under her arm. Janie called her OB/GYN and said, "Why didn't you offer me a breast MRI earlier?" He told her it was because MRIs often aren't covered by insurance. Janie told him she would have paid for the peace of mind and made him promise to offer MRIs to other women with dense and cystic breasts. Despite their relationship in and out of the office, her OB/GYN never followed up to find out how she was doing or to apologize for not treating her more aggressively at the beginning. Janie found another OB/GYN, who is a survivor of breast cancer and had empathy for her journey.

After her diagnosis, Janie called a meeting in her office, where she explained that she had cancer and would be undergoing chemo, surgery, and radiation, but she expected to keep working. She asked everyone to treat her the same as usual. She also called her clients and asked them to continue to send her business, as she wanted to keep working during her treatment. She succeeded in her goal of having her work continue in a normal fashion while she received treatment.

Chemotherapy

Janie got in touch with a friend whose father was a well-known Minneapolis oncologist. The friend's father was on vacation, returning in a few days, on a Sunday. He agreed to meet with Janie on Sunday when he returned. It was very rare and very kind. Janie showed up with a bit of an entourage: both of her sons, her sister, her mother, and her best friend, who was going to be her healthcare advocate. The oncologist wasn't fazed by the crowd. He talked to all of them about the breast cancer journey. He explained that Janie's cancer was estrogen and progesterone positive and HER2 negative. This meant that the long-term threat of recurrence could be managed by modulating the hormones in her body. The fact that it was HER2 negative was an excellent sign, as HER2 positive tumors tend to grow faster and are more likely to recur than HER2 negative tumors. He asked Janie what she was most afraid of. Janie told him she was most afraid of throwing up, and he told her he would manage her treatment and her chemo so she wouldn't get nauseous. He was reassuring and hopeful. He gave Janie his cell phone number and told her to call anytime, although he added, "But don't call me at 2 am when you're cleaning your closets because you can't sleep from the steroids!"

Because Janie's tumors were so large, her physicians suggested she have chemotherapy before surgery to shrink the tumors, which is known as neoadjuvant therapy. By shrinking the tumors there would be less chance they would cut into them when they did the surgery, reducing the risk that the cancer would spread. She had chemo every other week, eight sessions in all, from April to August. She was at work every day except Thursday/Friday of the weeks she had chemo. She took those days off to be with her sister who traveled from New York for most of the chemo sessions.

Normal protocol during chemotherapy is to implant a port in the patient's chest to administer the drugs as the process can be hard on the veins. Janie didn't want a scar on her chest, so they reluctantly agreed to administer the chemo through her veins unless and until she had a problem. Janie made sure she was working with the top chemo nurse to lessen the chance of complications when administering chemo through the veins in her arm, and she experienced no problems.

Before each chemotherapy treatment, Janie was given Aloxi, a relatively new antinausea medication from MGI Pharma. Because of Janie's job, she knew the marketing team for Aloxi, and they showered her with Aloxi tchotchkes. For each chemo treatment she brought all of her Aloxi-labeled paraphernalia for good luck: blanket, t-shirt, mug, flash drive, and water bottle. It worked, as she never got sick through the entire treatment.

During this stage of chemotherapy, Janie's white blood cell count went very low. Her doctor prescribed daily shots of Neulasta to increase white-blood-cell production. Neulasta is specifically formulated to increase white blood cell count during chemo. It worked, but caused intense nightly pain in her hips, where production of red blood cells generally occurs.

The second stage of Janie's chemotherapy involved four rounds of Taxol. One day when her parents were visiting from out of town, she got very hot. Her mother insisted on taking her temperature over Janie's protests—it was 104! She went to the ER to have it checked out, where her temperature eventually dropped while she was under observation. The next day, she began to have difficulty breathing—so much difficulty that she could barely walk. She went back to the ER. Her red-blood-cell count was 8.6. Although the cut-off is usually 8.0, they wheeled her to the infusion room. As they gave her a blood transfusion and she had oxygenated blood, she felt fine. Anemia can be one of the side effects of Taxol,[3] and shortness of breath is a frequent symptom.

Her oncologist told her they wouldn't do chemo the week she had the transfusion and told her to find something fun to do. Janie took her sister and two best friends up to Lutsen in Northern Minnesota and spent a long weekend playing at her ex-husband's family cabin: fun, friendship, and laughter made her feel much better and prepared her to go the rest of the distance.

After the first round of chemo, Janie's scalp started to hurt, especially while washing her hair in the shower. This is the first sign that one's hair is about to fall out. When she started losing her hair, she cut it short—and then shorter yet. When it was finally clear she was going to lose all of her hair, she held a hair shaving party. She bought a beautiful wig, but just couldn't wear it; it felt as if she was trying to be someone she wasn't. Instead, Janie bought beautiful scarves and learned to tie them really creatively. People often complimented her about them and it was fun for her. She also went to a makeup artist who taught her how to apply makeup so that she didn't look sick. It helped that Janie didn't lose her lashes or eyebrows until very late in the treatment, and they rebounded very fast.

Surgery and Radiation

By the end of chemotherapy, the tumors were considerably smaller. They no longer could find the tumor under her arm and the one in her breast was significantly smaller. Janie's doctor thought a lumpectomy would be sufficient, but Janie chose to have a double mastectomy as she didn't want to deal with the ongoing risks imposed by her dense, cystic breasts. Surgery was scheduled for a month after completion of her chemotherapy.

During surgery, her surgeon found another tumor behind the large one in her breast, which he also removed. It looked as if a piece of the tumor had broken off, but it was not clear where it had gone. During surgery, her doctor removed the sentinel lymph node and 13 surrounding nodes. The sentinel node was cancerous, but the rest were cancer free. It wasn't clear whether the chemo had eliminated cancer from the lymph nodes or whether the cancer had not spread beyond the sentinel node. Her doctor told her that none of the lymph nodes were misshapen, as they probably would have been had they been cancerous at any point. In any case, after 6 years with no additional symptoms, Janie and her doctor are comfortable that she is cancer free.

In order to have the best chance of survival Janie opted for radiation after her surgery. She interviewed four different radiation oncologists. Out of the four radiation oncologists Janie interviewed, two (who happened to be female) recommended that she receive radiation above the collarbone to radiate the supraclavicular nodes; this has been shown to increase survival time.[4] Two radiation oncologists (who happened to be male) downplayed the need for radiation of the supraclavicular nodes. Janie later found out that the two doctors who didn't recommend radiating the supraclavicular nodes worked at sites that didn't have the equipment to do it. Finding that out made her feel that they weren't her advocates, but were instead motivated by income. Janie chose one of the women oncologists and received radiation treatments daily for 33 days, timing the treatments to work with her schedule. During radiation, they created a mold for Janie to lie in during the therapy. Janie complained that it didn't feel right and her shoulder hurt, but they thought she was just being a complainer. It wasn't until her shoulder completely dislocated that they made a new mold for her—shoulder subluxation is one of the consequences of Janie's Ehlers-Danlos syndrome (EDS)—a disorder marked by overly flexible joints because of weakened connective tissue.[5]

Janie finished radiation on Christmas Eve. Her family greeted her at the radiologist's office with a 5-foot tall pink breast cancer ribbon balloon. They then took her out for a party at her favorite restaurant. It was a warm, welcoming celebration of life. They still celebrate December 24 as "boob day" in her family.

Breast Reconstruction

Janie started breast reconstruction during the mastectomy. Her doctor inserted breast "expanders" to make room for permanent implants later. Expanders start being pumped up within 2 weeks of being implanted. The first time that was done, Janie experienced intense pain, feeling like she was having a heart attack and her plastic surgeon sent her for acupuncture immediately. She was in so much pain that the acupuncturist sent her home without treatment. She didn't have that intense reaction again, but preparing for the permanent implants was difficult. Six months after her mastectomy, the expanders were removed and the permanent implants inserted. After another 6 months, she had nipples made. To make nipples, the surgeon pulls tissue from the inside of the breasts. The nipples are initially quite big, and Janie had to wear something like water bottle caps to protect them, but they flatten out over time. Two months later, she got tattoos to create the areola. Because her skin was so thin from radiation, she had to have the tattoos repeated three times. By the end of the process, her breasts looked somewhat normal, though Janie thought they looked like baseballs plastered to her chest. There was no fat around them at all so she had no cleavage.

Maintaining

At the end of cancer treatment and the beginning of maintenance, Janie was prescribed Tamoxifen to block the effects of estrogen in the body. On Tamoxifen Janie felt "like sludge" and got very depressed, although she'd never been depressed before. By November of the year after her treatments, she was miserable, coping with weight gain and depression that she knew had nothing to do with her "real" state of mind. She was 100 percent sure it was the Tamoxifen causing her terrible feeling. Her doctor suggested that she go to a well-known integrative cancer clinic outside Chicago.

There Janie and her family met with an internist, an oncologist, a psychologist, a nutritionist, and a physical therapist. These doctors stopped the Tamoxifen and retooled her diet. They taught her what to eat and not to eat, gave her extensive supplements, and introduced her to mindfulness meditation. They also put her on Arimidex, an aromatase inhibitor that, like Tamoxifen, works to reduce the effects of estrogen in the body but is usually given to women who are diagnosed with breast cancer after menopause. Janie was diagnosed before menopause. Within 3 days of stopping Tamoxifen, Janie felt better and quickly lost 7 pounds.

Janie went back to Minneapolis and took three courses of Jon Kabat Zinn's mindfulness meditation training. She also cleaned out her kitchen. Her parents had given her a gift certificate for $500 and she went through the co-op to buy supplies for an organic diet as instructed by her integrated physician team. She believes the combination of supplements, organic foods, mindfulness, and healthy living are keeping her well. Taking action on behalf of her own health also helps Jamie to feel in control of her health and her body.

The Arimidex wasn't keeping her estrogen low enough, however. She found a new oncologist who specialized in women's cancers. After seeing what was happening with her estrogen levels, her oncologist recommended removing her ovaries to better manage her hormones and reduce the threat of a recurrence of the cancer. A gynecological oncology surgeon was going to do the surgery shortly after Janie returned from New York for Passover. Janie was having some strange back pain, so her oncologist had her get an MRI to make sure she didn't have a recurrence of cancer. The MRI appeared to show a bone spur or some sort of hemangioma, so when she returned from New York, they also did a small slice CAT scan and a bone scan to be sure they knew what was causing the pain.

The gynecological surgeon who would be removing her ovaries called her two business days prior to her surgery and said, "I'm reading your CAT scans and it looks as if your cancer has metastasized to your spine—and given that, I need to know if I'm doing your surgery on Monday." In a panic, Janie called her oncologist, who said, "No, that's not right. I'm reading the report and it doesn't look like that at all."

That reassured Janie, but she was angry with the gynecological surgeon, who had sent her into a panic with an incorrect reading of the CAT scan. It was especially upsetting because it was Janie's oncologist's job to interpret the CAT scan, not the surgeon's, and the surgeon only seemed to be concerned about her schedule, not what it might mean to Janie if her cancer had recurred. A friend counseled Janie not to confront the surgeon until after her ovaries were removed. After that surgery—so uneventful that Janie was back at work 2 days afterward—Janie went back to the gynecological surgeon with a friend and a tape recorder. Janie carefully told the doctor that it wasn't her job to read the CAT scan or tell Janie the outcome, that she had read the report wrong in any case, and that there was no compassion in her approach—it was all about her surgery schedule rather than Janie's life or state of mind. Janie told her, "You have no idea what you put me through." The surgeon got teary, apologized profusely, and shortly after moved out of the area.

Lymphedema

Janie had been determined not to be one of the breast cancer patients who develop lymphedema. Lymphedema is an abnormal buildup of lymph fluid that causes swelling. The condition develops when lymph vessels or lymph nodes are missing, impaired, damaged, or removed. The occurrence of lymphedema has been reduced in recent years, seemingly because sentinel node biopsies are being used rather than *wholesale* removal of lymph nodes.[6] In an effort to prevent the development of lymphedema, Janie saw a lymphedema specialist before her surgery and afterward wore a compression sleeve every time she exercised or traveled by plane.

Immediately after surgery, Janie developed lymphatic or axillary cording in her left arm. Lymphatic cording is a poorly understood side effect of lymph node removal that creates tightness and pain from the shoulders through the arm.[7] Lymphatic massage helped relieve the pain of the cording and tightness. Almost exactly 3 years after her surgery, Janie put an elbow down on her desk and noticed that it felt "squishy." It was a small patch of fluid buildup, the beginning of lymphedema. Janie got additional lymphedema massages, which seemed to take care of the problem. Three weeks later, however, Janie took her sister and sons to the Atlantis on Paradise Island 17 days after major thumb surgery on her right hand. While they were there, her left arm and hand blew up like a balloon from lymphedema. She had a cast on one hand and the other arm was hugely swollen—not surprisingly, it was not the dream vacation she'd hoped for.

Janie knew about a new treatment for lymphedema, the Flexitouch machine, because a friend consulted to the company that made the device. The Flexitouch system is an advanced intermittent pneumatic compression device (lymphedema pump) that directs fluid away from affected areas of the body to functioning regions where it can be managed properly.[8] She made an appointment with her lymphedema specialist to ask about it. This doctor thought it would just push fluid into Janie's sensitive hand. Janie then talked to her oncologist's nurse about the Flexitouch, and, after some research to ensure it would cover her hand, the oncologist ordered one for her. The Flexitouch staff came to her house to fit her for the machine and teach her how to use it—and it worked well for Janie. Afterward, she went back to the lymphedema specialist and explained what she had done. Her doctor told her, "Janie, I am really proud of you for knowing what you needed and going for it. And I learned something."

Her lymphedema never goes away, but she now knows how to manage it. She gave a video testimonial for Tactile Medical, the maker of the Flexitouch system. She also put the company in touch with her oncologist, who recommended the conferences they should attend in order to expand awareness of the treatment. Janie is pleased to have found something that manages her symptoms so well. Tactile Medical has now asked Janie if she would like to be interviewed by the press to increase awareness of their unique treatment.

Hands

Before Janie was diagnosed with breast cancer, she'd been having slight episodes of numbness, pain, and tingling in her hands, especially the right one. During chemotherapy and radiation, the pain in her hands worsened to the point disrupting her sleep at night. It was excruciating. At one point, a friend brought over a massage table and Janie slept lying on her stomach on the table, a pillow under her breasts with her hands dangling on either side. It seemed the only way to relieve the pain in her hands at night.

Her lymphedema specialist sent her to a thoracic medicine doctor who diagnosed the pain in her hands as bilateral thoracic outlet syndrome. Thoracic outlet syndrome can cause pain in the arms and hands due to compression of nerves or blood vessels, or both, because of an inadequate passageway through an area (the thoracic outlet) between the base of the neck and the armpit.[9] This surgeon wanted to remove the first rib on both sides of her body. Janie didn't think her symptoms matched thoracic outlet symptoms very well, so she went to a second thoracic surgeon. He wasn't sure if it was thoracic outlet syndrome or not.

Janie's physical medicine doctor recommended she get an electromyogram, which measures the conductivity of nerves.[10] The doctor who read the study told her that she had severe carpal tunnel syndrome and would have permanent nerve damage if it wasn't treated immediately. Janie's radiation oncologist halted radiation for a day so a neurosurgeon could perform carpal tunnel surgery on her right hand. After Janie's radiation treatments were complete, she had carpal tunnel surgery on her left hand as well. At the same time, they relieved trigger fingers on the middle and third fingers on each hand. Janie was also experiencing terrible right thumb pain, which was diagnosed as severe osteoarthritis. This, combined with her Ehlers-Danlos, weakened the collagen in her thumb, which caused her thumb to be sitting outside the metacarpal joint. The surgeon also injected Synvisc, a treatment approved to relieve osteoarthritic knee pain. His hope was that the off-label use would help Janie's right thumb joint move back into the joint and move more smoothly.

The surgery relieved the carpal tunnel problem immediately (with no aftereffects) and the Synvisc helped the thumb pain for 21 months, but her hands had sustained significant damage from chemotherapy. The damage was compounded by the fact that Janie has Ehlers-Danlos syndrome. As mentioned earlier, Ehlers-Danlos Syndrome can cause joint hypermobility and tissue fragility. In November of 2011, the thumb on her right hand started hurting again, and she could feel it going in and out of joint. She got a steroid injection and another Synvisc injection. Neither helped for long, as her thumb kept falling out of joint because she didn't have enough connective tissue left to hold it in place.

That was the start of a series of difficult surgeries on Janie's hands. Each surgery was made more difficult by Ehlers-Danlos, which both created the problem of her thumb joint instability and impacted her recovery. There are indications that patients with EDS have more difficulty in surgical recovery than patients without a connective tissue disorder.[11]

Janie had a series of surgeries to support her thumb with thumbs, screws, and plates, but none of them worked and Janie was in constant pain. By now her doctor was frustrated and began suggesting that Janie's pain was psychological.

Janie insisted on a referral to a well-known Midwestern center of excellence. There her new hand specialist found that her right thumb hadn't fused and the hardware was jumbled up and not holding her thumb in place. The first repair was not altogether successful either, but after a second repair and a bone stimulator machine, her hand finally healed. Her thumb is now about 80 percent of normal, although her range of motion is still very limited; had Janie not been persistent, she might still be living in constant pain.

Janie has since had several surgeries on her left hand as well. The left hand took a lot of stress while her right hand went through previous surgeries. Pieces of her joint had broken off and needed to be cleaned out and the joint needed stabilization. On this hand, the doctor fused the thumb joint with a bone from her wrist and several pins to keep it in place. This surgery seems to have been successful, although her range of motion is low. She is having another surgery to help her thumb bend at the tip. It is stuck due to a lot of scar tissue buildup constricting the tendon from moving. After a total of 20 hand surgeries (including childhood surgeries for trigger finger),

Janie's hands seem to be working, although her left thumb has very little motion. Pain levels are significantly reduced (about 90 to 95 percent in her right hand, and 60 percent in her left).

Technology

Janie is not a fan of the portals provided at the many institutions where she has been seen—she sees them as a lot of hassle and not intuitively obvious. She asks her doctors for their e-mail addresses, however, and only sees physicians who will exchange e-mails with her. For her, it is much simpler to have a direct exchange via e-mails than cope with telephone messages that are garbled in translation or playing telephone tag with her providers or waiting for the delays in the portal. She collects copies of her MRIs, CAT scans, and x-rays, as she has learned that it is important to be able to share them with new doctors.

Observations for Policy and Practice

Through Janie's many different health conditions, one thing stands out: she learned how to be an advocate for herself and make sure that her physicians and their staff understood what she needed. She also learned how family and friends could support her on her journey.

- Listening to patients is a skill that needs to be taught in medical school, as it is not a natural outcome of current medical training, but has significant positive impacts on the relationship and on outcomes.
- Patients who are their own advocates need to be treated as partners in caring for themselves and their diseases.
- There's a need for better designed portals and for secure e-mail that works the way patients expect ordinary e-mail systems to work.
- Increasingly, patients expect the same convenient electronic capabilities they use in the rest of their lives in their interactions with the medical system.
- Patients also expect integrated care experiences that reflect their overall experience, and that means looking at the whole person in his or her experience with a particular disease.
- When patients tell you something is wrong, it is important to look for the cause; they are living 24×7 in the body in question and know the internal experience of it. In some situations the person may need to live with a level of pain, but it shouldn't be the first assumption physicians make.

Implications for Patients and Family Members

- Ask for what you need or what the patient needs to feel cared for and supported.
- Don't be afraid to get a second opinion—or more—to make sure you or your loved one are getting the best care.
- You know your body; don't be intimidated when someone suggests your pain or your symptoms aren't real.
- Behave like a partner with an equal stake in the outcomes of your disease. That means following the course of treatment you agree to with your doctor; it also means challenging doctors' recommendations when they don't work for you.

Conclusion

During this whole complicated journey, Janie has learned to listen to her body and to challenge doctors who don't pay attention to her or discount the symptoms she is experiencing. She has learned that doctors are not gods; they make mistakes like every human, and the relationship works best when it is truly a partnership between people who trust one another. Janie has had enough experience with the medical system to find a new doctor if she's dealing with someone who doesn't listen to her. She has built strong relationships along the way with doctors and also with the nurse practitioners and physician assistants who support them. In particular, Janie noted the strong and supportive relationship she developed with her oncologist's nurse practitioner, who was key to seeing her through treatment and recovery.

Notes

1. http://www.healthline.com/human-body-maps/semicircular-canals
2. http://vestibular.org/superior-canal-dehiscence-scd
3. http://www.chemocare.com/chemotherapy/drug-info/Taxol.aspx
4. http://www.ascopost.com/ViewNews.aspx?nid=8600
5. http://www.mayoclinic.org/diseases-conditions/ehlers-danlos-syndrome/basics/definition/con
   -20033656
6. http://ww5.komen.org/BreastCancer/Lymphedema.html
7. http://www.ncbi.nlm.nih.gov/pmc/articles/PMC2724805/
8. http://www.tactilemedical.com/products/flexitouch/
9. http://www.medicinenet.com/thoracic_outlet_syndrome/article.htm
10. http://www.webmd.com/brain/electromyogram-emg-and-nerve-conduction-studies
11. http://www.ncbi.nlm.nih.gov/pubmed/10426439

Story 21: Staying Abreast: Cancer and Community

Jan Oldenburg, FHIMSS with Beth, MEd, MBA

Introduction

Breast cancer wasn't in Beth's plans for 2010—or any year, for that matter. She was active, enjoying yoga, walking with friends, biking, taking spin classes, and occasionally swimming. She had recently lost her job and was in the beginning stages of a serious job search. But she could feel something that wasn't quite like typical breast tissue in her right breast. It had been there for a while, and if she hadn't been somewhat overwhelmed with stress in her life, she might have done something about it sooner.

She was a patient at an integrated delivery system and had access to her medical records online, but at the time, her mammography reports weren't available online and she was unsure when the next one was due. One night her husband said to her, "I think you'd better look into that." His confirmation that something wasn't right was the spur Beth needed to take action. She e-mailed her OB-GYN to ask about the problem. At the time, it seemed like a minor concern, and without the convenience of e-mail, she might not have taken action quite so quickly.

> I have noticed a tissue difference between my right and left breast. The left is more soft and flexible, but the right in the upper outer portion is harder. I read somewhere that this type of change may be menopause related, but I thought I should check. I wondered when I am due for a mammogram. Or whether a previous mammogram showed anything that might explain it.

Diagnosis

That was September 2, 2010. Her doctor recommended a mammogram, and she was able to get in that day. A week later, as follow-up to the mammogram, she went in for a sonogram. The radiologist saw something troubling and offered to do a biopsy while she was there. After having the tests done, Beth continued with plans to visit her parents and go to a class reunion in the Midwest. She was standing in a Walgreens store in her hometown 3 days after the biopsy when the call came from her doctor, telling her that the biopsy showed that she had cancer. The sonogram showed no signs of cancer in her lymph nodes, but it appeared that the lump was 2 cm by 5 cm. The cancer was lobular, which means that it begins in the milk-producing glands (lobules) of the breast.

The wonder of cell phones means that Beth was reachable across the country without playing a game of telephone tag. The difficulty of cell phones is that she got the news alone and was distracted enough by the diagnosis that driving home to her parent's house she missed the turn for the street she'd lived on for 10 years.

Beth received her diagnosis on September 17, a mere 15 days after her original e-mail to her doctor. She'd been out of town for 11 of those 15 days, but was able to coordinate the appointments and tests remotely.

Her care team planned tests and visits to start quickly. On September 23, just after returning home, she met with the team that would manage her treatment: nurse practitioner, breast care coordinator, and three doctors—a surgeon, a radiologist, and an oncologist. The team also included a nurse from the research center, to make sure that if she were eligible for any clinical trials she could be enrolled (she is currently participating in two clinical trials). They told her that the mass was 2.6 cm by 1.1 cm by 1.4 cm, of a low nuclear grade, estrogen receptor positive, progesterone receptor positive, and Her2neu negative: In short, there were positive signs that this was not an extremely aggressive tumor and it was likely that her health could be maintained long term. The team recommended that she have surgery (a choice between a lumpectomy and mastectomy) and removal of sentinel lymph nodes. After that, they would evaluate, determine if more surgery was needed, and begin chemo followed by radiation.

Beth had already done a lot of research on her own. Being in the room with the whole team, she was able to look each physician in the eye and ask, "Is this the treatment you would recommend if I was your wife or your sister?" and feel reassured by the answers.

Lumpectomy and Staging

Beth had an outpatient lumpectomy on October 8 along with the removal of lymph nodes. She recovered well and distracted herself from waiting for results by watching the San Francisco Giants win their way into the 2010 World Series. She saw her surgeon on October 14. In every way, the news was bad: The lumpectomy didn't have clear margins, so she would need additional surgery to remove the entire tumor. The mass was also larger than expected, and 21 out of 23 lymph nodes harvested showed signs of cancer. This meant the cancer was at least at stage 3.[1]

Even as Beth was processing this news, she swung into action. She began researching what it meant on her own, learning that her diagnosis was no longer "lobular breast cancer" but "invasive lobular breast cancer." Lobular breast cancers are more difficult to detect on mammograms, and 15 to 20 percent of women who get lobular breast cancers get it in both breasts.[2] Her second surgery was scheduled for October 27, so she had a limited time to decide whether she should have a double mastectomy. She began e-mailing her surgeon and oncologist immediately, asking more about what this meant, as you can tell from this e-mail to her oncologist:

> Once I picked myself up after meeting with my surgeon I organized my thoughts for the next steps. While I prefer this was not my reality, given what is… I want to be fully informed and involved as soon as possible all along the way.

My goals are:

- Be very aggressive.
- Move as quickly as possible to take appropriate action.
- Follow advice of my practitioners.
- Obtain second opinions where appropriate.

I am pleased my surgery will be 10/27 and appreciate your efforts to get the tests scheduled ahead of time. I have a PET scan on 10/23 and bone scan on 11/4, but I do not have the breast MRI scheduled. How do I get this scheduled in time? Per the surgeon's recommendation a right breast mastectomy is the appropriate action. I am 95 percent confident I want to be more aggressive and have a bilateral mastectomy. I know all too well the limitations of diagnosis for this type of tumor, and believe the occurrence rate bilaterally is approximately 15–20 percent. I do not want to live in fear. Is this something you would recommend?

Taking Charge

One of the things that is difficult to convey is just how assertive Beth was in her own care, and how much she used the secure messaging feature of her patient portal to get her needs met. Although during this intense period she was also talking to her doctors frequently, she was e-mailing them as well. In the 2 months between diagnosis and her surgical cancer-free status, she sent 20 e-mails to various members of her team including her doctors, nurses, the oncology pharmacist, and the physical therapist. She also found that it was significantly easier to e-mail than to call. It felt as if her calls were often triaged oddly and the messages the team received were garbled. Using e-mail, she got faster responses and they were more on point because she could express her questions directly. In general, if Beth initiated contact, she did so via e-mail; if the physician initiated contact he or she did so by phone, and about 50 percent of staff members responded by phone and 50 percent by e-mail. The knowledge that she could get answers and that her team was responsive was incredibly helpful in relieving her anxiety both at this stage and during the entire experience.

She had also created a CaringBridge.org site to keep her network up to date with her treatment. It relieved the burden on Beth and her husband to handle phone calls for status updates and meant that friends could support her with an understanding of what she was going through and what she needed at any given time. Beth also found that blogging about the experience was helpful to her in processing what was happening, and she did so with grace, clarity, and humor. CaringBridge.org helped Beth build and strengthen her already strong ties to her community, which helped alleviate some of the stress of the entire experience. In addition, Beth wanted to educate others. When she looked at her historical mammograms, it was clear that the "thickening" had been present for at least 10 years. It had never occurred to her that getting a mammogram wasn't "enough" insurance. After realizing that it wasn't and that the density of her breasts contributed to the difficulty of diagnosis, Beth wanted to spread the word to as many women as possible.

Her breast care nurse also told her about a local breast cancer support group. Beth signed up and went to her first meeting before the surgery, joining eight other women who had also just been diagnosed with varying stages of breast cancer. It was helpful to have a community of women going through the same process.

Because it was now clear the cancer had spread, Beth had other testing to determine how far, including the bone scan, PET scan, and MRI noted before. Finally, with the PET scan, there was good news: *no* metastases beyond the right lymph nodes! The MRI indicated two "suspicious enhancements" in her left breast. Once again, she got the news via cell phone in an inconvenient location: hiking on Mount Diablo. She was trying to get additional information on the call, but it kept breaking up, and the friend she was hiking with was getting impatient. Beth just wanted to be home, with her husband, processing the news together. Yes, it is good to get information quickly, but the very convenience of cell phones sometimes renders them uncomfortable channels for receiving difficult information.

Double Mastectomy

The decision whether or not to remove the left breast was a difficult one for Beth. There were no absolute indications either way, and tests are simply not good enough yet to give a definitive answer. In addition, her oncologist was encouraging her *not* to have the double mastectomy, while her surgeon was telling her it was her choice. She was also talking to plastic surgeons to understand her reconstruction options. Her cancer support group was helpful at this stage, as she was able to talk with other women who had had similar decisions to make. In the end, though, it was a decision that was Beth's alone.

She used e-mail to ask pointed questions to support her decision. After much contemplation, in accordance with her goal to live both cancer- and fear free, Beth chose to have a double mastectomy with a sentinel node biopsy on the left side. She took the indications from the MRI as guidance; although they didn't mean she had cancer in the left breast, it reminded her that if she didn't have the double mastectomy she would live in fear of a recurrence.

Beth made it through the surgery uneventfully, and the news after surgery was, almost for the first time in her journey, excellent. There was no evidence of cancer in the left breast or in the left lymph nodes, and the margins in the right breast looked completely clear. Despite the fact that there were no indications of current cancer in her left breast, Beth is confident that, for her, choosing to have it removed was the right decision. The total size of the tumor from the right breast was determined to have been 11 cm; this was significantly larger than anticipated, and it was surprising that a tumor of that size was undetectable by either mammogram or breast exam. It confirmed that even with frequent testing, she'd always be unsure if another cancer was developing in her left breast.

Beth also made plans to get a second opinion regarding the next phases of treatment. This wasn't for lack of trust in her physicians, but because she wanted to assure herself that she'd left no stone unturned in her goal of becoming cancer free. Getting a second opinion seemed like a good idea. Her care team supported her decision to obtain a consultation at an academic medical center and provided her with a combination of paper and digital records, along with a box of pathology slides to support the second opinion. Beth was a bit perturbed to find that notes about the consultation she'd had with the Oncology Department psychologist were included in the packet, apparently because her therapist was tagged to the Department of Oncology rather than the Department of Psychiatry. They were not of any great significance, but nonetheless, their inclusion made her uncomfortable. She removed them (easier to do with paper records than a CD, after all).

The academic medical center team was very helpful, although Beth's visit started on a down note. She had hand-delivered all the historical material to make sure it was available before her consultation. When she arrived, however, no one had looked at any of it, and the team told her it had "never arrived." After some time they located and returned the slides and Beth provided the history. Beth also found it somewhat irritating that the academic medical center didn't send a report directly to her, only to her doctor. After all, she had asked for the second opinion, not her doctor. For the most part, the recommendations were in sync with the recommendations from her original care team for chemo, radiation, and follow-on treatment. The one additional component they recommended was Zometa IV treatments to make the bones a less hospitable metastatic host. At the time the research was inconclusive as to the value of this treatment and her home clinic was no longer including it in their protocol. Beth read the primary research references provided by the second-opinion team and found the results for postmenopausal women were more conclusive. Her oncologist agreed and wrote the orders. The Zometa treatment would be provided every 6 months over the course of the next 3 years, beginning after completion of radiation.

Beth had 4 weeks to recover between her surgery and the start of chemo. Four weeks to cheer her beloved Giants on to a World Series win. Four weeks to enjoy life. Four weeks to have a wonderful Thanksgiving with family in Ohio.

Chemotherapy and Radiation

And then on to chemo. Beth chose the most intense options for her chemo treatments, as there was significant evidence that aggressive treatment had positive impacts on both survival and recurrence. Part 1 of chemo began with Adriamycin and Cytoxin (AC) treatment every 2 weeks: four treatments over 8 weeks starting in early December. Beth was influenced by research showing that this approach rather than the more typical 3-week cycles increased survival rates from 75 to 82 percent. In addition, the more intense approach reduced recurrence rates by 26 percent. Part 2 of the chemo was Taxol. Once again, Beth chose the most aggressive treatment plan, which would mean a higher dose of Taxol every 2 weeks for 8 weeks, starting in late January and running through late March. After that, Beth would get radiation treatments from May through mid-June, 5 days a week, followed by Zometa for 3 years and an aromatase inhibitor for the next 5 to 10 years.

Chemo was, as Beth's friend from the cancer support group called it, "inevitable, unspeakable, and unavoidable." Beth was on four medications including steroids to prevent nausea, along with home injections of Neupogen to stimulate her white-blood-cell count. After the first round of chemo caused migraines and agitation, doctors adjusted the doses of her outpatient meds and added three medications to prevent migraines and manage mouth sensitivity. The typical chemo-induced nausea was not an issue at all due to progress in managing this side effect.

Nearly 30 friends gathered to support Beth as her son shaved her head before her hair began falling out—yet one more way she took the initiative and her community supported her during her treatment.

Part 2 of chemo was easier than part 1, but hard in a different way. In the end, she elected to go with double doses every other week rather than a dose every week. All the way through chemo Beth was getting frequent lab tests to make sure all of her results were in normal range. Beth would review her results online as soon as they were available, graph them to see how they were trending, and then e-mail her doctors with any questions. It helped her to feel like a participant in her treatment.

As Beth was ending part 1 of chemo and beginning part 2, she developed a cold. Unfortunately, the cold turned into a cough and asthma, and eventually pneumonia, complicated by anemia from the chemo. She spent 7 days in the ICU as her care team aggressively managed the pneumonia. Once again, her experience was a good one. The only downsides were too many trips to the ER before she was admitted, and the fact that the pulmonary floor staff kept trying to room her with other patients who had pulmonary infections. With a compromised immune system, Beth had to be assertive to limit her exposure to additional germs.

Chemo, thankfully, ended in March, and Beth got a much deserved break for most of April. Many of the women in her support group ended chemo at nearly the same time, and they celebrated with a victory luncheon. The event finishing touch was provided on the street outside the restaurant where a young woman approached them to offer free shampoo service. They laughed and laughed at the irony of four bald women in wigs being offered shampoos, while the young woman in question couldn't understand what was so amusing.

Radiation started out feeling easy, but got harder as the treatment progressed and Beth began to experience radiation burn. The treatment needed to continue despite the burn, and it became increasingly painful. Thankfully, there were medications used by burn victims to reduce the pain and the risk of infection as layers of her skin peeled away, but Beth was relieved and ready to celebrate with a party when she was finally finished!

Living Well

It has now been nearly 6 years since her cancer was discovered. Beth is taking an aromatase inhibitor to suppress estrogen, as her cancer is an estrogen-dependent version. She is also in a clinical trial that involves taking the diabetes drug Metformin, which seems to have anticancer effects, as some cancers, including that of the breast, are linked to higher levels of insulin in the body. Through her participation with Army of Women in their recruiting for research projects, she has participated in several other research studies, including the use of acupuncture for joint pain issues related to aromatase inhibitor treatment, and post-treatment care planning among others.

Beth has also changed her life in ways that may reduce the likelihood of a recurrence: more vegetables and antioxidants, little to no alcohol, ongoing exercise and meditation, and a less stressful life. A year after her treatment, first allowing time for a trek on the Everest Road, she had reconstructive surgery. She's very happy with the outcome and is now going to a tattoo artist who specializes in nipples to finalize that part of her journey. Beth celebrates her cancer-free status daily and has gotten to the point where having had cancer is no longer top of mind.

Beth obviously used her access to her clinical records and to secure e-mail with her doctors to good effect during treatment, as well as her ability to communicate via CaringBridge.org with friends near and far. She is clear that the process would have been much more stressful and much more frustrating without those tools. Beth also had a wonderful experience with the caring and competent team that oversaw her care.

Observations for Policy and Practice

Nonetheless, there are additional digital tools and capabilities that would have simplified the process and further reduced stress. Policy makers, application developers, and physicians take note:

- It would have been very helpful to be able to e-mail her entire care team, rather than sending notes physician by physician, as her questions often crossed disciplines and she would have benefited from the dialogue between experts.
- Access to her clinical notes would have been useful in helping her recall key facts and recommendations. While the OpenNotes project is making access to clinical notes a reality for more patients, usage is still not widespread.

- Although her treatment was central in her mind, it still would have been helpful to be able to download appointment and follow-up schedules to her personal calendar, as coordination was complex.
- Her experience of hand-delivering her records for the second opinion, only to have them declared "lost," was frustrating and would have been helped significantly by better inter-operability tools.
- In an age of patient empowerment, hospitals, health systems and other doctors can't routinely assume that the recipients of their reports are other doctors. Beth's irritation when the second opinion report went to her doctor but not also to her illustrates the need to examine standard practices in areas like report distribution to include patients.
- There is ongoing dialogue in the medical community about how to make sure records aren't compromised by omissions or changes when they pass through patients' hands, but Beth's understandable desire to remove the record of her psychology visit highlights that patients may have very appropriate reasons for choosing to omit parts of their record during transmission from one system or doctor to another. In establishing policies and capabilities it is important to enable patients to protect their privacy as well as remind physicians that, even if records are obtained electronically, they may not tell the whole story.
- It would have been helpful to get a "clinical summary" of each stage of her treatment, much like the discharge summary completed after an inpatient stay. It would have enabled Beth to remember and communicate salient points more easily, and it clearly would have improved the second-opinion process and enabled successive rounds of physicians to understand her history quickly without wading through volumes of visit and treatment records.
- Similarly, it would have been helpful to be able to view all of her e-mails and responses in a summary narrative, rather than having to pull them up one e-mail at a time.
- When she was hospitalized, even in an integrated system, the pulmonary department had a hard time changing their protocols to accommodate the fact that she was immune-system suppressed, and Beth had to be alert and assertive to be safe from secondary infections.

Conclusion

It's clear from her journey that Beth was a true partner in planning her treatment and managing her cancer journey. Her access to digital tools, especially secure e-mail and online lab test results, supported her in playing an active role. She feels lucky to have been treated in a system that was able to welcome her as a partner and affirm and accommodate her involvement rather than experience her as disruptive or a problem patient. She felt her care team truly cared about her and was as invested in her recovery as she was. For Beth, healing was also supported by her community, enabled by CaringBridge.org. In observance of five cancer-free years after her diagnosis, Beth walked in the Avon Breast Cancer Walk in 2015 as a celebration of her survival, raising more than $5000 for the cause.

Notes

1. http://www.cancer.org/cancer/breastcancer/detailedguide/breast-cancer-staging
2. http://www.webmd.com/breast-cancer/lobular-carcinoma-invasive-and-in-situ?page=2#1

Story 22: Technology Can Make Pain Less Painful*

Rachel Katz[†]

Introduction

When I was 10 years old, I kicked a kid in the face in karate class. I remember the *sensei* made me kneel facing the wall while he tended to the boy's face, and the rest of the class looked on with the perverse giddiness of witnesses to a crime. In the end, the kid's face was fine, and I got a small bruise on my foot. The incident went by relatively unnoticed, though I quit karate and sustained a slight stiffness in the front of my right foot. For years, I only perceived this stiffness once in a while during those rare evening events when I opted for heels over four inches tall.

Delayed Consequences

A dozen years later, I was hiking with my dad on a narrow, flat path along the cliffs of the Northern California coastline, and the ball of my foot started hurting with each step. I sat down, took off my shoe, and massaged the spot. For the rest of the trip, I tried to ignore it, but the pain stuck like a little pebble in my hiking boot I couldn't shake out.

From that moment on, my foot has never stopped hurting. The karate injury had altered a joint in the front of my foot, so it grew in gnarled and lumpy instead of smooth and round. The pain was so delayed from the event that it seemed nonsensical. It made me frantic. I went to doctor after doctor, and I asked them all, "Why? Why now?" One doctor glanced at my x-ray and said: "Your foot is like a car that finally broke down."

It is terrifyingly final to have your body compared to a worn-out vehicle. And grossly morbid. I proceeded to diligently imagine my body as this car, one of the tires flat. Maybe my car body could flop along on the flat tire for a bit, the analogy went, but then it's pretty much going to be stuck in one place. One can imagine the rusted-over joints that would ensue, or the sagging belly, or the peeling paint. That may be one of the consequences of aging, but most 22-year-olds don't have to face it quite so soon.

---

* Story adapted from a blog post originally published on www.rachel-katz.com.

[†] @rachelthekatz

An Introduction to the World of "Can't"

After scattered consultations with podiatrists, orthopedists, physical therapists, rheumatologists, and on and on, I began to lose faith in any doctor's opinion. Each physician exclusively recommended solutions within his or her own specialty: The podiatrist told me to get orthotics, the physical therapist recommended physical therapy, the orthopedist, surgery. Clueless and desperate, I opted for surgery, too early and without sufficient information. The surgery failed and worsened the pain. By the time I was 24, I could no longer comfortably walk even the 20 minutes to work.

The physical pain was accompanied by even more traumatic emotional turmoil. After the surgery, I went through two years of trying to accept one "can't" at a time: Maybe I can't run again. Can't backpack again. Can't ever hike Mt. Kilimanjaro. Can't identify as an active person anymore. Can't ever go out dancing. Can't wear high heels again. Can't feel sexy. And throughout, I felt completely alone. I was seeing a slew of doctors, none of whom knew what the others were doing or saying to me. My friends and family were sympathetic but mostly unaware of the degree to which the pain permeated my every thought and dictated my state of mind.

Confusion and Conflicting Advice

My initiation into this world of chronic pain was made infinitely more painful by my constant confusion and indecision about what I should do. It has been two years and over 50 doctor visits since I first started experiencing the pain, and I feel I am only just starting to understand the condition and what I can do to relieve the pain and continue to live a full and vibrant life.

Now, thinking back, I ask—why did it take so long? Could this have been done in less time? With fewer unnecessary doctors visits? With more consistent and trustworthy support? With less time spent alone in my bed in tears? I don't think my chronic pain needed to be quite so painful. And, today, we have the tools to make sure that it isn't.

Observations for Policy and Practice

As I look back on this journey, there are five painful experiences that could have been avoided.

I Didn't Know Where to Find Answers to My Initial Questions

We have an incredible trove of information available to us on the Internet today. And it is great for many searches. But when it came to finding information about my own body, I could not navigate it. Searches about my foot pain turned up long, scary threads about Freiberg's disease or premature arthritis, with testimonial after testimonial, written in lower case letters and wrought with emojis, about living in pain for decades. After one particularly grueling search session where I was subjected to reading about "being in pain every single day always plz helppp:-(:-(!!!!" I found myself in a pile on the floor sobbing and vowed never to search again. I didn't for almost a year.

There are resources available that are beginning to help. WebMD gives legitimate descriptions of symptoms and diagnoses, with 80 million unique visitors every month. Patient networks such as PatientsLikeMe (www.patientslikeme.com) encourage people to share stories and tips about dealing with chronic diseases. But even these networks operate on a population level, sharing data about a crowd of sick people and requiring the individual to wade through the information to try to find what is relevant to her.

What I needed was a resource that could understand basic information about my specific symptoms and point me to reliable initial resources. This is the difference between going to the comedy section in Blockbuster and scrolling through your recommended picks on Netflix. If we can find movies this way, why not healthcare information and solutions? In that moment of life when we are most vulnerable and frantic, easy access to personalized, trusted resources could be life changing.

Once I Had Cursory Answers, I Didn't Find the Right Doctor

The process of finding the right specialists was costly and trying. I cycled through one after another: podiatrist, orthopedist, rheumatologist, physical therapists of different types, surgeon. I once visited New York City and saw an orthopedic surgeon recommended as the best in the world. I was in the office for all of 30 minutes, 20 of them spent filling out forms. The doctor looked at my x-ray and told me that there were no other viable surgical options, there was nothing he could do, and I should get rocker sneakers—the fat, chunky-soled shoes the old people wear. When I broke down in tears, he apologized, handed me a tissue box, and left to give me space to clean up. The appointment cost $500, paid in full by my insurance.

There were two dynamics at play: Firstly, I didn't know who the experts were for this condition and which fields they were in. Secondly, I didn't know how rare or serious the condition was, so I wasn't sure what level of specialization would be necessary to define the right path for me. The result was a haphazard set of appointments with all kinds of specialists, found through a mix of referrals and Yelp reviews. In his book, *The Creative Destruction of Medicine*, renowned cardiologist Eric Topol says:

> Not a week goes by without a friend, patient, or acquaintance asking me for a referral to the right doctor for a specific condition. This turns out to be one of the most privileged pieces of information I have....It might seem ironic that in the information era knowing which doctor is the best would be so difficult.[1]

Topol notes that in many hospital rankings such as the *US News and World Report*, hospitals are ranked based on reputation rather than reliable data about hospital outcomes. Similarly, Yelp reviews comprise a small sample of those patients who found the service excellent enough or poor enough to report on. *What we need instead is a matching service, like an OkCupid for doctors and patients, which can match the doctor and patient based on the condition, level of expertise needed, geography, and any number of other variables. If we can find love this way, can't we find doctors?*

With Each New Doctor, I Struggled to Bring Him Up to Speed

By the time I was on my fifth or sixth specialist, I was telling a wildly inconsistent tale of my foot care, impacted by my pain level and mood on any given day. In one embarrassing moment, I tried to tell a physical therapist what exactly the surgeon had done to my foot, since I was still waiting to get the surgery report I had ordered a week before and that was being mailed to my house. I told the therapist something the surgeon had mentioned once about taking some muscle and laying it between the collapsed joint to provide extra padding (which I described to the therapist in just those nontechnical terms). Later, when I got the report, my physical therapist told me that it didn't say anything about that procedure. I realized I didn't really know what the surgeon had done. And I had probably told a smattering of different surgery stories to specialists along the way.

I am an excruciatingly organized person, the type that makes long daily to-do lists and notes the duration in parentheses next to each item—for example, "clean out fridge (10 min)." But when it came to my body and my pain, I couldn't keep anything organized. It was like I had a huge black hole in my brain where this information might be stored. It makes sense that when something is painful, it is difficult to think rationally about it. And yet, when we are going through difficult health situations, it is our burden or our family's burden to keep track of everything and present it logically to each new doctor. This is not just inconvenient; it's dangerous.

From a doctor's perspective, it is frustrating as well. Doctor Leslie Kernisan wrote a post on The Health Care Blog about looking for a truly usable personal health record.[2] She identifies three things that constantly hinder her: records are not easily searchable, she struggles to trend the lab results, and it takes time and ongoing effort to get records from other providers. Is this what we want doctors to spend time doing?

We need our information to be collected and tracked in one location we can share with our doctors— a Facebook timeline for our health. I have a history of my life events, interests, and relationships conveniently laid out for me; can't I have the same for my health records and doctor relationships?

Once Testing Treatments, I Didn't Know How to Track Results

Eventually, I started trying things that were recommended to me by these various doctors. There was so much to try, recommended from so many different sources, that it took me a while to get over the paralysis of choice and act. As I started to try things—new shoes, new exercises, new dietary supplements—I had a difficult time identifying what was working because I didn't have an easy way to track my results.

In his book, Topol describes one heart patient who was extremely diligent about recording his own statistics. Multiple times a day he recorded number of steps taken, average heart rate, blood oxygen level, and other indicators. This is extremely useful, Topol says, but entirely unusual. Most people are like me. Call it lazy, or blocked, or confused, but most of us aren't going to manually track ourselves to the extent that this star patient did.

Today, though, we don't have to. *We have an explosion of sensors to measure everything from speed to temperature to heart rate. Soon these sensors will be in the Gatorade we drink and embedded in our skin to measure an extensive array of bioindicators. We can track ourselves without even trying. We are already doing this with fitness wearables like the Nike Fuelband or the Jawbone Up. Couldn't I collect data on movement in my foot or blood flow to the joint, correlate it with number of steps and pain level, and start understanding when and why my foot hurts?*

Throughout the Process, I Felt Completely Alone

Almost every account of chronic pain or illness I have read or heard touches on the experience of deep isolation. One that most resonated with me comes from an article in the *New Yorker* by Meghan O'Rourke on living with autoimmune disease[3]: "One of the hardest things about being chronically ill is that most people find what you're going through incomprehensible—if they believe you are going through it. In your loneliness, your preoccupation with enduring new reality, you want to be understood in a way that you can't be."

She quotes French writer Alphonse Daudet, from his book about living with syphilis, *In the Land of Pain*: "Pain is always new to the sufferer, but loses its originality for those around him... everyone will get used to it except me."[4]

More than anything, my pain made all happy things sad. It's like when you have to pee during a movie and can't enjoy the movie. Pain is like that all the time, tingeing every otherwise good experience with discomfort, anger, and fear of future pain. "Hopeless" is an understatement to describe those nights sitting hunched in my bed sobbing in the dark, considering my body as a broken-down car.

I needed a support system and I didn't know where to find it. Online groups felt too impersonal and scary. In my immediate community, I didn't know anyone else going through a similar experience. I most regret that I didn't have a personal and trusting relationship with any of my doctors, who may have been able to help me avoid the side effects of isolation and depression.

The field of telemedicine, or remotely connecting with a doctor over video chat, is only just emerging and promises to bring about huge changes in healthcare in the next decade. Though there is a sacrifice in giving up face-to-face visits, telemedicine could give us the capability to have more frequent contact with our doctors, with a richer relationship and more personalized care. *For me, consistency of care and an ongoing personal relationship with one point person would have transformed my experience.*

Conclusion

These improvements are completely feasible with today's technology. It is now a matter of will, willingness, and coordination. As patients, eventual patients, taxpayers, and humans, we will all be better off if we get these functions up and running more quickly—with a focus on the patient's problems and experience. The rapid expansion of technology into every part of life can be scary, and there are issues to work out related to data privacy as we track and share more of ourselves. But in healthcare, there is an obvious path for technology to reduce the terror, isolation, and pain that come with being sick and not knowing what to do about it. Let's make it happen!

Acknowledgments

Thanks to Steve Daniels, Greg Caplan, Bobbi Katz, and Francis Kubala for feedback and editing help. Writing is more fun with friends.

Notes

1. Topol, Eric. 2012. *The Creative Destruction of Medicine: How the Digital Revolution Will Create Better Health Care.* New York: Basic Books.
2. http://thehealthcareblog.com/blog/2014/01/11/in-search-of-a-really-usable-phr/
3. http://www.newyorker.com/magazine/2013/08/26/whats-wrong-with-me
4. Daudet, Alphonse. 2003. *In the Land of Pain*, trans. Julian Barnes. New York: Random House.

Story 23: Transformation Is Always Possible

Jan Oldenburg, FHIMSS with Don

Introduction

Don has had type 2 diabetes for nearly half his life, in part because he's always been fat. He also has several heart conditions partly triggered by his weight and eating habits. He says, "I've always been fat," and no matter what he has tried, he has never seemed to be able to lose weight or bring his diabetes fully under control.

A Plunge into Undiagnosed Depression

For Don, 2007 was a very difficult year. Five years earlier, his older brother had gone to the doctor for a routine physical. The nurse took him to a room, checked his blood pressure (normal), took his temperature (normal), asked him how he felt (fine), and left saying the doctor would be in a few minutes later. About 10 minutes later, when the doctor got no response to his knock on the door, he walked in to find Don's brother dead on the examining room table.

Don's shock and grief—as well as the fact that his brother had been his primary support system—pushed him into an undiagnosed depression. By late 2007, things were bleak: Don had lost his job, lost his house, and was living in his car. His weight was out of control, as was his diabetes. Hemoglobin A1C tests are used as a measure of current and past control of diabetes. A normal reading is between 4 and 6; anything above 6.5 indicates diabetes. In December of 2007, Don's HB AIC reading was 11.

In January of 2008, he was finally diagnosed with depression and began treatment. Don was able to obtain no-cost treatment because therapy services were offered on a sliding fee scale. Therapy was extremely helpful, but Don still did not have many ties to the community despite living in the town he grew up in.

A Supportive Community

His therapist recommended he join a group called Community Clubhouse (ICCD.org). Community Clubhouse is an international organization founded on the principle that people with mental illness can be partners in their own care and treatment, and that a supportive community is an essential part of healing.[1] The essential characteristics of a clubhouse include:

- Membership is voluntary.
- Members have a key role in organizing clubhouse activities. Staff and members work together as colleagues.
- The work and social activities in the clubhouse are meaningful and help members regain self-worth, confidence, and purpose, and help develop friendships.
- Clubhouses provide paid employment opportunities in local community businesses for members who want work; they help members become successful employees.
- Clubhouses help members successfully complete their education.

Don found those characteristics at his local clubhouse when he joined in early 2009. They helped him get an apartment and get Social Security disability payments set up. They also gave him a sense of community, as well as a place where he could get counseling and support for his depression and grief. In part due to the support the program provided at a key time, Don has been able to live on his own, find meaningful work, discover a supportive community, and have the space to recover other aspects of his life.

Heart Issues

In June of 2008, just as Don was starting to get his depression and his life under control, he began having some chest pains. They were followed by an episode of syncope, which is fainting caused by a drop in blood pressure. Testing showed that he had a congenital heart defect in his left anterior descending (LAD) artery; it was pinched between two other arteries so blood flow to his heart was limited. His doctor recommended that he receive a pacemaker/defibrillator (ICD), which was implanted that fall. Don had no insurance coverage and the procedure cost more than $100,000; he is still paying off the medical debt.

Despite the implanted pacemaker/defibrillator, Don continued to have episodes of atrial fibrillation (AFIB), which means the upper chambers of his heart would beat rapidly and irregularly. He had a heart ablation procedure in 2011. In heart ablation, doctors cauterize the part of the heart that is causing the irregular rhythms. The ablation didn't really stop Don's episodes of AFIB.

In late 2013 he had a coronary catheterization to assess his situation. Don's doctors discovered that he had two blocked arteries. This led to open heart surgery in which Don's doctors bypassed the two blocked arteries with veins from his legs. They also performed a cardiac maze procedure, which is an open heart variation on the ablation procedure he'd had in 2013.[2] In addition, doctors implanted an experimental CRYSTAL-AF monitor as a part of a clinical study. The CRYSTAL-AF monitor helps detect atrial fibrillation and appears to reduce long-term stroke risk. Early results from the study, published in February of 2014, show promise in detecting previously undetectable episodes of atrial fibrillation.[3]

Don's condition is monitored virtually by both the implanted ICD and the CRYSTAL-AF monitor. In both cases his devices are read via phone about every three months so that his doctor can see his history and determine if any changes are needed to his medication regimen.

Don's Clubhouse and Facebook communities were both really important in providing support, prayers, reassurance, and caring throughout the ordeal of open heart surgery and the recovery process.

Changing His Life

By the time Don went in for open heart surgery, he weighed 335 pounds and could only walk with a cane. You can see a picture of him from that time in Figure S23.1.

When he was in the hospital recovering, he got some serious counseling about his diet and his weight. Doctors said he was at risk for congestive heart failure, so he was put on a low-salt, restricted fluid, constant carb, high-protein diet. The diet only allowed him to have 64 ounces of fluid a day, including soup, ice cream, Jell-O, or anything else that turns liquid at room temperature.

Although Don had received lots of counseling about diet previously and understood the relationship between his diet and his diabetes, none of the other diets really "stuck." This time, however, something was different. He can't say exactly what caused the shift, whether it was the new lease on life from the cardiac procedures, the full recovery from depression, or the clarity that strict adherence to the diet was key to keeping him alive, but this time he really understood what he needed to do, felt motivated to do it, and had the tools and support to stick to it.

He began managing his diabetes more carefully. He tests his blood three times daily and takes two kinds of insulin to treat it—Lanits at bedtime and Novalog during the day. As he says, "I've always been fat" and his diabetes diagnosis in 1999 was one of the consequences of that.

He began walking and doing aqua therapy at the local health center. Although he no longer drives, there's a local bus that drops him off at the door of the center. He has stuck to the restrictive diet and has lost 65 pounds since the surgery in February of 2013. He's been able to stop using his cane. His diabetes is under control. He is off Warfarin. And he is feeling and looking great! It's the first time he's been at a normal weight since early childhood, and he's enjoying showing it off—it was especially fun to go to his fortieth high school reunion as "the new Don." You can see a picture of "the new Don" in Figure S23.2.

After Medicare and Medicaid managed the latest episode of care, Don's cost was $10—and most of the paperwork was handled by the hospital and clinic. He's just recently gained access to an online portal at his health system and uses it to keep in contact with his doctor via secure messaging and make appointments online.

Figure S23.1   Don before transformation, with cane.

Figure S23.2 The "new Don" after transformation.

Observations for Policy and Practice

It is not clear what the magic formula for long-lasting behavior change is, but some of the ingredients include:

- Caring supportive relationships in the context of community
- Appropriate diagnosis and treatment—in Don's case, for both a congenital heart condition and underlying depression
- Nutritional counseling and support in changing diet or other difficult-to-change behaviors
- Access to exercise facilities and support in using them
- Access to affordable mental health care as well as medical care and treatment
- A social infrastructure to cover the cost of treatment and to address basic issues such as housing and jobs

Conclusion

Often the healthcare community looks at people like Don, who have multiple serious conditions complicated by underlying depression and lifestyle choices, and concludes that nothing will ever change. Negative, judgmental thinking often is reflected in the approach to individuals who are being counseled, making it hard for the individuals to believe they can change or to trust their counselors. Don is proof that, with the right ingredients, change, growth, and transformation are possible at any stage of life.

Notes

1. http://iccd.org/ICCD_clubhouses.html
2. http://www.sts.org/patient-information/arrhythmia-surgery/atrial-fibrillation-surgery
3. http://newsroom.heart.org/news/insertable-heart-monitor-finds-elusive-atrial-fibrillation-after-unexplained-stroke

Story 24: Very Bad Genes and Very Bad Luck

Jan Oldenburg, FHIMSS with Jon, MA

With and in honor of her husband, Jon, MA

Introduction

Bad luck and bad genes certainly contributed to Jon's heart attack. But they weren't the only contributors. At 46, he didn't fit the profile of someone who would have an early heart attack, so no one, from the triage support nurse to the EMTs to the ER doctors, initially had a sense of urgency about his treatment. Jon and I were still "Minnesota nice" medical consumers, not realizing that our advocacy—or the lack of it—could have long-term consequences for Jon's life and health that would reverberate through our whole family and way of life.

Stress

It had been a very intense couple of weeks. My husband, Jon, was the middle school head at a private K-12 school and I was a partner in a small consulting business based in Minnesota. Our children were about to enter their eighth-grade and senior years in school. Jon was interviewing for a job as the headmaster of a K-8 private school in Palo Alto, California. We had lived in and around Minneapolis/St. Paul since college and had a deeply rooted network of friends, family, and colleagues that we would be leaving behind if he took the job in California.

The stress caused by Jon's job search was compounded by the fact that he'd been experiencing minor but persistent chest pain for a few weeks. On a Friday afternoon in April, he went to his primary care doctor to have it checked out. The doctor did an EKG, which looked normal. He told Jon, "You need a stress echocardiogram, but there's no rush. We'll schedule it in a couple of weeks." Jon came home from that visit on a Friday and told me, "I don't think I'll pass that stress test." We were both uncomfortable with the delay but neither of us wanted to believe something really serious was going on, and we ignored our discomfort.

Jon was offered the job the Sunday following his doctor's appointment. By that time, we'd decided he should take it if offered it, and we would figure out how to deal with the consequences later. Jon accepted the job Sunday night. On Monday he told the school headmaster and the board he was resigning at the end of the school year. On Tuesday he told the faculty and sent a letter to the parents of the middle school students.

Heart Attack—The Paramedics

At three on Wednesday morning, he woke me up saying, "I think I'm having a heart attack. Please get me an aspirin." I got him an aspirin; then, ever the dutiful health plan member, I called the nurse help line at our Health Maintenance Organization (HMO). The nurse explained the hospital options to me: one, a regional hospital near our house, and, the other, a major trauma center in downtown St. Paul. I did not think to ask which hospital would be better if it actually was a heart attack—nor did she advise me to go to the hospital with a level-one trauma center. Those unasked and unanswered questions would come back to haunt us. Before I hung up the nurse encouraged me to call 911.

While I was on the phone with 911, Jon got up, was sick in the bathroom, and fainted coming out. Numb with fear, I knelt at his side with a cold washcloth. He came back to consciousness, put on clothes, and went to the living room to wait for the paramedics. Moments later, there was a knock at the door. It was a police officer, who came in, started an IV, and took Jon's blood pressure. Then an ambulance came and with it several paramedics. They asked me where to take Jon, and I told them the regional hospital because the trauma hospital was in a rougher area of town and I was worried about our safety in the middle of the night. Like the triage nurse, they did not suggest that a level-one trauma center would be better if it was a heart attack.

Heart Attack—The Hospital and the Cardiologists

The paramedics loaded Jon into the ambulance and left. I dressed hastily, left a note for my sons, and drove myself to the hospital. At admitting, I provided insurance information and was reunited with my husband, who was already in an ED room. The doctor brought in an EKG machine for a few minutes every hour—but in those short bursts they couldn't see the heart attack that was happening. Jon was only 46, and no one really believed that someone so young and fit could be having a heart attack, despite what I described about his family history and cholesterol. The medical staff was researching drug interactions to see if that might be causing Jon's symptoms. Had they had access to his medical records electronically, they might have treated it as a heart attack more quickly based on the medical evidence that he was already on cholesterol-lowering medications, had a total cholesterol of 274, an HDL reading under 35, a family history of heart disease, and a scheduled stress echocardiogram to deal with recent angina.

Finally a cardiologist arrived and insisted they leave the EKG in the room and keep the leads attached continuously. At that point, they could see the heart attack happening and quickly administered tissue plasminogen activator (tPA), which is a clot-busting drug, to try to break up the clot. TPA is most effective if used within 3 hours of the start of a heart attack or stroke.[1] The attack had started around 3 a.m., we'd arrived at the hospital about 4, and it was now 5:30 or 6. Whatever its normal virtues, tPA did not work for Jon—or not well enough to relieve the symptoms he was experiencing. The nurses began looking for a hospital with a cardiac catheterization lab and a bed. While they were searching, it felt to me as if everyone had abandoned Jon. I went back and forth between the nursing station and Jon's room begging them to take action more quickly, as Jon was experiencing severe pain, and I was increasingly anxious about time passing without effective treatment.

Eventually they decided to send him to a sister hospital with a cardiac cath lab and inpatient beds available. The cardiologist explained that one of his partners would be taking care of Jon when he arrived. I rode in the front seat of the ambulance as we raced through Twin Cities traffic at morning rush hour. It was frustrating and frightening to watch how cavalier other drivers were about the sirens, and to see the ambulance driver try to navigate crowded freeway on-ramps and metering lights around drivers who didn't pull over to give him space, especially with Jon's life at risk during every moment of delay.

The Widow-Maker

When we arrived at the new hospital, I gave Jon a hug and told him I loved him. I watched as they carried him away on the stretcher, joking with the staff and waving goodbye to me. Someone showed me to the cardiac waiting room. There were others in the room, but it was quiet at that time of day. I waited, praying for Jon, feeling as if I was in some sort of surreal dream, trying to distract myself by reading a newspaper. At some point the cardiologist who had taken care of Jon at the first hospital stopped by. He told me Jon was being well taken care of and said, "That blockage your husband has—we call that one 'the widow-maker' because often people don't survive until they get to the hospital, especially when they're as young as he is. Your husband is a lucky man." It was ironic, because the last thing I felt just then was that Jon was lucky.

Later I heard them paging respiratory to the cath lab and then, not long afterward, "code blue" to the cath lab. I wondered how many cath labs they had in action at that hour of the morning, but I couldn't bear to imagine it was Jon who was in trouble. But then a woman came into the waiting room and introduced herself to me as a chaplain. She was very young and very nervous. She told me, "I'll call Sister Gerry for you. She works more with cardiac patients and their families." I remember looking around the waiting room, thinking, almost in slow motion, "There's a waiting room full of people here, and none of them has a chaplain with them. And I have two. That can't be good." When Sister Gerry came, she told me that I shouldn't be alone, that I needed a family member or friend to wait with me. I don't remember her telling me that anything untoward had happened with Jon, nor do I remember asking any questions.

While in the cath lab, Jon remembers feeling sensation leaving his feet, legs, and hands. He remembers hearing someone trying to insert a breathing tube say in frustration, "Am I going to have to break his teeth to get this down?" He also remembers hearing the surgeon say, "Get a chaplain to his wife. I think we're losing him!" Jon was lucky to be in the cath lab so that life-saving treatment could be administered immediately.

I called my sister Sue and asked her to join me. Luckily, she was available and came as quickly as she could. Before she arrived, a nurse took me to see Dr. J, the cardiologist who had worked on Jon in the cath lab. He was an interventional cardiologist and showed me the film they took while inserting the catheter into Jon's heart. At one point he stopped the screen and said, "Here. At this point there was a 50:50 chance we wouldn't get your husband off the table. We got him through the cardiac cath and were able to insert a stent to widen the left anterior descending artery, but you need to have your family standing by as there's still a 25 percent chance your husband won't make it through the night."

Another cardiologist came in as he was showing me the films. He said, "I know Jon—my daughter plays soccer on the school team with your son. Jon's my age. This shouldn't be happening to him." They explained that Jon likely would need open-heart surgery and that the stent wasn't going to be enough, but they thought he was too fragile for further surgery right then.

Diagnosis: Acute Myocardial Infarction with Cardiogenic Shock

Jon had suffered an acute myocardial infarction (AMI) in the left anterior descending (LAD) artery (the widow-maker) and had major blockages in three other vessels. When patients have had heart disease for a period of time, they often develop ancillary blood vessels that can help them survive in the event of a full blockage. Because Jon was so young, he had not formed those alternate routes around the blockage, raising the risk of death from the heart attack. I later came to understand that Jon had nearly died in the cath lab because he'd gone into cardiogenic shock. Cardiogenic shock develops in 5 to 10 percent of people with an AMI because the weakened heart isn't able to pump enough blood for the body's needs.[2] In the past, the mortality rate for cardiogenic shock was between 80 and 90 percent. With prompt and advanced treatment, the mortality rate has been lowered to around 50 percent, but it is still the leading cause of death following an AMI.

My sister, Sue, arrived soon after I'd talked to Dr. J. She has medical training as an EEG technician and was accustomed to hospitals, doctors, and surgeries. It was wonderful to have her there. She heard my story, reassured me, got me soup (how did it get to be noon?), sat with me, and managed things at home. I didn't know what I needed, but she did, and it was wonderful.

When they finally let me in to see Jon, he was in the cardiac intensive care unit with a full-time 1:1 nurse. He had an intra-aortic balloon pump in his heart to help it pump more effectively, was on a ventilator, and was also experiencing ventricular fibrillation, which is an electrical problem where the heart beats with rapid, erratic pulses. Instead of pumping blood effectively, the chambers (ventricles) quiver. It is often seen after an AMI with cardiogenic shock. Doctors and nurses were in and out of the room, clearly worried, adjusting machines and medications, huddling for consults just out of earshot. Jon surfaced into consciousness several times, and I tried to explain where he was and what was happening. I felt helpless and scared—able to help only by holding Jon's hand and reassuring him that I was present.

Each time he surfaced to consciousness, Jon would gesture for pen and paper, and write in a shaky hand, "Call the board chair." She was the board chair of the school he had said "yes" to just two joyous days before. I kept thinking, "Call the board chair? What am I going to say to her? I don't even know what is going on yet." I told him I would call, but perhaps the next day when we would have more information about his prognosis.

The Family Reaction

My sister brought our children to see Jon that evening. It was frightening for both of them: so many tubes and monitors going into him and coming out again; so many things beeping, buzzing, and whooshing. Their father looked small and frail in the bed, and he couldn't talk because the ventilator was still in place, but he wrote a note telling them how much he loved them. Somehow, seeing Jon through my children's eyes made it harder for me to cope. We huddled as a family, cried, told Jon how much we loved him, and then Sue took them home, got them food, and stayed with them overnight.

The nurses arranged for me to stay in an on-site apartment for family members of critically ill patients. It was a little eerie, as the apartment was on a floor of the hospital that was otherwise deserted, but I was grateful to be able to stay close. I called Jon's sister and brother. It was hard to break the news, but I was also hoping one of them would tell Jon's mother, critically ill herself with ovarian cancer, and his dad. I simply couldn't face making that call. My sister kept my family informed through phone calls and our extensive family participation in the MyFamily.com website. Although I knew that more people wanted updates, I had a hard time making those calls, as it felt as if I needed to reassure others about his condition, and that took more strength than I had.

I slept restlessly, surfacing several times during the night to check with Jon's nurse to make sure he was still alive. At moments like that, the whole world shrinks. The locus of everything is the hospital bed, the sounds of the ventilator and the machines, the voices of others in the corridor, and the prayers in your head.

The Importance of Community

Everyone on staff was very kind to us and clearly pulling for Jon to make it. Every day one or two people would stop by to ask how he was doing and to say some variant of, "I was in the cath lab, and one minute he was joking with all of us and the next he was dying. I have been in the chapel praying for him. I'm so glad he's doing better." Many doctors at the hospital had children at Jon's school, so word traveled fast that Jon was in the hospital. Many doctors stopped by to check on him and wish him well. Our pastors, church, and broader community of friends were also checking in, praying with us, and organizing meals and transportation for our children. It felt wonderful to be in a community that was so supportive, where friends new and old were rallying around to pray for Jon and help us make it through.

Managing Managed Care

The next day things looked a little less bleak. A case manager from Jon's HMO came by to check on him. I had worked at the HMO in the past and introduced myself. I gave her a card and told her to call me if there were any issues about Jon's care or any changes to the approach they were taking with him.

On the third morning, when I arrived at Jon's room about 8:30, the 1:1 nurse told me that I'd just missed the case manager from the HMO, and that they were going to move Jon to the downtown hospital that day. I was furious that the case manager hadn't had the courtesy to call me despite my introduction and card and furious that they were going to move him now that it was convenient for them. None of the doctors who had been caring for Jon were on staff at the downtown hospital, and we were going to have to build a whole new set of relationships with people who were coming in midtreatment. I remember thinking, "This is why people hate insurance companies."

I swung into action. I called everyone I'd worked with at the HMO, starting with my old boss. On his recommendation, I talked to a nurse navigator and then one of the medical directors. The medical director had worked with me and had attended medical school with the interventional cardiologist who was caring for Jon. They discussed Jon's case and what was planned. I also called a senior vice president who was on the board at Jon's school and managed contracted care for the

HMO. I was fueled by anger and concern for Jon, and it helped me be able to do something concrete to help. In the end, the HMO administrators agreed not to move Jon, and they even agreed that he should have follow-up surgery at the same hospital where we had already built trusted relationships.

Conversations

That day they weaned Jon from the ventilator, so we could finally have a conversation. It was such a relief to be able to talk together! He needed information about what had happened and what the prognosis was, and was trying to put together the bits and pieces that he remembered into a coherent story. He still wanted me to call the board chair at the new school to "find out if they still want me," so I did. It was one of the hardest conversations I've ever had. She listened, expressed sympathy, and told me she'd talk to the board. She called me back later in the day to say that the board was unanimous: "Jon is the head of school we want, and you are the family we want. Tell him to take as much time as he needs to heal, and we will welcome him when he's ready." It was a great relief, even though we were still unsure what recovery would look like.

We had almost the same conversation with every new doctor that came into Jon's room (and there were many). Those conversations went something like this:

Doctor: "Do you smoke?"
Jon: "No."
Doctor: "Do you drink?
Jon: "Maybe a drink or two a week."
Doctor: "Are you diabetic?"
Jon: "No."
Doctor: "You're not overweight—have you ever been?"
Jon: "No."
Doctor: "Do you have a family history of heart disease?"
Jon: "Yes, both my dad and my mom."
Doctor: "You must have very bad genes and very bad luck."

Homecoming

After 6 days in the hospital, Jon was finally able to come home. His doctors believed he needed coronary artery bypass surgery, but didn't feel he was stable enough to have it yet. They wanted him to rest and heal for a month first. I took him home with great trepidation. I wanted him home, of course, but we were going from 6 days of continuous intensive nursing support to no monitoring at all. I would have paid a premium for the reassurance that someone in addition to me was making sure Jon stayed alive. Each night of that month-long period I woke up several times and checked to make sure he was still breathing—occasionally, and much to his annoyance, waking him up in the process.

I remember sitting with Jon on the bed as we sorted through all the pills he needed to take. Some of them were mornings only, some morning and evening, some required double doses, some needed to be cut in half. It was incredibly confusing. We bought two daily pill dispensers and measured out both morning and evening pills for the week—but there were too many to fit in even two pill-keepers. For the first 6 months, just keeping track of the daily regimen of pills was a significant effort, one signal of the many ways our lives had changed.

During the month we waited for Jon's open-heart surgery, his mother went into hospice care for the ovarian cancer she had been battling for several years. Jon wanted to see her, but it was the Friday of Prom weekend for our oldest son, and it didn't seem right for both of us to abandon him on such a landmark occasion. With trepidation, I put Jon on the bus from Minneapolis to Wisconsin. He was able to spend the weekend with his mother and was present when she died Monday morning.

His mom's funeral was very hard. It was hard enough to lose her prematurely, but in addition, it was all too easy to imagine how close we had come to having it be Jon's funeral as well.

Open-Heart Surgery

After the funeral in Wisconsin, we returned to Minnesota, and waited for Jon's scheduled open-heart surgery. We had several decisions to make. One was about which cardiologist should perform the surgery; the other was whether he should have "still beating heart" surgery. Beating heart surgery is performed while the heart is still pumping and does not require the heart to be stopped and routed through a heart/lung machine. It was still quite experimental at the time, though the results were much better than traditional open-heart surgery in the reduced rate of cognitive issues. In the end, however, we decided Jon should have traditional surgery because the hospital simply didn't have enough experience with the new technique.

Nurses at the hospital where Jon was to have surgery were threatening to strike the week of his surgery. Since he had been discharged, open-heart surgery was now considered elective and would have been cancelled in the event of a strike. Luckily for all of us, the nurses settled the day before Jon's surgery, and it was possible to go forward with the surgery on May 25, exactly a month after his heart attack.

The hospital was running a test on the effectiveness of "healing touch" before surgery, and Jon volunteered to be a part of it. That meant that a healing touch practitioner spent time with him the day before surgery, the morning of surgery, and several times while he was in recovery. We later found an article that showed the outcomes of the study: statistically significant reductions in anxiety and length of stay in the healing touch group compared to the control group.[3]

Several people had volunteered to be with me during surgery: it was wonderful to have their support, but they were also working to distract me, and, while I appreciated their efforts, I had the superstitious fear that my attention was needed at all times to make sure Jon would survive. There is a terrible moment in open heart surgery when the nurse comes out to say, "We stopped the heart at 9:02. We will let you know when we restart it." We knew that the most dangerous part of the surgery came when they attempted to restart the heart, and the 90 minutes we waited were among the longest of my life. When the nurse came back out to say, "We successfully restarted the heart," I was so relieved I hardly knew how to react.

They bypassed Jon's left anterior descending artery with a graft from the mammary artery and took a vein out of his right leg to bypass two other blocked, but less critical, arteries. They cracked his chest and put him on the heart/lung machine. Despite the greater severity of the procedure, recovering from open-heart surgery was much easier than recovery from the heart attack had been. With the open-heart surgery, Jon had 1:1 nursing care for 4 hours compared to 3 days. The ventilator was removed the same day as the surgery took place. And, despite pain from the incision, Jon's recovery was more rapid than it had been after the heart attack.

Recovery

Jon went to cardiac rehab for a month in St. Paul. He had his goodbye party at school. He shopped for apartments in California online and the board chair of his new school visited the most promising ones until they found a place that would work. On July 1, he got on a plane to California without us to start his new job. That meant building new habits of exercise and healthy eating by himself in a new place.

The Toll of Caregiving

Sometime after the heart attack but before Jon left, my chest started to hurt. I am an asthmatic, but this was not the pain of a tight or wheezy chest. I kept quiet about it, wondering if it was some weird sympathetic reaction, or if I could possibly be having angina. Eventually, without telling Jon why, I went to the doctor, who diagnosed it as costochondritis, an inflammation of the cartilage where ribs attach to the sternum. It is the most common reason people go to the emergency room thinking they are having a heart attack and is thought to be exacerbated by stress. Relieved, I was able to put up with the pain, but it was a reminder of how easy it is to stop taking care of yourself in a crisis when the whole family is dependent on you. I had been strong the whole time because I needed to be. Shortly after Jon left, however, I started reacting. I sobbed in the car. I sobbed at sappy commercials and songs. Sometimes I cried myself to sleep. Jon was doing fine, but I needed to find ways to restore my own depleted resources in order to be able to continue to help our family heal—laughter, friends, family, love. Our journey back to wholeness included living a long distance apart across the country that first year—a situation made even more difficult by the 9/11 terror attacks, which made life feel both infinitely more precious and infinitely more precarious.

One day, we were living our lives with disease and death the furthest thing from our minds; the next, everything was different. We had to learn new ways of eating. Put a new focus on exercise. Rethink our priorities and what mattered in our lives. When Jon came home from the hospital, he remarked on how golden and alive the world looked. He had new eyes with which to see its beauty.

Aftermath—The Benefits of Digital Health/Care

Nearly every year we have at least one trip to the hospital because Jon is experiencing chest pain. His ejection fraction, a measure of the heart's pumping ability based on a theoretical score of 100, was only 45 after the heart attack. In 2006, doctors inserted a wider, drug-occluding stent in his LAD because it turned out the original stent had not kept enough blood flowing to the heart through the original artery that the mammary artery graph had failed for lack of blood flow. The stent needed to be bigger if it was to function as the LAD.

Several years ago, Jon's ejection fraction—a measure of the heart's pumping capacity—dropped under 35 and his doctor recommended he have an implantable cardiac defibrillator (ICD) inserted, as this was the standard of care for someone with such a low ejection fraction. He has been in the early stages of congestive heart failure for several years, but it is progressing very gradually. He has an AliveCor device that attaches to his phone and provides a single lead EKG, in the hopes that it will help clarify decisions about when to go to the ER and when not to. Because his heart rhythms are abnormal, the AliveCor is not especially helpful, but we hope for a day when he will have access to the readings from his ICD to help us decide whether or not to go to the ER when he is experiencing chest pain.

It has become clear that many factors contributed to Jon's heart attack. He had begun treatment for hypothyroidism about 6 months before his heart attack; his thyroid imbalance probably contributed to his risk of heart attack. While doctors suggested he take a nutrition class, it was Jon's reading that led us to try the Dean Ornish and Mark Hyman functional medicine diets. Despite the critical importance of diet and exercise, the medical establishment pays much more attention to procedures and drugs than diet. Due to my nagging, he finally was examined for sleep apnea in 2009 and found to have a severe case. The data are clear that sleep apnea is a significant contributor to heart disease—it increases the risk of heart failure by 140 percent, the risk of stroke by 60 percent, and the risk of coronary heart disease by 30 percent.[4] He tracks his blood pressure, weight, and diet using a simple app called BP Companion. Although Jon has received good and even great care throughout this journey, it hasn't been as well integrated and connected as would have been optimal for his health.

We have been lucky to be cared for in digitally connected health systems. Jon's had access to his electronic medical record since 2005 at three different health systems. He's been able to review his clinical information online and e-mail his doctors, and has learned to send questions ahead of his visits to make them more productive. He also had access to convenient tools ranging from prescription refill to appointment scheduling to online bill payment. He would like—but does not have—online access to readings from his ICD and the VPAP machine that regulates his sleep apnea, as well as the ability to correlate them with other events in his life and his health.

Observations for Policy and Practice

Our family's journey offers many lessons for about how the experience could have been different.

- Dr. Sandeep Jauhar discusses a scenario very like Jon's in his book, Doctored, the Disillusionment of an American Physician. He notes that he saw the scenario play out nearly daily where, "A heart attack victim [was] taken by ambulance to a community hospital that isn't equipped to perform angioplasty. If the man had been brought to LIJ, which has cardiac catheterization available twenty-four hours a day, the damage to his heart could have been averted, adding years to his life."[5]
- Home monitoring after surgery or an acute episode is likely not just to reduce costs by enabling patients to go home early; it is also important in relieving the stress on the patient and his or her family members.
- In the middle of an acute episode, it is important to provide resources to family members and loved ones, who may be managing the episode at the cost of their own health.
- There is value in finding ways to simplify medication management for the newly diagnosed. Shifting from being a patient who takes one or two medications daily to being a patient who takes 10 to 12 medications daily is traumatic in its own right and may contribute to the number of patients who don't fully follow their plan of care.
- Integrative medicine that looks at care of an individual across specialties really matters, especially in complex cases. We still have a long way to go to offer truly integrated care in most of our medical environments, yet it can be critical in truly addressing illnesses that complex and interconnected causes.

■ Jon is an activated healthcare consumer with a (highly) activated spouse—but it still took 8 years after the initial heart attack for him to be diagnosed with sleep apnea, and even then it was not a result of a physician's suggestion. Our sons know they are at risk and are taking preventive action, but how many other people need more help than they are getting to understand all of the possible contributing factors to their health?

■ Despite the wonderful care Jon has gotten from the medical system, it is the choices he makes on a daily basis—about what to eat, whether or how much to exercise, whether to take his meds or wear his VPAP—that have the most impact on his health. Those are family and individual choices, not health system choices. We still have a long distance to travel in supporting people in making healthy choices as well as helping them sort through the confusing "noise" of conflicting dietary advice.

Conclusion

In the intervening years, I have become a connoisseur of emergency room and hospital bedside chairs (most of which are awful). I have battled insurance about who pays for what and when. I have experienced the frustration of leaving Jon's bed to feed the dog only to miss the moment when the doctors make their rounds. I have become adept at the language of cardiac care and at advocating for Jon's needs when he can't. I am not Jon's caregiver; he is perfectly competent to care for himself and makes that clear whenever I get bossy. I am his supporter and wife and he is my beloved and my best friend. We are a team, supporting one another in the ways we eat, exercise, and celebrate being alive.

We are lucky to have had the 15 years since Jon's heart attack. Fifteen years of loving. Fifteen years in which to see our sons graduate from high school and college. Fifteen years of travel, adventures, and meaningful work. Our family knows not to take our lives and our love for granted. We say "I love you" to one another at every opportunity. We value our time together. We are not always successful at living as if each day will be our last, but we try. If the power was mine, I would absolutely give Jon his health back, but we also value the blessings that come from being acutely aware that life is fleeting.

Notes

1. https://www.nlm.nih.gov/medlineplus/ency/article/007089.htm
2. http://www.ncbi.nlm.nih.gov/pmc/articles/PMC2774583/
3. http://www.healingtouchprogram.com/articles/documents/HTBypassSurgery.pdf
4. http://www.ncbi.nlm.nih.gov/pubmed/11208620
5. Doctored: The Disillusionment of an American Physician, by Sandeep Jauhar, MD, published by Farrar, Straus and Giroux, 2014. p. 88.

Story 25: Visualizing Symptoms

Jan Oldenburg, FHIMSS with Katie McCurdy, MSI*

Introduction

Katie (Kathryn) is a user experience designer who is fascinated by the idea that visualizing symptoms or the course of an illness can help patients tell their stories. She has been working in healthcare design for 4 years and is passionate about improving the patient and clinician experience through design.

Diagnosis: Myasthenia Gravis

You might say that Katie has been on this path since she was 13, when she was first diagnosed with myasthenia gravis, nearly 23 years ago. Her mother noticed that her smile looked more like a grimace, which was both the first indication of the disease and the beginning of the path to diagnosis.

Myasthenia gravis is an autoimmune disorder. In it, the communication between nerves and muscles is faulty. Normally, as nerve impulses travel to the muscles, the nerve endings release a neurotransmitter called acetylcholine. Acetylcholine binds to receptors on the muscles, triggering the muscles to fire. In myasthenia gravis, that process is interrupted because the body forms antibodies that block or destroy the acetylcholine receptors on the muscles.[1]

The result is muscle weakness, often in the muscles that control facial expressions, eye and eyelid movements, chewing, talking, and swallowing. For Katie, it means that her smile is sometimes crooked, her voice weak, or her vision blurry. She had her thymus gland removed as a teenager, several months after she was diagnosed. Because she had the surgery so soon after her initial diagnosis, it is hard to tell how much removal helped to manage her symptoms. Katie's myasthenia gravis is managed with multiple medications including drugs that enhance communication between the nerves and muscles, drugs that reduce the autoimmune response, and other supplements that reduce inflammation, help her sleep, prevent osteoporosis, and more.

---

* @katiemccurdy

New Symptoms

When you have one autoimmune disease, you are more prone to develop another, which is what happened to Katie. Almost 10 years ago, she began to experience a series of weird symptoms: things like tingling in her fingers and toes and the feeling that the skin on her legs was crawling. She also began suffering severe irritable bowel syndrome (IBS) symptoms, and when her stomach was upset, all the rest of her symptoms seemed worse. She was living in New York City at the time and saw a number of gastroenterologists, neurologists, and rheumatologists: five, in all. Although she was seeing some of the best doctors in the world, her care was very fragmented. As soon as Katie's symptoms didn't fit into their neat mental map, her doctors would throw up their hands and refer her to yet another specialist. With each new doctor, Katie told her story again, hoping she remembered the right details and told it in a way that might highlight connections.

Visualizing Katie's World

Exhausted by her journey from doctor to doctor, Katie found a holistic doctor who she hoped would be able to treat all of her symptoms. He did not take any insurance, however, so she knew she'd be paying out of pocket for every minute she spent with him. To maximize the effectiveness of her time, Katie created a visual timeline of her life, showing the ups and downs of her autoimmune and stomach issues. She found the visualization helped her tell her story in a coherent way, and it seemed to help her provider understand the constellation of symptoms she was experiencing much more effectively than a purely verbal narration. Supported by all of her records, she was able to highlight salient points in her history, including the tests used to diagnose her disease as well as its progression. A part of her recent timeline is highlighted in Figure S25.1 so that you can see its power.

That visit marked a turning point for Katie—not in her disease as much as in the way she thought about it and about her life mission. She posted her timeline online, and a friend forwarded it to ePatient Dave (Dave DeBronkart), who in turn posted it on the Society for Participatory Medicine site (sp4m.org), to very positive feedback. She began finding other people like her, who had a proactive mind-set about taking charge of their medical care.

Katie moved out of New York City, to Burlington, Vermont, where it was easier to spend time outside and where her doctors actually talked to each other. She was amazed to find that her neurologist was willing to collaborate over e-mail with the herbalist she started seeing, both of them willing to stretch the boundaries to help her manage her condition in the most effective way.

The move to Vermont also marked a career turning point for Katie. She had been a user experience designer for a large agency, but she decided to become a consultant. She began working in healthcare, designing apps and websites for patients and doctors with clients like LabCorp and Medivo. She worked for a time with the nonprofit Open mHealth on ways of bringing together personally-generated health data (like the data that come from connected devices like a Fitbit or an app like Runkeeper) and making it more useful for doctors and patients. She now works with the University of Vermont Medical Center, an academic medical center in Burlington, designing better healthcare experiences for patients, families, and clinical staff.

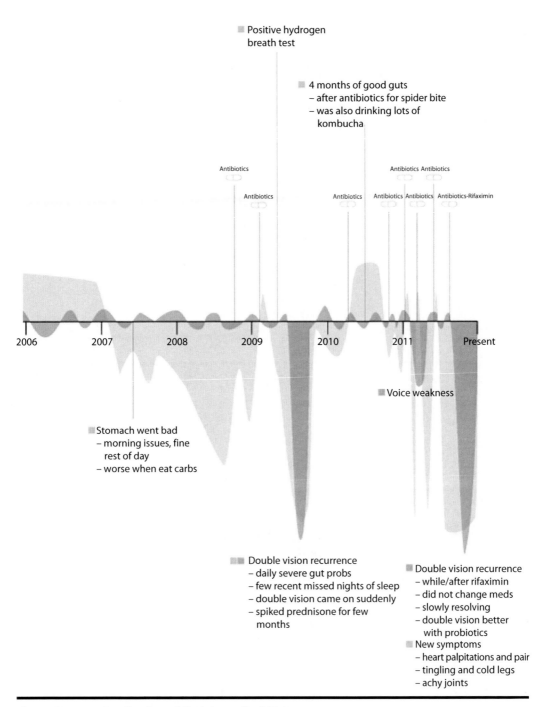

Figure S25.1   Visualization of Katie's medical history.

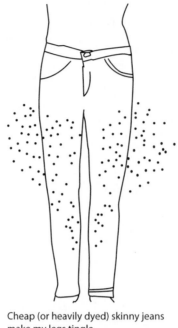

Cheap (or heavily dyed) skinny jeans
make my legs tingle.

Figure S25.2   How cheap jeans make Katie's legs feel.

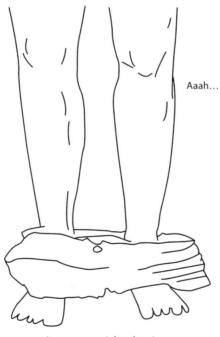

Aaah…

It goes away right when I
take those kind of pants off.

Figure S25.3   Relief when Katie takes off cheap jeans.

Various Visual Communication Approaches

Katie's efforts in visualizing aspects of her disease didn't stop with the timeline she created. She also has tried different communication formats to illustrate her symptoms, like cartoons and visual symptom maps. The cartoons in Figures S25.2 and S25.3 highlight her reaction to a new pair of jeans.

Katie also noted that when she is in a medical context such as a doctor visit, she talks at length about her symptoms and treatments; this gives the doctor a complete picture of her disease, but not of her as a person. She has been experimenting with a "vibrance" map, depicted in Figure S25.4, which she describes as, "an incomplete list of people and things that make me happy and joyful, that make me feel alive and vibrant, and that are my daily support. It would be great if I could share an at-a-glance view of my vibrance map, so that my doctors could quickly see if I was deficient in any important way." Katie is interested in the way her mobile phone or other digital technologies might be able to help her keep her vibrance map, displayed in Figure S25.4, up to date.

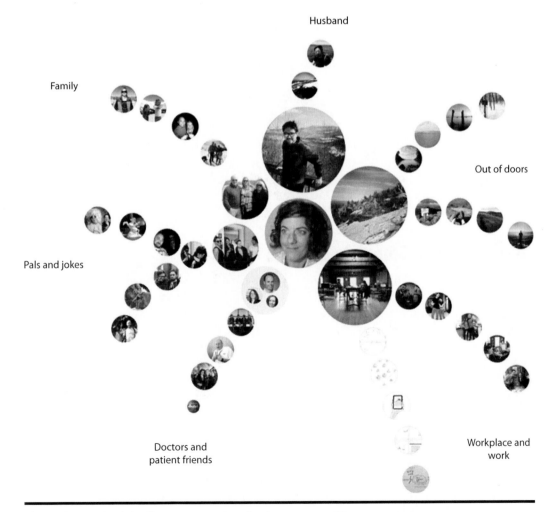

Figure S25.4   Katie's vibrance map showing her community.

Tracking and Correlating Symptoms

After all of this, Katie was still struggling with the collection of unruly and undiagnosed symptoms. She built what she called the "spreadsheet from hell" to track activities and symptoms so that she could try to find correlations between cause and effect. Her spreadsheet has 30 columns to enable her to track symptoms and possible triggers including such diverse things as weather, sleep quality, and alcohol and carbs consumed. It can be thought of as yet another way of visualizing her condition. She tried bringing the spreadsheet into one of her doctor's visits, but it seemed overwhelming and not particularly helpful for her doctor.

For a time Katie was a beta tester for an app/service called MyMee (www.mymee.com). MyMee helps clients set up a plan for what to track and then matches them with a coach to help interpret the resulting data. She had weekly meetings with her data coach, and during this time she was tracking everything she ate or drank as well as her symptoms. The tracking itself quickly became tiresome, but she kept going because she felt a commitment to her coach and wanted to see if she'd discover any insights. After a few weeks of that work, Katie's coach had a huge "aha" while looking at her data. It turned out about an hour after eating fruit or high-fructose sugars, the burning sensations in her hands and feet got much worse. As a result she stopped eating fruit, maple sugar, and honey, and she experienced significant reduction in her burning symptoms. This is a great example of a tracking success and, for Katie, the consequences were so immediate and impacted her health in such positive ways that it made it easy to make the lifestyle shift.

Despite the lasting insights that Katie got from tracking, she is all too aware that tracking fatigue is a real issue for patients. No one can keep up that level of focus for long, so it is important to figure out how to accommodate the "tracking fatigue" in designing applications and sensors to support patients. She thinks it's really important to time-box detailed tracking efforts so patients don't feel as if they will need to put so much effort into it for the rest of their lives. Katie is also acutely aware that the data that are helpful for her to track may not be helpful for her doctor.

Accessing Your Complete Medical Record

Katie requested copies of her medical record as part of her drive to understand and be able to communicate her health history. It was irritating to pay $50 for copies when there would have been no charge had one of her physicians requested the records, but she persisted. She needed her actual history in order to tell a coherent story about her past. She received copies of the records and was able to read through the history, see the tests that were used for diagnosis, and trace the ebb and flow of her symptoms. Katie used the data from her history to modify her timeline to make sure it accurately reflected her medical history.

Katie currently has access to parts of her medical record and lab tests online, but doesn't have the ability to easily download them or create a longitudinal view. For her, that limits the usefulness of online access. She can envision a future when it would not only be easy to get electronic access to your medical data, but when user-friendly tools also would help put it in a timeline and make sense of it.

She uses the ability to send secure messages to her doctor online, but is very careful how often she uses it as she doesn't want to be perceived as too demanding or too difficult.

Patient Participation and Multispecialty Diagnosis

Although tracking brought her insights and an ability to better manage her symptoms, she was still without a diagnosis that would help her understand what was happening. Katie signed up for a visit to a Midwestern multispecialty clinic, where she had five visits with different specialists in 2 days. In this setting, also offered at other multispecialty clinics, one physician acts as a "quarterback," coordinating the visits and testing, and bringing together the other specialists' thoughts.

Katie brought in copies of her symptom chart as well as her spreadsheet. She was prepared with facts and dates from her medical records as well as correlations between her symptoms, treatments, and exacerbations. Because she had been tracking, correlating, and visualizing her illness, she could answer virtually every question her doctors asked.

For Katie, the visit resulted in a diagnosis that finally made sense of some of the seemingly random symptoms she'd been suffering for more than 5 years. In addition to myasthenia gravis, she learned she also had Sjogren's syndrome—another autoimmune disorder in which the body attacks the glands that produce moisture in your body, primarily the eyes and mouth. It is, however, a systemic disorder, so it also may affect joints, the gastrointestinal tract, and a variety of other organs.[2]

Because Katie was already on immunosuppressants for her myasthenia gravis, her doctors didn't add medications to her regimen, but advised her to continue to manage the condition with food, lifestyle, and exercise, with the possibility of taking more medication in the future if needed. There was great relief in having a diagnosis even if there was no magic pill to manage the symptoms.

Community Support

Online patient groups have sometimes been helpful to Katie. Several years ago, when she first moved to Vermont, she had difficulty getting to a doctor while she was experiencing a severe flare in her visual symptoms. She was seeing double all the time, not just sporadically. Someone in the myasthenia gravis Facebook support group recommended a specific kind of eye drop that helped her get by until she got in to see the doctor. For the most part, however, the group has not been an important lifeline for her.

Her local doctors, her husband, and her friends have been a lifeline of support for Katie. She's also connected with and drawn great inspiration from other patient-designers and e-patient attendees she's met at conferences, especially Healthcare Experience Design and Medicine X. It has been helpful for her to talk with others who share her passion about the intersection of medicine, patient empowerment, and design, including Nina, a designer who shares some of Katie's autoimmune symptoms; Sean, who is a patient and entrepreneur; and Natasha, who created a symptom tracking app for other patients.

Redesigning the System

If Katie could redesign the medical system, she would focus on *both* high-tech and high-touch components. She notes that the human connection is still really important, and her best experiences with doctors are with those who create a space for conversation and storytelling that doesn't feel rushed or impersonal. She gives the example of her neurologist, who turns away from his computer to focus on her, and asks, repeatedly, "What else? What else?"

On the other hand, with complex illnesses and disconnected symptoms, it is hard for any one individual to put all the pieces together. She would have loved to put all of her symptoms into a computer and have a decision support engine sort through all the possible causes, relationships, and diagnoses. It could have spared her years of uncertainty.

Katie would also like more emphasis on collaboration: between doctors and patients, between doctors and doctors, and between patients, doctors, and other caregivers. Tools that maintain the connection between patient and doctor between visits would also be helpful—telemedicine, integrated tracking tools for communication of symptoms between patients and doctors between visits, secure messaging among the patient and all members of the care team. Katie's primary plea is for a system that understands she is a whole person, not a collection of symptoms and body parts.

How to Describe and Value Patients Like Katie?

Many of the terms used to describe activated and empowered patients like Katie bother her. For example, to her "patient engagement" sounds like a marketing term that implies that patients should be passive in relation to their health. Further, it implies that engagement is something that professionals bestow on patients by "getting them engaged" rather than something individuals do for themselves.

She is much more comfortable with terms that incorporate bidirectional communication, teamwork, and collaboration between patients and their medical teams, resulting in empowered, mindful, and trusting patients. Katie believes it is far more important to create the space for trust and where a meaningful dialogue can occur than to create one-size-fits-all solutions.

Observations for Policy and Practice

Katie's work highlights many opportunities for changes in the healthcare system—as well as accompanying tools and capabilities—that would support patients like her with disparate, complex, and interconnected symptoms:

- Build respectful processes that welcome patients' insights and collaboration in their own care. This involves many elements: the design of the space—putting patients at eye level for equalizing conversations. It also requires designing in-office workflows so that doctors and patients have time to spend in collaboration. Finally, it means providing patients with access to their clinical data so that they come into the discussion as partners.
- Visualization can both help patients tell their stories in a coherent way and enable doctors to process an enormous amount of diverse information quickly. We would all benefit from tools that enable us to better collect, summarize, and visualize our health histories and symptoms.
- Data are the foundation of visualization—comprehensive clinical data such as lab tests, diagnoses, and procedures as well as personal health data such as symptoms, exercise, food intake, lifestyle, and systemic data such as temperatures or pollution levels in the community. It is still far too challenging for many people to get access to their medical records—both the historical paper copies and the current electronic versions. Any and all efforts to

improve interoperability and provide patients with seamless access to their own data will significantly help patients to take responsibility for their own conditions. "Big data" tools applied to individual patients will aid in building correlations between a person's symptoms and factors in the external world.

- Understand that manual health tracking at a detailed level must be limited in scope and duration. Rather than considering it a failure when patients stop tracking, look at it as a normal part of the cycle and find ways to re-engage them to find different insights and data or extract more meaning from existing information. The best solution will be when sensors and wearables are so good that tracking your health and generating insights about it becomes a by-product of living your life.
- Tools that invite collaboration between the patient and all of the members of the medical team are more fruitful than "one-to-one" tracking capabilities or communication methods.

Conclusion

Katie's personal journey in using her visual and analytical skills to understand her own health has become her life mission, which she expresses in Haiku-like form:

My mission is to:
Help patients tell their stories
and help providers focus on the work they love
through thoughtful UX design
and research and close collaboration with fun, talented people.

Katie identifies as a professional as well as a patient. Until a few years ago, she was reticent to mention her medical issues, afraid that she would not be taken seriously as a professional if people knew she was also a patient. She has made peace with her mixed identity. She blogs about her health and uses the way she visualizes her health and symptoms as a teaching tool for others. She feels lucky that her health conditions give her perspective on her work, and that she can speak both as a patient and as a design professional. Katie uses her perspective as patient to add color and richness to her work as a professional. She is clear that her professional identity is not dependent on her status as patient.

Despite the fact that her conditions have helped Katie find her mission and focused her career, if she could wave a magic wand and eliminate them she would do so in a heartbeat.

Katie blogs often and eloquently, and her posts are highlighted by examples of her experiments with visual design and illustrations of aspects of her health. You can find her at http://sensical .wordpress.com/. All illustrations are Katie's work and can be found in her blog posts.

Notes

1. http://www.mayoclinic.org/diseases-conditions/myasthenia-gravis/basics/causes/con-20027124
2. http://www.mayoclinic.org/diseases-conditions/sjogrens-syndrome/basics/definition/con-20020275

Story 26: Wasting My Time

Jan Oldenburg, FHIMSS with Jessica Jacobs, MHSA, CPHIMS*

Introduction

Jess is no stranger to healthcare and health policy—she can trace memories of her illness to the age of 6 and began her foray into health IT welding ultrasound machines together after her high school classes. During her undergraduate studies, she developed a public health database for dual-eligible individuals diagnosed with both hepatitis C and HIV/AIDS to empower community health workers with timely outbreak information. Later she moved to Washington, DC, where she earned a graduate degree in health systems administration (HSA). Since this time she has worked inside the healthcare system in a number of roles: as a director with Aetna's Innovation Labs; within the department of Health and Human Services, where she cofounded the Food and Drug Administration's Center for Drug Evaluation and Research's Health IT Council, wrote the Health Resources and Services Administration's (HRSA) Text4baby promotional plan, and helped lay the groundwork for the Office of the National Coordinator for Health IT's (ONC) "Investing in Innovations" initiative. Additionally, she helped start up the federal mHealth and Telehealth collaboratives in coordination with the White House. Along the way, she has chaired committees, written white papers, and tweeted and blogged about health, healthcare, and consumer empowerment.

When Jess was diagnosed with postural tachycardia syndrome (POTS) in her early twenties, she became a student of the disease. She read everything about POTS in the medical literature from 2000 to 2010, becoming her own advocate and an expert in her condition. Yet, despite her deep knowledge of the healthcare system and her own condition, Jess does not always feel she is treated with respect and empathy as a patient. Her story highlights the way that knowledge and advocacy can sometimes make it more, rather than less, difficult to get empathetic and appropriate care.

Intertwined Conditions

Jess Jacobs fainted for the first time at the age of 12. And then it happened again. And again. It continued to happen at odd moments—sometimes in a restaurant after eating or when she stood up after sitting for a while, sometimes just from standing in one place. It took 8 years for her to be diagnosed with POTS; the average time between onset of symptoms and diagnosis of this rare condition is 7 years. With Jess' POTS, her heart rate is extremely variable—her normal heart rate

---

* jess_jacobs

is around 60, but with movement ranges between 35 (lying) and 240 (standing). Heart rate is an important indicator for POTS as the one criterion physicians agree upon is that the patient's heart rate speeds up 30 beats per minute or more when the person stands up, causing dizziness, fainting, and other symptoms.[1] Jess has been diagnosed with POTS three times through the gold-standard test for POTS: the tilt table test, which measures a patient's blood pressure and heart rate at various angles. In Jess's case the likely culprit for her POTS is Ehlers-Danlos syndrome (EDS), group of inherited disorders that affect the connective tissues—primarily the skin, joints, and blood vessel walls.[2] EDS causes easy bruising and joint hypermobility (loose joints), as well as skin and other tissues that are weak and stretch easily (skin hyperelasticity or laxity).

For Jess, the two are connected, as EDS causes her blood vessels to stretch, which amplifies the POTS problem of getting blood to her heart and head when she stands up. In addition, she has cyclic vomiting syndrome (CVS), which can be associated with both conditions.[3,4] As the name indicates, CVS results in episodes of severe vomiting that can last for weeks. EDS causes her joints to dislocate easily, which can easily happen if she falls during a POTS episode. Frequent dislocations hurt and mean she needs medication to reduce the pain. Her weak blood vessels mean that she often starts bleeding from medical procedures like having a tube up her nose. The bleeding means she needs frequent blood transfusions. This constellation of problems means Jess spends far too much of her time in the medical system.

In 2014 alone, as she recounts in her blog post, "Wasting My Time,"[5] Jess had 63 outpatient doctor visits, 24 emergency room visits, and spent 59 days inpatient (note that the numbers have been updated from the blog post to show the full year). The causes were a constellation of problems related to POTS, EDS, or treatments, including a kidney infection, shingles, pneumonia, a pulmonary embolism, a severe ankle sprain requiring an ankle cast, and eight blood transfusions.

It is astonishing how much Jess accomplishes despite the continuing barrage of symptoms and illness—and the hassles of trying to obtain appropriate care.

Coordinating Her Own Care

Both EDS and CVS are classified as rare diseases, and the addition of POTS to the mix means that there are very few patients with that combination of symptoms—and very few doctors who understand how to treat and coordinate care for any of them individually, much less the three of them in combination. Because each of them is complex, Jess is sent to multiple specialists in the hopes "someone else" will understand how to help her.

Because of this complexity, she has had multiple interactions with the medical system in the past year, including visits to the following doctors: primary care (16), psychology (12), pain specialist (8), cardiology (7), gastroenterology (8), gynecology (2), rheumatology (4), hematology (3), endocrinology (1), neurology (1), and ophthalmology (1). In the last year alone, she visited the emergency room 24 times, was hospitalized 10 times for 59 days, and had 8 ambulance rides. Clearly, it would be helpful to have a doctor or care coordinator working with her to make sense of it all: interpret the outcomes and coordinate the visits, communications, lab tests, medications, and exchange of medical records. Ideally, this is the role of a primary care physician (PCP), as described in the American Association of Family Physicians definition, which includes, "Primary care is performed and managed by a personal physician often collaborating with other health professionals, and utilizing consultation or referral as appropriate. Primary care provides patient advocacy in the health care system to accomplish cost-effective care by coordination of health care services."[6] This definition is also at the heart of recommendations for patient-centered medical home (PCMH) models and accountable care organizations (ACOs).

Jess did not have a PCP who was working in that fashion, despite moving all her specialists to one hospital and seeing the PCP the hospital suggested as the doctor best suited to coordinate her complicated care. Instead of taking charge and acting as the coordinating hub for medications, referrals, and assessment, her doctor added specialist after specialist and didn't take on medication coordination. She also never sent Jess's records to the disability management firm hired by her employer, so her request for disability was refused and her absences deemed "not medically justified."

As a consequence, Jess has been doing most of the coordination and advocacy herself. If you have ever been sick, you know how hard it is to explain your history or be clear about what you need when you are very ill. She has created a one-page sheet that summarizes her conditions and issues, as well as her medications and treatments. She has a supplemental 10-page list of lab tests and results. These allow her to summarize her story effectively, but she still finds that doctors are reluctant to start treatment before they have seen her several times. Given the difficulty of getting appointments with specialists who focus on her condition, this can really drag out the process of moving her treatment forward or addressing new issues. She finds that often no one talks about care coordination unless she brings it up.

Jess has recently switched from her unhelpful PCP to a concierge medicine practice in the hopes that she will be able to experience more empathetic and coordinated care from that type of practice.

Wasted Time

As noted earlier, Jess recently blogged about the time spent in all of those doctor and hospital visits last year. She downloaded all of her claims records and categorized each visit according to whether it was useful or useless. In her own words, the criteria she used to distinguish useful from useless included:

- Outpatient visits were useful if it resulted in a change to my treatment or I underwent a test/treatment.
- ER visits qualified as useful if they resulted in a new diagnosis or ended in a necessary hospitalization…some ER visits aren't useful (or are even harmful) usually for one of two reasons: (1) They refuse to manage my pain or (2) I have to make multiple visits for the same reason in a short time frame.
- Hospitalizations were designated as useful if they were unavoidable.
- Useful hospital days included a test or treatment; days where the only treatment was saline and Zofran do not count as useful.[4]

By these measures, 16 of her 56 outpatient visits were useful—only 29 percent of them actually furthered her treatment. By the same measure, only 9 of her 20 ER visits, 8 of 9 hospitalizations, 10 of 54 hospital days, and 3 of 7 ambulance rides were "useful." The tally by specialty is highlighted in Table S26.1.

Even if the medical establishment might quarrel with some of Jess's categorizations, that's still a lot of wasted time and expense for the healthcare system, not to mention days, hours, and years of Jess's life wasted—and that's without adding in the process inefficiencies that meant more hours waiting in waiting rooms, exam rooms, pharmacies, and hallways.

Jess gets deeply frustrated by the process of trying to fill prescriptions, especially prescriptions for opioids to manage the pain from the multiple dislocations and concussions she has each year. Recently, for example, her paper prescription was left on her physician's printer during her office

Table S26.1 Useful/Useless Visits by Specialty

	Total Visits	Useful Visits	Useless Visits
Outpatient			
Cardiology	7	3 (43%)	4 (57%)
Endocrinology	1	1 (100%)	0 (0%)
Gastroenterology	8	2 (20%)	6 (80%)
Gynecology	2	0 (0%)	2 (100%)
Hematology	3	1 (33.3%)	2 (66.7%)
Neurology	1	0 (0%)	1 (100%)
Ophthalmology	1	1 (100%)	0 (0%)
Pain specialist	8	3 (38%)	5 (63%)
Primary care	16	2 (13%)	14 (87%)
Psychology	12	2 (16%)	10 (83%)
Rheumatology	4	0 (0%)	4 (100%)
	63	**16 (25%)**	**47 (75%)**
Inpatient			
Emergency room	24	11 (45%)	13 (55%)
Hospitalizations	10	8 (80%)	2 (20%)
Hospital days	59	10 (17%)	49 (83%)
Ambulance	8	3 (38%)	5 (63%)

visit. (In many states, electronic prescribing of class II medications is still illegal because it is considered higher risk to send an electronic version than to provide a patient with a paper copy of the prescription.) Since the doctor's office is 45 minutes and 40 dollars in cab fare each way, she asked her physician to mail the prescription to her home. It took 7 days for the prescription to be mailed. She then had to find a pharmacy that was able to fill the prescription, which took several days as pharmacies often refuse to tell her by phone if they have sufficient supplies of the medication she needs to pick up, citing a fear of being robbed. This means the patient has to go, in person, pharmacy by pharmacy, to determine whether the pharmacy carries the prescription brand or dose and has sufficient quantity on hand to fill the prescription. If the pharmacy has the medication, then the local pharmacist decides whether to fill it exactly as state laws and policies indicate. Further, even if the prescription is legally correct, pharmacy stock and fill policy may require her to get a new prescription, which means starting the process over.

Some pharmacies will deliver the *medications* to her home, but the *prescription* still needs to be delivered in person by the patient. On more than one occasion, Jess has fainted from POTS while in line at the pharmacy, resulting in ambulance trips and hospitalizations. Oddly, despite the strictures around class II medications, pharmacies will dispense them to a friend or family member who shows up with information about Jess and the willingness to sign for them—but that means Jess often must ask friends and family for help and support just to get her medications.

Other examples of processes and policies that waste her time and highlight our lack of streamlined policies include:

- Coordinating care. Jess highlighted a situation where she called her PCP for a follow-up visit while she was in the hospital. She was told that it couldn't be scheduled because she was still an inpatient, yet when she was discharged an hour later, her PCP's appointment calendar was full and she couldn't get in for two additional weeks.
- Basic sterile procedures. She has a port in her chest to enable self-administration of Phenergan, an antinausea medication, and saline for rehydration (helps prevent fainting from dehydration). The port creates a risk of central line infections, which makes both Jess and the medical establishment nervous, yet she often finds herself needing to push hospital staff to follow proper sterile procedures while working with her port. Each time she does so, she is aware that she risks retaliation for embarrassing the staff—and yet it is a critical risk to her life and health that she can't tolerate after having had two central line infections that were directly connected to hospital incidents during which she did not speak up.
- Records transmission. While hospitalized, Jess needed a blood transfusion, but the hospital couldn't find her hematology records, despite the fact that the hematologist practices in the same location where she was hospitalized. She experienced a similar problem in getting her GI records sent to Cardiology, when GI was on the seventh floor and Cardiology was on the fifth.
- Useful tools. Although Jess has access to both her claims and clinical records via portals, she finds that they are relatively static records that don't help her track, correlate, and explain her conditions. She finds the summaries printed per "meaningful use" guidelines to be useless or even harmful, as they report "nothing of note since 2009." It's safe to say that significant events in her health have occurred since 2009, given all those visits and hospitalizations.
- Repeated tests. New doctors often want to repeat tests no matter how recently she has received them, as if the evidence from the medical records she carts to the visits isn't valid unless services have been performed for the doctor with a lab he or she knows. Jess challenges these inefficiencies when she can, but sometimes she is too weary to do so. When you multiply this penchant for new testing by the number of specialists she sees, the potential for waste of time and resources is enormous.
- Bring your own (BYO) devices. Jess has a Wi-Fi-connected scale, as well as a blood pressure cuff that links to the Wi-Fi and allows her to track and graph her conditions. Each doctor, however, wants her to use a blood pressure cuff he or she is familiar with, so she has five different blood pressure cuffs for home use. She has to double check her pressure and self-graph it to bring to her doctor, since he is not comfortable with the cuff that will connect to a spreadsheet and track automatically, despite the fact that the two give nearly identical results.

The Worst Hospital Experience Ever

A recent post from Jess went viral when she recounted a horrific hospitalization experience. One of the difficulties facing patients like Jess, with complex conditions that resist easy understanding and respond sporadically to treatments, is that they can be viewed as drug seekers or dismissed as crazy—imagining or contributing to their own conditions. In her blog, "On the Worst Healthcare Experience of My Life"[7] she recounts a difficult hospitalization experience. She was transferred to hospital X during an episode of CVS that hadn't responded to treatment in her previous hospital. Her history with hospital X wasn't good, as she'd called out a number of inadequacies in a previous hospitalization there the year before. Despite the promise of a new CVS specialist at hospital X, the reason for the transfer, she never saw him or her.

When Jess was admitted from the previous hospital, she was sent with all the things that had accumulated in the previous 3-week stay. These included supplies for her central line. Jess didn't pack the supplies herself; they were already in a bag a friend used to bring her clothes while she was in the hospital. The friend was unfamiliar with healthcare and didn't realize the supplies should have been left at home before packing clothes in the same bag. Jess disclosed those medications when she was admitted to hospital X and the admitting nurse gave the meds back to her after documenting that Jess had brought them. She also asked Jess to promise not to take any while she was an inpatient.

A few days into her stay, Jess fainted and fell in her room—a not unusual occurrence given she was admitted for syncope and vomiting. Another nurse at hospital X had noticed some vials in Jess' possession and assumed the cause of her fainting episode was a self-administered dose of morphine, rather than the POTS documented in her record.

The nursing staff sent the hospital security force to search Jess's room for illicit drugs. When asked where her needles were, Jess immediately pointed to the bag containing the central line supplies only to have the hospital police yell at her. Jess then took pictures of them ransacking her room while officers threatened to handcuff her and send her to jail if she didn't delete the pictures. The security office found two things: (1) empty vials Jess had collected for an art therapy project after a nurse had administered the medication in them, and (2) full vials of medications the charge nurse had let Jess keep upon admission. The drug the officers seized was Zofran, an antiemetic that she was already being given in the hospital. Zofran is almost impossible to over-dose on and offers no "high." Since Jess was already being given Zofran on a scheduled basis by the hospital, there was no reason for her to take more of it. Hospital X refused to return the meds to her, claiming that because the infusion company did not label each vial with her name and dosage, they could not confirm that they belonged to her—despite the fact that Jess produced her insurance claims for the medications and a photo of the prescriptions (from one of their own attending doctors) authorizing the medication. Despite these efforts the hospital still refused to return the medications when she was discharged—over a thousand dollars' worth of medications were involved.

After that incident, the hospital assigned a "sitter" to stay in Jess's room and ensure she wasn't taking medicines or getting out of bed on her own. Jess was told by one of the sitters that watching her was "silly," since in each instance where Jess lost consciousness Jess had called for help and a nurse was physically touching her. There is a distinct indignity to having every move watched with the assumption that you are not enough of an adult to call for help to get out of bed or that you are inventing or self-causing symptoms. The indignity was compounded by the sitters' discourteous behavior: loud chatter to other staff members in the middle of the night, eating foods that made Jess' sensitive stomach turn, and generally discourteous treatment.

Support of Community via Social Media

Jess tweeted about her situation while in hospital X and posted her blog, which quickly went viral. She has been steadfast about not naming the hospital in question, feeling that it would only make her own situation worse should she need to return. She received an outpouring of support as well as dismay that any patient—much less a healthcare colleague—would be subjected to such treatment. The support she received from friends and colleagues in the healthcare system was a small antidote to the way she was treated.

Jess has found support in the community of people who suffer from similar conditions and symptoms, though it is sometimes tiring to be the "elder statesman" explaining facts about her conditions to people who are not as well versed in the disease or the healthcare system as she is. And, given that these conditions are rare, it can be demoralizing to find those whose stories are similar. While it's wonderful to know that you are not crazy and the symptoms aren't all in your head, many of these people are desperate or have given up hope. She has tried PatientsLikeMe as well as several different Facebook groups, but she gets most of her support from her personal Facebook page and connected circle of friends and family.

Observations for Policy and Practice

Jess's situation bring to life the problems of being your own advocate in a system that is still struggling to incorporate patients as partners in their care, still uncomfortable with patients who are deeply knowledgeable about their diseases, and defensive about challenges to authority.

- We need to rethink the way we train doctors, nurses, and health administrators to embrace patient stories as part of the "facts" of the situation, and resist defensiveness when our treatments don't work or our patients hold us to account for the quality of care and level of empathy we deliver.
- Lack of true data interchange costs all of us in the form of repeated tests, delays in treatment, and guesswork about what has already been done.
- Many of our policies are shortsighted attempts to reduce risk that miss the broader picture of the need for convenience and empathy in dealing with patients. In particular, policies that prohibit e-prescribing for class II drugs actually add risk—both in the potential for lost paper prescriptions as well as significant amounts of hassle for patients and families that may mean delays or interruptions in medication therapy.
- Once the possibility of Munchausen's disease (a condition where patients self-harm in order to gain attention) is raised, or any other psychiatric syndrome is suggested as a part of a patient's condition, every legitimate symptom is called into question. Jess's situation exemplifies this complexity, as her pain could be viewed as an excuse for drug seeking or her vomiting a sign of self-induced attention-seeking behavior. Patients with severe illness often become hypervigilant about symptoms because the consequences of ignoring them can be severe. We must find better ways to distinguish between those with legitimate illnesses who may be hypervigilant about symptoms[8] and those with psychiatric disorders such as Munchausen's—and understand that empathy matters no matter what combination of physical or psychiatric symptoms are in play.
- Coordination of care requires both the time and the willingness to invest in understanding the patient, diligently following his or her care, and serving to coordinate aspects of care from medication renewals to follow-up visits. New policies that reward physicians for overall outcomes may help support primary care physicians in performing this role, perhaps with help from support staff. In patients with complex medical conditions, this kind of supportive oversight is essential to managing the patients' care, reducing the cost to the medical system, and easing the patients' distress.

- Telemedicine solutions that enable remote consultations between specialists from different disciplines hold some hope for reducing the hassle and improving care for patients like Jess, but procedures and policies that support its use in this way need to be put in place quickly. In Jess's case she used telemedicine a few times in the past year. In each use she was advised to go to the emergency room, turning something that might have been handled in the home into a medical emergency.
- Although Jess doesn't find her patient portal especially useful, she can envision a number of technologies that would support her care.
  - She would love a drug reminder program that allowed her to enter schedules and methods of administration for multiple drugs, so that she could be reminded appropriately what she needs to take and when. It would be even better if these reminder systems could update automatically, particularly for as-needed medications. For instance, with nausea you take a medication every 8 hours as needed. If you tell the application you took the medicine at 8 a.m., it'd be great to have an alert remind you at 4 p.m. that you can have another dose, if it's needed.
  - Tools that support Jess in aggregating and summarizing her medical history and symptoms would be helpful—especially if they helped categorize her symptoms and showcase their interactions. Keeping these tools open ended is important for documenting complex conditions.
- Streamlining and simplifying care for patients is not just convenient for them—a simpler and more streamlined system holds the promise of better and lower cost care for all of us.

Conclusion

Jess is weary and disillusioned with the healthcare system. Despite all her knowledge and experience—as a patient, as a healthcare activist, and as a healthcare executive—she hasn't been able to influence her own care and treatment in the ways she would like. She has learned the importance of having someone else present to be her advocate, so that she doesn't generate resentment from the very people whom she needs to care for and about her.

If we are going to do justice to the people like Jess, who have the knowledge and passion to advocate for themselves and affect their own care, we need to find better ways to help them tell their stories and support them in getting the care they deserve.

Notes

1. https://www.nymc.edu/fhp/centers/syncope/pots.htm
2. http://www.mayoclinic.org/diseases-conditions/ehlers-danlos-syndrome/basics/definition/con-20033656
3. http://www.ncbi.nlm.nih.gov/pubmed/20667005
4. http://www.ednf.org/sites/default/files/Collins.pdf
5. http://jessjacobs.me/on-wasting-my-time-the-numbers/
6. http://www.aafp.org/about/policies/all/primary-care.html
7. http://jessjacobs.me/worstexperience/
8. http://www.ncbi.nlm.nih.gov/pmc/articles/PMC3584492/

Story 27: When Lightning Strikes...A Family Story of the Impact of Disabilities*

Jan Oldenburg, FHIMSS with Paula, MA, Special Education with Endorsement in Visual Impairment

Introduction

Paula was in recovery after her C-section, still in a fog, when the doctor came in to tell her and her husband that their son would probably not live through the day. Paula knew, dimly, that her C-section had been an emergency and that a doctor had worked on reviving him afterward, but she wondered confusedly, "How did it come to this?" Paula and her husband passionately wanted a child and had gone through infertility treatments to get pregnant. Paula's pregnancy had been normal, though toward the end her doctor was a bit worried that she was developing signs of pre-eclampsia. When her water broke a month before her due date and they headed to the hospital, they were excited and nervous, like most about-to-be parents.

Emergency Cesarean Section

At the hospital, the staff put Paula on a fetal monitor and they all began waiting for something to happen. Paula had been in labor for some time when the doctor indicated that he was a bit concerned about the baby and thought they needed to do a C-section. "I'll just deliver the baby next door, and then we'll do your C-section," he said. While he was delivering the baby next door, their son's heart stopped. The doctors did an emergency C-section, but when they delivered her son, he was unresponsive, dead. They didn't have oxygen or a crash cart on hand, but a doctor from the neonatal intensive care unit (NICU) worked on him intensely.

Their baby was having nearly continuous seizures and was all tubes and devices. None of them knew what to do. Her husband, Frank, a graduate student and a scientist, was realistic about the implications of the doctor's words. He stayed with Paula for a while but neither of them knew how

---

* Names have been changed in this story at the request of the family.

to comfort the other, and he eventually went to campus to grade papers. Paula's father came that afternoon and she had to share that the baby was in dire straits. Paula didn't want to bond with a baby who might die, but when she saw him the nurses said, "We know who this baby looks like. He looks like his mom." She was falling in love, against her will.

Adjusting to a New Normal without a Roadmap

Paula and Frank named the baby Paul. It was one of the first steps of dealing with the new course of their lives. The photo in Figure S27.1 shows Paul in the NICU. Baby Paul was in the NICU for 35 days. They got used to the rhythm of going to the NICU to stay with him. At 10 days they were able to hold him. That's also when he began breathing on his own. Paula began wondering what his life would be like and what it meant for her and her husband. Several interns on NICU rotation happened to be around when she voiced her questions and one of them responded to her by saying, "He'll probably be a crib baby. You will learn to understand his cues and what he needs, but he won't be able to do any of the things that a normal child would." Paula was devastated and Frank was furious the intern said those things while no one was available to support her.

Paula began to think—and say—"I'll never teach again. I'll have to stay home with this baby." One of the nurses, however, told her, "No, in this state babies like Paul go to school." That made sense to Paula, with her history as a teacher. She and her husband understood that early intervention was critical. At that stage, Paula wanted someone to give her a clear path, to tell her, "This is what Paul will be able to accomplish." But there was no roadmap—the professionals not only didn't know what the journey would look like but also didn't want to set expectations that were either too high or too low. Even with their educational backgrounds, the journey through denial

Figure S27.1 Paul in the neonatal intensive care unit.

was hard for Paula and her husband. The first 18 months of Paul's life, every morning Paula woke again to the reality that the life they'd dreamed of with their son would never be theirs. Every day of the first 18 months it felt like a new assault. Gradually, however, acceptance crept in. They realized they had to give up their dreams of what life with Paul would be like in order to focus on the reality of helping him achieve as much as was possible for him.

Paula and Frank considered suing the hospital and the doctor. They went to Paula's hometown in the summer and talked to her former obstetrician, who said, "I've been on both sides of this process, and I tend to think that lawsuits are really a way for the lawyers to make money. No matter what the outcome, they aren't healing." When Paula and her husband seriously considered going forward with the lawsuit, they both had a gut feeling that they wouldn't survive the process. They were far from home, her husband was in a demanding graduate program, and they had a baby who needed them. They decided it was better to focus their energies on acceptance, healing, and working with baby Paul.

They contacted various services to help them work with Paul. One of the early challenges was to develop Paul's muscles, as he had "low tone." It was also clear that Paul couldn't see very well, so Paula spent a lot of time having him feel things and working with a bouquet of Christmas lights to stimulate him. At the time, Paul's visual condition, "cortical-visual impairment,"[1] was still a vague, misunderstood diagnosis. It means that his eyes could see but his brain couldn't process the input. Without understanding the true issue or what was at stake, Paula kept working with him, watching for the visual "click" that meant that Paul had made a connection between the world and something she was doing.

Paul's vision was one of the hardest blows because they couldn't get answers about what was happening or figure out how to help. The pediatric ophthalmologist they first saw was condescending, abrupt, and unhelpful. Paula once had the opportunity to read the doctor's notes and felt they were judgmental and unhelpful regarding Paul's prognosis.

At some point during those first few months, Paula was changing the sheets on their bed and Frank began bouncing Paul on the mattress. Paul shrieked with laughter. It was an "aha" moment—they realized that their energies had all been spent on caring for him, "fixing him" with therapies, worrying about him—they'd forgotten to have fun! That realization allowed them to relax and enjoy more of their time with Paul.

What Do You Want Your Child to Learn?

The medical school associated with Frank's graduate program contacted them. The school was sending interns out to interview families with special needs children to make sure doctors understood what it really was like to live with a child with special needs, and Paula found it was healing to her to describe her life and what it meant to her to care for Paul.

The infant team at the development center gave her tasks and orders rather than asking her, "What do you want your child to learn?" Paula realized that she was going to need to understand how to advocate for her son from cradle to grave. She became involved in parent training opportunities that focused on new federal laws to support families with infants needing medical and educational intervention. These federally funded programs mandated family-centered care, getting families involved, advocating for themselves and others. Paula appreciated the recognition that families needed to have a more balanced involvement, allowing them to be true partners in planning for their families and disabled children. Figure S27.2 shows Paul at age 9, walking with a little support.

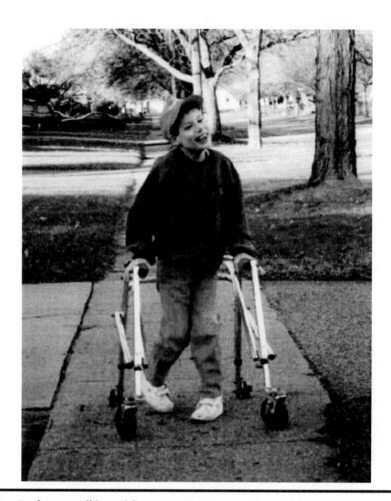

Figure S27.2   Paul at 9, walking with a support.

Finding Her Voice

Paula began talking publicly about what it was like to raise a child with disabilities. As an educator, she wanted others to learn from her family's experience. She explained what it was like as a family and how she felt about it. The school district created parenting groups and brought in infant mental health specialists who helped them as a couple and also helped them to help Paul. Paula and Frank were in a committed relationship, but for years were in very different places in their understanding of how very impaired Paul was. Frank didn't share her anxiety about Paul's future. He didn't believe in worrying and was focused on earning his PhD. That choice didn't work for Paula, who needed acknowledgment of the anxiety she was feeling and help working with it. It was a blessing that they got that support from the therapists the school district brought in. They also took advantage of respite programs from the start, realizing that they were on a long journey and would need breaks along the road.

Where They Are Now

Paul is now 26 years old and graduated from his center-based program in June of 2015. Their daughter, born 8 years after Paul, graduated from high school in the spring of 2015. Paul lives in a group home. From the beginning Paula understood Paul would always need care for daily activities. Timing the move away from home was important to Paul's success. Such a transition from a family home is more successful and healthy for all when the family and individual are not in crisis.

At 26, Paul is physically very strong. Gone is the "low tone" of his infancy. At five feet and about 105 pounds, he is solid from the waist up. He talks—Paula and Frank understand him—but he also does a lot of jabbering. Paul is very social and is beloved wherever he goes. He lives in the moment, laughs, and enjoys people. He loves to fly, especially to see his grandparents. He has played Challenger Little League baseball since he was eight, has a very personal relationship with Jesus, knows the words to all songs and every Disney movie he has ever seen. He is healthy, happy, and part of his community—and by the way, he sees just fine. All of Paula's work helped cement the connections between his visual cortex and the processing centers of his brain.

Paula's world is very different than it might have been had she never had Paul. As she says, "There are no coincidences in God's great economy." She had always been interested in the field of disability and rehabilitation, even before her marriage and Paul's birth. Paul's condition is by far the biggest grief of her life, but she also feels as if she has always been on this road. She became an advocate, speaking about Paul and speaking up about the needs of children with disabilities and their families. She was once excruciatingly shy. Speaking up for Paul helped her, in her parents' words, "blossom."

Paul's path also changed Paula's career choices. Fascinated by working with Paul's visual impairment, she enrolled in a special education graduate degree program focusing on visual impairment. She now works with visually impaired students from eight different school districts in rural Michigan. Her youngest student is 7 months and the oldest is 26, and their level of disability ranges from mild to severe.

Digital Tools

Paula can imagine a number of digital tools that would have supported her and their family on this journey. Prominent among them would be an organizational tool for managing the great variety of phone numbers, contact information, and support resources. Ideally this would come as a set of contacts—with notes that explain what they are for—that she could have downloaded into her own contact software and updated and managed from there. She also would have appreciated a scheduling tool that would enable her to incorporate her child's appointments, caregivers, schedules, exercises, and medications. Ideally, it would merge with her calendar and her husband's calendar, but would also be separable as well.

Nearly every specialist and therapist that they visited gave them handouts of information and exercises. It would have been most helpful to be able to store and categorize them online so they could have been easily accessed from anywhere and by other caregivers.

Paula would have liked to have an app to track symptoms and medications to figure out what symptoms the medications impacted. It would also have been helpful to get some coaching on what information about Paul's condition physicians would find helpful. Paula noted she would have loved to help co-design such tools.

It would have been wonderful to have had a social media community where she could have asked other parents, "What are you doing? What is helping?" Such a community would also have allowed her to give and get social support.

Paula would also have appreciated secure messaging with all members of Paul's care team and noted that often problems were caused because care team members didn't talk among themselves. As a teacher, Paula expanded on this idea to note that it would be helpful for her to be able to provide secure messages to both her students' parents and physicians, especially if she didn't have to worry about the threat of lawsuits.

Observations for Policy and Practice

Although Paula and Paul's story took place in a golden age of disability funding and acceptance, there are many lessons here for present-day policy makers, physicians, and parents:

- Professionals need to understand that they can't force acceptance on a family—they need to work with the family at whatever their stage; the best they can do is help them progress to the next level of acceptance.
- Many of Paula's friends with children with disabilities are more comfortable inside the disabled community because it is fundamentally kinder to them and their children than the "neurotypical" world.
- Hospitals and pediatricians both should have a social worker available to talk to parents about their emotions, provide them with support, and help them find community options.
- Physicians and caregivers need to assess where the family is and not condescend to them. Paula remembers making friends with a couple whose son had cerebral palsy. Their pediatrician didn't realize they were both PhD-level geneticists and had a conversation with them about "these things called germs." It broke trust.
- When physicians, social workers, and families work together on behalf of a disabled child, there are opportunities for an outcome greater than the sum of its parts. The partnership itself is empowering and relieves both stress and anxiety. Everyone comes to the table with a different perspective and sometimes that creates alternatives that dramatically impact care.
- In the early days of dealing with any significant change in health status, it is important to help educate parents about what they can ask for and what is reasonable. They need help in understanding what it means to be an informed consumer in the changed circumstances they find themselves in.
- In dealing with a complex health condition, it would have been very helpful to have a combined and digital version of the disabled person's medical record. It would also be helpful to have someone on the medical team who was putting the pieces together and functioning as the child's advocate.

Conclusion

Paula cannot now imagine who she would have been and what kind of family they would have been with a differently abled son. Paula describes their family as being like a tree that has been hit by lightning. The old tree withered and a new tree grew out of its base. If she could change her son to be neurotypical, she would, in a heartbeat, and yet she would not want to change anything about the essence of who he is or who she has become in caring for him.

Note

1. http://www.aapos.org/terms/conditions/40

Afterword

Throughout this book we have read perspectives about changes that are taking place in healthcare and the ways individuals interact with the healthcare system. We first read about the ways in which technology has catalyzed a new wave of healthcare consumerism. We then learned about the importance of behavior change and how both low-tech and high-tech solutions can help. Then we read how structural changes in our healthcare delivery and technologies can enhance healthcare, including chronic care. Next we explored the challenges and opportunities that accompany acute care and hospitalizations. Chapter 6 explored the multiple dimensions of "health" and urged us to think beyond traditional definitions of health, wellness, and healthcare. Next we read about the important role of informal caregivers (which includes 39% of adults in the United States) and how technologies can empower them and facilitate their work. Finally, we examined multiple programs and services that are helping to engage patients in their healthcare and promote partnership between patients and healthcare professionals.

This has been supplemented by an astounding array of patient and caregiver stories. These moving and powerful stories highlight the struggles that patients and their caregivers face with today's healthcare system. The stories highlight the opportunities for changes in our culture, technology, and policies that would significantly ease the frustration, pain, fear, cost, and hassle for patients and their caregivers.

What Can We Conclude from This Book?

First, to paraphrase Dickens, it is the best of times and the worst of times for healthcare. Thanks to medical and public health innovations, we are living longer and healthier lives than ever before in human history. The number of people over 65 will likely double in the next 25 years and it has been claimed that possibly half of all the humans who have ever been over 65 are alive today. In the developed world, we have declining rates of death due to infectious diseases and decreased hospitalizations for many acute (and some chronic) diseases. In addition, many previously fatal diseases, including HIV infection, coronary artery disease, and many cancers, have become chronic conditions.

But this has come at a cost. The cost of healthcare inexorably rises and governments, employers, and individuals have struggled to foot the bill. As a consequence, reimbursement to hospitals and healthcare professionals has declined or not kept up with inflation. In combination with other rising costs, this has forced healthcare providers to see more patients in less time, which generally results in a depersonalization of the healthcare experience, a lack of time to develop healing relationships, and curtailed time for listening and thoughtful decision making. This results in overprescription of drugs, overordering of diagnostic tests, and over-referral to specialists, all of which

297

further fragment healthcare and drive up healthcare costs while not delivering value to patients or payers. In addition, this fosters paternalism in medical practice because effective patient–provider collaboration can't be effectively done when practicing drive-by medicine.

But this has also had other impacts, which may ultimately lead to sustained improvements in medical practice.

For example, in the United States, we are seeing a shift to value-based care, in which payers are providing financial incentives to healthcare providers that encourage them to increase quality and reduce the costs of healthcare. This is prompting a reconsideration of current medical practice, which includes profligate diagnostic testing, a focus on the face-to-face visit for all delivery of healthcare services, and paternalism. Instead, diagnosis will be based less on reflexive testing and more on thoughtful questioning and listening; as Sir William Osler taught his students, "Listen to your patient, he is telling you the diagnosis."

Changes in healthcare payments are also spurring technology innovation in population health, care management, on-demand care delivery, and self-care, as well as models of practice that recognize the important role of the patient. Most importantly, savvy healthcare providers realize that improving outcomes and reducing costs must involve collaboration between the patient and physician—something called "participatory medicine."

Our next conclusion from this book is that high tech must complement high touch. Although technologists and so-called futurists call for a future of "digital healthcare," it's important to recognize that the human body is a highly complex analog system (as is the human mind). Almost all the tests that we do are imperfect and require context and nuance to interpret them. Prediction rules are generally true for populations but do not necessarily apply to individuals. Humans don't always respond the way we might expect, even when clinical trials might suggest otherwise and if such clinical trials included patients just like the one in front of us. Even the much vaunted "precision medicine" based on genomics is not adequate to direct clinical practice outside of a few narrow domains. Thus, many aspects of healthcare will continue to be delivered by humans. As my mentor, Professor Warner Slack from Harvard Medical School, once said (in the 1960s!), "Any physician who can be replaced by a computer should be."

In addition, technology is not a panacea. Technologic innovations in care delivery generally only produce the desired result when combined with a human intervention. In our rush to adopt technologies, we must appreciate the important synergy of high tech with high touch.

Finally, this book has shown us that despite the challenges, there are examples of success with patient-centered healthcare innovation taking place all over the world. We have a confluence of factors that has fostered these innovations: the crisis of healthcare cost and quality, the fact that information technology has achieved a tipping point in both capability and adoption sufficient for it to be applied to important health and healthcare problems, and the increased frustration of patients—the most important stakeholders—with their healthcare.

Now That You Have Read This Book, What Next?

It's imperative that each of us reflects on the lessons we have learned and the stories we have experienced: We must ask ourselves how we can make a difference. It may be by joining a patient/family advisory board at a local medical practice, hospital, or medical professional organization. It may be by serving on the editorial board of a medical journal. It may be by sharing your story with a broad audience through writing or through public speaking. It may be through serving as a consultant to hospitals or health systems or as an advocate serving patients and family caregivers.

It may be by participating in discussions, influencing public policy, educating healthcare professionals, or doing research. Or it may be giving direct feedback to the healthcare professionals and institutions you encounter.

I encourage you to get involved. There are a number of organizations working in this space, including the Society for Participatory Medicine (an organization I cofounded), MedicineX, the Patient Voice Institute, the National Partnership for Women and Families, and others. All are working in their own ways to push for health and healthcare that is more patient-and family centered, more collaborative, and more healing.

I urge you to be a part of this exciting transformation in healthcare, not just to change it for you and your loved ones, but so that everyone can have positive experiences in which they are able to be active participants in their care.

Daniel Z. Sands, MD, MPH

Index